SHAKESPEARE ON MASCULINITY

Masculinity was a political issue in early-modern England. Phrases such as 'courage-masculine' or 'manly virtue' took on a special meaning. As used by members of the Sidney–Essex faction, and later by admirers of the bellicose young Prince of Wales, they signified commitment to the ideals of militant Protestantism. Diplomacy and compromise were disparaged as 'feminine'.

Shakespeare on Masculinity is an original study of the way Shakespeare's plays engage with a subject that provoked bitter public dispute. Robin Headlam Wells argues that Shakespeare took a sceptical view of the militant-Protestant cult of heroic masculinity. Following a series of portraits of the dangerously charismatic warrior–hero, Shakespeare turned at the end of his writing career to a different kind of leader. If the heroes of the martial tragedies evoke a Herculean ideal of manhood, *The Tempest* portrays a ruler who, Orpheus-like, uses the arts of civilization to bring peace to a divided world. Other plays receiving close readings include *Henry V*, *Troilus and Cressida*, *Hamlet*, *Othello*, *Macbeth*, and *Coriolanus*.

ROBIN HEADLAM WELLS is Professor of English at the University of Surrey Roehampton. He has held visiting posts in Canada, France, Italy, the United States, and the West Indies and has written on Shakespeare, Spenser and Renaissance mythography. He is author of *Elizabethan Mythologies: Studies in Poetry, Drama and Music* (1994).

SHAKESPEARE ON MASCULINITY

ROBIN HEADLAM WELLS

CAMBRIDGE
UNIVERSITY PRESS

PUBLISHED BY THE PRESS SYNDICATE OF THE UNIVERSITY OF CAMBRIDGE
The Pitt Building, Trumpington Street, Cambridge, United Kingdom

CAMBRIDGE UNIVERSITY PRESS
The Edinburgh Building, Cambridge CB2 2RU, UK   www.cup.cam.ac.uk
40 West 20th Street, New York, NY 10011–4211, USA   www.cup.org
10 Stamford Road, Oakleigh, Melbourne 3166, Australia
Ruiz de Alarcón 13, 28014 Madrid, Spain

© Robin Headlam Wells 2000

This book is in copyright. Subject to statutory exception and to the provisions of relevant collective licensing agreements, no reproduction of any part may take place without the written permission of Cambridge University Press.

First published 2000

Printed in the United Kingdom at the University Press, Cambridge

Typeface Baskerville 11/12.5pt   *System* 3B2   [CE]

A catalogue record for this book is available from the British Library

Library of Congress Cataloguing in Publication data
Wells, Robin Headlam.
Shakespeare on masculinity / Robin Headlam Wells.
p. cm.
Includes bibliographical references and index.
ISBN 0 521 66204 4
1. Shakespeare, William, 1564–1616 – Characters – Men.   2. Masculinity in literature.
3. Kings and rulers in literature.   4. Heroes in literature.   5. Men in literature.   I. Title.
PR2992.M28 W45 2000
822.3′3–dc21   00-028952

ISBN 0 521 66204 4 hardback

Contents

Preface	*page*	vii
Abbreviations		ix
	Introduction	1
1	The chivalric revival: *Henry V* and *Troilus and Cressida*	31
2	'Tender and delicate prince': *Hamlet*	61
3	'O these men, these men': *Othello*	86
4	'Arms, and the Man': *Macbeth*	117
5	'Flower of warriors': *Coriolanus*	144
6	'Rarer action': *The Tempest*	177
	Afterword: historicism and 'presentism'	207
Select bibliography		219
Index		243

Preface

A search of the Modern Language Association of America's electronic database of scholarly articles and book reviews using the keyword 'masculinity' yields over 850 hits for the years 1981–99. A common theme in many of these items is summed up in such title phrases as 'the construction of masculinity in', or 'masculinity, trauma, and psychoanalysis in', or 'the cultural construction of femininity and masculinity in'. Only a small number of these works is concerned with early-modern literature. However, one book on the psychodynamics of gender construction that does deal with this period is Mark Breitenberg's *Anxious Masculinity in Early Modern England* (Cambridge University Press, 1996). Using post-Freudian psychoanalysis to uncover the processes by which the masculine subject is constructed in the early-modern period, Breitenberg aims to expose the contradictions and anomalies in patriarchal culture. My own approach to the question of masculinity is very different from Breitenberg's, as I hope will be clear from my Introduction. But I do not want to detain the reader with talk about what I am *not* going to say. Those who are interested in a discussion of the difference between a historicist and what is sometimes termed a 'presentist' approach to literature may begin by turning to the Afterword.

A number of people have been generous with their time either in answering questions on topics about which I was all too conscious of being ignorant, or in reading drafts of chapters and putting me right on matters about which I did not know that I was ignorant. These include: Helen Baron, James Booth, Glenn Burgess, Mandy Capern, Tom Clayton, Lesley Coote, W.L. Godshalk, A.C. Hamilton, Jenny Headlam Wells, Owen Knowles, Peter Lamarque, Richard Levin, Tom McAlindon, Steven Marx, Lionel North, Anita Pacheco, Derek

Roper, Lisa Rodriguez, Wendy Scase, Raymond Tallis, Blair Worden, and Rowland Wymer. I am grateful to all of them, but especially to Helen Baron who gave me so much of her time. I also benefited enormously from the late Peggy Muñoz Simonds' encyclopaedic knowledge of Renaissance iconography. My anonymous readers gave me invaluable advice, for which I am profoundly grateful.

I am grateful also to the newly established Arts and Humanities Research Board for granting me a Study Leave award for 1999. This enabled me to finish a project that I started some years ago and had to lay aside when I was asked to take on a major managerial job.

Finally, I wish to thank my editor, Victoria Cooper, for her encouragement and support.

Chapters 1, 4, 5 and 6 first appeared in a different form in *Shakespeare and History*, ed. Holger Klein and Rowland Wymer (Edwin Mellen Press: Lewiston, Queenstown and Lampeter, 1996), the Proceedings of the 8th International Conference of the Spanish Society for English Renaissance Studies (Seville: SEDERI, 1997), *Review of English Studies*, and *Neo-Historicism: Studies in Renaissance Literature, History and Politics*, ed. Robin Headlam Wells, Glenn Burgess and Rowland Wymer (D. S. Brewer, 2000), respectively. I am grateful to the Edwin Mellen Press, SEDERI, Oxford University Press, and Boydell & Brewer Ltd for permission to reprint material in revised form.

Note: in quotations from early books and other documents I have retained original spelling, but have modernized 'u', 'v', 'i', and 'j'. All quotations from Shakespeare are from *The Complete Works* (modern spelling edn.), ed. Stanley Wells and Gary Taylor (Oxford: Clarendon Press, 1986).

Abbreviations

PERIODICALS

AHR	*American Historical Review*
AST	*Assaph Studies in the Theatre*
BJJ	*Ben Jonson Journal*
BJRL	*Bulletin of the John Rylands Library*
BNYPL	*Bulletin of the New York Public Library*
CEAC	*CEA Critic*
CR	*The Centennial Review*
CD	*Comparative Drama*
CQ	*Critical Quarterly*
DH	*The Dalhousie Review*
Dia	*Diacritics*
ELH	*Journal of English Literary History*
ELR	*English Literary Renaissance*
ES	*English Studies*
EC	*Essays in Criticism*
Exp	*Explicator*
HS	*Hamlet Studies*
HJ	*The Historical Journal*
HT	*History and Theory*
JBS	*Journal of British Studies*
JEGP	*Journal of English and Germanic Philology*
JSH	*Journal of Social History*
JSP	*Journal of Social Philosophy*
JWCI	*Journal of the Warburg and Courtauld Institutes*
JWI	*Journal of the Warburg Institute*
MSHS	*Miscellany of the Scottish History Society*
MLQ	*Modern Language Quarterly*
MLR	*Modern Language Review*

NET	*Nordisk Estetisk Tidskrift*
NQ	*Notes and Queries*
PBA	*Proceedings of the British Academy*
PEAS	*Papers in English and American Studies*
PMLA	*Publications of the Modern Language Association of America*
PTRSC	*Proceedings and Transactions of the Royal Society of Canada*
Renforum	*Renaissance Forum*
RenQ	*Renaissance Quarterly*
RS	*Renaissance Studies*
Rep	*Representations*
RES	*Review of English Studies*
RP	*Review of Politics*
RUS	*Rice University Studies*
Rin	*Rinascimento*
SC	*The Seventeenth Century*
SewR	*Sewanee Review*
SQ	*Shakespeare Quarterly*
SStud	*Shakespeare Studies*
SST	*Shakespeare Studies Tokyo*
ShS	*Shakespeare Survey*
SAQ	*South Atlantic Quarterly*
SEL	*Studies in English Literature*
SP	*Studies in Philology*
TRI	*Theatre Research International*
TS	*Theatre Studies*
TD	*Themes in Drama*
TLS	*Times Literary Supplement*
TAPS	*Transactions of the American Philosophical Society*
UMSE	*University of Mississippi Studies in English*
UTQ	*University of Toronto Quarterly*
UCROW	*The Upstart Crow*
YR	*The Yale Review*
YSS	*Yearbook of Shakespeare Studies*

SHAKESPEARE'S PLAYS AND POEMS

Ant.	*Antony and Cleopatra*
Cor.	*Coriolanus*
Cym.	*Cymbeline*
Ham.	*Hamlet*

1H4	*Henry IV, Part 1*
2H4	*Henry IV, Part 2*
H5	*Henry V*
1H6	*Henry VI, Part 1*
JC	*Julius Caesar*
Jn.	*King John*
Luc.	*The Rape of Lucrece*
Mac.	*Macbeth*
MM	*Measure for Measure*
MND	*A Midsummer Night's Dream*
MV	*The Merchant of Venice*
Oth.	*Othello*
Per.	*Pericles*
R3	*Richard III*
Rom.	*Romeo and Juliet*
Son.	*Sonnets*
Tit.	*Titus Andronicus*
Tmp.	*The Tempest*
Tro.	*Troilus and Cressida*
WT	*The Winter's Tale*

Introduction

> It is fayned that ... Orpheus assembled the wilde beasts to come in heards to harken to his musicke, and by that meanes made them tame, implying thereby, how by his discreete and wholsome lessons uttered in harmonie and with melodious instruments, he brought the rude and savage people to a more civill and orderly life.
> George Puttenham, *The Arte of English Poesie*, p. 6

> Long ago, when rude primitive men lived in the woods, naked, without ramparts, roofless, it sometimes happened that they were attacked by wild beasts. And so it was on them that man first made war, and the one who defended the human race from the onslaught of the wild animals was held to be a man of mettle, and taken for leader. Indeed it seemed entirely right that the stabbers should be stabbed, the butchers butchered, especially when they were attacking us without provocation. Since these exploits won high praise – for that was how Hercules was made a god – spirited youth began to hunt the animals far and wide, and to show off their skins as a trophy.
> Erasmus, 'Dulce bellum inexpertis', *Adages*, p. 317

> The story of Orpheus, which though so well known has not yet been in all points perfectly well interpreted, seems meant for a representation of universal philosophy. For Orpheus himself – a man admirable and truly divine, who being master of all harmony subdued and drew all things after him by the sweet and gentle measures – may pass by an easy metaphor for philosophy personified. For as the works of wisdom surpass in dignity and power the works of strength, so the labours of Orpheus surpass the labours of Hercules.
> Francis Bacon, *The Wisdom of the Ancients, Philosophical Works*, p. 835

This book is about Shakespeare's heroes. That is to say, it is about men. There are, of course, heroines in the plays, and some of them die tragically. But they are not heroic in the sense in which Henry V or Macbeth or Coriolanus are heroic, or in which it sometimes seems that Hamlet would like to be heroic. For the Renaissance the heroic ideal is essentially masculine. The qualities it evokes – courage, physical strength, prowess in battle, manly honour, defiance of fortune – may be summed up in a word whose Latin root means 'a man'. As English Renaissance writers understand the term, *virtus* signifies an ideal of manhood that derives partly from classical epic, partly from medieval chivalry, and partly from Italian *realpolitik*. Though women may occasionally display heroic qualities, they are exceptions that prove the rule. Heroes in Shakespeare are, by definition, men.

THE HEROIC IDEAL

In the Renaissance most critics agree that heroic poetry is the highest literary form. By providing an ideal pattern of human conduct it serves, in theory at least, as a source of moral inspiration. 'For as the image of each action stirreth and instructeth the mind,' wrote Sir Philip Sidney, 'so the lofty image of [the classical] worthies most inflameth the mind with desire to be worthy.'[1] But Sidney's didactic theory does not match literary practice. Listing some of the greatest heroes of classical and Renaissance poetry, Sidney asks how anyone could speak evil of such champions when they are capable of making 'magnanimity and justice shine throughout all misty fearfulness and foggy desires' (119). The answer is that characters like Achilles and Turnus are not just paragons of 'magnanimity and justice'; they are remarkable also for their ferocity. Even Aeneas, Sidney's supreme example of the epic hero, combines steadfast piety with a savage and vindictive brutality (see below, Chapter 4, pp. 130–3). Tasso gets closer to the truth about the peculiar fascination of the epic hero when he admits that heroes defy conventional morality. Following Aristotle, he distinguishes between moral virtue, which consists in a mean between extremes, and heroic virtue, which is a kind of greatness that defies description, an excess, as it were, of virtue ('un eccesso, per cosi dire, della virtù').[2] As Eugene Waith explains in *The Herculean Hero*, essential to the heroic

---

[1] Sir Philip Sidney, *An Apology for Poetry*, ed. Geoffrey Shepherd (London: Nelson, 1965), p. 119.
[2] Torquato Tasso, 'Della Virtù Eroica e Della Carità', *Prose Filosofiche* (Florence: Alcide Parenti, 1847), p. 355.

Introduction 3

ideal is a sense of awe and wonder at the transgression of normal limits. The exploits of the classic hero of mythology, writes Waith,

> are strange mixtures of beneficence and crime, of fabulous quests and shameful betrayals, of triumph over wicked enemies and insensate slaughter of the innocent, yet the career is always a testimony to the greatness of a man who is almost a god . . . That is not to say that tales about the hero excuse his moral defects, but rather that they point to a special morality.[3]

The sense of awe and wonder that is integral to the heroic ideal is an essential ingredient in Shakespearean tragedy. The spectacle of men of great courage or exceptional idealism destroying their own and others' lives may not be unique to Shakespeare. But the conflicting feelings generated by this paradox are arguably more intense in his tragedies than in any other body of drama. According to Paul Jorgensen, 'one of the miracles of Shakespeare's tragedies is how we can learn to love, when he suffers, a man whom we disliked'.[4] But *are* we expected to love Shakespeare's heroes? Feminism has taught us to be suspicious of men who claim to be like gods, especially when 'slaughter of the innocent' is justified by appeal to a 'special morality'.[5] Waith is right in saying that an important dimension of Shakespearean tragedy is lost when the hero's nobility and idealism are underplayed.[6] But the fact that Shakespeare emphasizes the heroic stature of his male protagonists and the awe they inspire does not necessarily mean that he accepts heroic conventions uncritically.

Many scholars have written on the heroic ideal in Renaissance literature. Some believe that Shakespeare was essentially in sympathy with heroic values and make it their task to recover an imaginative understanding of those values for our own unheroic age;[7] others draw attention to contemporary distinctions between

---

[3] Eugene M. Waith, *The Herculean Hero in Marlowe, Chapman, Shakespeare and Dryden* (London: Chatto & Windus, 1962), p. 16.
[4] Paul Jorgensen, *William Shakespeare: The Tragedies* (Boston: Twayne, 1985), p. 8.
[5] Commenting on the widely reported case of a man who was exonerated by a High-Court judge after killing his wife in a domestic argument, Una Freeley of London Women's Aid writes: 'the avenues of escape from justice for men who kill women are many, varied and endlessly imaginative. They change according to fashionable social thought at any one time, but the results change little. She is dead and he gets the sympathy for having been so provoked as to kill her. Women who kill men are seen as mentally ill or just plain vicious, and this is reflected in their sentencing' (letter to *The Guardian*, 31 October 1994, p. 19).
[6] *Ideas of Greatness: Heroic Drama in England* (London: Routledge & Kegan Paul, 1971), p. 105.
[7] Waith writes: 'Few literary forms seem more remote than heroic drama in the age of the anti-hero and the common man, yet no age is truly against heroes, however distrustful it may be of heroic rhetoric' (*Ideas of Greatness*, p. xi). See also Waith, 'Manhood and Valor in Two Shakespearean Tragedies', *ELH*, 17 (1950), 262–73; *The Herculean Hero*; Curtis Brown

true and debased forms of manly honour, arguing that the fall of Shakespeare's heroes can usually be attributed to a decline from the former to the latter.[8] From the mid 1970s feminist critics began to consider the previously invisible issue of gender in the plays.[9] The body of work that followed in the next decade was, as Ann Thompson rightly says, the most lively, productive, and influential

---

Watson, *Shakespeare and the Renaissance Concept of Honor* (Princeton: Princeton University Press, 1960); G.K. Hunter, 'The Heroism of Hamlet', *Hamlet*, ed. John Russell Brown and Bernard Harris, Stratford-upon-Avon Studies 5 (London: Arnold, 1963), pp. 90–109; David Riggs, *Shakespeare's Heroical Histories: Henry VI and its Literary Tradition* (Cambridge, Mass.: Harvard University Press, 1971); Alice Shalvi, *The Relationship of Renaissance Concepts of Honour to Shakespeare's Problem Plays* (Salzburg: University of Salzburg, 1972); James C. Bulman, *The Heroic Idiom of Shakespearean Tragedy* (Newark, N.J.: University of Delaware Press, 1985).

[8] Contrasting 'true honour' with 'empty versions of honour', Theodor Meron writes: 'I show Shakespeare's sympathy for chivalry as an ideal, a sharp contrast to his sarcasm for vain and excessive chivalry and exaggerated and dangerous notions of honour' (*Bloody Constraint: War and Chivalry in Shakespeare* (New York and Oxford: Oxford University Press, 1998), p. 8. See also Norman Council, *When Honour's at the Stake: Ideas of Honour in Shakespeare's Plays* (London: Allen & Unwin, 1973); Richard S. Ide, *Possessed with Greatness: The Heroic Tragedies of Chapman and Shakespeare* (London: Scolar Press, 1980); Charles Barber, *The Theme of Honour's Tongue: A Study of Social Attitudes in the English Drama from Shakespeare to Dryden* (Göteborg: University of Göteborg Press, 1985). In *The Heroic Image in Five Shakespearean Tragedies* (Princeton: Princeton University Press, 1965), Matthew N. Proser makes a different kind of distinction, arguing that each of Shakespeare's heroes is torn between a heroic self-image and his 'full humanity' (p. 3).

[9] Juliet Dusinberre, *Shakespeare and the Nature of Women* (London: Macmillan, 1975). See also Carol Thomas Neely, 'Women and Men in *Othello*', *SStud*, 10 (1977), 133–58; Janet Adelman, '"Anger's my meat": Feeding, Dependency and Aggression in *Coriolanus*', *Shakespeare: Pattern of Excelling Nature*, ed. David Bevington and Jay L. Halio (Newark, N.J.: University of Delaware Press, 1978), pp. 108–24; Adelman, *Suffocating Mothers: Fantasies of Maternal Origin in Shakespeare's Plays, 'Hamlet' to 'The Tempest'* (London and New York: Routledge, 1992); Carolyn Ruth Swift Lenz, Gayle Greene, and Carol Thomas Neely, *The Woman's Part: Feminist Criticism of Shakespeare* (Urbana, Chicago, and London: University of Illinois Press, 1980); Irene Dash, *Wooing, Wedding, and Power: Women in Shakespeare's Plays* (New York: Columbia University Press, 1981); Marilyn French, *Shakespeare's Division of Experience* (London: Jonathan Cape, 1982); Coppélia Kahn, *Man's Estate: Masculine Identity in Shakespeare* (Berkeley, Los Angeles, and London: University of California Press, 1981); Kahn, *Roman Shakespeare: Warriors, Wounds, and Women* (London and New York: Routledge, 1997); Linda Bamber, *Comic Women, Tragic Men: A Study of Gender and Genre in Shakespeare* (Stanford: Stanford University Press, 1982); Lisa Jardine, *Still Harping on Daughters: Women and Drama in the Age of Shakespeare* (New York and London: Harvester Wheatsheaf, 1983); Marianne Novy, *Love's Argument: Gender Relations in Shakespeare* (Chapel Hill: University of North Carolina Press, 1984); Peter Erickson, *Patriarchal Structures in Shakespeare's Drama* (Berkeley, Los Angeles, and London: University of California Press, 1985); Kathleen McLuskie, 'The Patriarchal Bard: Feminist Criticism and Shakespeare', *Political Shakespeare: New Essays in Cultural Materialism*, ed. Jonathan Dollimore and Alan Sinfield (Manchester: Manchester University Press, 1985) pp. 88–108; Jeanne Addison Roberts, *The Shakespearean Wild: Geography, Genus, and Gender* (Lincoln, Nebr. and London: University of Nebraska Press, 1991); Jean E. Howard and Phyllis Rackin, *Engendering a Nation: A Feminist Account of Shakespeare's English Histories* (London and New York: Routledge, 1997); Curtis Perry, *The Making of Jacobean Culture: James I and the Renegotiation of Elizabethan Literary Practice* (Cambridge: Cambridge University Press, 1997), pp. 115–49.

aspect of Shakespeare criticism in the 1980s.[10] With continuing disagreement over the question of whether or not Shakespeare was in sympathy with the misogynist ideas expressed by so many of his characters, Jonathan Dollimore is probably right when he says that the question that unites the diverse body of feminist Shakespeare scholarship is: 'do these plays endorse the conservative and, to us, oppressive views of gender which prevailed in their society, or do they challenge them'.[11] Finally, following seminal work by Francis Barker, Catherine Belsey, Jonathan Dollimore, and Louis Montrose in the mid 1980s,[12] materialist criticism has concerned itself in recent years with what Megan Matchinske calls 'the cultural dynamics of gender construction' in the early-modern period.[13]

However, none of these critics explains that masculine honour was a political issue throughout the period when Shakespeare was writing his tragedies and tragi-comedies. Indeed it is something of a paradox that materialist criticism, with its Foucault-inspired interest in the dynamics of power, should show less interest in the overt and well-reported political conflicts of the period than in the more metaphysical question of how an emergent capitalist state acquires

---

[10] Ann Thompson, '"The warrant of womanhood": Shakespeare and Feminist Criticism', *The Shakespeare Myth*, ed. Graham Holderness (Manchester: Manchester University Press, 1988), p. 74.

[11] 'Critical Development: Cultural Materialism, Feminism and Gender Critique, and New Historicism', *Shakespeare: A Bibliographical Guide*, ed. Stanley Wells (Oxford: Clarendon Press, 1990), p. 416.

[12] Francis Barker, *The Tremulous Private Body: Essays in Subjection* (London and New York: Methuen, 1984); Jonathan Dollimore, *Radical Tragedy: Religion, Ideology and Power in the Drama of Shakespeare and his Contemporaries* (1984; repr. Brighton: Harvester Press, 1986); Catherine Belsey, *The Subject of Tragedy* (London and New York: Methuen, 1985); Louis Montrose, 'Renaissance Literary Studies and the Subject of History', *ELR*, 16 (1986), 5–12.

[13] Megan Matchinske, *Writing, Gender and State in Early Modern England: Identity Formation and the Female Subject* (Cambridge: Cambridge University Press, 1998), p. 6. See also Thomas Laqueur, *Making Sex: Body and Gender from the Greeks to Freud* (Cambridge, Mass. and London: Harvard University Press, 1990); Valerie Wayne ed., *The Matter of Difference: Materialist Feminist Criticism of Shakespeare* (New York and London: Harvester Wheatsheaf, 1991); Valerie Traub, *Desire and Anxiety: Circulations of Sexuality in Shakespearean Drama* (London and New York: Routledge, 1992); Laura Levine, *Men in Women's Clothing: Anti-theatricality and Effeminization, 1579–1642* (Cambridge: Cambridge University Press, 1994); Deborah Barker and Ivo Kamps, eds., *Shakespeare and Gender: A History* (London and New York: Verso, 1995); Mark Breitenberg, *Anxious Masculinity in Early Modern England* (Cambridge: Cambridge University Press, 1996); Richard Hillman, *Self-Speaking in Medieval and Early Modern English Drama: Subjectivity, Discourse and the Stage* (Basingstoke and New York: Macmillan, 1997); Kahn, *Roman Shakespeare*; Elizabeth Hanson, *Discovering the Subject in Renaissance England* (Cambridge: Cambridge University Press, 1998); Eve Rachele Sanders, *Gender and Literacy on Stage in Early Modern England* (Cambridge: Cambridge University Press, 1998); Andrew P. Williams, ed., *The Image of Manhood in Early Modern Literature: Viewing the Male* (Westport, Conn. and London: Greenwood Press, 1999).

control over individuals by constructing them as seemingly autonomous subjects.[14] Yet, as I shall explain, the conflicting political positions signalled by such coded phrases as 'courage-masculine' and 'manly virtue' caused deeper divisions in Elizabeth's and James' Privy Councils than any other topic of public debate in late-Elizabethan and early-Stuart England. Those conflicts very nearly resulted in the deposition of a reigning monarch, and later provoked a bitter and embarrassingly public rift between her successor and the crown prince. Shakespeare's tragedies are not allegories. But they do engage closely with these political issues, increasingly so after 1603 when Shakespeare wrote a series of plays dealing with matters of government and policy that seem to have a close bearing on James' own concerns.[15] Though all the tragedies and most of the comedies and histories inevitably concern themselves in one way or another with the question of 'manhood and honour' (*Tro.*, II.ii.46), the plays I shall deal with in the chapters that follow have a particular bearing on the politics of masculinity. James himself showed no great enthusiasm for the theatre and does not seem to have been particularly interested in plays as a way of shaping public opinion.[16] But the fact that public debate of foreign policy was forbidden only encouraged playwrights to devise oblique ways of dealing with these issues.[17] Judging from the volume of plays on historical and political topics that were performed in the 1590s and 1600s,[18] the playgoing public's appetite for political drama was insatiable. The bulk of plays dealing with matters of state in this period were tragedies. And since

[14] Francis Barker writes: 'The defining feature of the bourgeois discursive regime is the *in situ* control . . . of the newly interiorated subject' (*The Tremulous Private Body*, p. 52).
[15] On the political dimension of Shakespeare's Stuart plays see Jonathan Goldberg, *James I and the Politics of Literature: Jonson, Shakespeare, Donne, and Their Contemporaries* (Baltimore and London: Johns Hopkins University Press, 1983); Leah Marcus, *Puzzling Shakespeare: Local Reading and its Discontents* (Berkeley, Los Angeles, and London: University of California Press, 1988), pp. 106–59; Alvin Kernan, *Shakespeare, the King's Playwright: Theater in the Stuart Court 1603–1613* (New Haven, Conn. and London: Yale University Press, 1995); Constance Jordan, *Shakespeare's Monarchies: Ruler and Subject in the Romances* (Ithaca and London: Cornell University Press, 1997).
[16] J. Leeds Barroll, *Politics, Plague, and Shakespeare's Theater: The Stuart Years* (Ithaca and London: Cornell University Press, 1991), pp. 25–31. See also Paul Yachnin, 'The Powerless Theatre', *ELR*, 21 (1991), 49–74.
[17] Tristan Marshall, '"That's the Misery of Peace": Representations of Martialism in the Jacobean Public Theatre, 1608–1614', *SC*, 13 (1998), 1–21.
[18] In the twenty-year period from 1590 to 1610 approximately sixty-five tragedies or historical plays were performed at court and the public playhouses (G.K. Hunter, *English Drama 1586–1642*, *The Oxford History of English Literature* (Oxford: Clarendon Press, 1997), pp. 554–68).

the heroic ideal is never far away in English Renaissance tragedy, it is not surprising that Shakespeare's political plays should return repeatedly to Hamlet's question: 'What is a man?' (*Ham.*, IV.iv.33).

'COURAGE-MASCULINE'

In a recent socio-historical study of gender entitled *Manhood in Early Modern England* Elizabeth Foyster explains that she uses the word 'manhood' rather than 'masculinity' because 'the latter was only employed by contemporaries from the mid-eighteenth century'.[19] Though it is true that early-modern writers do not use the word in its substantive form, the adjective 'masculine' was a familiar term in Shakespeare's working lifetime. Seventeenth- and eighteenth-century poets who aspired to an Horatian ideal of urbanity were expected to show what Addison called 'a good Fund of strong Masculine Sense'.[20] But in Shakespeare's lifetime the word masculine was often used to signify martial or heroic qualities.[21] When the Duke of Burgundy asks Talbot and Bedford about Joan of Arc's character in the first part of *Henry VI*, Talbot replies, 'A maid, they say'. Bedford interjects, 'A maid? And be so martial?', to which Burgundy responds, 'Pray God she prove not masculine ere long' (*1H6*, II.i.21–2). Complimenting another paragon of chastity on her seemingly impregnable honour, Tharsalio, the opportunistic fortune hunter in George Chapman's *Widow's Tears* (*c.* 1605), speaks banteringly of Eudora's 'Masculine and Heroicall vertues'.[22]

The relative worth of qualities thought to be peculiar to men or women is a stereotyped Elizabethan debating *topos*. In the anonymous University Satire *Return from Parnassus* (*c.* 1602) Sir Raderick says to Immerito, 'Very learnedly in good faith, I pray now let me aske you one question that I remember, whether is the Masculine gender or the feminine more worthy?'.[23] Repeated again and again

---

[19] Elizabeth A. Foyster, *Manhood in Early Modern England: Honour, Sex and Marriage* (London and New York: Longman, 1999), p. 5. See also Anthony Fletcher, *Gender, Sex and Subordination in England, 1500–1800* (New Haven, Conn.: Yale University Press, 1995).
[20] *The Spectator*, no. 618, ed. Donald F. Bond, 5 vols. (Oxford: Clarendon Press, 1965), vol. V, p. 113.
[21] Watson notes that 'Manhood or manliness was in the Renaissance a popular synonym for valor' (*Shakespeare and the Renaissance Concept of Honor*, p. 245).
[22] *The Widow's Tears*, II.iv.187, *The Plays of George Chapman: The Comedies*, ed. Allan Holaday and Michael Kiernan (Urbana, Chicago, and London: University of Illinois Press, 1970), p. 505.
[23] *The Return from Parnassus, or the Scourge of Simony*, III.i, ed. Edward Arber (London: English Scholar's Library, 1879), p. 36.

in debate plays and courtesy books, often with identical phrasing,[24] this formulaic question has more to do with a medieval tradition of polemic on marriage and the nature of women than with any contemporary political issue. However, for a brief period the collocation of 'martial' and 'masculine' took on a very specific and local meaning. In militant-Protestant circles it formed part of a pattern of praising martial values by characterizing them as masculine and depreciating eirenic values as feminine.[25] In *A Fig for Fortune*, Anthony Copley's bizarre allegorical tribute to Elizabeth, the dreamer is told by the spirit of Revenge that

> To be faire Fortunes ever Carpet-darling
> Is female glorie: But Reveng'd disgrace
> That's truly Masculine, and rich triumphing:
> Al peace-content is too too cheap and base:
> What manhood is it still to feed on Chickins
> Like infant nurse-boys in nice Fortunes kitchins.[26]

On the accession of James I, John Davies of Hereford wrote a panegyric to the young Prince of Wales in which he took a more sympathetic view of such assertive masculinity, praising the prince as inheritor of that 'Courage-masculine' which the legendary Brutus had bequeathed to his ancestors. It was Brutus' martial spirit, Davies tells Henry, which made the ancient British a proud and noble people; for that was a time

> When with our Swordes we did the Land convince.
> Wee were a People free, and freely fought
> For glorie, freedome, and preheminence.[27]

---

[24] Sir Raderick's question is a standard debating *topos*. In Greene's *Friar Bacon and Friar Bungay* the irreverent Miles warns Bacon's visitors of his master's predictable disputing questions: 'Marry, sir, he'll straight be on you pick-pack to know whether the feminine or the masculine gender be the most worthy' (Scene ii.88–90, New Mermaid edn., ed. J.A. Lavin (London: Ernest Benn, 1969), p. 17). The same formula appears in Lyly's *Midas* (1592): 'Thou servest Mellacrites, and I his daughter, which is the better man?', asks Licio. Petulus returns the pat answer: 'The Masculin gender is more worthy then the feminine' (I.ii.1–4, *The Complete Works of John Lyly*, 3 vols., ed. R. Warwick Bond (Oxford: Clarendon Press, 1902), vol. III, p. 119). The same question is debated in George Whetstone's colloquium on marriage. When Ismarito claims that 'Sovereigne Vertue is Feminine, and . . . Yrksome Vice is Masculine' the ladies laugh at him and tell him that his countrymen must be effeminate (*An Heptameron of Civill Discourses* (London, 1582), p. 118).

[25] On 'masculine' wartime values and 'feminine' peacetime values see Linda Woodbridge, *Women and the English Renaissance: Literature and the Nature of Womenkind, 1540–1620* (Brighton: Harvester Press, 1984), pp. 161–2. Woodbridge does not discuss the political implications of these designations.

[26] *A Fig for Fortune* (1596) facsimile edn. (London: Spenser Society, 1883), p. 12.

[27] John Davies of Hereford, *Microcosmos* (London, 1603), p. 37.

Davies' panegyric was one of many tributes commissioned over the following nine years by politicians and aristocrats who saw in the young prince a symbolic focus for the political aspirations of militant Protestantism. For Henry's supporters, as for members of the old Sidney–Essex alliance, the terms 'masculine' and 'manly', together with 'chivalrous', 'virtuous', and 'honourable', were a code that signalled allegiance to a well defined political agenda.[28] Involving, as it did, an aggressively interventionist foreign policy, that agenda was in direct conflict with James' openly declared commitment to the realization of peace in Europe. To praise a courtier for his manly honour or his chivalric virtue was to acknowledge his sympathy with the aims of the war party. In 1605 Samuel Daniel published a poem called 'Ulisses and the Syren'. The poem is a dialogue in which the hero, who represents the war party, is tempted by the siren voice of peace. 'Come worthy Greeke, *Ulisses* come / Possesse these shores with me', pleads the siren,[29]

> Here may we sit, and view their toile
> That travaile on the deepe,
> And joy the day in mirth the while,
> And spend the night in sleepe.

Ulysses replies that fame and honour are won, not in idleness and sleep, but through active pursuit of danger. When the siren tells him that honour is not worth the candle, he replies that even if there were no honour or fame to be won, 'Yet manlines would scorne to weare / The time in idle sport' (28–9). Sir Philip Sidney had been praised by contemporary admirers for his 'manlie' acts on the battlefield.[30] As a supporter of the Sidney–Essex faction, Daniel habitually identified true manliness with a warlike spirit.[31] In such a

---

[28] The counterpart of these heroic epithets is a cluster of words to do with sleep, dreams, enchantment, and idleness. Blair Worden notes that, 'Sidney's party use "sleep" as a metaphor for the fatal sense of "security" which, they held, was blinding [Protestant] princes to dangers at home and abroad' (*The Sound of Virtue: Philip Sidney's 'Arcadia' and Elizabethan Politics* (New Haven, Conn. and London: Yale University Press, 1996), p. 62). See also Worden, 'Ben Jonson Among the Historians', *Culture and Politics in Early Stuart England*, ed. Kevin Sharpe and Peter Lake (Basingstoke: Macmillan, 1994) pp. 67–89.

[29] 'Ulisses and the Syren', 1–2, 5–8, *The Complete Works in Verse and Prose of Samuel Daniel*, 5 vols., ed. Alexander B. Grosart (London, 1885–96), vol. I (1885) pp. 270–1.

[30] Angel Day, *Upon the life and death of the most worthy, and thrise renowned knight, Sir Phillip Sidney* (London, 1586), Sig. B^v.

[31] See, for example, 'To The Lord Henrie Howard', Daniel, *The Complete Works*, vol. I, p. 201, line 78; *The Civile Wars*, Book IV, *Complete Works*, vol. II, p. 156, lines 439–40; Book VIII, vol. II, p. 304, lines 147–8; Book VIII, vol. II, pp. 333, lines 852–3.

context, where manliness is usually associated with aggressive militarism, Lady Macbeth's characterization of regicide as an act of heroic manhood would have had a pointed significance for Shakespeare's new peace-loving patron: 'When you durst do it, then you were a man;' she tells Macbeth, 'And to be more than what you were, you would / Be so much more the man' (I.vii.49–51). But *Macbeth* is no simple condemnation of heroic values (see below, Chapter 4). In dramatizing the story of James' dynastic origins in the violent world of medieval Scotland, Shakespeare shows that the revolution that transformed an inherently unstable society of warring nobles into an hereditary monarchy of unprecedented longevity was itself accomplished, ironically, by heroic violence. 'Let grief / Convert to anger; blunt not the heart, enrage it' (IV.iii.228–9), Malcolm tells Macduff as he urges him to avenge, in an act that Anthony Copley would have described as 'truly Masculine', the murder of his wife and children. No play is written in an intellectual vacuum, least of all Shakespeare's tragedies. It may help to clarify some of the public issues that Shakespeare deals with in these plays if we review the political history of heroic masculinity in sixteenth- and early seventeenth-century England.

'ENGLISSHE CHEVALRIE'

During the last years of Elizabeth's reign, and particularly after Burghley's death in the summer of 1598, there was deep unrest at court as political rivals jostled for power in an atmosphere of slander, calumny, and backbiting. 'See how these great men cloath their private hate / In those faire colours of the publike good', wrote Daniel in a play based closely on the Essex rebellion.[32] One result of the disillusionment with court life which this decline of standards inevitably led to was a vogue for Tacitean drama and Juvenalian satire in which the corruption of the rich and powerful is exposed to cynical scrutiny.[33] As a number of revisionist historians have shown, the real intellectual and political debates of the period were not

---

[32] *Philotas*, III.iii.1135–6, *Complete Works*, vol. III, p. 144.
[33] Blair Worden, 'Classical Republicanism and the Puritan Revolution', *History and Imagination: Essays in Honour of H.R. Trevor-Roper*, ed. Hugh Lloyd-Jones, Valerie Pearl and Blair Worden (London: Duckworth, 1981), pp. 182–200; Worden, 'Ben Jonson Among the Historians'; Malcolm Smuts, 'Court-Centred Politics and the Uses of Roman Historians c. 1590–1630', *Culture and Politics in Early Stuart England*, ed. Sharpe and Lake, pp. 21–43.

between the court and its opponents, or even, more broadly, between absolutists and constitutionalists, but between rival factions within the court.[34] Chief among the policy issues that were disputed in the 1590s and 1600s was England's relations with Spain. The final decade of the century saw the spectacular rise and fall of the most charismatic and the most dangerous of all Elizabeth's courtiers. Robert Devereux, the second Earl of Essex, was the central figure of an aristocratic faction that wanted to restore military values to a society that had, in Essex's words, grown generally 'unwarlicke, in love with the name, and bewitched with the delight of peace'.[35] Renewal of the war with Spain was one of Essex's chief objectives. To his admirers Essex was a symbol of national pride, the 'Faire branch of Honor' and 'flower of Chevalrie'.[36]

Originating in the Middle Ages as the code of values of a military aristocracy, chivalry placed paramount emphasis on the masculine virtues of physical courage and military prowess as the guarantors of justice and honour.[37] Where this involved dynastic rights of the kind that were at issue in the Hundred Years War, chivalry provided justification for aggressive international action. In exhorting Edward IV to defend his territorial rights, William of Worcester appealed to 'ye noble Englisshe chevalrie . . . to take armes and enterprinses [sic], seeing so many good examples before yow of so many victorius

---

[34] See Alan G.R. Smith, 'Constitutional Ideas and Parliamentary Developments in England 1603–1625', *The Reign of James VI and I*, ed. Alan G.R. Smith (London: Macmillan, 1973), pp. 160–76; chapters by Munden and Sharpe in Kevin Sharpe, ed., *Faction and Parliament: Essays on Early Stuart History* (Oxford: Clarendon Press, 1978); Conrad Russell, *Parliaments and English Politics, 1621–1629* (Oxford: Oxford University Press, 1979), pp. 4–10; *Unrevolutionary England, 1603–1642* (London and Ronceverte: Hambledon Press, 1990); Barry Coward, *The Stuart Age: A History of England 1603–1714* (London and New York: Longman, 1980); R. Malcolm Smuts, ed., *Court Culture and the Origins of a Royalist Tradition in Early Stuart England* (Philadelphia: University of Pennsylvania Press, 1987); Mervyn James, *Society, Politics and Culture: Studies in Early Modern England* (1978; repr. Cambridge: Cambridge University Press, 1986), pp. 460–1; R.B. Wernham, *The Making of Elizabethan Foreign Policy, 1558–1603* (Berkeley, Los Angeles, and London: University of California Press, 1980), pp. 8–9; Glenn Burgess, *The Politics of the Ancient Constitution: An Introduction to English Political Thought, 1603–1642* (Basingstoke and London: Macmillan, 1992), pp. 109–14; *Absolute Monarchy and the Stuart Constitution* (New Haven, and London: Yale University Press, 1996); David Cressy, *Birth, Marriage, and Death: Ritual, Religion, and the Life-Cycle in Tudor and Stuart England* (Oxford: Oxford University Press, 1997), p. 11.

[35] *An Apologie of the Earl of Essex* (London, 1603), Sig. E^v.

[36] Edmund Spenser, *Prothalamion*, 146, *The Poetical Works*, ed. J.C. Smith and E. de Selincourt (London, New York, and Toronto: Oxford University Press, 1912), p. 602.

[37] See M.H. Keen, *Chivalry* (New Haven, and London: Yale University Press, 1984); Huizinga, *The Waning of the Middle Ages*, ch. 4; Malcolm Vale, *War and Chivalry: Warfare and Aristocratic Culture in England, France and Burgundy at the End of the Middle Ages* (London: Duckworth, 1981).

dedis in armes done by youre noble progenitoures'.[38] One of chivalry's most enduring legacies was the honour code, a system of values characterized above all by a stress on competitive assertiveness. As Mervyn James explains, the honour code both legitimized and provided moral reinforcement for 'a politics of violence'.[39] It was this medieval code of values that the Essex circle hoped to revive.[40] In a pamphlet in praise of the aristocratic leaders of the Essex faction Gervase Markam described honour as 'the food of every great spirit, and the very god which creates in high minds Heroical actions'.[41] Writing in pseudo-medieval verse George Peele described how, when he jousted at the Accession Day tilt in 1590, Essex appeared 'Yclad in mightie Armes of mourners hue, / And plume as blacke as Ravens wing' as a sign of mourning for Sidney, the man 'whose successor he / In love and Armes had ever vowed to be'.[42] In calling for a return to the heroic values of the past, the Essex faction was self-consciously rejecting three generations of anti-chivalric thinking.

With changing methods of warfare and the gradual disintegration of the feudal system of land tenure in which chivalry was rooted, the old martial values had been in decline at the end of the fifteenth century. 'O ye knyghtes of Englond,' complained Caxton in his *Book of the Ordre of Chyvalry* (an expanded translation of Ramón Lull's *Libre del Orde del Cavayleria*) 'where is the custome and usage of noble chyvalry that was used in those days?'.[43] What Arthur B. Ferguson calls 'The Indian Summer of English Chivalry' is the literary rear-

---

[38] William of Worcester, *The Boke of Noblesse: Addressed to King Edward IV on his Invasion of France*, with an introduction by John Gough Nichols (London: J.B. Nichols, 1860), p. 29.
[39] James, *Society, Politics and Culture*, p. 309.
[40] On the revival of chivalric values see Arthur B. Ferguson, *The Chivalric Tradition in Renaissance England* (Washington, London, and Toronto: The Folger Shakespeare Library, 1986). See also Sydney Anglo, ed., introduction to *Chivalry in the Renaissance* (Woodbridge, Suffolk: Boydell Press, 1990), pp. xi-xvi; Ferguson, *The Indian Summer of English Chivalry: Studies in the Decline and Transformation of Chivalric Idealism* (Durham, N.C.: Duke University Press, 1960); Richard C. McCoy, *The Rites of Knighthood: The Literature and Politics of Elizabethan Chivalry* (Berkeley, Los Angeles, and London: University of California Press, 1989); Roy Strong, *The Cult of Elizabeth* (London: Thames & Hudson, 1977); Frances Yates, *Astraea: The Imperial Theme in the Sixteenth Century* (London and Boston: Routledge & Kegan Paul, 1975), pp. 88-111.
[41] Gervase Markham, *Honour in his Perfection* (London, 1624) p. 4.
[42] 'Polyhymnia', *The Life and Works of George Peele*, 3 vols., ed. Charles Tyler Prouty (New Haven, Conn. and London: Yale University Press, 1952-70), vol. 1 (1952, ed. David H. Horne), pp. 235-6.
[43] Ramón Lull, *The Book of the Ordre of Chyvalry*, trans. William Caxton (c. 1483-5) (London: Early English Text Society, 1926), p. 122.

guard action of men like Malory and Hawes who wanted to revive an antiquated system of values that bore increasingly little relationship to contemporary social and military reality. By the second decade of the sixteenth century that system had been superseded by an entirely different code of values.

Fundamental to Renaissance humanism is a new sense of historical perspective. For the generation of Colet, Erasmus, and More, a medieval culture of violence had no place in the new world of civic humanism. The sword and shield of Erasmus' Christian knight were those, not of the medieval warrior, but of St Paul's metaphoric 'armour of God'(Eph. 6:13).[44] Of the early sixteenth-century anti-militarists Erasmus was the most passionate in his denunciation of war.[45] He conceded that war may be justified under exceptional circumstances, for example a Turkish attack against a Christian state.[46] But wars between Christian states are inexcusable. When Henry VIII came to the throne he had been praised by his contemporaries for his learning and his artistic accomplishments. But it quickly became apparent that his real ambition was to win honour and glory through a revival of chivalric military ideals.[47] In a barely concealed attack on the young king's expansionist policies, Erasmus denounced wars between Christian states as unmitigated folly:

Almost all wars between Christians have arisen from either stupidity or wickedness. Some young men, with no experience of life, inflamed by the bad examples of our forbears told in the histories that fools have compiled from foolish documents, and then encouraged by flatterers and stimulated by lawyers and theologians, with the consent and connivance of bishops, and even at their desire – these young men, I say, go into war out of rashness rather than badness; and then they learn, to the suffering of the whole world, that war is a thing to be avoided by every possible means.[48]

---

[44] Desiderius Erasmus, *Enchiridion Militis Christiani: An English Version*, ed. Anne M. O'Donnell, SND (Oxford: Early English Text Society, 1981), ch. 2, 'The wepons of a chrysten man', pp. 41–55.
[45] See Robert P. Adams, *The Better Part of Valor: More, Erasmus, Colet, and Vives on Humanism, War, and Peace 1496–1535* (Seattle: University of Washington Press, 1962), pp. 88–121; Philip C. Dust, *Three Renaissance Pacifists: Essays on the Theories of Erasmus, More, and Vives* (New York: Peter Lang, 1987), pp. 13–61. See also Steven Marx, 'Shakespeare's Pacifism', *RenQ*, 45 (1992), 49–95.
[46] 'Dulce bellum inexpertis', *The 'Adages' of Erasmus*, ed. and trans. Margaret Mann Phillips (Cambridge: Cambridge University Press, 1964), p. 348.
[47] J.J. Scarisbrick, *Henry VIII* (London: Eyre & Spottiswoode, 1968), pp. 21–4.
[48] *The 'Adages'*, p. 348.

Erasmus' friend More, though equivocal as always, was clearly satirizing chivalric attitudes when he described how the Utopians despise the notion of honour in battle, counting 'nothynge so much against glorie, as glory gotten in war'.[49] As C.S. Lewis disapprovingly put it, 'the military methods of More's Utopians are mischievously devised to flout the chivalric code at every turn'.[50] The powerful influence of Erasmus' thinking can also be seen in Sir Thomas Elyot's *The Governour*. Though not a pacifist, Elyot upheld the humanist emphasis on the primacy of learning. Comparing social values in the modern world with the 'doctryne of auncient noble men', he claimed that the reason for the decay of learning in the modern world was contempt for education among the aristocracy. Elyot's model of princely virtue was Henry I, known as Henry Beau Clerke for his learning. Contrasting him with his brother Robert, 'a man of moche prowesse, and right expert in martial affayres', Elyot praised Henry as the superior leader because his wisdom and learning enabled him to add 'polycie to vertue and courage'.[51] In drawing up a scheme of education for a newly emerging governing class Elyot omitted from his list of physical exercises suitable for noblemen any discussion of the tournaments that for Castiglione's courtier are a way of acquiring martial prowess.[52] For Elyot honour was to be won, not through battle, but through public service. The purpose of studying 'morall philosophie' was to create a just society based on 'vertues, maners, and civile policie'.[53] Later in the century Elizabeth's tutor Ascham showed a similar scorn for the militaristic element in medieval chivalry when he complained that Malory's *Morte D'Arthur* was nothing but 'open mans slaughter and bold bawdrye'.[54] For Erasmian humanists chivalry was a denial of their most fundamental beliefs.[55]

---

[49] Thomas More, *Utopia*, trans. Raphe Robinson (1551) with an introduction by John O'Hagan (London and Toronto: Dent, 1910), p. 91.
[50] C.S. Lewis, *English Literature in the Sixteenth Century Excluding Drama* (London, Oxford, and New York: Oxford University Press, 1954), p. 29.
[51] Sir Thomas Elyot, *The Boke Named the Governour*, ed. Foster Watson (London: Dent, 1907), p. 49.
[52] Baldassare Castiglione, *The Book of the Courtier*, trans. Sir Thomas Hoby, ed. W.H.D. Rouse (London: Dent, 1928), p. 41.
[53] *The Governour*, p. 69.
[54] Roger Ascham, *The Scholemaster*, ed. W.A. Wright (Cambridge: Cambridge University Press, 1904), p. 231.
[55] See Norman Council, 'Ben Jonson, Inigo Jones, and the Transformation of Tudor Chivalry', *ELH*, 47 (1980), 259–75.

Though it cannot be said that the sixteenth century saw very significant advances in the social position of women, humanism did provide some foundation for sexual equality. Erasmus and Vives' programme for women's education may have been designed primarily to produce better wives,[56] but at least it showed, as Elizabeth's own example proved, that women could also be scholars. By contrast, the honour code is unequivocally masculine; its appeal is, as William of Worcester put it, to 'corage, feersnes, manlinesse and strength'.[57] Inspired by Erasmus' example, Elizabethan humanists spoke metaphorically of figures of rhetoric as 'martiall instruments both of defence & invasion', explaining that 'what the sword may do in war, [rhetoric] may performe in peace'.[58] It was the pacifist element in English civic humanism, with its contempt for masculine chivalric values that Sidney, and later Essex, wanted to reform.[59] Essex wanted to see a return to a national culture where 'martiall instruments' were not metaphoric but literal. In his *Apologie* he compared the unheroic present with 'those former gallant ages' when England did not hesitate 'to atchieve great conquests in Fraunce'.[60] Underlying his quarrel with Elizabeth was a masculinist belief that women were by nature unfitted for government. In his view the queen's failure to adopt a more aggressive foreign policy was due to the simple fact that she was a woman.[61] In the world of medieval romance, polarization of gender is taken to its ultimate extreme: men undertake heroic quests and surmount impossible obstacles; women serve as their inspiration and reward. In such a world, where women are idealized as spiritually superior beings, misogyny is never far away.

When Essex wrote his *Apologie* the simmering rivalry between the two main factions in the Privy Council was rapidly approaching

---

[56] Ruth Kelso, *Doctrine for the Lady of the Renaissance* (Urbana: University of Illinois Press, 1956), pp. 78–135.
[57] *The Boke of Noblesse*, p. 9.
[58] Henry Peacham the Elder, *The Garden of Eloquence* (1593), with an introduction by William G. Crane (Gainesville, Fla.: Scholars' Facsimiles and Reprints, 1954), Sig. ABiv.
[59] On Sidney's belief in the importance of national honour and his commitment to an aggressive policy towards Spain see Worden, *The Sound of Virtue, passim*.
[60] Devereux, *An Apologie*, Sig. D3ᵛ.
[61] James, *Society, Politics and Culture*, p. 444. Ironically, Essex's prejudices concerning women's unsuitability for rule are endorsed by a woman's advice. Lady Macbeth's words to her husband as she urges him to overcome his scruples about murdering Duncan – 'When you durst do it, then you were a man' – echo the values of the Essex circle and its revivalist interest in heroic manhood.

crisis point.⁶² On one side were the Cecils, astute and scheming politicians, but concerned above all to contain conflict, both at home and abroad. On the other was Essex, arrogant, mercurial, paranoid, and desperate for military glory. Where the Cecils instinctively favoured civilian rule, Essex would have liked to have done away with civil magistracy altogether and to have replaced it with martial law. His dream was of a military society ruled by an aristocratic élite. Matters came to a head in 1598 with the Treaty of Vervins: the Cecils urged acceptance of Spain's proposals; Essex, hoping no doubt that history would repeat itself and that a war faction would once again triumph as it had done in 1513, insisted on an all-out offensive against the dominant power on the continent: 'now, now is the fittest time to make warre upon the Spaniard', he wrote in his *Apologie*.⁶³ Like Shakespeare's Henry V, Essex was a zealot with a heroic conviction in the justice of England's cause.

If the glamorous and bellicose young Henry VIII was a source of practical inspiration for the Elizabethan war party, the great Lancastrian ancestor on whom he conspicuously modelled himself⁶⁴ enjoyed an almost mythical reputation in the popular mind.⁶⁵ For the Essex faction Henry V was the perfect symbol of national pride. Here was not only an inspirational type of what Lydgate called 'the prowesse of olde chivalrie',⁶⁶ but also an embodiment of just the kind of aggressive military action that Essex himself so passionately advocated. Samuel Daniel, who praised Essex in the *Civile Wars* as a rare example 'Of ancient honor neere worne out of date',⁶⁷

---

[62] See Wallace T. MacCaffrey, *Elizabeth I: War and Politics 1588–1603* (Princeton: Princeton University Press, 1992), pp. 453ff; see also Wernham, *The Making of Elizabethan Foreign Policy*, *passim*; John Guy, *Tudor England* (Oxford and New York: Oxford University Press, 1988), pp. 439ff; Penry Williams, *The Later Tudors: England 1547–1603*, The New Oxford History of England (Oxford: Clarendon Press, 1995), p. 364.

[63] *An Apologie*, Sig. D4.

[64] See Dominic Baker-Smith, '"Inglorious glory": 1513 and the Humanist Attack on Chivalry' in *Chivalry, in the Renaissance*, ed. Anglo, p. 135.

[65] Henry's reputation as the mirror of Christian chivalry owes much to his brother Humphrey, Duke of Gloucester, who commissioned the Italian historian Tito Livio to write his life (*Vita Henrici Quinti*); to the anonymous *Gesta Henrici Quinti*; and to William of Worcester, author of the chauvinistic *Boke of Noblesse*. In the sixteenth century the myth of Henry as the 'floure of kynges passed' (Edward Hall, *Hall's Chronicle* (1548; repr. London, 1809), p. 113) was kept alive by the chroniclers Fabyan, Grafton, Hall, and Holinshed. Their patriotic view of Henry found ready acceptance in militant-Protestant circles, and is reflected in the crudely jingoistic *Famous Victories of Henry V*.

[66] *Lydgate's Troy Book*, Prol., lines 76–85, ed. Henry Bergen, 4 vols. (London: Early English Text Society, 1906–35), vol. I (1906), p. 3.

[67] *The Civile Wars*, II, stanza 130 (cancelled in 1601), *The Complete Works*, vol. II (1885), p. 98.

imagined the ghost of Henry V returning (like Hamlet's father) to reprove the present age for its neglect of the 'wondrous Actions' of the heroic past. In defending Henry's campaigns, he put the emphasis, not on the reassertion of hereditary rights, but on 'joyes of gotten spoyles', 'thoughts of glorie', and 'conquests, riches, Land, and Kingdome gain'd' (v. stanzas 1, 3, 40). For Essex's admirers the 'dreadful and yet lovely' Henry was the supreme example of chivalric heroism, inspiring both 'terror and delight' (v. stanza 2).

Such blatantly militarist sentiments inevitably attracted criticism. There is always a danger of reading modern assumptions into the debates of the past. But if our own century has particular reason to be wary of charismatic military leaders, we know from the success of such plays as *Tamburlaine* and *Locrine* that the sixteenth century was fascinated as well as repelled by the cult of the megalo-psyche. Humanists were fully aware of the opposition between their own ideal of honour through public service and commitment to civic ideals, and what they regarded as a false cult of neo-chivalric honour.[68] Sidney's friend Hubert Languet is typical of those humanists who had reservations about the culture of violence fostered by militant Protestantism. Warning him of the temptations of seeking honour through military achievement, Languet wrote to Sidney: 'It is the misfortune, or rather the folly of our age that most men of high rank think it more honorable to do the work of a soldier than of a leader, and would rather earn a name for boldness than for judgment'.[69] Essex received similar, though less friendly, advice from the Privy Council when it debated the Spanish peace proposals in 1598. Warning the earl of the dangers of his obsession with war, Burghley reminded him of the psalmist's prophecy: 'Men of blood shall not live out half their days'.[70]

Burghley's prediction proved true. By February 1601 the man of blood was dead and his supporters humiliated by the farcical outcome of the abortive rebellion (see below, Chapter 1, pp. 50–1).

---

[68] Paul N. Siegel, 'Shakespeare and the Neo-Chivalric Cult of Honor', *CR*, 8 (1964), 43. See also Herbert Howarth, *The Tiger's Heart: Eight Essays on Shakespeare* (London: Chatto & Windus, 1970), pp. 24–44; R.R. Bolger, 'Hero or Anti-Hero: The Genesis and Development of the *Miles Christianus*', *Concepts of the Hero in the Middle Ages and the Renaissance*, ed. Norman T. Burns and Christopher J. Reagan (Albany: State University of New York Press, 1975), pp. 120–46; Council, 'Ben Jonson, Inigo Jones, and the Transformation of Tudor Chivalry', 259–75.

[69] Hubert Languet, *The Correspondence of Sir Philip Sidney and Hubert Languet*, ed. S.A. Pears (London, 1845), p. 138.

[70] Quoted by MacCaffrey, *Elizabeth I: War and Politics*, p. 516.

Three years later, in March 1604, James I made his belated progress through the City of London. In dramatic contrast to the extravagant displays of chivalry at Elizabeth's Accession Day tilts, the central figure in the pageant designed to celebrate James' accession was the goddess Eirene, attended by the nine muses and the seven liberal arts.[71] James was repeatedly hailed in the royal progresses as *Augustus redivivus* restoring a new age of peace and artistic accomplishment. For some years it has been fashionable, particularly in materialist criticism, to deride James for his absolutist political tendencies (though in reality these were more a matter of words than of actions). Alan Sinfield even suggests that there is little to choose between him and a tyrant like Macbeth.[72] Yet for all his personal weaknesses and his less than tactful treatment of parliament, James was also a far-sighted political leader who was determined to put an end to the factionalism that had threatened national stability in the final years of Elizabeth's reign.[73] Concluding peace with Spain in 1604, he successfully avoided war with Europe until 1619. Though the Gunpowder Plot ruined his plans for an ecumenical council, he remained committed to his Erasmian vision of a peaceful Europe united, not by conquest, but by the arts of civilization – a mission that was recognized even by those who did not share his anti-militarist beliefs. 'He enters not with an Olive Branch in his hand, but with an whole Forrest of Olives about him,' wrote Essex's former captain Gervase Markham, 'for he brought Peace, not to this Kingdome alone, but almost to all the Christian Kingdomes in Europe.'[74] Writers like Daniel and Davies were suspicious of James' conciliatory attitude towards Spain and would have preferred to see a more aggressive foreign policy.[75] But with Sidney and Essex dead, the war party lacked a symbolic focus. For a few years it looked as if militant Protestantism, with its grandiose vision of 'conquests, riches, Land, and Kingdome gain'd' and its fantastic neo-medieval military rituals, had lost all credibility. Looking back to Elizabeth's reign Daniel described himself in 1605 as 'the remnant of another time'.[76]

---

[71] See Graham Parry, *The Golden Age Restor'd: The Culture of the Stuart Court, 1603–42* (Manchester: Manchester University Press, 1981), ch. 1.
[72] 'Macbeth: History, Ideology, and Intellectuals', in *Faultlines: Cultural Materialism and the Politics of Dissident Reading* (Oxford: Clarendon Press, 1992), p. 102.
[73] W.B. Patterson, *King James VI and I and the Reunion of Christendom* (Cambridge: Cambridge University Press, 1997), *passim.*
[74] *Honour in his Perfection*, p. 24.   [75] See Smuts, *Court Culture*, pp. 24–6.
[76] Dedicatory Epistle to *Philotas*, *The Complete Works*, ed. Grosart vol. III, p. 101.

Shakespeare's *Troilus and Cressida* catches, arguably better than any other play of the period, the spirit of the anti-chivalric reaction that inevitably followed the collapse of the Essex rebellion. Agamemnon's heroic catalogue of the glorious slain (v.v.6–16) is pointedly juxtaposed against the crude reality of Achilles with his mangled Myrmidons, 'noseless, handless, hacked and chipped' (34), seeking personal vengeance against Hector.

ROMAN VIRTUE

The Elizabethan Accession Day tilts were pure pageantry and bore no relation to contemporary military realities. But the religious and political ambitions that the Sidney–Essex faction sought to express through chivalric contest were anything but sentimental. Militant Protestants, too, were inspired by the ideal of a united Europe, but a Europe tamed by conquest rather than peaceful negotiation. Essex's behaviour both before and after his trial may have helped to expose the more bizarre trappings of Elizabethan chivalry as self-indulgent make-believe, but the principles underlying the pageantry were anything but dead.[77] In a masque entitled 'The Vision of the Twelve Goddesses' (1604) Samuel Daniel claimed that 'Empire and Dominion' are 'the ground and matter whereon [the] glory of State is built'.[78] Francis Bacon was also keenly interested in the 'glory of State' and in the early years of James' reign wrote a series of papers and speeches on the subject.[79] Where Spenser had praised Essex as the 'Faire branch of Honor' and 'flower of Chevalrie' (see note 36 above), Bacon clearly had a Roman model in mind. His account of that model was inspired by Machiavelli's glorification of Roman military *virtù*.[80]

---

[77] See Marshall, '"That's the Misery of Peace": Representations of Martialism in the Jacobean Public Theatre, 1608–1614', 1–21. See also J.S.A. Adamson, 'Chivalry and Political Culture in Caroline England', *Culture and Politics in Early Stuart England*, ed. Sharpe and Lake, pp. 161–97.
[78] *The Complete Works*, vol. III, p. 189.
[79] See Ian Box, 'Politics and Philosophy: Bacon on the Values of War and Peace', *SC*, 7 (1992), 113–27; 'Bacon's Moral Philosophy', *The Cambridge Companion to Bacon*, ed. Markku Peltonen (Cambridge: Cambridge University Press, 1996), pp. 260–82; Markku Peltonen, 'Politics and Science: Francis Bacon and the True Greatness of States', *HJ*, 35 (1992), 279–305.
[80] See Mark Hulliung, *Citizen Machiavelli* (Princeton: Princeton University Press, 1983), *passim*. On Machiavelli's influence in England see Felix Raab, *The English Face of Machiavelli: A Changing Interpretation 1500–1700* (London: Routledge & Kegan Paul, 1964); F.J. Levy, *Tudor Historical Thought* (San Marino, Calif.: The Huntington Library, 1967), pp. 238–42.

In the celebrated passage from the second book of the *Discourses on Livy* Machiavelli regretted the decline of ancient heroic values in the modern world, complaining that the Christian religion had glorified humble and contemplative men rather than men of action. He wrote:

> It hath plac'd the cheife good in humility and in the rejecting and contempt of worldly things. That other [i.e., ancient Roman religion] imagined the cheife happinesse to consist in the greatnesse of courage, in the strength of body and in all things fit to make men exceedingly valiant.[81]

Though Machiavelli's originality as a political thinker should not be underestimated, the celebration of military *virtù* was not a new phenomenon in sixteenth-century Florence. Identifying human action rather than providence or fortune as the ultimate determining force of events, fifteenth-century historians like Coluccio Salutati and Leonardo Bruni were self-consciously writing for the glorification of the state:[82] the rise of great nations, they argued, is the result, neither of blind fortune nor even of heaven's will, but of the self-assertion of heroic individuals. For Poggio Bracciolini it was the Mongol warlord Timur (Marlowe's Tamburlaine) who epitomized the ruthlessly aggressive military spirit that had once made Rome great;[83] for Machiavelli it was the Luccan military dictator Castruccio Castracani.[84]

That Marlowe was fascinated by the figure of the charismatic and fabulously successful warlord who defies fortune is well known: *Tamburlaine the Great* owes much to Petrus Perondinus' *Vita Tamerlanis*[85] and probably also to Machiavelli's *Vita di Castruccio Castracani*.[86] Gabriel Harvey was also an admirer of Machiavelli, confiding to himself that what matters in life is 'heroical valour, nothing else'.[87] In his marginalia on Ramus' *Oikonomia* he wrote: 'The Marii and the Sforzas – men of great power, more endowed with a fiery

---

[81] *Machiavels discourses upon the first Decade of T. Livius*, trans. E. Dacres (London, 1636), p. 267.
[82] Eric Voegelin, 'Machiavelli's Prince: Background and Formation', *RP*, 13 (1951), 152–3. On Bacon's interest in the debate on *virtus* versus *fortuna* see John F. Tinkler, 'Bacon and History', *The Cambridge Companion to Bacon* (Cambridge: Cambridge University Press, 1996), pp. 232–59.
[83] Voegelin, 'Machiavelli's Prince', pp. 156–61.
[84] Ibid., pp. 165–8.
[85] *Tamburlaine the Great*, ed. U.M. Ellis-Fermor (London: Methuen, 1930), pp. 31–4.
[86] *Tamburlaine the Great*, Revels Plays, ed. J.S. Cunningham (Manchester and Baltimore: Manchester University Press and Johns Hopkins University Press, 1981), p. 15.
[87] *Gabriel Harvey's Marginalia*, ed. G.C. Moore Smith (Stratford-upon-Avon: Shakespeare Head, 1913), p. 156.

spirit than with intellect . . . it is these passionate spirits who are truly counted as men'.[88] Bacon shared Harvey's enthusiasm for Machiavelli's political vision, and believed that great nations are characterized by a warlike spirit. Indeed much of his essay on 'The True Greatness of Kingdoms' reads like a paraphrase of Machiavelli. Contrasting 'sedentary and within-door arts' with the military life, Bacon rehearsed the familiar claim that, while 'slothful peace' results in effeminacy and corrupt manners, foreign wars are like exercise to a healthy body.[89] 'Above all,' he wrote, 'for empire and greatness, it importeth most, that a nation do profess arms as their principal honour, study and occupation.'[90] In a conspicuous echo of the *Discourses*, Bacon compared the unheroic present with 'the glory and honour which reflected upon men from wars in ancient time',[91] adding, in a clear endorsement of Machiavelli's insistence on the importance of an expansionist military policy, 'it is in the power of princes or estates to add amplitude and greatness to their kingdoms'.[92]

Bacon's paper on 'The True Greatness of Kingdoms' was first published in 1625 in the final edition of the *Essays*. But it has its origins in a speech to parliament in 1607 in which Bacon cited Machiavelli on the importance to any kingdom with pretensions to greatness of an army of 'valiant men'.[93] In the following year he expanded the speech as an unfinished essay on 'The True Greatness of the Kingdom of Britain'. The essence of the 1625 essay's insistence on military assertiveness can clearly be seen in the 1608 fragment. Appealing to the example of ancient Rome, Bacon claimed that true greatness consists in 'the valour and military disposition of the people it breedeth: and in this, that they make profession of arms'.[94] He also discussed means of 'securing of large territories',[95] though he is more guarded in his references to the Machiavellian principle of expansion than he was in the later essay.

The discourses of Machiavellian *virtù* and neo-medieval chivalry

---

[88] 'Marii, et Sfortiae, magna Vi, magni: animi quam ingenii pleniores . . . feruidis hominibus applaudit vulgus; eosque solos, reputat Viros' (*Marginalia*, p. 156). For discussion of other contemporary defences of military values see Paul Jorgensen, *Shakespeare's Military World* (Berkeley and Los Angeles: University of California Press, 1956), pp. 169–207.
[89] 'Of the True Greatness of Kingdoms', *The Essayes or Counsels Civill or Morall* (London and Toronto: Dent, 1906), p. 95.
[90] Ibid., p. 94.   [91] Ibid., p. 96.   [92] Ibid., p. 97.
[93] *The Works of Francis Bacon*, 7 vols., ed. James Spedding, Robert Leslie Ellis, and Douglas Denon Heath (London: Longman, 1879–87), vol. VII (1879), p. 40.
[94] Ibid., p.48.   [95] Ibid., p.49.

may appear to belong to entirely different worlds: one was the product of fifteenth- and early sixteenth-century Florentine republican *realpolitik*;[96] the other apparently lay in a sentimental desire to recreate the glamour of a lost age of knightly enterprise. In reality they were inspired by the same political ideals. Like Essex, Bacon believed that the key to international prestige lay in military strength. And though he had no choice but to condemn Essex's folly in attempting to overthrow a reigning monarch, he shared his former patron's belief in the importance of an expansionist foreign policy. Machiavellian *virtù* and the chivalric honour of the neo-medievalist amount in practice to the same thing. Both are about that 'courage-masculine' which militarists believed to be the hallmark of a glorious nation. Improbably, the two were combined in the person of a boy who, according to his supporters, had been marked out by providence as the future leader of the Protestant cause and scourge of England's Continental enemies.

From the earliest years of James' reign, Prince Henry was hailed by the surviving members of the old Sidney–Essex faction as a figure of destiny (see below, Chapter 5). He was praised both as an embodiment of English chivalry and as a type of Roman military *virtus*: while the engraving by Simon van de Passe used by Drayton in the dedication to *Poly-Olbion* shows the prince in shining medieval armour with a fantastically decorated helmet, the miniature by Isaac Oliver in the Fitzwilliam Museum, Cambridge, represents him in the austere guise of a Roman general.[97] But whether Henry was portrayed as medieval knight or as military general, the consistent theme of all the panegyrics that were written to the young prince was that of the future conqueror. As one biographer remarks, 'rarely had such a young boy managed to surround himself so with the odor of masculinity'.[98]

So inimical to James' own eirenic ideals was the cult of heroic masculinity promulgated by Henry's supporters that it was bound to cause friction within the royal family. Disturbed in 1608 by a pamphlet entitled 'Arguments for War' put together by a group of

---

[96] Felix Gilbert, *Machiavelli and Guicciardini: Politics and History in Sixteenth-Century Florence* (Princeton: Princeton University Press, 1965), pp. 129–37.
[97] J.W. Williamson, *The Myth of the Conqueror: Prince Henry Stuart: A Study of 17th-Century Personation* (New York: AMS Press, 1978), p. 66; Roy Strong, *The English Icon: Elizabethan and Jacobean Portraiture* (London: Routledge & Kegan Paul, 1969), p. 55.
[98] Williamson, *The Myth of the Conqueror*, p. 32.

Henry's military advisors, James commissioned Sir Robert Cotton to write a reply warning of the dangers of the new cult of military assertiveness associated with the prince. Shakespeare's *Coriolanus* forms part of this embarrassingly public debate on military values. For his portrait of the martial hero at his most unlovable, Shakespeare turned, not just to a state renowned above all others in the ancient world for its military adventurism, but to a time when internal order in that state had broken down altogether. In doing so he effectively gave the lie to one of the most frequently repeated arguments of the war party, namely, the claim that 'when Wars are ended abroad, Sedition begins at home'.[99]

AN ORPHEUS FOR A HERCULES

Insofar as most of them portray nations and cities either actively prosecuting foreign wars or defending themselves against incursions from abroad, Shakespeare's tragedies and histories inevitably reflect the kind of problems that were debated in Elizabeth's and James' Privy Councils. But there was no contemporary consensus on those problems. In this period foreign policy caused deeper rifts than any other political issue. It is therefore, perhaps, not surprising that the plays do not leave us with a sense either that they are endorsing some supposedly unitary body of thought that E.M.W. Tillyard called 'orthodox doctrine' and Cultural Materialists call 'dominant ideology', or that they are subverting establishment opinion.[100] With Milton we know pretty much where we are on the question of martial heroism.[101] Having created a portrait of the charismatic

---

[99] Sir Walter Ralegh, 'A Discourse of War', *The Works*, 2 vols. (London, 1751), vol. II p. 65.

[100] Some years ago Jonathan Dollimore suggested that the question we should ask about Shakespeare's plays is 'did [they] reinforce the dominant order, or do they resist it to the point of subversion?' ('Critical Development', *Shakespeare: A Bibliographical Guide*, ed. Wells, p. 414). Refined and reworded, Dollimore's critical strategy continues to command approval among more recent materialist critics. In *The Stage and Social Struggle in Early Modern England* (London and New York: Routledge, 1994), Jean Howard tells us that her primary concern is the question 'what interests are served and power relations constituted by [theatrical] representations?' (p. 8). In *Shakespeare's Troy: Drama, Politics, and the Translation of Empire* (Cambridge: Cambridge University Press, 1997), Heather James asks: can 'cultural legitimacy . . . coexist with autonomy' or does Shakespeare's 'immersion in the courtly system of patronage mean that he, chief playwright of the King's Men, must treat his theater as an instrument of royal authority' (p. 189).

[101] See John M. Steadman, 'Heroic Virtue and the Divine Image in *Paradise Lost*', *JWCI*, 22 (1959), 88–105; *Milton and the Paradoxes of Renaissance Heroism* (Baton Rouge and London: Louisiana State University Press, 1987).

warlord with 'Browes / Of dauntless courage, and considerat Pride / Waiting revenge' (*Paradise Lost*, I, 602–4), Milton then cuts his Homeric hero down to size, making it clear that the kind of heroism he is going to celebrate reveals itself, not in the 'long and tedious havoc' (IX, 30) of chivalric warfare, but in the 'better fortitude / Of Patience and Heroic Martyrdom' (IX, 31–2).[102] But with a writer as self-consciously ambivalent as Shakespeare it is more difficult to determine his politics.[103] The plays leave us with a sense of the intractability of the political problems that beset their characters: to what extent are governments or individuals justified in using violent methods to defeat barbarism? Are martial values necessary to preserve peace at times of national insecurity? If a beleaguered society needs strong military leaders, how do you ensure that the sort of heroic qualities that make for effective leadership in time of war do not undermine the very values that you are defending? Is it wise to remove a criminal, but highly effective, ruler at a time of national crisis? If I have no answers to these questions it is because I believe that Shakespeare offers none.

But though there may be no easy solutions to the political and ethical questions that Shakespeare deals with, there is in the tragedies and histories a consistently sceptical view of the kind of heroic masculinity that was exemplified by the Earl of Essex and, in his imagination at least, by the Prince of Wales. It is a view of the heroic ideal that Shakespeare inherited from a humanist tradition

[102] *The Poetical Works of John Milton*, 2 vols., ed. Helen Darbishire (Oxford: Clarendon Press, 1952–55), vol. I (1952), pp. 20, 183.
[103] According to a distinguished line of twentieth-century critics from A.P. Rossiter in 1951 to Graham Bradshaw in 1993 the quality that is most characteristic of Shakespeare's plays is their ambivalence. W.R. Elton speaks for this body of criticism when he argues that Shakespeare's plays are best seen as 'a dialect of ironies and ambivalences, avoiding in its complex movement and dialogue the simplification of direct statement and reductive resolution' ('Shakespeare and the Thought of his Age' (1971), *The Cambridge Companion to Shakespeare Studies*, ed. Stanley Wells (Cambridge: Cambridge University Press, 1986), p. 32). See also A.P. Rossiter, 'Ambivalence: The Dialectic of the Histories' (1951), *Angel with Horns: Fifteen Lectures on Shakespeare*, ed. Graham Storey (1961; repr. with an introduction by Peter Holland, London and New York: Longman, 1989), pp. 40–64; Helen Gardner, 'The Historical Approach' (1953), in *The Business of Criticism* (Oxford: Clarendon Press, 1959), pp. 25–51; Norman Rabkin, *Shakespeare and the Common Understanding* (1967; repr. Chicago and London: University of Chicago Press, 1984); Bernard McElroy, *Shakespeare's Mature Tragedies* (Princeton: Princeton University Press, 1973), Emrys Jones, *The Origins of Shakespeare* (Oxford: Clarendon Press, 1977); Robert Grudin, *Mighty Opposites: Shakespeare and Renaissance Contrariety* (Berkeley, Los Angeles, and London: University of California Press, 1979); Graham Bradshaw, *Shakespeare's Scepticism* (Brighton: Harvester Press, 1987); *Misrepresentations: Shakespeare and the Materialists* (Ithaca and London: Cornell University Press, 1993).

that goes back through More and Erasmus to Seneca and Cicero and that is expressed in terms of a contrast between two mythological figures.

The symbolic opposition between Mars and Venus is a well-known *topos* in medieval and Renaissance literature: Chaucer uses it in *The Knight's Tale* to represent the rival powers of love and war; Marlowe and Shakespeare employ it for similar purposes in *Tamburlaine* and *Antony and Cleopatra*.[104] A similar opposition is that between Mars and Mercury who Hamlet tells us were wonderfully combined in the figure of his father (III.iv.58–63).[105] The reconciling of love and war, or of the arts of peace and those of war, is a commonplace of Renaissance humanist thought and is an expression of the classic Stoic theory of the well-tempered mind.[106] But there is another pair of linked mythological figures in classical and Renaissance art and literature who serve to illustrate, not so much an ethical and psychological ideal, as a political principle. In *Hercules furens* Seneca invites us to compare the two archetypal heroes, Hercules and Orpheus (see Chapter 3, p. 90). Both heroes are peacemakers; both heroically risk a journey to Hades where they subdue the gods of the underworld and disrupt the course of nature; both lose a wife and are tormented by grief; both suffer an agonizing death. But Seneca also asks us to consider the differences between the two heroes: though both are renowned as peacemakers, one achieves his ends through violent conquest, the other through the arts of peace. In *Hercules furens* Seneca makes it clear that the heroic rage typically associated with the martial hero causes more problems than it solves. His *furor* is symbolic of the madness of war itself.

For Renaissance mythographers, Hercules and Orpheus are two of the most important heroes in the Greek pantheon. The former, as

---

[104] T. McAlindon, *English Renaissance Tragedy* (Basingstoke and London: Macmillan, 1986), pp. 93–9; *Shakespeare's Tragic Cosmos* (Cambridge: Cambridge University Press, 1991), pp. 230–2, 248.

[105] Roland Mushat Frye, *The Renaissance 'Hamlet': Issues and Responses in 1600* (Princeton University Press: Princeton, 1984), p. 172–7.

[106] An example is Lyly's *Campaspe* (1584), where the rival values of war and peace and the conflict between love and duty is the play's central debating *topos*. *Campaspe* begins with Parmenio asking whether one should 'more commend in *Alexanders* victories, courage, or curtesie'. The question is resolved when Alexander decides to abandon all claims on his beautiful captive and devote himself to learning: 'needes must that common wealth be fortunate, whose captaine is a Philosopher, and whose Philosopher is a Captaine', says Hephestion of the king who combines learning with military expertise (I.i.1–2; 86–8, *The Complete Works*, ed. Bond vol. II, pp. 317, 319).

Ben Jonson explained in a note to *The Masque of Queens*, was one of the principal figures in whom the ancients expressed 'a brave & masculine virtue'.[107] A man of inordinate passions and exceptional physical prowess, Hercules is associated above all with success in battle.[108] In his *Boke of Noblesse* William of Worcester claimed that the labours of Hercules 'were writen in a figure of a poesy for to courage and comfort alle noble men of birthe to be victorious in entreprinses [*sic*] of armes'.[109] Spenser described Hercules as conqueror of 'all the West'.[110] Because it was Hercules who first taught men to subdue savage beasts, he is regarded as a founder of civilization through warfare.[111] His antithesis in Renaissance mythography is Orpheus, symbolic representative of the arts of civilization.[112] Orpheus too was regarded as a founder of civilization, though in his case it was not by force, but by the magical power of eloquence that he persuaded men to abandon their barbaric practices and accept the constraints of civic life.[113] Though both heroes are claimed by mythographers as symbolic founding fathers, they represent opposing ideals of community: one stands for order imposed by physical conquest, the other for peaceful persuasion. Discussing the different ways in which the two types of leader were celebrated in antiquity, the notoriously inconsistent Bacon explained (notwithstanding his Machiavellian ideas on national glory) that, whereas Hercules and Theseus are inevitably associated 'with strife and perturbation', the Apollonian leader 'hath the true character of divine presence, coming in *aura leni* ['like a gentle breath from heaven'] without noise or agitation'.[114] It was this classic contrast

[107] Ben Jonson, *The Complete Masques*, ed. Stephen Orgel (New Haven, Conn. and London: Yale University Press, 1969), p. 542. The other two heroes whom Jonson cites as embodiments of 'heroic virtue' (p. 134) are Perseus and Bellerophon.

[108] See Waith, *The Herculean Hero*; G.Karl Galinsky, *The Herakles Theme: The Adaptations of the Hero in Literature from Homer to the Twentieth Century* (Oxford: Basil Blackwell, 1972).

[109] *The Boke of Noblesse*, p. 21.

[110] *The Faerie Queene*, v.i.2, *The Poetical Works*, ed. Smith and de Selincourt, p. 277.

[111] Erasmus, 'Dulce bellum inexpertis', *The 'Adages'*, ed. Phillips, p. 317. See also Francis Bacon, *The Advancement of Learning*, ed. William A. Armstrong (London: Athlone Press, 1975), p. 88.

[112] See Kirsty Cochrane, 'Orpheus Applied: Some Instances of his Importance in the Humanist View of Language', *RES*, n.s. 19 (1968), 1–13. See also Robin Headlam Wells, *Elizabethan Mythologies: Studies in Poetry, Drama and Music* (Cambridge: Cambridge University Press, 1994), pp. 2–8.

[113] George Puttenham follows Horace *(Ars poetica*, lines 391–401) in representing Orpheus, together with Amphion, as the founder of civilization *(The Arte of English Poesie*, ed. Gladys Doidge Willcock and Alice Walker (Cambridge: Cambridge University Press, 1936), p. 6).

[114] *The Advancement of Learning*, pp. 88–9. On Bacon's inconsistencies with regard to war and

between rhetorical and physical forms of persuasion that Fynes Moryson, Mountjoy's chief secretary in Ireland, was referring to when he complained of the Irish rebels: 'If Orpheus himself could not make these stones and trees dance after his harp, then Hercules and Theseus must make them follow with their clubs'.[115] In Shakespeare the two figures can be seen in their most stylized form in Coriolanus and Prospero. Many of Shakespeare's tragedies contain echoes of Seneca's *Hercules furens*.[116] But it is Coriolanus who is Shakespeare's most extreme example of the Herculean hero. Prospero, by contrast, is a type of the Orphic tamer of human passions. Having anatomized the Herculean hero in a series of tragedies, Shakespeare turns, at the end of his writing career, to an entirely different kind of leader.

On his accession James I made it clear that he wished to be identified, not with the heroic archetypes of Elizabethan political mythology, but with an alternative tradition, that of the musician–king who, Orpheus-like, civilizes the unruly elements in his kingdom 'by the sweet Harmony of his harp'.[117] At his coronation pageant James was greeted with an 'Orphean quire', while emblematic devices foretold a new dispensation under which the 'Arts that were threatened to be trod under foot by Barbarisme' would now be 'advanced to most high preferment'.[118] Shakespeare turns this Orphic theme into a central motif of *The Tempest*. Alluding to Seneca's contrast between Herculean and Orphic forms of conquest, he portrays a ruler who renounces the 'rough magic' of destructive vengeance in favour of a more 'airy charm' (v.i.54) that relies on 'heavenly music' (52) for its civilizing effects. Directed by providence to an enchanted island, Prospero is less interested in establishing a colony than in using his magical powers to reconcile old enemies. Like James, who spent many years negotiating political

---

learning see Peltonen, 'Politics and Science: Francis Bacon and the True Greatness of States'.

[115] *An Itinerary* (1617) in James P. Myers Jr., ed., *Elizabethan Ireland: A Selection of Writings by Elizabethan Writers on Ireland* (Hamden, Conn.: Archon Books, 1983), p. 235.

[116] On Shakespeare's use of Seneca in the tragedies see Robert S. Miola, *Shakespeare and Classical Tragedy: The Influence of Seneca* (Oxford: Clarendon Press, 1992). See also Waith, *The Herculean Hero*.

[117] The phrase comes from George Marcelline's *The Triumphs of King James the First* (London, 1610), p. 35. Marcelline makes an extended comparison of James with Orpheus (see Chapter 6). On the musician-king see Headlam Wells, *Elizabethan Mythologies*, pp. 2–8.

[118] Thomas Dekker, *The Whole Magnifycent Entertainment Given to King James* (London, 1604), Sigs. B2, G3^v.

marriages for both Henry and Elizabeth, Prospero plans to accomplish his political mission by means of a dynastic alliance. To point to these topical elements in *The Tempest* is not to say that the play is a panegyric to the patron of the King's Men. Indeed, given the obvious similarities between Prospero and James, it might be thought that Shakespeare was sailing dangerously close to the wind in portraying his pacifist duke as not only neglectful of his political responsibilities, but irritable, vindictive, and, if we can believe Caliban, hated by his fellow islanders. Rather than asking whether *The Tempest* is for or against James, it would probably make more sense to see the play as a dramatist's imaginative alternative to the heroic model of leadership. The heroes of Shakespeare's martial and political tragedies are destructive figures. They are leaders who are either responsible for the collapse of the state or city whose safety they are supposed to be safeguarding, or else place it in extreme jeopardy. Prospero, for all his personal failings, is a visionary. His ideal is not conquest, but an Italy united by the arts of peace.

THE ETHIC OF HEROISM

In *The Mask of Command* the military historian John Keegan argues that the modern world needs 'an end to the ethic of heroism in its leadership for good and all'.[119] Erasmus said much the same in his pacifist essay 'Dulce bellum inexpertis'. When Henry VIII planned his campaign against France in 1513 he knew perfectly well that a successful battle in which he could appeal to the glorious memory of his heroic namesake Henry V, England's greatest chivalric leader, would do wonders for his reputation. But for Erasmus, a neo-medieval culture of violence had no place in the new world of enlightened civic humanism. William of Worcester had interpreted the labours of Hercules as an allegory of the martial life. But in Erasmus' view the only truly Herculean task for the modern world was the recovery of classical culture: 'The nature of this kind of work', he wrote in an essay entitled 'Herculei labores' (1508), 'is that it brings profit to everyone, and the only person to suffer hardship is the one who undertakes to do it'.[120] A century later Bacon compared

---

[119] John Keegan, *The Mask of Command* (London: Jonathan Cape, 1987), p. 350.
[120] *The 'Adages'*, p. 209.

Otto van Veen, 'Amor addocet artes', *Amorum emblemata* (Antwerp, 1608)

the labours of Hercules with those of Orpheus. In *The Wisdom of the Ancients* (1609) he wrote: 'as the works of wisdom surpass in dignity and power the works of strength, so the labours of Orpheus surpass the labours of Hercules'.[121] Otto van Veen, or Vaenius as he is usually known, made a similar point in a device from his *Amorum emblemata* – 'Emblems of Love' (1608).[122]

The moral of Vaenius' emblem is summed up in its title: 'Amor addocet artes' – 'Love is the schoolmaster of the arts'. It is a variation on a familiar theme: the taming and redirection of the violent side of human nature by the arts of civilization. But in this emblem, instead of the usual figure of Orpheus taming man's innate savagery, it is Hercules who is being taught to subdue his own passions. Adapting the story of Omphale, usually moralized as a satire on termagant

---

[121] *The Philosophical Works*, ed. John M. Robertson (London: George Routledge, 1905), p. 835.
[122] Otto van Veen, *Amorum emblemata* (Antwerp, 1608), p. 83.

women,[123] Vaenius shows the civilizing of heroic masculinity in a more positive light. Hercules has now laid aside his club, and while Cupid sings from a music book, the hero learns how to transform the natural fibre of humanity into the thread from which the fabric of civilization is woven.[124] It is a similar transformation of hero into artist that we see as we move from Shakespeare's later tragedies to *The Tempest*. Written at a time when ideas of greatness were the subject of heated debate, these plays represent the age's most sustained and most complex analysis of the dangers of heroic masculinity.

[123] For Sidney 'the scornfullness of the [Hercules and Omphale story] stirreth laughter' (*An Apology for Poetry*, ed. Shepherd, p. 136). In *The Faerie Queene* Spenser describes Hercules with his 'distaffe vile', adding: 'Such is the crueltie of womenkynd, / When they have shaken off the shamefast band, / With which wise Nature did them strongly bynd, / T'obey the heasts of mans well ruling hand' (v.v.25, *The Poetical Works*, ed. Smith and de Selincourt, p. 298).

[124] Peggy Muñoz Simonds, 'The Herculean Lover in the Emblems of Cranach and Vaenius', *Acta Conventius Neo-Latini Torontonensis: Proceedings of the Seventh International Congress of Neo-Latin Studies*, ed. Alexander Dalzell, Charles Fantazzi, and Richard J. Schoeck (Binghamton, N.Y.: Medieval and Renaissance Texts and Studies, 1991), pp. 708–9.

CHAPTER I

The chivalric revival: 'Henry V' and 'Troilus and Cressida'

> Now help, o Mars, þat art of kny3thod lord,
> And hast of manhod the magnificence!
> John Lydgate, *Lydgate's Troy Book*, Prologue, lines 36–7, vol. I, p. 2

Introducing the second act of *Henry V*, Shakespeare's Chorus paints a striking picture of a country on the eve of a foreign campaign:

> Now all the youth of England are on fire,
> And silken dalliance in the wardrobe lies;
> Now thrive the armourers, and honour's thought
> Reigns solely in the breast of every man.   (II. Chorus.1–4)

No intelligent audience can fail to respond to such imaginative scene painting. But for contemporary playgoers the most remarkable thing about the Chorus' words must have been not the ekphrasis but the politics. The reference to 'honour's thought', together with the allusion in the Act V Chorus to the Earl of Essex's anticipated return from Ireland – the single explicit topical allusion in Shakespeare – must have sounded like a surprisingly audacious endorsement of Essex and all that he stood for. But if the earl's supporters were encouraged by such a stirring evocation of national war fever, they must have been less pleased by the distinctly unheroic scene that immediately follows. In place of the Chorus' idealized picture of England's youth on fire with noble thoughts of war, we have the unromantic reality of brawling soldiers, broken promises, and 'wilful adultery and murder' (II.i.36). Unimpressed by Pistol's heroic posturing, Bardolph offers to act as mediator in the absurd quarrel between him and Corporal Nym: 'Come, shall I make you two friends?' Then reminding them that they are about to embark for France, he asks: 'Why the devil should we keep knives to cut one another's throats?' (86–8). The audience is left to decide for itself whether Bardolph is thinking about France or Mistress Quickly's tavern when he reflects on the futility of fighting.

The subplot of *Henry V* looks very much like a parody of the play's heroic main plot.[1] Its characters are pilferers, fools, and braggarts motivated by self interest and an absurd sense of pride in the dignity of the 'manly heart' (II.iii.3). The resulting ambivalence makes it one of Shakespeare's most puzzling plays. Critical opinion is broadly divided between those who see the play's hero as a mirror of all Christian kings, and those who see him as a cynical deceiver who, according to Mistress Quickly, has killed his friend's heart (II.i.84). For J.H. Walter, Shakespeare's Henry combines the character and action of the epic hero with the moral qualities of Erasmus' Christian prince;[2] for Norman Rabkin he is 'the kind of exemplary monarch that neither Richard II nor Henry IV could be, combining the inwardness and the sense of occasion of the one and the strength of the other with a generous humanity available to neither';[3] for Gary Taylor he is 'a study of human greatness'.[4] But New-Historicist and materialist criticism takes a very different view of Henry. In one of his most influential essays[5] Stephen Greenblatt argues that throughout the three plays in which he appears Henry is a Machiavellian 'juggler' and 'conniving hypocrite'. The final play of the series, says Greenblatt, 'deftly registers every nuance of royal hypocrisy, ruthlessness, and bad faith'.[6] Neither of these positions will bear close scrutiny.

It is true that Shakespeare's portrait of Henry is in many ways a notably sympathetic one. Henry's rhetoric is exhilarating; his courage in battle is exemplary; his piety seems indisputable, and his

---

[1] Graham Bradshaw writes well on what he calls 'dramatic rhyming' in *Henry V* in *Misrepresentations: Shakespeare and the Materialists* (Ithaca and London: Cornell University Press, 1993), pp. 63–80.

[2] J.H. Walter, ed., Introduction to Arden edition of *Henry V* (London and Cambridge, Mass.: Methuen and Harvard University Press, 1954), p. xvi.

[3] Norman Rabkin, *Shakespeare and the Common Understanding* (1967; repr. Chicago and London: University of Chicago Press, 1984), p. 98. However, Rabkin later revised this view: see *Shakespeare and the Problem of Meaning* (Chicago and London: University of Chicago Press, 1981), pp. 33–62.

[4] Gary Taylor, ed., Introduction to *Henry V* (Oxford and New York: Oxford University Press, 1982), p. 72.

[5] Arthur Kinney describes 'Invisible Bullets' as 'perhaps the most important and surely the most influential essay of the past decade in English Renaissance cultural history' (Arthur F. Kinney, ed., *Rogues, Vagabonds and Sturdy Beggars: A New Gallery of Tudor and Stuart Rogue Literature* (Amherst, Mass.: University of Massachusetts Press, 1990), p. 1).

[6] Stephen Greenblatt, *Shakespearean Negotiations: The Circulation of Social Energy in Renaissance England* (Oxford: Clarendon Press, 1988), pp. 41, 56.

honour bright. By the final scene of the play any lingering doubts about the legitimacy of his claims to France are easily forgotten in the superficially playful charm of the wooing of Katharine. When even the French king and queen seem delighted with 'brother England' and the terms of his proposed alliance, what reason is there to doubt the integrity of this now plain-speaking soldier with a heart that 'never changes, but keeps his course truly' (v.ii.164–5)? But as many critics have pointed out, this concluding scene of international and domestic harmony, almost like a comedy in its stylized conviviality,[7] has many ironies. Unlike the typical Elizabethan romantic comedy, which ends with an unfulfilled promise of future happiness, the final Chorus of *Henry V* takes us back to a future that is already past. We know all too well that not one of Henry's hopes will be realized: Katharine will never be a 'soldier-breeder'; the king himself will not live to see old age; the peace between England and France will hold only a few short years. As the Chorus reminds us of the English blood that will soon be shed in the Wars of the Roses, it is difficult to suppress memory of all the other disquieting events we have witnessed in the play: the scheming clergy so eager to support a war that is conveniently in their own interests; Henry's brutal threats to the citizens of Harfleur; the casuistical argument with Williams; the cold-blooded killing of the prisoners at Agincourt.

But if it is true that Henry's militant brand of Christianity is a far cry from the pacifism of Erasmus' Christian prince, there is little evidence in the play to support the claim that he is a Machiavellian hypocrite. Modern historians speak of the historical Henry's 'messianic streak'[8] and his religious bigotry.[9] Even Allmand, his most admiring biographer, describes him as 'a man with an obsession'.[10] Henry was identified by his contemporaries with the world conqueror of popular apocalyptic prophecy.[11] According to early fifteenth-century millenarian writers, the last universal emperor

---

[7] Rabkin compares the play to a comedy in *Shakespeare and the Common Understanding*, pp. 99–100.
[8] G.L. Harriss, ed., Introduction to *Henry V: The Practice of Kingship* (Oxford: Oxford University Press, 1985), p. 24.
[9] J.R. Lander describes Henry as 'a bigot of near-heroic mould whose intense religiosity equalled only his intense legalism over feudal property rights' (*Conflict and Stability in Fifteenth-Century England* (London: Hutchinson, 1969), p. 58).
[10] C.T. Allmand, 'Henry v the Soldier, and the War in France' in *Henry V*, ed. Harriss, p. 129.
[11] Lesley A. Coote, *Prophecy and Public Affairs in Later Medieval England* (York: York Medieval Press, 2000), ch. 5.

would free the Holy Land from the infidel and yield up his throne in Jerusalem, after which the world would be consumed by fire in 1500.[12] Henry seems to have believed in that prophetic, imperial vision and to have seen himself as the instrument of providence. For the author of the propagandist *Gesta Henrici Quinti* (1416), writing almost certainly under Henry's direction, England's warrior–king is 'the true elect of God';[13] for Henry's uncle and political mentor, Henry Beaufort, Bishop of Winchester, he is a divinely favoured warrior greater even than Alexander the Great or Judas Maccabaeus.[14]

Fifteenth-century writers fostered the myth of the reformed prodigal[15] and drew parallels between Henry and Sextus, the world-conqueror of the *Prophecia Merlini*, who was also supposed to have reformed after a misspent youth.[16] Shakespeare's Henry also has that obsessive, single-minded zeal that is characteristic of the religious convert who sees himself as an instrument of heaven's will. It is not hypocrisy but a heroic conviction in the justice of his cause that is his most disturbing quality. That too is something that must have had an ironic resonance for contemporary audiences. *Henry V* and *Troilus and Cressida* are highly topical plays. Written at a time when apocalyptic belief in England's role in a universal providential programme was once again attracting popular assent (see below, pp. 36–7), they are both about that kind of nationalistic sense of honour which the Elizabethan armorist Gerard Legh defined as 'glory gotten by courage of manhood'.[17] *Henry V* was written when Essex's career was in the balance. The earl was a man of whom, in Gervase Markham's words, 'it behove[d] every man to be careful how to write'.[18] Two years later, after Essex had betrayed not just the queen but his own supporters, and after the bubble of Elizabethan chivalry had burst, Shakespeare returned to the question of military honour. Now he could afford to be less ambivalent. Where

---

[12] London, British Library MS Cotton Cleopatra BI, cited by Coote, ch. 5.
[13] *Gesta Henrici Quinti: The Deeds of Henry the Fifth*, ed. and trans. Frank Taylor and John S. Roskell (Oxford: Clarendon Press, 1975), p. 4.
[14] *Letters of Queen Margaret of Anjou, and Bishop Beckington, and others*, ed. Cecil Monro, Camden First Series 86 (London: Camden Society, 1863), p. 4.
[15] Charles Lethbridge Kingsford, *English Historical Literature in the Fifteenth Century* (Oxford: Clarendon Press, 1913), p. 66.
[16] *The Historia Regum Britannie of Geoffrey of Monmouth*, ed. Neil Wright (Cambridge: D.S. Brewer, 1985), pp. 384–97, cited by Coote, *Prophecy and Public Affairs*, ch. 5.
[17] Gerard Legh, *The Accedens of Armory* (1562; repr. London: 1597), fol. 13.
[18] Gervase Markham, *Honour in his Perfection* (London, 1624), p. 26.

Henry V is necessarily guarded in its critique of military values, *Troilus and Cressida* is a devastating satire on that exaggerated sense of manly honour that is the essence of chivalry.[19]

THE CHIVALRIC REVIVAL

When the Act II Chorus tells us that all the youth of England are on fire with thoughts of war, and that 'honour's thought / Reigns solely in the breast of every man', it looks very much as if Shakespeare is alluding to the warlike 'General of our gracious Empress' (v. Chorus.30) who was expected shortly to return from Ireland 'Bringing rebellion broachèd on his sword' (32). But if the Chorus *was* alluding to Essex, he was grossly overstating his case. Though honour's thought certainly reigned supreme in the breasts of Essex and his followers, the earl's aggressive militarism was by no means universally welcomed in 1599. After twenty years of heavy expenditure on the war with Spain, and with Tyrone's rebellion in Ireland making increasing demands on the exchequer, there was widespread resentment at the relentless increase in taxation. Not only had direct levies risen threefold during the war years, but the government was forced to resort to various indirect ways of raising income, all of them highly unpopular. These included ship money, disposing of crown lands, control of church revenues, and the hated sale of monopolies. In 1599 the exchequer's balance had fallen to its lowest level ever.[20] Faced with the embarrassment of continual complaints from their constituents, members of parliament protested their disapproval of England's continued involvement in foreign wars. W.B. Wernham writes: 'there was a crescendo of complaint and criticism, rising from the grievances voiced in 1589 and the restrictions attempted in 1593 to the great outcry in the monopolies debates of 1601'.[21] Nor is it surprising that among the populace in general support for war was less than overwhelming. The main beneficiaries of a new campaign in Europe would have been a nobility eager for offices and appointments. For the common soldier the reward of victory would no doubt

---

[19] I would accept, with reservations, Jan Kott's description of the play as 'a sneering political pamphlet', but not his equation of the Trojans with Spain and the Greeks with England (*Shakespeare our Contemporary*, trans. Boleslaw Taborski (London: Methuen, 1964), p. 65).
[20] Penry Williams, *The Later Tudors: England 1547–1603*, The New Oxford History of England (Oxford: Clarendon Press, 1995), p. 382.
[21] *The Making of Elizabethan Foreign Policy, 1558–1603* (Berkeley, Los Angeles, and London: University of California Press, 1980), p. 90.

have been much like that of Pistol: no honours and titles, but a life of begging and stealing (v.i.81–5). Little wonder that those unfortunate enough to be conscripted to fight England's foreign wars expressed their resentment by desertion and mutiny.[22] To suggest that honour's thought reigned in the breast of every Englishman in 1599 – assuming, that is, that these lines were indeed intended as an oblique allusion to contemporary events – is grotesque misrepresentation, and further evidence of the unreliability that many critics have seen as one of the chief characteristics of *Henry V*'s Chorus.[23] For the majority of English men and women the possibility of an escalation of the war with Spain was not a welcome prospect.

However, that is not to deny that honour played an important part in the contemporary debate on foreign policy. The Privy Council was deeply divided. Although both sides recognized the need for military preparedness, one side favoured a defensive strategy, while the other argued for an aggressive approach towards Spain. Supported by her Secretary of State, Elizabeth was anxious to avoid committing English troops on the Continent if she could possibly help it; her natural inclination was to maintain a balance of power in Europe by playing off the two Continental superpowers against each other. Essex was passionately opposed to this policy of caution. From the late 1580s he had assiduously built up his power and influence at court by surrounding himself with professional soldiers and intelligence agents. His spectacular success in destroying the Spanish fleet in Cadiz harbour in 1596 did much to redeem the failure of the siege of Rouen in 1592 and to establish his reputation as a national hero and leader of the war party. His personal campaign to persuade the government to adopt a more assertive foreign policy was in tune with the mood of apocalyptic hysteria that characterized extreme militant Protestantism in the 1590s.[24] In 1596 George Gifford argued that the faithful servants of God must seek

---

[22] Ibid., p. 91.
[23] See Andrew Gurr, ed., *Introduction to 'King Henry V'* (Cambridge: Cambridge University Press, 1992), pp. 6–16.
[24] Bernard Capp, 'The Political Dimension of Apocalyptic Thought', *The Apocalypse in English Renaissance Thought and Literature*, ed. C.A. Patrides and Joseph Wittreich (Manchester: Manchester University Press, 1984), pp. 93–124. See also Richard Bauckham, *Tudor Apocalypse: Sixteenth-Century Apocalypticism, Millenarianism and the English Reformation* (Abingdon: Sutton Courtenay, 1978); Paul Christianson, *Reformers and Babylon: English Apocalyptic Visions from the Reformation to the End of the Civil War* (Toronto: University of Toronto Press, 1978); Katharine R. Firth, *The Apocalyptic Tradition in Reformation Britain 1530–1645* (Oxford: Oxford University Press, 1979).

revenge 'even to the full' on Rome for its corruption of the church.[25] Even more violent in its anticipation of militaristic vengeance is Arthur Dent's *The ruine of Rome*. Dent prophesied that 'when the armies of the [Catholic] Leaguers . . . and all other Popish armies shall joyne & band themselves together against the christian kings and defenders of the Gospell: their dead carkasses shall even cover the earth'.[26] In 1598 Essex wrote his own pamphlet praising the heroic mind and arguing the case for an all-out attack on Spain.[27] Though the apocalyptic sermons of clerics like Gifford provided religious support for the ambitions of the war party, Essex himself was less interested in eschatology than in the personal glory that would accrue from a successful Continental campaign. Essex saw himself as the inheritor of an ancient chivalric tradition that had been allowed to decay under the influence of civic humanism. He believed that England, like Claudius' Denmark, should declare itself a 'warlike state'.

It was in the context of this highly politicized quarrel between the war party and its opponents that *Henry V* was written. By beginning the play with an invocation to Mars, patron god of chivalry, attended by 'famine, sword and fire' straining like leashed greyhounds at his heels (Prol. 1–8), Shakespeare could hardly have given a clearer indication of the topical issues he meant to address.

HOLY WARRIOR

Because Shakespeare's Henry is a natural autocrat, post-Foucauldian criticism has portrayed the play, perhaps predictably, as an essay on power. For Stephen Greenblatt *Henry V* is a classic example of the way authority produces and contains subversion. Insofar as it is concerned to illustrate a transhistorical paradigm of power politics, Greenblatt's essay is, strictly speaking, a-historicist. For all its rhetorical persuasiveness, it suffers from the inevitable limitations of its analogical methodology. When flexible use is made of the text,[28] and when external appeal is made, not to proven source material or contemporaneous political debate, but to unconnected 'reiterations'

---

[25] George Gifford, *Sermons upon the Whole Booke of the Revelation* (London: 1596), p. 346.
[26] Arthur Dent, *The ruine of Rome* (London: 1603), p. 240.
[27] Robert Devereux, 2nd Earl of Essex, *An Apologie of the Earl of Essex* (London: 1603).
[28] On Greenblatt's rhetorical strategies, analogical method, and flexible treatment of texts see Tom McAlindon, 'Testing the New Historicism', *SP*, 92 (1995), 411–38.

of an *a priori* principle, it becomes difficult either to prove or disprove his thesis. A more truly historicist case for seeing Henry as scheming Machiavel has recently been made by Steven Marx.[29] The idea of the benign Machiavel using deception for the good of the state is not a new one in Shakespeare criticism.[30] But Marx goes, not just to Machiavelli, but to one of Machiavelli's own sources for his political analogues. Noting the presumably intentional parallel between the miracle of Agincourt and God's deliverance of Israel (the *Non nobis* that Henry orders to be sung after the battle is the Latin title of Psalm 115 celebrating the defeat of the Egyptian armies at the Red Sea), he argues that the Old Testament provided Renaissance humanists with a political history as rich and revealing as those of the classical world. Citing a number of biblical figures who use trickery to defeat their enemies, Marx suggests that Shakespeare shows Henry deliberately and cynically using holy war as a political device to inspire faith in his followers and awe in his enemies.

Based as it is on proven sources rather than on tendentious readings of entirely unconnected texts, Marx's argument is a much more convincing one than Greenblatt's. But again the play itself does not support the claim that Henry is unscrupulously manipulating religion for political ends. Ruthless Henry undoubtedly is, but to accuse him of bad faith is to deny him his most outstanding and most dangerous characteristic, namely his frank and single-minded fidelity to his cause.

It is true that in *Henry IV* the prince uses deception to enhance his reputation, announcing at the beginning of Part 1 that he will 'falsify men's hopes' by 'redeeming time' when people least expect it (*1H4*, 1.ii.208–14). Whether or not his reformation at the end of Part 2 is authentic, he appears, when we see him at the beginning of *Henry V*, to have all the characteristics of the reborn Christian of fifteenth-century prophetic writings about Henry. From the conversation between Canterbury and Ely in the first scene we learn that he does indeed seem to be the 'new man' described in *The First English Life of Henry V* (1513), and rehearsed by the sixteenth-century chroniclers:[31]

---

[29] Steven Marx, 'Holy War in *Henry V*', *ShS*, 48 (1995), 85–97.

[30] John F. Danby, *Shakespeare's Doctrine of Nature: A Study of 'King Lear'* (London: Faber & Faber, 1961), pp. 81–101.

[31] For discussion of Pauline allusions in Henry IV see J.A. Bryant, 'Prince Hal and the Ephesians', *SewR*, 67 (1959), 204–19; D.J. Palmer, 'Casting off the Old Man: History and St Paul in Henry IV', *CQ*, 12 (1970), 267–83. See also Robin Headlam Wells, *Elizabethan*

> Never was such a sudden scholar made;
> Never came reformation in a flood,
> With such a heady currance scouring faults;
> Nor never Hydra-headed wilfulness
> So soon did lose his seat – and all at once –
> As in this king. (1.i.33–8)

As well as showing an impressive grasp of theological and political matters, the reborn king is a compelling orator, especially on the subject of war. 'List his discourse of war,' says Canterbury, 'and you shall hear / A fearful battle rendered you in music' (1.i.44–5). It is Henry's passion for war that particularly interests the bishops. Seeing in this a way out of the church's own problems, Canterbury makes the king an offer: if he will guarantee the security of church lands, the clergy will support a re-opening of the war against France. But before Henry will agree to this proposal he insists on satisfying himself that he does have a legitimate claim to the French crown. The ground is thus prepared for the notorious debate on Salic Law.

If it was Shakespeare's intention to portray Henry as the mirror of Christian kings and to justify his aggressive military policies, Canterbury's exposition of Salic Law seems an odd way of going about it. To establish the legality of Henry's claim to France, Shakespeare could easily have had a group of courtiers discussing the Plantagenet dynasty. One of them might begin by reminding the court that English kings had ruled the Angevin empire since time immemorial (that is to say, since the eleventh century); another might say that Edward III had a better claim to the French throne than anyone else, better certainly than Philip VI; a third might rejoin that Philip's confiscation of the Duchy of Aquitaine in 1337 was quite illegal; a fourth might point out that when Henry's father met the dukes of Berry, Bourbon, and Orléans in Bourges in 1412 all had agreed that Aquitaine was rightfully English. All this could have been done quickly and emphatically. Alternatively, Shakespeare could have followed the example of the *Famous Victories of Henry V* where the question of Henry's legal claims to France is dealt with in two sentences. In response to the king's request for advice Canterbury simply says 'Your right to the French crown of France came by your great-grandmother, Isabel, wife to King Edward the third, and sister to Charles, the French King. Now, if the French King deny it, as

Mythologies: Studies in Poetry, Drama and Music (Cambridge: Cambridge University Press, 1994), pp. 44–62.

likely enough he will, then must you take your sword in hand and conquer the right'.³² What could be simpler? The king has a clear legal right and he must defend it. By contrast, Shakespeare reproduces more or less word for word from Holinshed a forensic argument of such tortuous casuistry that no theatre audience could possibly follow it. Holinshed's own view of Canterbury's tactics comes across fairly clearly. Winding up what Holinshed calls 'his prepared tale', the archbishop shifts to a different register as he exhorts Henry to 'advance forth his banner to fight for his right' and 'spare neither bloud, sword, nor fire' in defence of his inheritance. Parliament responds to this emotive rhetoric with cries of 'Warre, warre; France, France'. Carried away by its own jingoism, the House forgets the more mundane question of church lands, and votes enthusiastically for war. Holinshed comments dryly: 'Hereby the bill for dissolving of religious houses was cleerelie set aside, and nothing thought on but onelie the recovering of France, according as the archbishop had mooved'.³³

With his keen interest in the unscrupulous use of political oratory – *Julius Caesar* was probably written in the same year as *Henry V* – Shakespeare clearly saw the dramatic potential of such material. But if Canterbury's motives are dishonourable, this does not mean that Henry is necessarily a conniver. Indeed he is insistent that the archbishop explain the crown's legal position 'justly and religiously' (1.ii.10). Warning him not to 'fashion, wrest, or bow' the facts to suit convenience (14), Henry soberly reminds the court of the consequences of going to war. In contrast to Canterbury's casuistical exposition of Salic Law, the king's response is a simple question: 'May I with right and conscience make this claim?' (96). As in Holinshed, Canterbury's reply is an emotive appeal to national pride:

> Gracious lord,
> Stand for your own; unwind your bloody flag;
> Look back into your mighty ancestors.
> Go, my dread lord, to your great-grandsire's tomb,
> From whom you claim; invoke his warlike spirit.   (100–4)

---

[32] *The Oldcastle Controversy: Sir John Oldcastle, Part I and the Famous Victories of Henry V*, Revels Plays edn., ed. Peter Corbin and Douglas Sedge (Manchester and New York: Manchester University Press, 1991), p. 175.

[33] Raphael Holinshed, *Holinshed's Chronicles* revised edn. (1587), 6 vols, ed. John Vowell (London, 1807–8), vol. III (1808), p. 66.

Taking up the archbishop's theme, Ely urges Henry to think of 'exploits and mighty enterprises' (121). Unlike Hamlet, whose reaction to an appeal to dynastic honour is an impassioned declaration of vengeance, Henry remains cool, quietly reminding the court of the need to prepare, not only for a foreign campaign, but also for the possibility of an attack from Scotland. The debate concludes with the archbishop's emollient parable of the beehive. Obedience to the rule of nature, says Canterbury, is the key to social harmony: just as members of a beehive work together under the direction of a king, so national success depends on each member of society working for the common good.

Canterbury's parable is meant as an illustration of the general principle that Exeter has just stated in the preceding speech. 'Government,' says Exeter,

> though high and low and lower,
> Put into parts, doth keep in one consent,
> Congreeing in a full and natural close,
> Like music. (180–3)

Musical harmony is a key metaphor in political debate in this period.[34] In formulating their constitutional arguments both apologists for and critics of the crown appeal to the laws of a nature whose characteristic feature is 'harmonicall agreement' and 'due proportion'.[35] That Exeter's appeal to these familiar Pythagorean principles should make Canterbury think of bees is not in itself surprising. The association is conventional. The *inscriptio* of an early seventeenth-century emblem illustrating the principles of social harmony explains that

> As busie Bees unto their Hive doe swarme,
> So do's th' attractive power of *Musicke* charme . . .
> This *Harmony* in t' humane *Fabricke* steales
> And is the sinewes of all Common-weales.[36]

---

[34] See below ch. 6.
[35] Pierre de La Primaudaye, *The French Academie* (London, 1586), p. 743.
[36] *The Mirrour of Maiestie: or, The Badges of Honour* (1618), facsimile copy, ed. Henry Green and James Croston (London, 1870), Sig. F2. The beehive analogy is a commonplace in classical, medieval, and Renaissance political writing (see J.H. Walter's notes to 1.ii in his Arden edition of *Henry V*, p. 22). In the *Education of a Christian Prince* (trans. with introduction by Lester K. Born (New York: Columbia University Press, 1936)), which Shakespeare is known to have used when he was writing *Henry V*, Erasmus uses the beehive analogy to caution the prince against the temptation to enlarge his territories (cited in Andrew Gurr, '*Henry V* and the Bees' Commonwealth', *ShS*, 30 (1977), 61–72).

The significant thing about the archbishop's little clerical homily is not its content – which is conventional enough – but the context in which it is made and the lesson that Canterbury draws from it. The irony of Canterbury's speech is that he should appeal to harmonist principles, not in order to defend the Orphic arts of peace, but to argue for war. In what seems no less of a *non sequitur* than Hector's abrupt volte-face at the end of his eloquent exposition of natural law in *Troilus and Cressida* (II.ii.173–92), the archbishop concludes his parable of social harmony with a call to arms: 'Therefore to France, my liege' (I.ii.213).

Behind Canterbury's speech lies a long debate on the arts of war and peace.[37] At the end of the play there is another reminder of that debate. In an extended natural image, ironically of great beauty, the Duke of Burgundy reflects sadly on the way peace, the 'nurse of arts', has been 'mangled' by war. As nature reverts to wildness, so humanity seems to return to its primal savagery:

> An all our vineyards, fallows, meads, and hedges,
> Defective in their natures, grow to wildness;
> Even so our houses and ourselves and children
> Have lost, or do not learn for want of time,
> The sciences that should become our country;
> But grow, like savages – as soldiers will
> That nothing do but meditate on blood.   (v.ii.54–60)

But Henry, unlike the effeminate Richard II, is no 'nurse of arts'. Above all he is a holy warrior. Having satisfied himself that he has good legal and religious grounds for going to war, he announces his decision. With calm deliberation he declares that once France is his he will either bend it to his will or 'break it all to pieces' (I.ii.224–5). When the French ambassadors arrive he informs them that he is 'no tyrant, but a Christian king' (241). J.H. Walter has shown that Shakespeare knew Erasmus' *Education of a Christian Prince* well and was probably working closely with it when he wrote *Henry V*.[38] But Henry's notion of what it means to be a Christian king could not be more different from Erasmus'. For Erasmus clemency is one of the prince's cardinal virtues.[39] So too is it for Shakespeare's Portia. If

---

[37] See Robert P. Adams, *The Better Part of Valor: More, Erasmus, Colet, and Vives on Humanism, War, and Peace 1496–1535* (Seattle: University of Washington Press, 1962); Philip C. Dust, *Three Renaissance Pacifists: Essays on the Theories of Erasmus, More, and Vives* (New York: Peter Lang, 1987).

[38] Introduction to *Henry V*, pp. xvii–xviii.

[39] *The Education of a Christian Prince*, trans. Born, p. 209.

mercy 'becomes / The thronèd monarch better than his crown' it is because 'It is an attribute of God himself' (*MV*, IV.i.185–192). By contrast Henry sees himself as the scourge of a vindictive God. In retaliation for the Dauphin's insult, Henry tells the ambassadors to warn their prince that

> his soul
> Shall stand sore chargèd for the wasteful vengeance
> That shall fly at them – for many a thousand widows
> Shall this his mock mock out of their dear husbands,
> Mock mothers from their sons, mock castles down;
> Ay, some are yet ungotten and unborn
> That shall have cause to curse the Dauphin's scorn.
> But this lies all within the will of God,
> To whom I do appeal, and in whose name
> Tell you the Dauphin I am coming on
> To venge me as I may, and to put forth
> My rightful hand in a well-hallowed cause.   (I.ii.282–93)

It would be difficult to think of a more aptly ironic comment on such cold savagery than Exeter's 'This was a merry message'(298).

Dramatically the whole scene is of crucial importance in establishing one of the play's central thematic concerns, that is the dangers of single-minded idealism. Many critics and historians – including, I suspect, Holinshed – are suspicious of Canterbury's motives. Legally his arguments may be sound,[40] but the effect of his speech is not to clarify matters but to confuse them. That Henry himself seems to be satisfied with the archbishop's exposition of Salic Law does not mean that he is a 'conniving hypocrite'. What we see of Henry in this scene is in keeping with fifteenth-century apocalytic interpretations of his providential role as the scourge of God: first he confirms that he has a 'well-hallowed cause'; then he coolly and openly tells his enemies what they can expect if they dare to oppose his will. The truly frightening thing about him is the sense he has of the absolute rightness of his cause. Having 'whipped th' offending Adam out of him' (I.i.30), he is now a man driven by a powerful sense of missionary zeal. Though he claims to be a Christian king, it is really Mars who is his true god, and Henry is his scourge. By contrast, the clergy with whom he deals are not idealists inspired by a divine mission, but cynical politicians who are prepared to see

---

[40] See Theodor Meron, *Henry's Wars and Shakespeare's Laws: Perspectives on the Law of War in the Later Middle Ages* (Oxford: Clarendon Press, 1993), pp. 27ff.

England go to war rather than lose their lands. Defending Canterbury's speech against the usual charges of tedium and incomprehensibility, Gary Taylor argues that the archbishop's performance is 'both comprehensible and dramatically necessary': comprehensible because Elizabethans were apparently interested in Salic Law and were used to listening to long speeches, and dramatically necessary because if one wants to build up to a thrilling climax (Henry's riposte to the Dauphin) one has to begin at a low pitch.[41] Taylor needs to defend the archbishop's speech because he believes that Shakespeare approved of Henry's policies and wanted to justify them. Dramatically, however, what comes over most strongly in these crucial opening scenes is not the transparent justice of Henry's cause, but the inherent danger of unholy alliances between unscrupulous cynicism and single-minded idealism, a motif that Shakespeare was later to develop to devastating effect in another tale about an idealistic soldier and a Machiavellian cynic.

But Henry is no Othello; a steely self control is one of his most impressive characteristics. It is not just that he is good at mastering his feelings; as he admits when he learns of the killing of the luggage boys, normally he is simply not prone to strong emotions. But in this case anger is an entirely appropriate response. The other occasion when he allows his anger to show is in the argument with Williams.

The disguised king who shows his true humanity by mingling with his people in a brief interlude of benevolent deception is a common motif in Elizabethan fiction.[42] It is just such a stereotype that the Chorus evokes as he asks us to imagine Henry passing among his 'ruined band' of soldiers and raising their spirits with his 'cheerful semblance and sweet majesty' (IV. Chorus.29, 40). But the reality is rather different. Instead of cheering his men, Henry quarrels with them, provoking Bates to call him and Williams a pair of 'English fools' (IV.i.220). It is Bates who triggers the argument by innocently suggesting that at a moment like the present the king is probably wishing he were anywhere but at Agincourt. Henry tells him that, 'his cause being just and his quarrel honourable' (126–7), it is unlikely that the king would want to be anywhere else. Bates is not interested in challenging the point, but Williams immediately picks it

---

[41] Introduction to *Henry V*, pp. 34–8.
[42] Anne Barton, 'The King Disguised: Shakespeare's *Henry V* and the Comical History', in *The Triple Bond: Plays, Mainly Shakespearean, in Performance*, ed. Joseph G. Price (University Park and London: Pennsylvania State University Press, 1975), pp. 92–117.

up: 'But if the cause be not good, the King himself hath a heavy reckoning to make' (133–4). We thus return to the play's central politico-religious problem. In an apocalyptic image of dismembered bodies joining together at the day of judgment, Williams speculates on the horror of dying unattended on the battlefield knowing that wives and children are left unprotected and debts unpaid. If the cause for which these men are about to die is not a good one, he says, 'it will be a black matter for the King that led them to it' (143–4). Unknowingly Williams has touched on something that is dear to Henry's heart. Little wonder that he becomes angry, for who is Williams, a common soldier, to question the scourge of God? Henry's response is a long speech absolving the king of any responsibility for the souls of men who die with 'irreconciled iniquities' (152); such men, he tells Williams, cannot expect to escape the wrath of God, for 'War is his beadle. War is his vengeance' (167–8). Williams and the king are clearly talking at cross-purposes: one is thinking about soldiers dying with unprotected dependants; the other is concerned to obey the will of a vindictive 'God of battles'. Henry's theology is harsh and, so far as Williams is concerned, irrelevant. But it is not said in bad faith. If Henry fails to answer Williams' worries it is because he is apparently incapable of understanding the concerns of a common soldier. As he admitted when he threatened the citizens of Harfleur with 'heady murder, spoil, and villainy' (III.iii.115), 'What is it then to me' if the innocent suffer? 'What is 't to me?' (98, 102). Henry's mind is on loftier things than the sufferings of common people. As we hear him pray to his God of battles at the end of the scene there is no question of his sincerity. Henry's fault is not 'juggling' hypocrisy, but an apocalyptic idealism that is incapable of doubting its own validity. If there is a moral in this play it must be: beware of men with visions.

The debate with Williams does not show Henry to good advantage. But the following morning he is in his true element. His rallying cry to his troops in the Crispin's Day speech is not a piece of cynical bravado, but an expression of unaffected joy in doing the one thing that, for the chevalier, gives meaning and purpose to life:

> We few, we happy few, we band of brothers.
> For he today that sheds his blood with me
> Shall be my brother. (IV.iii.60–2)

For the medieval knight war provides the ultimate test of his virtue; it is something for which his whole training in the chivalric arts has been a preparation. This is why Henry tells Westmoreland that he would not wish for any additional men, since that would diminish the glory of the hour:

> I would not lose so great an honour
> As one man more methinks would share from me
> For the best hope I have. O do not wish one more. (31–3)

War does not just provide a test of a knight's prowess; to die well is a consummation devoutly to be wished. Johan Huizinga quotes a passage from Jean de Bueil's *Le Jouvencel* (*c.* 1466) that captures wonderfully the idealized sentiments that war is capable of inspiring:

It is a joyous thing, is war . . . You love your comrade so in war. When you see that your quarrel is just and your blood is fighting well, tears rise to your eye. A great sweet feeling of loyalty and of pity fills your heart on seeing your friend so valiantly exposing his body to execute and accomplish the command of our Creator. And then you prepare to go and die or live with him, and for love not to abandon him. And out of that there arises such a delectation, that he who has not tasted it is not fit to say what a delight it is. Do you think that a man who does that fears death? Not at all; for he feels so strengthened, he is so elated, that he does not know where he is. Truly he is afraid of nothing.[43]

Idealization of battle is the very core of medieval chivalry. It is the knight's moment of true glory. The same sentiments as those described by Jean de Bueil are expressed in Exeter's account of the deaths of Suffolk and York in Scene vi. Exeter's speech is a powerfully moving piece of theatre. In dramatic contrast to the disorder and confusion among the demoralized French (Scene v), we are now given a picture of heroic self sacrifice and sublime emotion as two noble warriors, brothers in chivalry, are united in death. Exeter reports how, tenderly kissing the torn and bleeding face of his companion in arms, York cries

> 'Tarry, dear cousin Suffolk.
> My soul shall thine keep company to heaven.
> Tarry, sweet soul, for mine, then fly abreast,
> As in this glorious and well-foughten field
> We kept together in our chivalry.' (IV.vi.15–19)

---

[43] J. Huizinga, *The Waning of the Middle Ages* (1924; repr. Harmondsworth: Penguin, 1982), p. 73.

Holding Exeter's hand, the dying York asks him to commend him to the king. Then he kisses the lips of his dead companion once more;

> And so espous'd to death, with blood he sealed
> A testament of noble-ending love. (26–7)

No conventional love scene in Shakespeare is so affecting. Indeed so moving is Exeter's story that even Henry is almost moved to tears – almost, but not quite (IV.vi.33–4). If this battle scene had been written in the fifteenth century it might just have been possible to take it seriously. A century later it is the purest kitsch.[44]

But Shakespeare, always the self-conscious dramatist, distances us from the artfully constructed pathos of the scene. As if to signal the fact that Exeter's romantic chivalry is no more than theatrical sentimentality, the mood of maudlin heroism is abruptly broken by an alarum signalling that the French have regrouped, and we are brought back abruptly from a dream of heroic romance to the killing field. With brutal efficiency Henry immediately orders the prisoners to be killed. Since the prisoners are actually on stage at the time the order is given, Gary Taylor is probably right in suggesting that the killing would have taken place in front of the audience.[45] Whether or not circumstances on the battlefield at Agincourt meant that it was tactically necessary to kill the prisoners is something that no theatre audience would have time to consider. Dramatically, though, its impact is powerful. This time it is Gower who provides the commentary. Supposing, wrongly, that Henry had ordered the killing of the prisoners in retaliation for the slaughter of the luggage boys, he says, 'O, 'tis a gallant king' (IV.vii.10).

THE DANGERS OF IDEALISM

One effect of the meeting between Henry and his bishops at the beginning of the play is to make us warm to Henry's integrity. Confronted with such blatant episcopal cynicism, it is not difficult to admire the man of honour. As Robert Ashley wrote in a treatise entitled *Of Honour* (*c.* 1600):

By honour are vertues kindled and incouraged, by honour are vices eschewed, by honour ignoraunce, error and folly, sloth and sluggishness,

---

[44] On kitsch in *Henry V* see also Robin Headlam Wells, 'Neo-Petrarchan Kitsch in *Romeo and Juliet*', *MLR*, 93 (1998), 913–14.
[45] Introduction to *Henry V*, p. 32.

hatred and fear, shame and ignoraunce, and all evill affeccions are alayed.[46]

Henry is a man inspired by a heroic ideal. At Agincourt his integrity and his valour are set off to even greater advantage by the foolish boasting of the Dauphin (III.vii). When the man of honour is as gifted an orator as Henry is, the combination of missionary zeal and impassioned eloquence is almost irresistible. Against our better judgment we respond to his inspiring words and forget for the moment the cruel reality behind the noble rhetoric. Yet repeatedly the play brings us back to that reality. Even as the Act II Chorus describes how England's youth are fired with thoughts of war, he tells us that they follow Henry to battle like 'English Mercuries' (II. chorus.3–4, 7). Like so many of his Olympian clients, Mercury has a double nature. He is both peacemaker and thief.[47] Which of them Henry is depends on one's point of view. Lydgate described the historical Henry as a 'prince of pes' resolving an ancient dynastic dispute (*Troy Book*, v.3416); the author of the *Gesta Henrici Quinti* says he is 'the true elect of God'. Shakespeare's Henry also sees himself as a peacemaker. Ironically it is on the eve of a battle in which some ten thousand men are about to lose their lives that Henry reflects on his peacemaking role. As he ponders the cares of office he thinks ruefully how the peasant little knows 'what watch the King keeps to maintain the peace' (IV.i.280). But Erasmus had no time for millenarian fantasies. He saw Henry's campaigns as a classic example of the folly of attempting to extend territory. To him the chivalric ideals that endorsed them were simply a means of promoting war under a veneer of glory. What Shakespeare thought about Henry we can only guess. However, it is interesting that, having given us a heroic image of chivalrous English warriors setting off to do battle for their country's honour, he then immediately produces some English Mercuries of a very different kind in Scene ii. The ironic parallel between Henry's exploits and those of his soldiers is underlined by Fluellen's comparison of him to Alexander the Great: 'If you mark

---

[46] Robert Ashley, *Of Honour*, edited with an introduction by Virgil B. Heltzel (San Marino, Calif.: The Huntington Library, 1947), p. 30.

[47] On Mercury as a symbolic representative of peace, government, and control see Douglas Brooks-Davies, *The Mercurian Monarch: Magical Politics from Spenser to Pope* (Manchester: Manchester University Press, 1983), p. 2; see also Edgar Wind *Pagan Mysteries in the Renaissance* (London: Faber, 1958), p. 91n2. On his thieving habits see the Homeric *Hymn to Hermes*; see also Ovid, *Metamorphoses*, II.685ff.; II.815ff.

Alexander's life well, Harry of Monmouth's life is come after it indifferent well' (IV.vii.30–2).

There are several allusions to Alexander in the play (I.i.46; III.i.19; IV.vii.13ff). But the anecdote from Alexander's life that is most damaging to Henry is the general's meeting with a pirate he has taken prisoner. In St Augustine's version of the story Alexander asks Dionides how he dare 'molest the seas'. Dionides replies: 'How darest thou molest the whole world? But because I doe it with a little ship onely, I am called a theefe: thou doing it with a great Navie, art called an Emperour'.[48] In the light of Erasmus' deprecation of war between neighbouring rulers when disagreements could easily be settled by arbitration,[49] Bardolph's complaint at the pointless brawling of his companions sounds very much like an oblique comment on his betters.

If, as Fluellen says, 'there is figures in all things' (IV.vii.32), we have to ask what the function of these subplot scenes is with their foolish squabbling, petty thieving, and preposterous heroics. Is it to reveal 'true things by what their mock'ries be' (IV. Chorus.53), and in this way to show to advantage the 'gret manhode' for which Henry was praised by his contemporaries?[50] Or is it to suggest that, for all Henry's noble rhetoric, his foreign policy is merely thievery on an international scale? In 1599 Shakespeare had good reasons for not declaring his hand.

THE COLLAPSE OF CHIVALRY

Henry V was written and performed while Essex was out of the country. Until news began to filter back to London of the truce that he had been forced to conclude with Tyrone in September 1599, no one could have predicted with certainty the outcome of the earl's mission to suppress the Irish rebellion. Success might lead to a reconciliation with the queen and the rehabilitation of his own reputation as crusading national hero; failure would in all probability mean the end of his political career, at least while Elizabeth

---

[48] St Augustine of Hippo, *Of the Citie of God*, trans. J. Healey (London, 1610). For this point I am indebted to Janet M. Spencer, 'Princes, Pirates, and Pigs: Criminalizing Wars of Conquest in *Henry V*', *SQ*, 47 (1996), 160–77.
[49] *The Education of a Christian Prince*, trans. Born, pp. 252–3.
[50] William of Worcester, *The Boke of Noblesse: Addressed to King Edward III on his Invasion of France*, with an introduction by John Gough Nichols (London: J.B. Nichols, 1860) p. 20.

was alive. In dealing with a historical figure with whom the earl was so closely identified, Shakespeare had to tread with extreme caution. The dangers of linking oneself too closely with the earl are vividly illustrated by the imprisonment of Sir John Hayward in July 1600. Hayward's crime was that of publishing what Elizabeth regarded as a seditious history of Henry IV. His injudicious choice of subject matter was compounded by the extravagant praise he offered to Essex in the dedication of *The First Part of the Life and Raigne of King Henry IIII*. At Hayward's trial it was put to him that, by dealing with the deposition of a reigning monarch by a group of discontented noblemen, and by writing about it in a way that seemed to invite readers to draw parallels with contemporary events, he was in effect inciting rebellion.[51] Whatever Shakespeare's personal views of Essex were, the Hayward trial cannot have been reassuring. Not only was Hayward dealing with precisely the same period of history that he himself had already dramatized in the first three plays of his second historical tetralogy, but Hayward's allegedly seditious theory of history was actually no more pointed than the Tacitean views that Shakespeare had put into the mouth of Warwick in the second part of *Henry IV* (iii.i.75–87). With Hayward still in the Tower, the Chamberlain's Men were understandably reluctant when they were asked by Essex's supporters in February 1601 to put on a performance of a play called *Richard II*. Had they known that a military coup would be attempted the very next day, it is unlikely that they would have agreed.

Essex's supporters knew that their leader's political career depended on the outcome of the Irish campaign. What no one could have predicted in the summer of 1599 was the extraordinary nature of the events that would follow his return from Ireland.[52] While Essex's quarrel with the queen; his house arrest; the trial in June 1600; his plans for seizing the centres of power – while all these were the ingredients of high political drama, the coup itself was more like farce. Instead of rallying to his cause, as Essex had expected, the

---

[51] *The First and Second Part of John Hayward's 'The Life and Raigne of King Henrie IIII'*, ed. with an introduction by John J. Manning, Camden Fourth Series, vol. 42 (London: Royal Historical Society, 1991), pp. 31–2.

[52] The story of the rebellion has been told many times. See especially G.B. Harrison, *The Life and Death of Robert Devereux, Earl of Essex* (London, Toronto, Melbourne, and Sydney: Cassell, 1937); Robert Lacey, *Robert, Earl of Essex: An Elizabethan Icarus* (London: Weidenfeld and Nicolson, 1971); Mervyn James, *Society, Politics and Culture: Studies in Early Modern England* (1978; repr., Cambridge: Cambridge University Press, 1986), pp. 416–65.

people of London stood by in silent amazement as he led his little cavalcade up Fenchurch Street crying 'for the Queen, for the Queen'.[53] But it was not the failure of the coup itself so much as the earl's behaviour after his arrest that exposed neo-chivalric honour for the anachronistic folly that it was.[54] It might be imagined that a man who had championed the cause of masculine honour would resolve to die a hero's death, displaying that manly fortitude which so moved Ralegh's audience when he addressed the crowd from the scaffold seventeen years later. But Essex did not stand by his principles. In his confession he not only repudiated all his former ideals, but even denounced his supporters, including his own sister. Neo-chivalric idealism had been revealed as an empty sham; and, most damaging of all to the war party, the exposure had come from within. With Essex disgraced, Shakespeare could afford to drop his guard. Returning to satirize the false ideals of masculine chivalry,[55] he chose a story that was one of Henry's own favourites.

MANHOOD AND HONOUR

Shortly before his accession Henry V commissioned a translation of Guido delle Colonne's *Historia destructionis Troiae*. The result was John Lydgate's *Troy Book*. In his Prologue Lydgate explained that it was Henry's enthusiasm for 'verray kny3thod' and 'al that longeth to manhood' that was responsible for the prince's interest in a story that was held to be an epitome of 'the prowesse of olde chivalrie'.[56] Praised by his contemporaries as the flower of knighthood,[57] Henry

---

[53] P. M. Handover, *The Second Cecil: The Rise to Power 1563–1604 of Sir Robert Cecil* (London: Eyre & Spottiswoode, 1959), pp. 222.

[54] See James, *Society, Politics and Culture*, pp. 455–65, for a brilliant analysis of the political significance of Essex's volte-face.

[55] It is a commonplace of earlier twentieth-century criticism that in *Troilus and Cressida* Shakespeare was satirizing the England of Elizabeth's final years. As Tucker Brooke puts it: 'within the wall the febrile Essex type of decadent chivalry; without, the strident go-getters of the newer dispensation: Cecil–Ulysses and Ralegh–Diomed' ('Shakespeare's Study in Culture and Anarchy', *YR*, 17 (1928), 576. See also James E. Savage, '*Troilus and Cressida* and Elizabethan Court Factions', *UMSE*, 5 (1964), 413–66. For a survey of earlier twentieth-century topical readings of the play see the New Variorum edn., ed. Harold N. Hillebrand (Philadelphia and London: J.B. Lippincott, 1953), pp. 377–82.

[56] *Lydgate's Troy Book*, Prol., lines 76–85, ed. Henry Bergen, 4 vols. (London: Early English Text Society, 1906–35), vol. I (1906), p. 3.

[57] In the first line of his Envoy John Lydgate praises Henry as the 'sours & welle' of knighthood (*Lydgate's Troy Book*, vol. III (1908), p. 876). Thomas Hoccleve describes him as the 'welle of honur' and 'flour of Chivalrie' (*Hoccleve's Works*, 3 vols., ed. Frederick J. Furnival (London: Early English Text Society, 1892–7), vol. I, p. 41).

inevitably became linked in the popular mind with the great Trojan exemplars of chivalry. Reminding Edward IV that the English had 'their first originalle of the noble blood of Troy', William of Worcester exhorted his prince to recall the 'victorious conquestis of youre noble predecessours', especially the 'gret manhode' of Henry v. 'And let also be brought to mynde', he wrote, 'to folow the steppis in conceitis of noble courage of the mighty dedis in armes of the vaillaunt knight Hector of Troy, whiche bene enacted in the seige of Troy for a perpetuelle remembraunce of chevalrie.'[58]

Linking the two stories, Shakespeare gives to *Troilus and Cressida*'s Prologue lines that echo *Henry V*. Asking us to imagine Henry's heavily armed fleet setting out for the siege of Harfleur, the Act III Chorus had painted a picture of ships drawing their huge hulls through the furrowed sea, and breasting the lofty surge (12–13). *Troilus and Cressida*'s Prologue also describes a fleet of 'deep-drawing barques' (Prol.12) 'fraught with the ministers and instruments / Of cruel war' (4–5) bound for a foreign siege. And as *Henry V* contrasts the ascetic idealism of the besieging army with the decadence of its opponents, so we have in Priam's palace a court dedicated, like the Dauphin's, to epicurean pleasures, though as Troilus indulges in voluptuous dreams of pleasures to come, he is reminiscent more of Orsino than of the Dauphin:

> I am giddy. Expectation whirls me round.
> Th'imaginary relish is so sweet
> That it enchants my sense. What will it be
> When that the wat'ry palates taste indeed
> Love's thrice-repurèd nectar? Death, I fear me,
> Swooning destruction, or some joy too fine,
> Too subtle-potent, tuned too sharp in sweetness
> For the capacity of my ruder powers.
> I fear it much, and I do fear besides
> That I shall lose distinction in my joys,
> As doth a battle when they charge on heaps
> The enemy flying.   (III.ii.16–27)

Like Orsino and his courtiers, Shakespeare's Trojans are 'idle shallow things' (*TN*, III.iv.121–2) who spend their time, when they are not at war, in sexual scheming and over-ingenious word games. The setting of *Troilus and Cressida* is of course more complex than that of *Twelfth Night*. Instead of the world of Elizabethan country-house

---

[58] *The Boke of Noblesse*, pp. 20, 16, 20.

parties – thinly disguised as a timeless Illyria – we are now taken back to antiquity. But Shakespeare makes no attempt at historical authenticity; the characters who inhabit this antique world are camped up medieval knights and ladies as imagined by a satirist exposing the follies of Elizabethan revivalism. In that neo-chivalric world men live by an idealized code of military honour that has no time for effeminacy,[59] and women are impossibly fair. But it is all a shameless illusion. The extravagant rituals of courtesy do not conceal the barbarity of what is actually being performed in the name of honour; the women are not paragons of chaste beauty, but frivolous coquettes. At the root of Essex's quarrels with the queen was a neo-medieval view of women. According to the masculine code of values that Essex espoused, women were to be served, obeyed, and adored as pseudo-religious symbols, but not as military commanders. While Essex feigned helpless susceptibility to Elizabeth's beauty, in reality he deeply resented being subject to a woman's authority.[60] *Troilus and Cressida* shows very clearly the price women had to pay for their idealized status in the world of chivalry. Helen and Cressida are powerless ciphers.

The discrepancy between outward show and hollow reality – so scandalously exposed at Essex's trial – is one of *Troilus and Cressida*'s central motifs. For all Troilus' talk of honour and renown, the Trojan war is actually, as Thersites puts it, a 'war for a placket' (II.iii.19). The motif is also articulated at a more intellectual level in the philosophic debate that is such a characteristic feature of *Troilus and Cressida*. The play's characters are inveterate arguers. Between them they discuss natural law (I.iii; II.ii), honour (II.ii), reason and ethical relativism (II.ii), selfhood and self knowledge (III.iii), reputation (III.iii), and time and memory (III.iii; IV.v). They express their ideas in language of extreme abstraction. Yet the impressive, wise-sounding *sententiae* are not matched by wise action. Consistently Shakespeare's characters either contradict themselves, or produce apparently cogent arguments in support of untenable positions. The dispute between Hector and Troilus on value epitomizes this paradox. It is Shakespeare's philosophically most penetrating critique of the anti-rationalism that is at the heart of heroic masculinity.

---

[59] For discussion of Patroclus' warning to Achilles of the dangers of effeminacy see Gary Spear, 'Shakespeare's "Manly" Parts: Masculinity and Effeminacy in *Troilus and Cressida*', *SQ* 44 (1993), 409–22.
[60] James, *Society, Politics and Culture*, p. 444.

The debate on the nature of value is prompted by Greek proposals for a truce based on the return of Helen (II.ii.3–7). Reminding his brothers of the thousands of men who have died in defence of a 'thing' that is of no value to them, and is not theirs in the first place (21), Hector asks what rational grounds there can conceivably be for refusing to give her up: 'What merit's in that reason which denies / The yielding of her up?' (23–4). In reply Troilus asks how Hector can think of comparing the lives of insignificant soldiers with something as momentous as kingly honour:

> Fie, fie, my brother!
> Weigh you the worth and honour of a king
> So great as our dread father in a scale
> Of common ounces? (24–7)

Helenus tells him he is being irrational. But Troilus makes no attempt to justify his position on logical grounds: what is at stake is a matter of 'manhood and honour', and these are things that are inimical to reason: 'Nay, if we talk of reason,' he says,

> Let's shut our gates and sleep. Manhood and honour
> Should have hare hearts, would they but fat their thoughts
> With this crammed reason. Reason and respect
> Make livers pale and lustihood deject. (45–9)

When Hector reminds him that Helen is not worth the keeping, Troilus offers the glib reply: 'What's aught but as 'tis valued?' (51).

It might seem at first glance that Troilus is echoing Portia's words to Nerissa about value – 'Nothing is good, I see, without respect' (*MV*, v.i.99). But Portia is not making a case for ethical relativism. The fact that we may mistake a deputy for the real thing ('A substitute shines brightly as a king / Until a king be by') does not mean they are of equal value. On the contrary, it is failure to allow for the fact that 'things by season seasoned are' (107) that leads to such simple errors of judgment. In reality all things have their 'right praise and true perfection' (108). Like Portia, Hector believes in objectivity in value judgments. Value, he tells Troilus, cannot simply be reduced to a matter of personal preference. If we place inordinate value on something that is intrinsically worthless we merely make fools of ourselves (52–8).[61]

---

[61] Hector's defence of objective value is echoed by Ulysses: 'Nature, what things there are, / Most abject in regard and dear in use. / What things again, most dear in the esteem / And poor in worth' (III.iii.122–5).

Did Shakespeare change his mind between the writing of *The Merchant of Venice* and *Troilus and Cressida*? Is he now satirizing Hector's belief in objectivity? Hugh Grady believes he is. E.M.W. Tillyard has been taken to task countless times for naively assuming that Ulysses' defence of hierarchical order is an expression of Shakespeare's own views. It is surprising therefore – the more so in view of Shakespeare's pointed satire on relativist anti-rationalism – to find postmodern criticism doing exactly the same thing with Troilus' ethical relativism, and assuming that character and author speak with one voice. But now Shakespeare has been transformed from a supposedly conservative upholder of natural law into a precursor of postmodernism's own radical distrust of objectivity and reason. Grady writes:

> Hector, like Ulysses in the Greek camp, can still evoke what Horkheimer called Objective Reason and Derrida logocentrism – that mainline of Western rationality stretching from Plato through Hegel – which 'solves' the problem of value through the glorious fiction of a transcendental, objective rationality which can be discovered and once discovered must be submitted to. And yet underneath that glorious autonomous fiction, the play of 'will' exerts its force, bending the supposed autonomous rationality where it lists.[62]

The assumption that Troilus' relativism was Shakespeare's own is not a new one. 'The writer of this play is a man to whom values have become suspect', wrote Una Ellis-Fermor in 1945.[63] But where Ellis-Fermor recognized the fallaciousness of Troilus' relativist arguments, believing that they reflect a vision of chaos that Shakespeare himself experienced during his own 'dark night of the soul',[64] Grady now hails that same anarchic relativism as a true account of the problem of value. In exposing the 'false universality of traditional objective reason', *Troilus and Cressida* seems, says Grady, 'to prefigure several central discourses of modernity'[65] – most notably Adorno and

---

[62] *Shakespeare's Universal Wolf: Studies in Early Modern Reification* (Oxford: Clarendon Press, 1996), p. 91. Cf Heather James: 'In the play's dramatic construction Shakespeare reiterates Troilus' notorious query, "What's aught but as 'tis valued?"' (*Shakespeare's Troy: Drama, Politics, and the Translation of Empire* (Cambridge: Cambridge University Press, 1997), p. 90). For a defence of Shakespeare's supposed anti-rationalism from a psychoanalytic point of view see Emil Roy, 'War and Manliness in Shakespeare's *Troilus and Cressida*', *CD*, 7 (1974), 107–20. Roy writes: 'More than in any other play, Shakespeare offers the subtleties of intellection as a self-defeating way of handling moral instabilities' (p. 119).
[63] *The Frontiers of Drama*, 2nd edn. (London: Methuen, 1964), p. 67.
[64] Ibid., p. 72.
[65] *Shakespeare's Universal Wolf*, pp. 93, 59.

Horkheimer's neo-Romantic, quasi-mystical, anti-rationalist hatred of the Enlightenment and its supposed legacy of 'totalitarianism'.[66]

Shakespeare is fond of conundrums, and the contest between relativism and objectivity is one of the most intractable topics that he deals with. For the youthful philosopher – Hector tells Troilus and Paris that they sound like a couple of intellectual novices (II.ii.162–6) – extreme relativism has a certain shocking bravado about it. What better way of subverting establishment morality than to expose the philosophic groundlessness of its rules? Short of appealing to a transcendent being whose edicts are in some inexplicable way universally and eternally true, there is no logical way of proving that one set of moral values is preferable to another; all values are relative to particular cultures. However, a moment's thought will reveal that extreme relativism is itself logically untenable. For if we claim that under no imaginable circumstances can moral truths be absolute or objective, we are asserting precisely what relativism denies, namely, a universal truth.[67]

Relativism poses a logical riddle to which philosophy has so far not found a satisfactory answer. Unlike many philosophical conundrums, it has social, and indeed international, consequences; they are ones that the United Nations Security Council regularly has to confront. If, with postmodernism, we reject the grand narratives of reason and objectivity as oppressive instruments of an arrogant Western imperialism, we may well find ourselves having to defend regimes that are themselves intolerant and ethnocentric.[68] The inevitable consequence of extreme relativism is social anarchy, which is exactly what we see in *Troilus and Cressida*. For all his scabrous cynicism, it is Thersites who provides the play's most apt summary of the moral condition of two nations that have abrogated reason:

> Here is such patchery, such juggling and such
> knavery. All the argument is a whore and a cuckold.
> A good quarrel to draw emulous factions and bleed to
> death upon.   (II.iii.70–3)

[66] 'Enlightenment is as totalitarian as any system' write Adorno and Horkheimer. 'In the anticipatory identification of the wholly conceived and mathematized world with truth, enlightenment intends to secure itself against the return of the mythic' (Theodor W. Adorno and Max Horkheimer, *Dialectic of Enlightenment*, 1944; trans. John Cumming (London: Allen Lane, 1973), pp. 24–5).
[67] Ernest Gellner, *Relativism and the Social Sciences* (Cambridge: Cambridge University Press, 1985), pp. 84–5.
[68] Ibid., p. 84. See also Raymond Tallis, *Enemies of Hope: A Critique of Contemporary Pessimism* (Basingstoke and London: Macmillan, 1997), p. 367.

Logical knots of the kind in which Hector and Troilus are entangled need a Gordian sword of common sense if intellectual, or in worst cases military, paralysis is to be avoided. Isaiah Berlin's solution is to appeal to a universal framework of human moral thought that is common to all human societies and that transcends local cultural differences.[69] As good an illustration as any of such a moral framework is Hector's reply to Troilus' and Paris' anti-rationalism:

> There is a law in each well-ordered nation
> To curb those raging appetites that are
> Most disobedient and refractory. (II.ii.179–81)

Hector is not, *pace* Grady, appealing to a transcendent principle; with little of the verbosity that is characteristic of his more bombastic speeches,[70] he is simply making an empirical observation. We know as a matter of fact that, in contrast to pre-civilized heroic societies, where disputes are typically resolved by appeal to an honour code that demands vengeance for personal or national injury, 'well-ordered nation[s]' have legal systems designed to restrain barbaric behaviour. We also know, unless we are radical anti-essentialists, that a desire for order and justice appears to be just as much a part of our universal human nature as the raging appetites which our laws are designed to curb. Based, as it is, partly on traditional notions of natural law, and partly on social observation, Berlin's universal framework of values is no more satisfying theoretically than the postmodernist's anarchic relativism. Pragmatically, however, there can be little doubt which is to be preferred. The relativist alternative, as Hector points out to Troilus and Paris, is ultimately an abandonment of the principle of independent moral choice:

> The reasons you allege do more conduce
> To the hot passion of distempered blood
> Than to make up a free determination
> 'Twixt right and wrong; for pleasure and revenge
> Have ears more deaf than adders to the voice
> Of any true decision. (167–72)

---

[69] See John Gray, *Isaiah Berlin* (London: Harper Collins, 1995), pp. 38–75.
[70] The classic essay on the relation between style and meaning in *Troilus and Cressida* is T. McAlindon, 'Language, Style, and Meaning in *Troilus and Cressida*', *PMLA*, 84 (1969), 29–41.

Having argued so persuasively that the 'moral laws / Of nature and of nations speak aloud / To have her back returned' (183–5), Hector then concludes this impressive defence of universals by denying everything that he has just been saying: 'My sprightly brethren, I propend to you / In resolution to keep Helen still' (189–90). Why the abrupt volte-face? For all his wise words, Hector is no less a dupe of the honour code than Troilus is. While his challenge to the Greeks at the beginning of the play – he claims he has 'a lady wiser, fairer, truer, / Than ever Greek did compass in his arms' (I.iii.272–3) – merely looks like foolish boasting, his insistence on doing battle, despite his father's warnings, on the grounds that he must keep faith with the enemy (v.iii.74) is absurd. When Andromache adds her voice to Priam and Cassandra's he brushes her fears aside, telling her that the worthy man 'Holds honour far more precious-dear than life' (v.iii.28). So important to Hector is 'the faith of valour' (71) that it takes precedence over all other considerations. As Larry Clarke rightly says, 'Hector changes his mind because he shares in the systematically irrational validation of "honor" by the Trojan ruling class, regardless of the good of society as a whole'.[71]

Hector's justification for refusing Nestor's peace proposals sounds very much like that which keeps Orangemen marching in Northern Ireland, namely masculine honour. 'For 'tis a cause,' he says, 'that hath no mean dependence / Upon our joint and several dignities' (II.ii.191–2). Troilus is delighted. 'Why, there you touched the life of our design', he tells his brother,

> Were it not glory that we more affected
> Than the performance of our heaving spleens,
> I would not wish a drop of Trojan blood
> Spent more in her defence. But, worthy Hector,
> She is a theme of honour and renown,
> A spur to valiant and magnanimous deeds.   (193–9)

The dramatic effect of Hector's volte-face is stark. Abandon reason and you inevitably revert to a pre-civilized code of values based, not on law and a 'free determination / 'Twixt right and wrong', but on honour and the sword. As Greeks and Trojans exchange extravagant courtesies before the play's only battle, Hector's antique chivalry and his innocent belief in 'fair play' (v.iii.43)

---

[71] Larry R. Clarke, '"Mars his heart inflam'd with Venus": Ideology and Eros in Shakespeare's *Troilus and Cressida*', *MLQ*, 50 (1989), 216.

may seem like nothing worse than a charming, other-worldly eccentricity. But Cassandra knows that it is dangerous make-believe: 'Thou dost thyself and all our Troy deceive', she tells him (93). The brutal reality that lies behind the chivalric façade of 'honour and renown' is spelt out in the killing of the unarmed Hector by Achilles and his myrmidons. With the embittered Troilus appealing to the gods to avenge his brother's death, this cynical and often very funny satire on masculine chivalry takes on an altogether more sombre tone as we are left with the prospect of an endless cycle of Senecan vengeance. Cursing Achilles for his cowardice, Troilus cries:

> No space of earth shall sunder our two hates.
> I'll haunt thee like a wicked conscience still,
> That mouldeth goblins swift as frenzy's thoughts.
> Strike a free march! To Troy with comfort go:
> Hope of revenge shall hide our inward woe.   (v.xi.27–31).

It is Troilus himself who acknowledges that the kind of 'manhood and honour' celebrated in the chivalric tradition is in the most fundamental sense anti-rational. However, what comes across with great clarity in the debate on relativism is not just the irrationality of the honour code, but the destructive power of its appeal. In 1601 this was a highly topical question. Had Essex's revolt succeeded there is every likelihood that England would have been committed to an escalation of a 'cormorant war' that had already caused so much 'loss of time, travail, expense, / Wounds, friends' (II.ii.4–6).[72] That Essex himself was emotionally unstable is well known; some contemporaries actually began to doubt his sanity.[73] But how did he manage to persuade so many of his aristocratic supporters that 'valiant and magnanimous deeds' were a serious basis on which to construct foreign policy in a modern state? The answer is not very far to seek. 'Honour and renown' are a feature of many pre-civilized cultures and are probably the manifestation of some deeply rooted feature of the ancestral male psyche. In most 'well-ordered nation[s]' they are able to find harmless expression through the ritualized battles of sport, or in the case of Elizabethan England, the mock

---

[72] Eric S. Mallin compares the 'besieged and paralised' final years of Elizabeth's reign with Troy ('Emulous Factions and the Collapse of Chivalry: *Troilus and Cressida*', *Rep*, 29 (1990), 146). See also Christopher Highley, *Shakespeare, Spenser, and the Crisis in Ireland* (Cambridge: Cambridge University Press, 1997), p. 136.
[73] Handover, *The Second Cecil*, p. 187.

tournaments of the Accession Day tilts.[74] But if notions of 'manhood and honour' of the kind promoted by Essex and the Elizabethan war party are given official sanction, as their modern equivalents are in countries like Afghanistan and Serbia, they are capable of corrupting whole cultures.

[74] Frances A. Yates, 'Elizabethan Chivalry: The Romance of the Accession Day Tilts', *JWCI*, 20 (1957), 4–25.

CHAPTER 2

'Tender and delicate prince': 'Hamlet'

When the imaginary . . . hero moves us most deeply, it is the moment when he awakens within us for an instant our own heroism.
  W.B. Yeats, *The Irish Dramatic Movement 1901–1919, Explorations*, p. 96

Give homage and allegiance to a hero, and you become yourself heroic. It is the law of men.
  D.H. Lawrence, *Apocalypse*, p. 27

The notion of King James and Queen Anne seated in state in the Great Hall at Hampton Court in January 1604 watching a play in which, as in a mirror, a Player King and Queen enact a story of betrayal and murder in front of another royal couple is an interesting one. Imagining the scene, Alvin Kernan writes: 'it must have been one of the great moments in Western theater, a true coup de theatre . . . causing all thoughtful spectators then and since to wonder which was stage and which was reality'.[1]

Whether or not James was moved by the experience of watching *Hamlet* (or indeed whether *Hamlet* was actually performed at Hampton Court) we do not know. In general James showed no great interest in the theatre. Reporting the 1603/4 winter season, one courtier wrote: 'The first holy days we had every night a public play in the great hall, at which the King was ever present and liked or disliked as he saw cause, but it seems he takes no extraordinary pleasure in them'.[2] Nevertheless, there was plenty in *Hamlet* to catch the king's attention. The play was probably written two years before

---

[1] Alvin Kernan, *Shakespeare, the King's Playwright: Theater in the Stuart Court 1603–1613* (New Haven, Conn. and London: Yale University Press, 1995), p. 32.
[2] Letter from Dudley Carleton to John Chamberlain, quoted by J. Leeds Barroll, *Politics, Plague, and Shakespeare's Theater: The Stuart Years* (Ithaca and London: Cornell University Press, 1991), p. 27.

James came to England. Of the numerous claims to the throne his was the strongest,[3] and it was widely assumed that he would succeed his cousin. Shakespeare had done his homework on the man who seemed most likely to be England's new king, and included in *Hamlet* a scene that bore a striking similarity to one of the most traumatic events in post-Reformation Scottish history.[4] In 1567, only three months after the murdered body of the king had been found in an orchard,[5] Queen Mary married the man universally thought to have been her husband's assassin. The queen's suspected involvement in the Darnley murder and her 'o'er-hasty marriage' to the hated Earl of Bothwell scandalized Catholics as well as Protestants and led to her deposition a month later in June 1567. In their outrage James' grandparents, the Earl and Countess of Lennox, commissioned the so-called *Darnley Memorial*, a narrative painting in which the murder was recorded and moralized. An inscription in the painting exhorted James to 'shut not out of his memory the recent atrocious murder of the King his father, until God should avenge it through him'.[6] Like Hamlet, James had had laid upon him, with all the solemnity of a sacred occasion, a family command to avenge a 'foul and most unnatural murder'. To watch that occasion apparently being re-enacted in a play dealing with 'carnal, bloody, and unnatural acts . . . [and] deaths put on by cunning and forced cause' (v.ii.334–6) must have aroused strong feelings for James.

The Darnley murder and the deposition of Mary took place when James was an infant, and although these events were to have terrible consequences for him throughout his childhood – he was the victim of repeated and often violent plots by ambitious nobles trying to wrest control from his regents – he could have had no first-hand memory of them. And anyway, that was in another country; and

---

[3] Joel Hurstfield, 'The Succession Struggle in Late Elizabethan England', *Elizabethan Government and Society*, ed., S.T. Bindoff, J. Hurstfield, and C.H. Williams (London: Athlone Press, 1961), pp. 369–96; Hurstfield, *Freedom, Corruption and Government in Elizabethan England* (London: Jonathan Cape, 1975), pp. 104–34. See also Penry Williams, *The Later Tudors: England 1547–1603*, *The New Oxford History of England* (Oxford: Clarendon Press, 1995), pp. 383–6.
[4] The most detailed account of the parallels between *Hamlet* and the events of James' life are by Lilian Winstanley, *'Hamlet' and the Scottish Succession* (Cambridge: Cambridge University Press, 1921). See also Roland Mushat Frye, *The Renaissance Hamlet: Issues and Responses in 1600* (Princeton: Princeton University Press, 1984), pp. 31–7; 102–10.
[5] William McElwee, *The Wisest Fool in Christendom: The Reign of King James I and VI* (London: Faber & Faber, 1958), p. 26.
[6] Quoted by Frye, *The Renaissance Hamlet*, p. 32. For analysis of the painting's iconography see Oliver Millar, *The Tudor and Stuart and Early Georgian Pictures in the Collection of Her Majesty the Queen*, 2 vols. (London: Phaidon, 1963), vol. II, pp. 75–7.

besides the murderer and his wife were long since dead. But there were other analogues in *Hamlet* of more recent events that were fresh in people's minds.

On 24 March 1603 Elizabeth died and word was immediately sent to Edinburgh. James came south to a broadly sympathetic welcome from his new subjects. After a lengthy delay caused by worries of plague, he made his formal entry into the capital in March 1604 proclaiming himself a prince of peace.[7] Within five months the Treaty of London had been signed and for the next fifteen years England was at peace with Spain. But things could easily have turned out very differently.

As an experienced ruler and a Protestant, James was the most popular of the many claimants to the English throne. But his mother's treason, combined with the fact that he himself was a foreigner, meant that there were legal difficulties in the way of his succession. In the atmosphere of uncertainty and suspicion created by Henry VIII's will (which effectively excluded a Stuart succession) and Elizabeth's refusal to name her successor, rival power groups sought to promote their own candidates.[8] One of these groups was the Essex faction. Suspecting, or at least claiming that he suspected, that the Cecils favoured the Infanta Isabella, Essex saw James as the best hope for the Protestant cause. The plan was that, with the support of Lord Mountjoy in Ireland and Essex's men in London, James should muster an army and insist on his right to the English throne. In 1599 rumours of Scottish war preparations were rife. Some of these claimed that James was plotting an alliance with Spain, others that he was negotiating with Denmark, others again that he was relying primarily on English support.[9] James' correspondence with Sir Robert Cecil makes it clear that he had at least considered the possibility of using arms to insist on his right to the English throne.[10] But James was warned that, far from aiding his cause, association with Essex would probably wreck it.[11] Under the

---

[7] 'I found the state embarked in a great and tedious war,' James told his first parliament, 'and only by mine arrival here, and by the peace in my person, is now amity kept where war was before' (*Political Writings*, ed. Johann P. Sommerville (Cambridge: Cambridge University Press, 1994), p. 133).

[8] Williams, *The Later Tudors*, pp. 384–5.

[9] Stuart M. Kurland, '*Hamlet* and the Scottish Succession?', *SEL*, 34 (1994), 279–300.

[10] Ibid., p. 282.

[11] P. M. Handover, *The Second Cecil: The Rise to Power 1563–1604 of Sir Robert Cecil* (London: Eyre & Spottiswoode, 1959), p. 191.

terms of the Bond of Association of 1584 private citizens were entitled 'to take the uttermost revenge' on anyone involved in a plot against the queen.[12] James must have known that, in the event of a failed coup that involved him however indirectly, he would be a legal target for avengers. At any rate, he dropped his military plans, and in February 1601 Essex mounted his own coup. Had the rebellion succeeded, and had Essex's Machiavellian vision of a military aristocracy become a reality, England's relations with Europe would have been very different. The country would indeed have become a 'warlike state'. The image of James presented on the Elizabethan stage had not been an entirely positive one.[13] With Essex's failed coup fresh in the public mind, it must have been a potentially unsettling experience for him to watch a play that not only contained disturbing echoes of his own violent childhood, but also dealt with a succession crisis ending with an unscrupulous military adventurist being welcomed into the kingdom. Many years ago Lilian Winstanley suggested that Hamlet was intended as a portrait of James.[14] With the theme of military intervention in a neighbouring state given such prominence, James must have been relieved to find that Hamlet's actions and his political intuitions were in certain crucial respects so different from his own. In particular it is Hamlet's fascination with heroic masculinity that was remote from his own ideals.

WELCOMING THE IRREDENTIST

Hamlet has the reputation of being Shakespeare's most enigmatic play.[15] Even Hamlet himself provocatively challenges Rosencrantz and Guildenstern to pluck the heart out of his mystery (III.ii.353–4). While post-Romantic criticism focused on Hamlet's character and the psychological reasons for his delaying vengeance on Claudius, modern historical scholarship has considered the ethics of revenge and the related problem of tyrannicide. The latter was a problematic and widely debated political issue in Elizabethan England that I will

---

[12] J.E. Neale, *Elizabeth I and her Parliaments 1584–1601* (London: Jonathan Cape, 1957), p. 17.
[13] James Shapiro points out that 'King James VI and the Scots had [in 1598] been the subject of ridicule on the London stage, leading to quiet diplomatic protests' ('*The Scot's Tragedy* and the Politics of Popular Drama', *ELR*, 23 (1992), 430).
[14] Kurland, '*Hamlet* and the Scottish Succession?', pp. 72–101.
[15] The best discussion of the theme of indeterminate meaning in *Hamlet* is still T. McAlindon, *Shakespeare and Decorum* (London and Basingstoke: Macmillan, 1973), pp. 44–79.

return to shortly. But the play's most difficult interpretative problem – Hamlet's dying endorsement of Fortinbras – is one that is seldom discussed.[16] Having himself written on the subject of succession, emphasizing the importance of the legal transfer of power, 'no[t] by conquest, but by right and due discent',[17] King James would have recognized the inherently problematic nature of Hamlet's proposal.

As Hamlet is dying he asks Horatio to report his cause and tell the world of all the things that still stand unknown. Before Horatio can reply they are interrupted by the sound of gunshots. Hamlet asks the meaning of this 'warlike noise' (v.ii.301), and Osric tells him that it is Fortinbras returning from Poland. Hamlet then speaks his last words:

> O, I die, Horatio!
> The potent poison quite o'ercrows my spirit.
> I cannot live to hear the news from England,
> But I do prophesy th' election lights
> On Fortinbras. He has my dying voice.
> So tell him, with th' occurrents, more and less,
> Which have solicited. The rest is silence. (304–10)

Fortinbras enters with his military retinue and, after a formal exchange of words with Horatio, announces his intentions. He has come, he says, to embrace his fortune: 'I have some rights of memory in this kingdom, / Which now to claim my vantage doth invite me' (342–3). Shakespeare's Denmark is an elective monarchy,[18] though there is a traditional preference for hereditary succession (1.ii.109). As the play twice reminds us (IV.v.100–6; v.ii.66), under normal circumstances any new contender for the throne would need the support of the people. In this situation Hamlet's voice would be a valuable asset. But Fortinbras was too late to hear Hamlet's endorsement of his political ambitions, and there has been no time for Horatio to report them. So we must suppose that, having achieved his military objectives in Poland, Fortinbras now intends to

---

[16] The best recent discussion of Fortinbras and the constitutional problems he raises is Kurland, 'Hamlet and the Scottish Succession?' For a survey of critical discussion of Fortinbras to 1986 see Rudiger Imhof, 'Fortinbras Ante Portas: The Role and Significance of Fortinbras in *Hamlet*', HS, 8 (1986), 8–23. See also Neil Graves, ' "Even for an eggshell": Hamlet and the Problem of Fortinbras', UCROW, 2 (1979), 51–63.

[17] *Basilicon Doron, Political Writings*, ed. Sommerville.

[18] For discussion of the constitutional world of the play see E.A.J. Honigmann, 'The Politics of *Hamlet* and the "World of the Play" ', *Hamlet*, ed. John Russell Brown and Bernard Harris, Stratford-upon-Avon Studies 5 (London: Edward Arnold, 1963), pp. 129–47.

take advantage of the present confusion in Denmark to assert his 'rights of memory' whether or not he has popular support. (Fortinbras' 'rights of memory' are not actually rights at all, his father having lost his lands in 'sealed compact / Well ratified by law and heraldry' – 1.i.85–6.)[19] The fact that Hamlet's approval coincides so neatly with his own plans confirms Fortinbras as a man of destiny who happens, providentially, to be in the right place at the right time. Or so a number of critics would have us believe.

Many modern critics from Bradley onwards, including Harold Jenkins in his revised Arden edition of 1982 and Philip Edwards in the New Cambridge edition of 1985, have simply ignored the puzzle of Hamlet's endorsement of Fortinbras. Modern productions of *Hamlet* often cut Fortinbras altogether.[20] Those critics who do address the problem sometimes go to some length to justify Hamlet's choice. On the face of it this is not an easy thing to do: the terrifyingly aggressive irredentist with his ability to instil fear in the hearts of professional soldiers, who has been waiting for an opportunity to seize Danish lands by 'strong hand / And terms compulsative' (1.i.101–2), is now welcomed as the new king. One of the few modern critics who does acknowledge that Hamlet's choice may not be in Denmark's national interest is Eleanor Prosser. Prosser sees little hope for Denmark in the fact that Fortinbras will now be in charge: 'His past actions give little assurance that he will be a temperate and judicious ruler who seeks only peace and stability... Order has been restored, but not by a figure representing the rule of reason and integrity. A strong man has taken over'.[21] Terence Hawkes has similar misgivings about Hamlet's choice of Fortinbras: 'Military rule, by a foreigner, is what lies in store for the Danish state. The war promised at the beginning has not taken place, but at the end the results are just the same as if it had'.[22] But these sceptical readings of the play's ending have not met with general approval.

---

[19] For a helpful discussion of this point see Martin Coyle, 'Shakespeare's Hamlet', *Exp*, 43 (1984), 12–13.

[20] Nancy M. Lee-Riffe, 'What Fortinbras and Laertes tell us about Hamlet', *HS*, 3 (1981), 103–9; Daniel Gerould, 'Enter Fortinbras: Shakespeare's Strongman in Modern Eastern European Theatre', *AST*, 1 (1984), 5–27; Robert F. Willson Jr., 'Fortinbras: The Unkindest Cut', *UCROW*, 6 (1986), 105–10; Gregg Dion, 'Fortinbras our Contemporary', *TS*, 38 (1993), 17–27.

[21] Eleanor Prosser, *'Hamlet' and Revenge*, 2nd edn. (Stanford: Stanford University Press, 1971), pp. 239–40.

[22] Terence Hawkes, *That Shakespeherian Rag: Essays on a Critical Process* (London and New York: Methuen, 1986), p. 93.

Martin Dodsworth feels that Prosser's interpretation is 'too depressed'. Surely the fact that Hamlet himself gives Fortinbras his dying voice means that we need not question his rights too closely, says Dodsworth: 'what matters is that Fortinbras enters as it were with Hamlet's blessing'. And though we may not exactly feel that all's well that ends well, nevertheless, by and large the situation in Denmark now seems 'perfectly satisfactory'.[23] Dodsworth's sense of reassurance in the events of the play's finale is shared by Roland Frye. It is true, says Frye, that Fortinbras would seem to be a less than ideal choice, 'but Shakespeare is holding a mirror up to nature, and human societies usually find themselves forced to make less than ideal choices'. Quoting du Plessis-Mornay – 'we should not look for perfect princes, but consider ourselves fortunate if we have men of middling virtue as our rulers' – Frye concludes that, of the various choices open to him, Hamlet takes the only one creditable to his judgment. Thus, 'all things considered, Shakespeare has done everything necessary to satisfy his own contemporaries, who constituted the audience which concerned him. Elizabethans would have accepted the end of the play as insuring the restoration of order'.[24] In a rare discussion of Fortinbras' claim in the context of contemporary concern with the succession problem Leonard Tennenhouse reminds us that *Hamlet* is, in part at least, about a power struggle between a member of the ruling dynasty and a successful usurper: 'if Hamlet cannot translate the claims of blood into the exercise of force, it is also true that Claudius cannot command the symbolic elements of his culture which testify to the magic of blood'. This political stalemate is resolved by Fortinbras. Appearing in the final scene as 'the product of human history and providence as well', Fortinbras 'acquires authority not only through material conflicts which display the effective use of force, but also through the

---

[23] Martin Dodsworth, *'Hamlet' Closely Observed* (London: Athlone Press, 1985), p. 295. Norman Kelvin also believes that Hamlet's blessing must indicate that Fortinbras is the right man for the job, arguing that 'when Hamlet recognizes that Fortinbras is warring against Poland over a principle of honor, we eliminate suspicion that he may be hot-headed, and we acquire instead an impression of a level-headed, firm-willed prince . . . [who is] fit to rule Denmark' ('Fortinbras' Links with Hamlet', *BNYPL*, 66 (1962), 660). In a more sophisticated attempt to justify Hamlet's endorsement of Fortinbras, Harold Jenkins argues that during the course of the play Fortinbras changes from reckless adventurer to calm, efficient commander. In his latter role he is clearly 'a ruler to whom Denmark may safely be left' ('Fortinbras and Laertes and the Composition of *Hamlet*', *RUS*, 60 (1974), 106).
[24] Frye, *The Renaissance 'Hamlet'*, pp. 267–8.

metaphysics of blood which he embodies'.[25] I assume Tennenhouse means that Fortinbras' takeover is likely to be successful partly because he is strong and people are afraid of him, and partly because he is a member of the Norwegian royal family, though what this explains is not clear. It certainly does not tell us why a Danish prince should apparently want to encourage the very man who was the cause of so much anxiety at the beginning of the play.

That criticism should have largely overlooked this problem is in one sense understandable: after all, throughout the play Hamlet has seemed oddly unaware of the political consequences of his actions. Horatio's first thought on meeting the ghost is of Denmark's security. 'If thou art privy to thy country's fate', he says to the ghost, 'Which happily foreknowing may avoid, / O, speak!' (I.i.114–16). But Hamlet never confronts the question of national security. He considers, in an oblique way, the ethics of revenge; he philosophizes about the nature of wise action; he considers the morality of suicide; and he regrets the fact that the time is out of joint. But never does he address the question of 'the country's fate'. His one overtly political decision is the most surprising thing he does in the whole play. His endorsement of Fortinbras' claim to the Danish throne is the more baffling since he gives no reason for his choice. However, the fact that Hamlet seems generally to be unaware of the political consequences of his actions does not mean that the play itself is indifferent to them. Indeed, it insists on them. As Laertes leaves for France he reminds Ophelia that even if Hamlet is genuinely in love with her, he cannot act as if he were a private citizen:

> He may not, as unvalued persons do,
> Carve for himself, for on his choice depends
> The sanity and health of the whole state;
> And therefore must his choice be circumscribed
> Unto the voice and yielding of that body
> Whereof he is the head.   (I.iii.19–24)

Though Laertes is talking about the choice of a wife, his words have an unintended bearing on the question that is uppermost in Hamlet's mind – what to do about the man who killed his father; whatever Hamlet decides to do will affect the whole country. Rosencrantz also spells out, again with unconscious irony, the far-

---

[25] *Power on Display: The Politics of Shakespeare's Genres* (New York and London: Methuen, 1986), pp. 86; 93.

reaching political consequences of killing a king: 'The cease of majesty / Dies not alone, but like a gulf doth draw / What's near it with it' (III.iii.15–17). Hamlet may be strangely unaware of the political consequences of a prince's actions, but the play reminds us that this is essentially a tragedy of state.

CONSTITUTIONAL CRISIS

The period in which *Hamlet* is set is indeterminate. Like many of the histories (Roman and British) and tragedies, the play portrays a state at or near a time of transition between two political systems. Under Claudius' Machiavellian rule Denmark has all the protocol of a Renaissance state, while her southern neighbour enjoys an early-modern university system. But under Hamlet's father the Danish court was a very different place. Compressing several centuries into one generation – Alfred liberated London from the Danes in 886; Wittenberg University was founded in 1502 – Shakespeare takes us back to the time of the Viking invasions of Britain. In fact, as Claudius reminds us, English cicatrices are still raw and red from Danish swords (IV.iii.62) and Danegeld is still being demanded (III.i.173). This imaginative compression of history serves primarily as a way of contrasting two antithetical cultures: where only a generation ago disputes between neighbouring warlords full of 'emulate pride' were being settled by personal duels that involved the wagering of lands in accordance with heraldic law, Claudius' world is one of diplomatic negotiation. His Denmark may be a 'warlike state', but when the stakes are high, national interest can be protected by skilful diplomacy. And for Denmark the stakes are high.

In the Middle Ages Elsinore occupied a strategic position of major international significance. Its location on the narrowest part of the strait that separates Denmark from what is now Sweden (but in the Middle Ages was part of Denmark) gave its rulers enviable power; for whoever controlled the Sound of Denmark controlled the Baltic and the north-eastern Atlantic trade routes.[26] Little wonder that the guards on the battlements of Elsinore's heavily fortified castle are anxious: an ominous supernatural being has appeared just at the time when the country is defending, not simply a parcel of land won from Norway in an earlier skirmish, but its supremacy in the whole

[26] Keith Brown, 'Hamlet's Place on the Map', *SStud*, 4 (1968), 160.

region, a point that would not have been lost on an audience whose own national sovereignty had recently survived a potentially devastating threat from a foreign invader. The far-reaching political implications of the Norwegian threat to Denmark are intimated by Horatio in his allusion to the unnatural portents that prefigured the collapse of civil order in ancient Rome following Caesar's murder. Sensing that the ghost 'bodes some strange eruption to our state' (1.i.68), Horatio fears it may be a harbinger of doom 'preceding still the fates / And prologue to the omen coming on' (122–3). So if the guards on Elsinore's battlements are edgy, they have good reason: Denmark is facing a challenge to both sovereignty and regional supremacy. That is why the country is urgently reinforcing its navy and re-equipping its army with the aid of foreign arms traders (1.i.71ff).

To complicate matters, Denmark has its own internal difficulties. It is these problems that have led the opportunistic Fortinbras to press his advantage while the state is 'disjoint and out of frame' (1.ii.20) as the result of the apparently natural death of the old king. In reality, a silent coup has taken place: as in Saxo Grammaticus' chronicle, the king has been murdered by his brother and a usurper now occupies the throne,[27] though only Hamlet knows this, and even he is uncertain about the reliability of his evidence. Hamlet's response to this situation is to plan the murder of Claudius.

It used to be thought that Elizabethans regarded resistance against an anointed ruler as unthinkable even when the ruler was a tyrant. For, as the 1570 *Homilie Agaynst Disobedience and Wylful Rebellion* put it, 'what a perilous thing were it to commit unto the subjectes the judgement whiche prince is wyse and godly, and his government good, and whiche is otherwyse?'.[28] According to E.M.W. Tillyard this essentially 'simple' doctrine was universally accepted by the Elizabethans.[29] Two decades later Eleanor Prosser considered the related question of private vengeance. That too was utterly proscribed by the church and condemned by all right thinking people.[30]

---

[27] The story of Amleth is told in Books III and IV of Saxo's chronicle (Saxo Grammaticus, *The History of the Danes*, ed. H.E. Davidson, trans. P. Fisher, 2 vols. (Cambridge: D.S. Brewer, 1979), vol. I, pp. 82–101).
[28] *An Homilie Agaynst Disobedience and Wylful Rebellion* (London, 1570), Sig. Bi. James VI echoes this principle in *The Trew Law of Free Monarchies* (1598), *Political Writings*, ed. Sommerville, p. 79.
[29] *Shakespeare's History Plays* (London: Chatto & Windus, 1944), p. 66.
[30] *'Hamlet' and Revenge*, pp. 3–35.

Neither of these claims is true. The later sixteenth century was a period of vigorous intellectual and political debate in England.[31] 'In learned treatises and popular pamphlets alike', wrote James Phillips in *The State in Shakespeare's Greek and Roman Plays* (1940), 'a variety of theories and attitudes were developed concerning such individual political problems as the authority of the king, the function of the law, the duties of subjects and the right of rebellion.'[32] Not only was there a long tradition going back to the Middle Ages of defending the principle of responsible tyrannicide,[33] but the Bond of Association drawn up by Elizabeth's own councillors flatly contradicted the Christian principle of passive acceptance of divine prerogative in matters of vengeance. In 1570 the pope had absolved Elizabeth's Catholic subjects of any obligation of obedience, thus effectively inciting them to rebellion. Appealing to the same retributive principle, the Bond of Association gave private individuals the right under law to avenge any attempt to harm the queen. Far from being quite clear in their minds on the question of tyrannicide and vengeance, Elizabethans seem to have been exceptionally ambivalent. Some measure of that confusion can be seen in a book called *A Short Treatise of Politic Power* (1556) by the Marian exile John Ponet. In his tortuous discussion of tyrannicide Ponet explains that, although Christians and pagans take different views of revenge, some Christian countries do allow private acts of retaliation. For his own part

---

[31] J.W. Allen, *A History of Political Thought in the Sixteenth Century* (London: Methuen, 1928); George H. Sabine, *A History of Political Theory* (New York: Holt, 1937); Franklin le van Baumer, *The Early Tudor Theory of Kingship* (New Haven and London: Yale University Press, 1940).

[32] *The State in Shakespeare's Greek and Roman Plays* (1940; repr. New York: Octagon Books, 1972), p. 20.

[33] Writing shortly after the deposition of Richard II, Henry Knighton argued that

> From ancient statute and a precedent of times not long past which might be invoked again, though it was a painful thing, the people have an established principle that if, because of evil counsel of any kind, or silly obstinacy, or contempt, or singular impudent willfulness or irregular behavior, the king should alienate himself from his people and refuse, despite the sane advice of the lords and most celebrated men of the realm, to be governed and regulated by the laws, statutes, and praiseworthy ordinances of the realm, but would impudently exercise in his insane counsels his own singular willfulness, then it is allowable for them, with common assent and with the consensus of the people of the realm, to depose the king himself from the royal throne and to raise to that throne in his place someone near at hand from the royal stock.

(*Chronicon Henrici Knighton*, ed. Joseph Rawson Lumby (London, 1895), vol. II, p. 219, quoted and trans. Russell A. Peck, *Kingship and Common Profit in Gower's 'Confessio Amantis'* (London: Feffer and Simons, 1978), p. 9.)

Ponet says he would find it difficult to endorse acts of private vengeance except in certain very particular circumstances:

Forasmuche as all thinges in every christen common wealthe ought to be done decently and according to ordre and charitie: I thinke it can not be maintained by Goddes worde, that any private man maie kill, except (wher execucion of iuste punishment upon tirannes, idolaters, and traiterous gouvernours is either by the hole state utterly neglected, or the prince with the nobilitie and counsail conspire the subversion or alteracion of their contrey and people) any private man have som special inwarde commaundement or surely proved mocion of God . . . or be otherwise commaunded or permitted by common autoritie upon iuste occasion and common necessitie to kill.[34]

It is all very well to talk of a 'special inward commandment' to take action against a tyrant. But as Hamlet discovers, guaranteeing that one's commandment is a 'surely proved motion of God' is no simple matter. Indeed it is even less simple than he seems to imagine. Though Hamlet recognizes that the ghost may be a devil, he believes that if he can prove that it is telling the truth he will be able to act with a clear conscience. But truth-telling is no guarantee of integrity. As Banquo says, 'The instruments of darkness tell us truths, / Win us with honest trifles to betray 's / In deepest consequence' (*Mac.*, I.iii.122–4). Even assuming that it were possible to prove that an inward command is a motion of God, what would the national consequences be of acting on such a command at a time when the country is facing the threat of invasion by a hostile power? In *The Trew Law of Free Monarchies* James had warned of the risks involved in removing tyrants, arguing that 'a king cannot be imagined to be so unruly and tyrannous, but the common-wealth will be kept in better order, notwithstanding thereof, by him, then it can be by his way-taking'.[35] But Hamlet does not address this question. Nor is Ponet much help. Indeed on every aspect of vengeance his advice is so hedged about with qualifications that the only thing we can say with certainty is that he thinks tyrannicide is a risky business. While that may not be a satisfying answer for someone looking for evidence of orthodox Elizabethan doctrine or a dominant state ideology, such ambivalence is the very stuff of drama. Hamlet's own feelings about

---

[34] John Ponet, *A Short Treatise of Politic Power*, facsimile edn. (Menston: Scolar Press, 1970), Sigs. Gviii–Gviii^v.
[35] James VI and I, *Political Writings*, ed. Sommerville, p. 79.

revenge seem to be as mixed as Ponet's and are closely bound up with his attitude towards heroic values.

VIKING HONOUR

Paul Cantor has argued that Hamlet's ethical dilemma is expressed in the form of a conflict between two incompatible cultures: the heroic world of classical epic and Norse saga, and the modern world of Christian-humanist values.[36] It is the latter to which Hamlet appeals when he declares his admiration for Horatio's Stoical resignation:

> blest are those
> Whose blood and judgement are so well commingled
> That they are not a pipe for Fortune's finger
> To sound what stop she please. Give me that man
> That is not passion's slave, and I will wear him
> In my heart's core, ay, in my heart of heart,
> As I do thee. (III.ii.66–72)

Horatio's Christian Stoicism may have a privileged place in Hamlet's heart, but it is an entirely different set of values that his father's ghost impresses on him.

In his *Apologie* of 1598 Essex had recalled 'those former gallant ages' when England had 'atchieve[d] great conquests in Fraunce', complaining that the English were now 'in love with the name, and bewitched with the delight of peace' (see Introduction, pp. 11, 15). The following year, in a new edition of the *Civile Wars*, Samuel Daniel took up the same theme. He imagined the ghost of Henry V returning to reprove an unheroic age for its indolence:

> Out of the clowdy darkenes of the night
> I do behold approache with Martiall cheere,
> And with a dreadful (and yet lovely) sight:
> Whose eye gives courage, and whose brow hath feare;
> Both representing terror, and delight.

The ghost of Henry then 'fiercely speakes':

> 'Ungrateful times, that impiously neglect
> That worth, that never times againe shall shew;

---

[36] *Hamlet* (Cambridge: Cambridge University Press, 1989), pp. 32–53. See also Reuben A. Brower, *Hero and Saint: Shakespeare and the Graeco-Roman Heroic Tradition* (Oxford: Clarendon Press, 1971), pp. 277–316; William F. Hansen, *Saxo Grammaticus and the Life of Hamlet* (Lincoln, Nebr. and London: University of Nebraska Press, 1983), pp. 81–2.

> What? Merits all our toyle no more respect?
> Or else standes Idlenesse asham'd to knowe
> Those wondrous Actions, that do so object
> Blame to the wanton, sinne unto the slowe?'[37]

Like Daniel's spirit returning from the heroic past, the ghost of Hamlet's father appears in 'fair and warlike form' inspiring 'fear and wonder' to goad the prince into action (I.i.45, 42). When it first reveals itself to Hamlet its tactics are similar to those of Claudius when he urges Laertes to avenge the deaths of his father and sister (IV.vii). Appealing, neither to his reason, nor to his sense of political responsibility, the ghost works cunningly on Hamlet's susceptibilities. It hints at the horrors of purgatory; it asks him rhetorically if he truly loved his father; it describes in horrific detail the action of the poison on Old Hamlet's body; it appeals to Hamlet's sense of family honour; and it urges vengeance. All of which is necessary to fire the emotions, for only a psychopath can murder in cold blood. It is when he is able to relish the thought of drinking 'hot blood' that Hamlet feels ready for murder (III.ii.377–81). His response to the ghost's appeal is to erase from his memory everything that 'youth and observation has copied there' and take on the role of avenger (I.v.92–103).

Shakespeare took the outlines of the Hamlet story from Saxo Grammaticus' *History of the Danes*. The world described by Saxo is the heroic world of Norse saga filtered through the mind of a medieval Latinist.[38] The values celebrated in Viking myth and legend are those of a warrior society: courage, physical endurance, daring, and above all a quasi-religious belief in the obligation to uphold family and national honour. The duty to avenge a slight to the honour of one's family or one's king was inflexible; failure to do so would infallibly incur the wrath of the gods. In Book III Saxo tells the story of a deceitful Swedish plot to murder the wise and magnanimous King Rolf in his sleep. In urging the Danish princes to avenge this insult to their king, the warrior-hero Hialti appeals to their manly desire for honour and glory. 'This moment calls us to conflict,' he cries,

---

[37] *The Civile Wars*, v, stanzas 2–3, *The Complete Works in Verse and Prose of Samuel Daniel*, 5 vols., ed. Alexander B. Grosart (London, 1885–96), vol. II (1885), pp. 178–9.

[38] In 'Wit and Eloquence in the Courts of Saxo's Early Kings', *Saxo Grammaticus: A Medieval Author Between Norse and Latin Culture*, ed. Karsten Friis-Jensen (Copenhagen: Museum Tusculanum Press, 1981) Hilda R. Davidson argues that Saxo consciously stressed the parallels between Norse heroic tales and Virgil's *Aeneid* (pp. 39–52).

> Seize arms every man who claims to love his king,
> for the scales of battle are ready to weigh our souls.
> So, let the brave cast out their tremors or mildness;
> pleasure must forsake our minds and yield to weapons.
> Our wages are glory. Each of you controls
> his own reputation, illustrious by his right hand.
> No room here for sensual promptings, all
> must learn sternly to undo the present mischief.
> A man who covets the title of fame or the prizes
> cannot grow faint with lethargic fear, but must tackle
> bold men, nor now pale at the icy steel.[39]

In her recent *Shakespeare and the Loss of Eden* Catherine Belsey says that 'The Ghost appeals to Hamlet in the name of family values'.[40] One can see what she means. But the play makes it clear that it is a very particular and dated kind of 'family values' that the ghost appeals to. Hamlet's father typifies the exaggeratedly masculine world of heroic values that Saxo described in his chronicle; he was, says Hamlet with eloquent simplicity, 'a man' (1.ii.186). As Daniel had pictured the ghost of Henry V returning to remind the present unheroic age of the 'wondrous Actions' of England's warlike past, so the martial figure of Old Hamlet's ghost embodies 'the majesty of buried Denmark' (1.i.46). Though Hamlet recognizes that he is no Hercules himself (1.ii.153), he is strongly drawn to that heroic ideal.[41]

Many generations of Romantic and post-Romantic critics have encouraged us to think of Hamlet as a philosopher–prince trapped in a violent world that is alien to his true nature. But the truth is that, despite his declared admiration for Horatio's Stoic wisdom, Hamlet is irresistibly drawn to the successful avenger. His fascination with heroic violence reveals itself most starkly in the speech he has memorized from a play based on the *Aeneid* about another son avenging the death of his father. Welcoming the travelling players to Elsinore, Hamlet asks for a sample of their wares. He requests a favourite speech of his about a killer of legendary ferocity. To prompt the players Hamlet begins with a passage describing Pyrrhus inside the Trojan horse. 'Roasted in wrath and fire', and covered from head to foot in the 'coagulate gore' of fathers, mothers,

---

[39] *The History of the Danes*, trans. Fisher, vol. 1, p. 57.
[40] *Shakespeare and the Loss of Eden* (Basingstoke and London: Macmillan, 1999), p. 24.
[41] For discussion of the use Shakespeare makes of Seneca's *Hercules furens* in *Hamlet* see Robert S. Miola, *Shakespeare and Classical Tragedy: The Influence of Seneca* (Oxford: Clarendon Press, 1992), pp. 43–4.

daughters, and sons, the 'hellish' Pyrrhus is the very personification of heroic violence (II.ii.454–66). After some dozen lines Hamlet invites one of the players to take over. There follows an account of how, enraged by an incompetent blow from Priam's sword, Pyrrhus kills the old man:

> But as we often see against some storm
> A silence in the heavens, the rack stand still,
> The bold winds speechless, and the orb below
> As hush as death, anon the dreadful thunder
> Doth rend the region: so, after Pyrrhus' pause,
> A rousèd vengeance sets him new a-work;
> And never did the Cyclops' hammers fall
> On Mars his armour, forged for proof eterne,
> With less remorse than Pyrrhus' bleeding sword
> Now falls on Priam.   (II.ii.485–94)

This is heroic violence in its most savage and stylized form. In Marlowe's version of the story, which Shakespeare probably drew on for the player's speech, even Jove's statue frowns in loathing at Pyrrhus' 'wicked act' in killing an old man.[42] It is a speech that Hamlet says he 'chiefly loved' (448–9).

Given Hamlet's fascination with heroic masculinity both in life and in poetry, it is not surprising that he should be drawn to Fortinbras. At his court conference in Act I Scene ii Claudius announces that he intends to put diplomatic pressure on Norway to deflect Fortinbras' ambitions. By Act II Scene ii we learn that his diplomatic efforts have been successful and that Old Fortinbras has bribed his nephew to keep his mercenaries out of Denmark and busy his mind instead with other foreign quarrels. We discover what these are when Hamlet meets the Norwegian captain in Act IV Scene iv and hears about the new Norwegian military objective. When the captain tells him that they are marching on Poland, Hamlet assumes that the Norwegians must be planning a full-scale attack on the country, or at the least on one of her frontiers. But the captain tells him that it is a valueless piece of land that they plan to seize, one that is scarcely worth the taking:

> Truly to speak, and with no addition,
> We go to gain a little patch of ground
> That hath in it no profit but the name.

---

[42] *Dido, Queen of Carthage*, II.i.258, *The Complete Works of Christopher Marlowe*, 2 vols., ed. Fredson Bowers (Cambridge: Cambridge University Press, 1981), vol. I, p. 23.

> To pay five ducats, five, I would not farm it,
> Nor will it yield to Norway or the Pole
> A ranker rate, should it be sold in fee.   (IV.iv.24–9)

In that case, replies Hamlet, surely the Poles won't bother to defend it. On the contrary, the captain tells him, it is already garrisoned.

Fortinbras and his troops are engaged on a major military campaign to destroy an armed garrison and seize a piece of land that is of little good to anyone but the people who happen to scratch a living from it. It is a symbolic image expressive of barbaric futility, rather like the pointless shelling of a nameless stretch of jungle in Conrad's *Heart of Darkness*. The sole purpose of the enterprise is apparently to satisfy Fortinbras' 'divine ambition'. Yet Hamlet's response is ambivalent. He appears to recognize that there is something absurd in the spectacle of two armies fighting over a straw, but attributes the folly, in a familiar militarist argument, to 'th' impostume of much wealth and peace' (28). Faced with the example of a brutal militarist sacrificing thousands of lives for a mere 'fantasy and trick of fame' (61), he persuades himself that true greatness lies, not in an overscrupulous picking over of moral issues, but in the willingness to 'find quarrel in a straw / When honour's at the stake' (55–6).

Fascinated, as he is, with heroic violence, it is perhaps understandable that Hamlet should be drawn to the hot-blooded, and appropriately named,[43] young neo-Viking warrior who has 'Sharked up a list of landless resolutes' (I.i.97) to redeem *his* father's honour and seize by force what he regards as his rightful inheritance. Hamlet does not say what he expects the outcome will be for Denmark of a military takeover by Fortinbras. Nor does the play tell us, at least not directly. But it does give two possible hints as to the consequences of welcoming in the invader.

One of these is the tale of Pyrrhus' vengeance on Priam. On one level Hamlet's meeting with the players serves simply to illustrate his interest in the art of theatre. But this does not explain the length of the episode. Even the garrulous Polonius complains that the player's speech is 'too long' (II.ii.500). The answer may lie in its subject

---

[43] Cherrell Guilfoyle suggests that Fortinbras' name might have recalled Fierebras, the steward of Antichrist in the twelfth-century *Le Tourneiment Antichrist* ('King Hamlet's Two Successors', *CD*, 15 (1981), 126). She also suggests parallels with the figure of Gog in Ezek. 38:15, 12: 'Gog, like Fortinbras, comes from a "place out of the North partes", "Thinking to spoile the pray and take the bootie"' (p. 127).

matter. Generally regarded in the Middle Ages and the Renaissance as the greatest civic and military catastrophe of the ancient world, the Trojan war is commonly alluded to by both poets and politicians wanting to point up a moral about the dangers of seductive women or the cunning of a deceitful enemy.[44] In his *Apologie* the Earl of Essex had compared England's war with Spain to the Trojan war, warning that the Treaty of Vervins was nothing more than a Trojan Horse: 'Their first maine attempt against England was in 88; from that time to this present is full tenne yeares, the just time of the siege of Troy. And now they see open force cannot prevaile, they in shewe retire and give over armes, but they have prepared a Sinons horse, which cannot enter if we cast not downe our walles'.[45] In a play about treachery and murder in a city besieged by an avenging army one might almost assume that there would be some allusion to Troy. Traditionally the blame for the city's fall was pinned on two men: 'Some say *Antenor* did betray the towne,' wrote Marlowe in *Dido, Queen of Carthage*, 'Others report 'twas *Sinons* perjurie'.[46] The better known of these two is the man Essex referred to in his *Apologie*. It was Sinon who allowed himself to be captured by the Trojans, assuring them that if they took the Wooden Horse into the city, Troy would be invulnerable. In the Middle Ages his name was synonymous with treachery. But Sinon can hardly be blamed for his act of deception. He was, after all, only supporting his country's interests. The real traitor was a man who betrayed his own people. According to some versions of the story, it was Antenor who sealed Troy's fate by secretly advising the Greeks to steal the city's guardian statue of Pallas Athene and to build the Wooden Horse. How ironic, says Chaucer, that the Trojans should be so eager to exchange Criseyde for Antenor, the very man who 'was after traitor to the town / Of Troye'.[47] There is no mention of either Sinon or Antenor in *Hamlet*. But with Essex's attempted negotiations with James now public knowledge, explicit allusion to Troy would probably have had a resonance for contemporary audiences that it lacks for the modern

[44] Noting the allusion to Troy, Richard A. Levin writes: 'Elizabethans had long lived in fear of invasion, and they understood that a nation became vulnerable to attack as a consequence of such internal division as *Hamlet* depicts ('Fortinbras and the "Conveyance of a Promised March"', *CEAC*, 58 (1996), 10).
[45] Robert Devereux, *An Apologie of the Earl of Essex* (London, 1603), Sig. B4.
[46] *Dido*, II.i.110–11, ed. Bowers, vol. I, p. 19.
[47] 'Troilus and Criseyde', IV.204–5, *The Works of Geoffrey Chaucer*, 2nd edn., ed. F.N. Robinson (London: Oxford University Press, 1957), p. 443.

playgoer. Troy is the archetypal example of a city that fell as a consequence of help from within.

But perhaps by imposing order, albeit a military order, Fortinbras would bring stability to a country that has had a surfeit of 'carnal, bloody and unnatural acts'?[48] Modern Viking scholars emphasize the artistic achievements of Norse culture. However, Elizabethans were interested less in Viking art than in the legendary brutality of the invader. Omitting any mention of Viking artistic culture, Elizabethan history books told how, for the best part of a century, barbarian hordes ransacked towns and villages, pillaged monasteries, and devasted the English countryside, killing and raping as they went, so that, in Richard Grafton's words (1569), 'all of the Countrye, along the coast, from the North part of England, unto the Isle of wight, was by them eyther utterly destroyed, or greatly empayred'.[49] Just as Fortinbras' threatened attack reminds Horatio of the portents that foreshadowed the collapse of civil order in Rome, so Grafton rehearses the well-known story of the omens that preceded the first Viking invasion of Britain: 'Sodeynly as men walked in the streete, Crosses lyke unto blood fell upon their clothes, and blood fell from heaven lyke droppes of raine. This after some expositors, betokened the comming of the Danes into this lande, the which entered shortly after'.[50] The barbarian invader from across the North Sea with his band of landless resolutes was a potent figure in English national mythology. Indeed when Shakespeare wrote his play it was still vividly present in the national consciousness: in the annual festival of Hocktide Elizabethans still celebrated 'the deliverance of the English from the tyranny of the Danes'.[51] Elizabethan theatre audiences were sufficiently familiar with this episode in their own history for dramatists to be able to make it the subject of jest. John Lyly began one of his court comedies with a mock-serious allusion to the curse of plundering Danish armies (*Gallathea*, 1.i.21ff). To start with a night-watch nervously anticipating a Viking raid was a sure way of gripping an English audience's imagination. Whether Shakespeare took his narrative material directly from Saxo, from Kranz's

---

[48] Robert F. Willson believes that 'Fortinbras restores a chivalric world that was poisoned by Claudius' cowardly, politic deed' ('Fortinbras: The Unkindest Cut', p. 107).
[49] *Grafton's Chronicle*, 2 vols. (London, 1809), vol. I, p. 136.
[50] Ibid., vol. I, p. 103.
[51] John Nichols, ed., *The Progresses and Public Processions of Queen Elizabeth*, 3 vols. (London: Society of Antiquaries, 1823), vol. I, p. 446 n3.

sixteenth-century version of the *History of the Danes*, from an early draft of Belleforest's *Histoires*, or simply from the hypothetical *Ur-Hamlet* is immaterial: Fortinbras is the typical Viking marauder of popular legend. Yet this is the man to whom Hamlet gives his dying voice. If his prophecy is right, it will mean that Denmark will now in effect be under Norwegian rule and Norway will control the Sound of Denmark. What will that loss of national sovereignty mean for Danish citizens? What political rights will they have under the new dispensation? Will they have to pay tributary taxes to Norway as Britons did to Denmark in the ninth century (as the play reminds us with its allusion to Danegeld in Act III Scene i)? Will their wives and daughters be any safer from the attentions of the occupying soldiers than those of the English were under Viking rule? The play gives us no answers to these questions; the rest is silence.

'THE TEFLON FACTOR'

Hamlet is a man of many parts: courtier, soldier, scholar, glass of fashion, mould of form. Of all his remarkable talents, perhaps the most astonishing is what irreverent Reagan observers used to call 'the teflon factor', that is the wonderful knack of preserving an unsullied reputation no matter what acts of violence (or imbecility) one might actually have committed. Robert Ornstein, writing apparently without irony, puts it like this: 'Although [Hamlet] commits rash and bloody deeds . . . [he remains] beautiful in mind and spirit, noble in thought and feeling, alert, high-spirited, superior to the accidents and passions that corrupt lesser men'.[52] Like Conrad's Nostromo, Hamlet is seemingly incorruptible.

However, the belief that Hamlet is in a real sense essentially and truly 'a good man',[53] whose own responses offer the best guide to interpretation of the events he is caught up in, would not necessarily have been shared by contemporary playgoers. It is a view of Hamlet that has its origins in the later eighteenth century.[54] Where the seventeenth century was inclined to see him as a malcontent,

---

[52] Robert Ornstein, *The Moral Vision of Jacobean Tragedy* (Madison and Milwaukee: University of Wisconsin Press, 1965), p. 237.
[53] A.C. Bradley, *Shakespearean Tragedy*, 2nd edn (1904; repr. London: Macmillan, 1963), p. 63.
[54] For discussion of eighteenth- and nineteenth-century interpretations of Hamlet see T.J.B. Spencer, 'The Decline of Hamlet', *Hamlet*, ed. Russell Brown and Harris, pp. 185–99.

embittered and alienated by a corrupt world,⁵⁵ the age of sensibility invented a new Hamlet – sensitive, delicate, distressed. For Henry Mackenzie Hamlet was the original Man of Sensibility. His misfortune was to be 'placed in a situation in which even the amiable qualities of his mind serve but to aggravate his distress and to perplex his conduct'.⁵⁶ But it is Goethe who best describes the sentimental Hamlet. In *Wilhelm Meisters Lehrjahre* he considered the tragic irony of a sensitive nature crushed by a task for which he is by nature unfitted: 'a beautiful, pure, noble, and most moral nature, without the strength of nerve which makes the hero, sinks beneath a burden which it can neither bear nor throw off; every duty is holy to him, – this is too hard'.⁵⁷

For all his delicacy, the sentimental Hamlet has proved amazingly durable. Two centuries after Mackenzie made emotion rather than reason the defining mark of our essential humanity, and sensibility the true test and guarantor of virtue, one still finds critics characterizing *Hamlet* as a portrait of the sensitive individual crushed by the weight of responsibility. What distinguishes *Hamlet* from other revenge tragedies, said Helen Gardner, is 'the heroism and nobility of its hero . . . and his capacity to suffer the moral anguish which moral responsibility brings'.⁵⁸ So powerful, apparently, is the need to believe in Hamlet's essential virtue that it becomes a kind of *a priori* principle governing our reading of the whole play. Paul Cantor warns that we 'must be wary of critical approaches which are in effect patronizing to Hamlet, and which cut him down to manageable size'. The challenge to any interpretation, he says, 'is to find a way of explaining the delay in Hamlet's vengeance without undermining our sense of him as a heroic figure'.⁵⁹

Whatever we may think of Hamlet's heroic qualities, one thing is certain: he is not cut out for politics. In the final scene of the play Fortinbras says that, had Hamlet become king, he would 'have proved most royally' (v.ii.352). His judgment is as perverse as Hamlet's own description of Fortinbras as 'a tender and delicate

---

⁵⁵ Paul S. Conklin, *A History of 'Hamlet' Criticism 1601–1821* (New York: Humanities Press, 1968), p. 9; Philip Edwards, ed., *Hamlet* (Cambridge: Cambridge University Press, 1985), pp. 32–3.
⁵⁶ *Hamlet*, New Variorum edn., 2 vols., ed. Horace Howard Furness (London and Philadelphia: J.B. Lippincott, 1877), vol. II, p. 148.
⁵⁷ Ibid., vol. II, p. 273.
⁵⁸ Helen Gardner, *The Business of Criticism* (Oxford: Clarendon Press, 1959), p. 50.
⁵⁹ Cantor, *Hamlet*, p. 26.

prince'. Popular though Hamlet may be with the 'general gender' (IV.vii.18), he lacks both Claudius' diplomacy and his cunning. Admitting that he is 'proud, revengeful, ambitious' (III.i.126–7), he swings from a passionate desire for personal vengeance to a passive fatalism and back again, with apparently no thought of how his actions might affect his country's future. Either policy would be a disastrous one for a ruler to adopt in the new Machiavellian world of Renaissance Denmark. If *Hamlet* had a political lesson for its own time, that lesson is probably best summed up in Aquinas' words in *De Regno* concerning the dangers of unconstitutional action: 'to proceed against the cruelty of tyrants is an action to be undertaken, not through the private presumption of a few, but rather by public authority'.[60] Writing from a pagan standpoint, Machiavelli reached much the same conclusion in the *Discourses on Livy*. Discussing the impeachment of Coriolanus he considered the destabilizing consequences of acts of private vengeance:

What mischeife thereby had falne on the Commonwealth of Rome, if in a tumult he had been slaine; for thereupon had growne offences betweene particular men, offences cause feare, feare seekes defence, for defence men make partisans, and thus parties grow in cities, and from them the ruine of cities. But the matter being order'd by publique authoritie, they tooke away all those mischeifes, which might have happn'd, had it been carried by private power.[61]

Not only does heroic vengeance have no place in the modern world of Renaissance *realpolitik*; according to Machiavelli it does not even belong in the fiercely militaristic world of early republican Rome. But Hamlet has little sense of these political realities. It is his admiration for Fortinbras and 'the big wars / That makes ambition virtue' *(Oth.*, III.iii.353–4) that disqualifies him most decisively as a potential political leader in the new Denmark. In *Gorboduc* the evil Hermon urges Ferrex to have no scruples about seizing his brother's share of the kingdom:

> When kings on slender quarrels run to wars,
> And then in cruel and unkindly wise
> Command thefts, rape, murders of innocents,
> The spoil of towns, ruins of mighty realms,
> Think you such princes do suppose themselves

---

[60] Thomas Aquinas, *On Kingship: To the King of Cyprus*, trans. Gerald B. Phelan, revised by I.Th. Eschmann (Toronto: Pontifical Institute of Medieval Studies, 1949), p. 27.
[61] *Machiavels discourses upon the first Decade of T. Livius*, trans. E. Dacres (London, 1636), p. 39.

> Subject to laws of kind, and fear of Gods?
> Murders and violent thefts in private men
> Are heinous crimes and full of foul reproach,
> Yet none offence, but decked with glorious name
> Of noble conquests, in the hands of kings.[62]

It is precisely the spectacle of a prince running to wars on the slenderest of quarrels that impresses Hamlet with a sense of true greatness. In Saxo's chronicle a triumphant Amleth is hailed as a national saviour. Appealing to the people for their support, Amleth says: 'It is I who have stripped you of slavery and dressed you in freedom, set you back on the heights, repaired your renown, evicted the despot . . . Since you know my merits, I ask you . . . to bestow the reward'.[63] Hamlet also wants the world to know of his exploits (v.ii.340–1), though in welcoming in the enemy, he could hardly be said to have repaired his country's renown.

Earlier I compared Hamlet with Conrad's Nostromo. Beyond the fact that they are both 'lov'd of the distracted multitude' (iv.iii.4) the two characters have little in common; my point was that their reputation – in one case with theatre audiences and critics, in the other in the minds of fictional characters in the novel – is at odds with the way they act. Conrad's anatomy of heroism has much to tell us about Shakespeare's own. Conrad was fascinated by popular heroes and their ability to inspire devotion. And he recognized what a dangerous thing charismatic heroism could be. Nostromo, the 'incorruptible Capataz', is anything but incorruptible. By the end of the story he is the antithesis of what he seems. Superficially glamorous, romantic, and buccaneering, he is in reality a heartless sham who cares more about preserving his own reputation than he does about the feelings of a dying woman. Yet for his followers he remains *nostro uomo*; he is 'our man' in the sense that Kurtz is 'our man': he is the hero that has been created by popular acclaim. Heroes do not exist in a vacuum. They depend for their existence on an admiring public; and they tell us as much about ourselves and our own will-to-myth as they do about themselves. Conrad was writing at a time when there was a widespread revival of interest in the idea of the heroic individual who is seen as a national saviour. Excited by what they found in Nietzsche, writers like Yeats and

---

[62] Thomas Sackville and Thomas Norton, *Gorboduc, or Ferrex and Porrex*, ii.i.146–55, ed. Irby B. Cauthen, Jr. (Lincoln, Nebr.: University of Nebraska Press, 1970), pp. 31–2.
[63] *The History of the Danes*, trans. Fisher, 1.96.

Lawrence were strongly attracted by the heroic ideal. 'When the imaginary . . . hero moves us most deeply,' wrote Yeats, 'it is the moment when he awakens within us for an instant our own heroism.'[64] Lawrence too was fascinated by heroes. 'Give homage and allegiance to a hero,' he said, 'and you become yourself heroic. It is the law of men.'[65] Conrad had also read his Nietzsche. He too recognized this phenomenon and distrusted it. It is the irresistible charm of characters like Nostromo, Kurtz, and Lord Jim that makes them so dangerous.

Shakespeare also wrote at a time when there was a revival of interest in the heroic ideal. In the sixteenth century it was Robert Devereux, the flamboyant and charismatic second Earl of Essex, who embodied most vividly the popular ideal of the warrior-hero. The heroic values he espoused had wide support among militant-Protestant aristocrats. At the end of the *Arcadia*, as Sidney's two young princes review their lives in the face of what they believe is certain death, Musidorus tells Pyrocles: 'In this time, place and fortune, it is lawful for us to speak gloriously'.[66] Shakespeare too was deeply interested in the honour code, though he was more critical of its values than Sidney was. In play after play we see heroic military ideals in collision with more pragmatic values. With characters like Hotspur, or Troilus, or Fortinbras, the drastic limitations of a moral code that glorified violence and masculine self-assertion are clear enough. However, the heroes of the major tragedies are more complex. Like Conrad's heroic figures, these are radically ambivalent characters who combine great folly or wickedness with irresistible appeal. When Conrad wanted to convey something of the dangerous magnetism of the charismatic hero, he used the device of an ambivalent fictional narrator whose own emotions cloud his better judgment. But in the theatre, where there is no interposing narrator, the dramatist has got to make his audience feel for themselves that spellbinding power which Conrad is able to convey in part through Marlow's ambivalent response. Dover Wilson was right when he argued that

Shakespeare asks every spectator, every reader, to sympathize with his hero, to feel with him, to place himself in his shoes, to understand his situation,

---

[64] W.B. Yeats, *The Irish Dramatic Movement 1901–1919, Explorations* (London: Macmillan, 1962), p. 196.
[65] D.H. Lawrence, *Apocalypse* (London: Martin Secker, 1932), p. 27.
[66] Sir Philip Sidney, *The Countess of Pembroke's Arcadia*, ed. Maurice Evans (Harmondsworth: Penguin, 1977), p. 803.

and to attempt, in his imagination, a solution. That is, in part, the meaning of tragic drama, for without complete *sympatheia* full *katharsis* is impossible.[67]

But it is an unreflecting audience that does not ponder the meaning of the magic spell that the theatre casts on us, especially in the case of a body of drama as self-reflexive as Shakespeare's. It is in the final scenes of the martial tragedies that the most moving appeal is made to our *sympatheia*. Echoing epideictic convention, those scenes evoke a sense both of the fallen hero's wasted potential and of his true nobility of spirit. Our natural response – to redeem the hero's memory – is primarily an emotional one. It is a phenomenon that many critics have noticed since T.S. Eliot's famous essay on 'Shakespeare and the Stoicism of Seneca';[68] indeed Shakespeare himself calls attention to it. '[T]he ebb'd man,' says Caesar, commenting dryly on the vicissitudes of Roman public life, 'Comes deared by being lacked' *(Ant.* I.iv.43–4). Antony makes much the same point, but in rather blunter language, when he says of Fulvia: 'she's good being gone' (I.ii.120). Having been reminded repeatedly of the fickle nature of reputation, it should come as no surprise to find that Antony himself is the subject of extravagant encomium after his death; nor that the response of a disinterested servant to that encomium should be simple disbelief.

There has been endless critical debate on the question 'Was Hamlet a good man or was he a bad one?'.[69] To point out, as Rebecca West did, that Hamlet is 'an exceptionally callous murderer' who shows no compunction in murdering old men,[70] gets us no nearer to an answer than the eighteenth century did with a Hamlet who exemplified 'purity of moral sentiment . . . eminent abilities . . . [and] manners most elegant and becoming'.[71] More to the point is to see what a powerful hold on the imagination the rhetoric of heroic masculinity can exercise, and to recognize its potential for creating political instability. Having observed the unfolding of the Essex drama from a safe distance, James must have been reassured to see that there was little chance of his being mistaken for Hamlet's original.

---

[67] J. Dover Wilson, *What Happens in 'Hamlet'*, 3rd edn (1951; repr. Cambridge: Cambridge University Press, 1970), p. 44.
[68] *Selected Essays* (London: Faber & Faber, 1932), pp. 126–40.
[69] Patrick Cruttwell, 'The Morality of Hamlet: "Sweet Prince" or "Arrant Knave"?', *Hamlet*, ed. Russell Brown and Harris, p. 110.
[70] Rebecca West, *The Court and the Castle: A Study of the Interactions of Political and Religious Ideas in Imaginative Literature* (London: Macmillan, 1958), pp. 11–12.
[71] William Richardson, *Essays on Shakespeare's Dramatic Characters* (London, 1786), pp. 138–9.

CHAPTER 3

'O these men, these men': Othello

> Faire Phebus is the god of sapience;
> Caliopee, his wyf, is eloquence;
> Thir twa maryit gat Orpheus belyve,
> Quhilk callit is the part intellective
> Of mannis saule and under-standing, free
> And separate fra sensualitee.
> Erudices is oure affection,
> Be fantasy oft movit up and doun;
> Quhile to reson it castis the delyte,
> Quhile to the flesch settis the appetite.
> Robert Henryson, *Orpheus and Erudices*, 425–34, *Poems*, pp. 146–7

> O, these men, these men!
> Dost thou in conscience think – tell me, Emilia –
> That there be women do abuse their husbands
> In such gross kind?
> *Othello*, IV.iii.58–61

> The avenues of escape from justice for men who kill women are many, varied and endlessly imaginative. They change according to fashionable social thought at any one time, but the results change little. She is dead and he gets the sympathy for having been so provoked as to kill her. Women who kill men are seen as mentally ill or just plain vicious, and this is reflected in their sentencing.
> Una Freeley (London Women's Aid), Letter to *The Guardian*, 31 October 1994

On a mountain in Cameroon lives a tribe called the Bakweri. The mountain is covered in forest (at least it was thirty years ago when the social anthropologist Edwin Ardener was studying the Bakweri) and is extremely wet. In fact so dense are the rain clouds covering the forest that visibility is often reduced to a few yards. In this inhospitable environment the Bakweri women spend their day collecting firewood and tending their plantations. The men sit at home in their leaking huts waiting for the women to return, streaming wet and loaded with wood and other spoils of the forest, to cook their dinners. Being good structuralists, the Bakweri naturally divide up their world into binary opposites. The village represents culture; outside its palisade is the wild forest inhabited by beasts, spirits, and, during the day, women. The inescapable link between women and the wild is reconfirmed every evening when the women stumble back to the village bedraggled and cursing after their day in the sodden forest. Such, at least, is Ardener's reading of Bakweri society.[1]

In *The Shakespearean Wild* Jeanne Roberts takes Ardener's structuralist paradigm as a model for interpreting Shakespeare. Culture is a masculine region, and everything that lies beyond its purlieus – untamed nature, the sea, forests, brutes, cannibals, foreigners – belongs to the domain of the wild. Roberts' particular interest is Shakespeare's women and the way socially constructed notions of culture and the wild shape our perceptions of the female. Her aim is to show that 'for Shakespeare the Wild is the locale for the male's necessary, seductive, and terrifying confrontation with the female'.[2]

Roberts' approach is both suggestive and illuminating. As they repeatedly contrast the worlds of civilization and untamed nature, Shakespeare's plays give imaginative expression to one of the great controlling narratives of Renaissance culture, namely, the power of the arts of civilization to restrain and order the barbarous passions of our fallen nature. It is this axiomatic principle of humanist thought that Iago sums up when he tells Roderigo that, 'If the beam of our lives had not one scale of reason to peise another of sensuality, the blood and baseness of our natures would conduct us to most preposterous conclusions' (1.iii.326–9). In its most familiar form the myth of the birth of civilization has a nasty misogynist sting in the tale: as Renaissance mythographers well knew, the fate of Orpheus was brutal dismemberment by a group of fanatical shrieking women 'Tearing the Thracian singer in their rage' (*MND*, v.i.49).[3] In

---

[1] Edwin Ardener, 'Belief and the Problem of Women', *Perceiving Women*, ed. Shirley Ardener (London: Malaby Press, 1975), pp. 7–8.
[2] Jeanne Addison Roberts, *The Shakespearean Wild: Geography, Genus, and Gender* (Lincoln, Nebr. and London: University of Nebraska Press, 1991), p. 24.
[3] 'And (wicked wights) they murthred him, who never till that howre / Did utter woordes in vaine, nor sing without effectuall powre' (*Shakespeare's Ovid*, trans. Arthur Golding, ed. W.H.D. Rouse (London: Centaur Press, 1961), p. 219).

Henryson's version of the Orpheus story the fate of the innocent Erudices is presented as a solemn warning of the dangers of 'warldly lust',[4] even though she had been trying to escape a rapist when she received the fatal snake bite.[5] The corrupting power of a seductive woman is one of the reasons that Othello gives for murdering Desdemona: 'Yet she must die, else she'll betray more men' (v.ii.6). His other reason is more personal: he burns with a desire to avenge the imagined loss of his masculine honour. The way he proposes to accomplish this sounds every bit as brutal as the way the Thracian Maenads took their revenge on Orpheus: 'I'll tear her all to pieces ... I will chop her into messes' (III.iii.436; IV.i.195).

Insofar as feminism has taught us to reread the literature of the past, it has helped us to see that great writers are just as likely to deconstruct as to endorse male mythologies. It is true that the Orpheus story may be read as an archetypal myth of social order in which masculine civility confronts, and is tragically destroyed by, the female wild. But we need to be careful about the way we apply formulaic models to a writer who subverts conventional paradigms as often as Shakespeare does. In *The Winter's Tale* it is not a woman but a man who poses a threat to social order, and it is left to Antigonus' wife to employ the arts of civilization to tame the brutal heart and purge it of its barbaric fantasies. In *Othello* too it is a man who abandons civilized principles. As Othello's resolve to punish Desdemona hardens, we seem to hear echoes of the Orpheus story. But as so often happens in Shakespeare, gender roles are reversed. Acknowledging his wife's virtues, Othello praises Desdemona as an 'admirable musician', and suggests that she will 'sing the savageness out of a bear' (IV.i.185). But there is an unconscious irony in his words: when it comes to saving her own life from an assailant who is deaf to her pleas for mercy, Desdemona, like Orpheus, is helpless. Emilia completes these Ovidian allusions. As she herself 'die[s] in music' (v.ii.225), she thinks of the prophetic symbolism of Desdemona's own Orphic song of valediction with its talk, as in Ovid, of stones

---

[4] 'Orpheus and Erudices', 444, *The Poems of Robert Henryson*, ed. Denton Fox (Oxford: Clarendon Press, 1981), p. 147.

[5] Following Nicholas Trevet's allegorization of Boethius (see John MacQueen, *Robert Henryson: A Study of the Major Narrative Poems* (Oxford: Clarendon Press, 1967), p. 30), Henryson justifies this bizarre interpretation of the story by explaining that Aristius, the goatherd who had tried to rape Erudices, represents 'gude vertue', and that her attempt to escape from her rapist signifies the feckless soul's flight from virtue to the vain but fatal pleasures of the world.

softened by compassion, and a mourning stream that echoes the singer's lament (IV.iii.38–50).[6] Unlike Desdemona and Emilia, Othello has a reputation among the clowns and musicians for not caring for music (III.i.16–17). In contrast to Ovid's hero, he is not the victim of savagery, but its perpetrator.

HERCULEAN HERO

When Lorenzo entertains Jessica with the story of Orpheus in the final act of *The Merchant of Venice*, he finishes with a piece of conventional cautionary wisdom:

> The man that hath no music in himself,
> Nor is not moved with concord of sweet sounds,
> Is fit for treasons, stratagems, and spoils.
> T̶ ̶ ̶ ̶ ̶ ̶ ̶ ̶ ̶ ̶ ̶ ̶ ̶ night,
> A̶
> L̶ (v.i.83–8)

If there seem to be traces of the Orpheus myth in *Othello*, with its tale of 'affections dark as Erebus', they are oblique and ironic. But there is another hero, closely linked with Orpheus, with whom Othello has far more in common.

In *The Herculean Hero* Eugene Waith argues that the paradoxical sense of awe and wonder generated by certain Renaissance tragic heroes as they transgress conventional morality has its origins in classic representations of Hercules, the hero whose legendary virtues were matched only by his insensate passions, and whose fabulous labours were imposed on him as atonement for the murder of his wife and children in a fit of madness sent by the gods. It would be difficult to find a Renaissance tragic hero who approximates more closely to the ancient ideal of the heroic demi-god[7] than Othello. Like Hercules, he is a warrior dedicated to a noble ideal. And when that ideal is destroyed he takes upon himself the role of the gods in punishing human error. In an influential essay entitled 'The Noble Moor' Helen Gardner argued that *Othello* is not a play about a flawed personality whose fatal weakness leads to his downfall, but

---

[6] Cf Ovid: 'And through that mouth of his . . . which even the stones had heard . . . / His ghost then breathing intoo aire, departed'; 'And both the banks in moorning wyse made answer to [his song]' (*Shakespeare's Ovid*, pp. 219–20).

[7] Eugene M. Waith, *The Herculean Hero in Marlowe, Chapman, Shakespeare and Dryden* (London: Chatto & Windus, 1962), pp. 16–38.

rather the spectacle of a man suffering the penalties of his own heroic nature. For Gardner, Othello is no ordinary mortal; he is 'like a hero of the ancient world in that he is not a man like us, but a man recognized as extraordinary. He seems born to do great deeds and live in legend. He has the obvious heroic qualities of courage and strength . . . He has [above all] the heroic capacity for passion'.[8] Many critics have shared Gardner's sense that, in his pride, his suffering, his rage, and his insensate slaughter of innocence Othello is somehow above or beyond the common race of men: excessive in his passions, he is a type of the antique tragic hero. And his penalty for living like a hero, the argument goes, is that he must die like one.

The classical tragedy that Othello owes most to is Seneca's *Hercules furens*. Robert Miola has recently suggested that Seneca provided Shakespeare not just with a paradigm of tragic *furor*, but also a complex structural pattern involving an unstable opposition between the hero and his enemy: 'In his *furor* Hercules becomes Lycus, a raging tyrant who slays Megara and his children. And in his *furor* Othello becomes the Turk, a raging barbarian who murders the loyal and civilized Desdemona'.[9] *Hercules furens* is no simple endorsement of heroic values. Central to Seneca's play is an ironic contrast between Hercules and Orpheus. The dramatic presentation of Hercules as a peacemaker who heroically risks a journey to Hades, who subdues the gods of the underworld and controls nature, who loses his wife and is tormented by grief, cannot help but evoke echoes of Orpheus; and in the play's second Chorus Seneca underlines the parallels between the two heroes. Where Hercules uses force to conquer the underworld, Orpheus shows that, in Heywood's translation, the 'cruell lordes of spryghtes' can be 'subdew'de with song' (569–71).[10]

---

[8] Helen Gardner, 'The Noble Moor', *Interpretations of Shakespeare: British Academy Shakespeare Lectures*, ed. Kenneth Muir (Oxford: Clarendon Press, 1985), pp. 164–5.
[9] Robert S. Miola, *Shakespeare and Classical Tragedy: The Influence of Seneca* (Oxford: Clarendon Press, 1992), pp. 124–43.
[10] *Hercules furens*, trans. Jasper Heywood, *The Tenne Tragedies of Seneca* (1581), 2 vols. (Manchester: The Spenser Society, 1887), vol. I, p. 22. Erasmus makes a similar point in his discussion of the meaning of the labours of Hercules. The phrase, he says, can mean two things, either a task requiring great physical strength, or, if we interpret the legend metaphorically, some great intellectual endeavour. As one would expect, it is the latter meaning that Erasmus favours: 'if any human labours ever deserved to be called Herculean, it is certainly the work of those who are striving to restore the great works of ancient literature' (*The 'Adages' of Erasmus*, ed. and trans. Margaret Mann Phillips (Cambridge: Cambridge University Press, 1964), p. 194.

Hercules' murderous passions are the result of Juno's curse. Believing that he has been cuckolded by Lycus, and deaf to his father's warnings about the folly of vengeance, Hercules murders first his children, and then his wife. When his fit of madness has passed, he resolves to redeem the 'honour and renowne' of his sullied manhood (1270) by an act of suicide. But in what is arguably the most important speech in the play Theseus tells the world's greatest exemplar of heroic *virtus* that true manliness lies not in heroic rage, but in self-control:

> surge et adversa impetu
> perfringe solito. Nunc tuum nulli imparem
> animum malo resume, nunc magna tibi
> virtute agendum est: Herculem irasci veta. (1274–7)[11]

> aryse thou up, and with thy wonted myght
> Subdue thyne yls: now such a mynde unmeete to beare upright
> No evill hap, receyve againe loe now with manhode gret
> Thou must prevayle even Hercules forbyd with yre to fret.[12]

Miola is right when he says that Othello's terrible *anagnorisis* owes more to Seneca than it does to Cinthio: 'like Hercules, Othello calls for retributive thunder, wishes himself in hell, laments his loss. He agonizes about his name, experiences dislocation, calls for his weapons, suffers sorrows too deep for tears'.[13] (In Giraldi Cinthio's *Hecatommithi* there is none of this, only a bald account of the way the Moor is tried, imprisoned, and eventually killed by Desdemona's relations, 'as he richly deserved'.)[14] But though the rhetoric of Othello's *furor* is clearly Senecan in origin, it is an ironic view of 'manhode gret' that Shakespeare takes from *Hercules furens*. That irony, as well as the mythological framework through which it is articulated, is an important key to the meaning of *Othello*.

NOBLE SAVAGE?

In his vindictive rage Othello has all the hallmarks of the Herculean hero. But he is no mere stereotype of tragic *furor*. His combination of

---

[11] *Seneca's Tragedies*, trans. Frank Justus Miller, 2 vols. (London: Heinemann, 1927), vol. I, p. 112.
[12] Heywood, *The Tenne Tragedies of Seneca*, vol. I, p. 42.
[13] *Shakespeare and Classical Tragedy*, p. 137.
[14] Trans. Geoffrey Bullough, ed., *Narrative and Dramatic Sources of Shakespeare* (1957–75), 8 vols. (London: Routledge & Kegan Paul, 1973), vol. VII, p. 252.

natural dignity and outstanding professional competence so impresses the Venetian Senate that, even after the truth has emerged about his betrayal of Brabantio's trust, the duke does not hesitate to place the safety of the republic in Othello's hands. As a middle-aged husband Othello has little interest in the 'light-winged toys / Of feathered Cupid' (1.iii.268–9), preferring instead to pay 'free and bounteous' homage to his wife's qualities of mind (265). Even as a murderer he tugs at our heart strings. After he has got over his initial rage for vengeance, he approaches his terrible task tormented by conflicting emotions: 'O balmy breath, that dost almost persuade / Justice to break her sword! One more, one more' (v.ii.16–17) he whispers as he kisses her sleeping body. Little wonder that Othello has divided critics more sharply than any other Shakespearean hero.[15]

It used to be a widely held view that Othello's tragedy is, as Matthew Proser puts it, 'neither political nor historical'.[16] In its concern to resolve the question of Othello's true nature – noble hero, or self-deceiving barbarian – such character criticism paid little attention to a symbolic pattern that can hardly have failed to impress contemporary audiences with its topicality, that is the confrontation between civilization and the non-European other.[17]

Many critics have discussed Othello's colour.[18] It is something the

---

[15] On the one hand there is a long line of twentieth-century critics going back to A.C. Bradley (*Shakespearean Tragedy* (1905; repr. London: Macmillan, 1963), pp. 142–98), who believe that the essence of *Othello*'s tragedy lies in the paradox of a noble figure whose very virtues are ironically the cause of his downfall, and who see in the hero's recognition of the enormity of his error true testimony of what McAlindon describes as 'the greatness of his heart and the power of his moral imagination' (*Shakespeare's Tragic Cosmos* (Cambridge: Cambridge University Press, 1991), p. 145). On the other there are those critics who share T.S. Eliot's and F.R. Leavis' view that Othello is in truth a self-deceiving barbarian concerned only with redeeming his own reputation (Eliot, 'Shakespeare and the Stoicism of Seneca', *Selected Essays* (London: Faber & Faber, 1932), pp. 126–40; Leavis, 'Diabolical Intellect and the Noble Hero', *The Common Pursuit* (London: Chatto & Windus, 1958), pp. 136–59).

[16] Matthew N. Proser, *The Heroic Image in Five Shakespearean Tragedies* (Princeton: Princeton University Press, 1965), p. 6.

[17] T. McAlindon and Virginia Mason Vaughan consider *Othello* in the context of the Turco-Christian wars (*Shakespeare's Tragic Cosmos*, pp. 127–35; *'Othello': A Contextual History* (Cambridge: Cambridge University Press, 1994), pp. 13–34, though neither discusses this question as part of the wider contemporary debate on primitivism.

[18] The question of race in *Othello* divides critics along similar lines to the broader question of the hero's character. For example, while the Sierra Leonean critic Eldred Jones believes that Shakespeare avoided racial stereotyping and emphasized Othello's dignity as well as his obvious character flaws (*Othello's Countrymen: The African in English Renaissance Drama* (London: Oxford University Press, 1965), pp. 86–109), the Ghanaian Royal Shakespeare Company actor Hugh Quarshie argues that *Othello* rehearses all the period's worst racial myths (*Second Thoughts about Othello*, International Shakespeare Association Occasional Paper 7 (Stratford-

play does not allow us to ignore. In emphasizing Othello's blackness, the play echoes the conventional associations of blackness with the devil and all his works. 'When devils will the blackest sins put on,' says Iago, 'They do suggest at first with heavenly shows' (II.iii.342–3). More significantly, it is Othello himself who complains that his sullied reputation 'is now begrimed and black / As mine own face' (III.iii.392–3). And when he swears vengeance for the wrong he believes Desdemona has done him he cries 'Arise, black vengeance, from the hollow hell' (451). Though modern criticism has spent a great deal of time discussing the problem of race in *Othello*, it has tended to neglect the political and mythological contexts that gave that problem meaning for contemporary audiences.

Before Othello appears on stage Iago gives us two quite different images of Othello. One is the Othello that Iago himself actually hates: this Othello is vain, proud, boastful and, in Iago's view, a poor judge of character and ability. The other is the Othello with whom Iago wants to torment Brabantio, and this is the African of popular Elizabethan myth. Iago wants a violent response from Brabantio, so he deliberately presents him with an image that the white man is going to find most threatening. He describes Othello as an old black ram servicing Brabantio's white ewe (I.i.88–9), and as an Arab stallion engaged in an act of bestiality with Brabantio's daughter (113–14). A few lines further on he refers to their copulation as making the beast with two backs (118–19). Brabantio responds in exactly the way Iago had intended: the idea of his daughter held in

---

upon-Avon: International Shakespeare Association, 1999). See also G.M. Matthews, 'Othello and the Dignity of Man', *Shakespeare in a Changing World*, ed. Arnold Kettle (London: Lawrence & Wishart, 1964), pp. 123–45; G.K. Hunter, '*Othello* and Colour Prejudice', *PBA*, 53 (1967), 139–63; K.W. Evans, 'The Racial Factor in *Othello*', *SStud*, 5 (1969), 124–40; Karen Newman, '"And wash the Ethiop white": Femininity and the Monstrous in *Othello*', *Shakespeare Reproduced: The Text in History and Ideology*, ed. Jean Howard and Marion F. O'Connor (New York and London: Methuen, 1987), pp. 143–62; Martin Orkin, '*Othello* and the "plain face" of Racism', *SQ*, 38 (1987), 166–88; Ania Loomba, *Gender, Race, Renaissance Drama* (Manchester: Manchester University Press, 1989), pp. 38–64 *passim*; Michael Neill, 'Unproper Beds: Race, Adultery, and the Hideous in *Othello*', *SQ*, 40 (1989), 379–412; Harriett Hawkins, *Classics and Trash: Traditions and Taboos in High Literature and Popular Modern Genres* (New York and London: Harvester Wheatsheaf, 1990), pp. 131–8; Emily C. Bartels, 'Making More of the Moor: Aaron, Othello, and Renaissance Refashionings of Race', *SQ*, 41 (1990), 433–54; Dympna Callaghan, '"Othello was a white man": Properties of Race on Shakespeare's Stage', *Alternative Shakespeares 2*, ed. Terence Hawkes (London and New York: Routledge, 1996), pp. 192–5; Walter S.H. Lim, *The Arts of Empire: The Poetics of Colonialism from Ralegh to Milton* (London: Associated University Presses, 1998), pp. 104–41.

the 'gross clasps of a lascivious Moor' (128) is torture to him; it's a treason of the blood.

However, the Othello whom we see in the second scene of the play is neither braggart nor barbarian; he is a dignified and graceful commander of men. Even when Brabantio heaps abuse on him, calling him a foul thief, and accusing him of enchanting Desdemona with magic spells, Othello retains his dignity and self restraint. It's the disparity between conventional Elizabethan associations of blackness with barbarity, and the man we actually see on the stage that makes him, symbolically, what he appears to be, that is a noble savage. Like the term itself, he is an oxymoron, a figure who unites incompatible ideas in a single image.

The noble savage has appeared at many times in literary history, and particularly at those times when the meaning of civilization and its values is being questioned or reassessed. But always he stands for man's natural innocence, for primitive virtue contrasted with the corruptions of civilization. In 1603, when Shakespeare was writing *Othello*, the theme happened to be a topical one. There are two reasons for this contemporary interest in the non-European other. The first is the publication in English translation of Montaigne's *Essays*.

Elizabethans had access to a wide variety of myths, legends, and reports about primitive peoples,[19] some almost entirely fanciful, others, such as Leo Africanus' *History and Description of Africa* (published in English translation in 1600), based on authentic sociological evidence. With increasing numbers of black servants and slaves being brought to England by traders, Elizabethans also had the opportunity for observing non-Europeans in the flesh. Yet despite the gradual replacement of fantasy with factual information, Africans, and Moors in particular, continued to be represented in fiction as embodiments of cruelty and treachery. The self-confessed villainy of Aaron in *Titus Andronicus* is typical of the Elizabethan stage Moor:

> O, how this villainy
> Doth fat me with the very thoughts of it!
> Let fools do good, and fair men call for grace:
> Aaron will have his soul black like his face.   (III.i.201–4)

---

[19] See Eldred D. Jones, *The Elizabethan Image of Africa* (Washington: The Folger Shakespeare Library, 1971); Vaughan, *'Othello': A Contextual History*.

Nor, apparently, were such stereotyped views confined to literature. Queen Elizabeth felt sufficiently strongly about the undesirability of the 'great numbers of Negars and Blackamoors which . . . are crept into this realm' to give orders for them to be transported.[20]

However, Montaigne painted a very different picture of non-Europeans in his celebrated essay 'Of the Caniballes'. Adopting a primitivist position,[21] Montaigne claimed that, far from leading lives of savage brutality, some supposedly savage peoples enjoy a society that is in reality superior to our own. South-American Indians are innocent of the corruptions of European civilization: among them 'the very words that import lying, falshood, treason, dissimulations, covetousnes, envie, detraction, and pardon, were never heard'.[22] People have always been interested in making comparisons between civilized and primitive societies. In the sixteenth century Europe's expanding trade with Africa, Asia, and the New World created new opportunities for observing primitive peoples at first hand. Of the flood of books on the remote and the marvellous that were published in this period, some were of an idealizing character, others were critical of what they portrayed as barbarian savagery.[23] Comparing reports of the lives of South-American Indians with classical accounts of the primal age, Montaigne suggested the possibility that the legendary golden age was not just a poetic fiction or even a historical period of remote antiquity, but a contemporary reality.

The second reason why supposedly barbaric peoples were of topical interest in 1603 was political rather than purely anthropological. The view of civilization embodied in this political theme is the antithesis of Montaigne's primitivism. Shortly after his accession James I republished his uninspired heroic poem on the battle of Lepanto. When it was first written in 1585, *Lepanto* quickly became famous and was widely commented on by contemporary poets.[24] James represented the naval victory at the centre of his poem as having apocalyptic significance. In his *Generall Historie of the Turkes*,

---

[20] Quoted by Jones, *The Elizabethan Image of Africa*, p. 20.
[21] William M. Hamlin notes that Montaigne was by no means consistent in his primitivism (*The Image of America in Montaigne, Spenser and Shakespeare: Renaissance Ethnography and Literary Reflection* (New York: St Martin's Press, 1995), pp. 50–5). See also David Lewis Schaefer, *The Political Philosophy of Montaigne* (Ithaca and London: Cornell University Press, 1990), pp. 177–88.
[22] 'Of the Caniballes', *The Essayes of Montaigne*, trans. John Florio (1603), 3 vols. (1910; repr. London: Dent, 1928), vol. I, p. 220.
[23] Hamlin, *The Image of America*, pp. 3–23.
[24] Emrys Jones, 'Othello, "Lepanto" and the Cyprus Wars', *ShS*, 21 (1968), 48.

also published in 1603, Richard Knolles complimented James on *Lepanto* and described the battle as 'the greatest and most glorious victorie that ever was by any of the Christian confederat princes obtained against these the *Othoman* Kings or Emperors'.[25] In evoking a sense of the anagogic significance of the Turkish defeat, James and Knolles were building on recent anti-Muslim iconography.

In the sixteenth century the European view of Islam was mixed. With the growth of Arabic studies scholars were increasingly aware of the West's intellectual debt to Islam.[26] The importance of Avicenna, Averroes, and other great medieval Arabic philosophers in transmitting Greek philosophy and science was well known to English intellectuals through John Trevisa's late fourteenth-century translation of Bartholomaeus Anglicus' *De proprietatibis rerum* (reprinted in 1582 under the title *Batman uppon Bartholome*).[27] In the sixteenth century too the old crusading belief that Islam was a barbarian heresy to be obliterated with unrelenting missionary violence was replaced by a more informed understanding of Muslim political and military systems;[28] indeed the Turks had diplomatic relations with most European countries, including England.[29] When it suited her, Elizabeth was quite happy to confide to the Ottoman emperor that she regarded Spain as their common enemy and 'head of all the idolaters'.[30]

Notwithstanding these diplomatic realities, the Turks could be relegated to their old role of barbaric infidel when propaganda required it. Under Suleiman the Great (*c.* 1495–1566) the Ottomans had become a world power, systematically plundering Western Europe and posing a potentially devastating threat to the Christian

---

[25] Richard Knolles, *The Generall Historie of the Turkes* (London: 1603), Epistle Dedicatorie, Sig. Aiii^v.
[26] Norman Daniel, *Islam, Europe and Empire* (Edinburgh: Edinburgh University Press, 1966), p. 10. See also David Knowles, *The Evolution of Medieval Thought* (London: Longman, 1962), p. 197; W.Montgomery Watt, *The Influence of Islam on Medieval Europe* (Edinburgh: Edinburgh University Press, 1972), pp. 78–9; M.C. Seymour and Colleagues, *Bartholomaeus Anglicus and his Encyclopedia* (Aldershot: Variorum, 1992), p. 23.
[27] Trevisa's translation was completed in 1398/9 and printed by Wynkyn De Worde in 1495. See *On the Properties of Things: John Trevisa's Translation of Bartholomaeus Anglicus 'De proprietatibis rerum'*, 3 vols., ed. M.C. Seymour (Oxford: Clarendon Press, 1975–1988), vol. 1 (1975), p. xi.
[28] When Machiavelli discusses the need for rulers to ensure the support of either the army or the people in *The Prince* he compares Ottoman military society with the typical modern European state (*The Prince*, ed. Quentin Skinner and Russell Price (Cambridge: Cambridge University Press, 1988), p. 71).
[29] Daniel, *Islam, Europe and Empire*, p. 12.
[30] *Calendar of State Papers* (Foreign Series), 9 February 1588, p. 508.

world. European polemic represented the Turks as barbarians who would not be satisfied until they had brought the whole world under their subjection. Following the siege of Vienna in 1529, the subjugation of Islam became a popular motif in Protestant iconography. One of the prints in Hans Collaert's *The Virtues* (1576) shows Mohammed at the feet of a female figure in idealized classical costume representing Faith. The same iconography, imitated from Collaert's engraving, appears in a wall hanging (*c.* 1580) at Hardwick Hall. Though Faith now stands stiffly dressed in contemporary Elizabethan costume, Mohammed kneels at her feet in exactly the same position as Collaert's figure, bowing his turbaned head in abject submission.[31] Given their legendary treachery and their supposedly barbaric customs it was easy enough to identify the Turks with Antichrist.[32]

Christian polemic represented the extraordinary scale of the Turkish success as a portentous omen. 'If you consider the beginning, progresse, and perpetuall felicitie of this the Othoman Empire,' wrote Knolles, echoing Luther's prediction[33] that Christendom would be engulfed by Islam,

> there is in this world nothing . . . more dreadfull or dangerous: which wondering at nothing but the beautie of it selfe, and drunke with the pleasant wine of perpetuall felicitie, holdeth all the world in scorne, thundering out nothing but still bloud and warre, with a full persuasion in time to rule over all, prefining unto it selfe no other limits than the uttermost bounds of the earth, from the rising of the Sunne unto the going downe of the same. (Sig. Aiv^v)

Though Lepanto signalled a turning point in Turkish fortunes, it did not, as contemporaries hoped, represent the end of the Ottoman peril.[34] Despite the truce of 1581, the possibility remained that the Turks might realize their predatory ambitions while Europe was

---

[31] Anthony Wells-Cole, *Art and Decoration in Elizabethan and Jacobean England: The Influence of Continental Prints, 1558–1625* (New Haven, Conn. and London: Yale University Press, 1997), pp. 257–61.

[32] Nabil Matar, *Islam in Britain 1558–1685* (Cambridge: Cambridge University Press, 1998), pp. 158–62.

[33] See R.W. Southern, *Western Views of Islam in the Middle Ages* (Cambridge, Mass.: Harvard University Press, 1962), pp. 105–6.

[34] Paul Coles, *The Ottoman Impact on Europe* (London: Thames & Hudson, 1968), p. 97. See also Stanford Shaw, *History of the Ottoman Empire and Modern Turkey*, 2 vols. (Cambridge: Cambridge University Press, 1976), vol. 1, p. 178; Halil Inalcik, *The Ottoman Empire: The Classical Age 1300–1600*, trans. Norman Itzkowitz and Colin Imber (New Rochelle: Orpheus Publishing, 1989), p. 42; Matar, *Islam in Britain*, p. 6.

divided by religious differences. Only by uniting under a Christian prince and presenting a common front, Knolles told James in 1603, could the barbarian be kept at bay.[35]

Knolles' message to James could hardly have presented a greater contrast to Montaigne's primitivism. Where Montaigne compared the unsullied life of the South-American savage with the decadence of European civilization, Knolles echoed James' own lines about an apocalyptic conflict between 'the baptiz'd race' and the 'circumsised' barbarian.[36] Historian and patron both saw Islam as a barbarous force that threatened 'the unspeakable ruine and destruction of the Christian Religion and State'.[37] The great naval battle of 1571 symbolized nothing less than a conflict between pagan savagery and Christian order. It was that anagogic conflict that Sir Thomas Browne was referring to when he took Lepanto as a figure for the inner battle between barbarity and civility: 'Let me be nothing,' he wrote in the famous aphorism from *The Religio Medici*, 'if within the compass of my self I do not find the battail of Lepanto, Passion against Reason, Reason against Faith, Faith against the Devil, and my Conscience against all'.[38] In the popular mind there was little to choose between Turks and their Moorish co religionists.[39] For a new king whose greatest ambition was to be the architect of a united Europe,[40] the idea of an 'erring barbarian' employed in the defence of European interests in Cyprus must have seemed like a very strange paradox, particularly in view of the fact that the island had fallen to the Turks in 1570.[41]

To ask whether *Othello*'s charismatic Moorish hero is truly noble or essentially savage makes little more sense than it would to ask whether Shylock's Venetian adversary really is the kindest gentleman who treads the earth (*MV*, II.viii.35), or whether he is actually an unpleasant anti-Semite. Both characters display such fantastic con-

---

[35] Knolles, *The Generall Historie of the Turkes*, Sig. Aiii^v.
[36] *The Lepanto*, 10–11, *The Poems of James VI of Scotland*, ed. James Craigie (Edinburgh and London: William Blackwood, 1955), p. 202.
[37] Knolles, *The Generall Historie of the Turkes*, Sig. Aiv.
[38] Sir Thomas Browne, *The Religio Medici* (London: Dent, 1962), p. 76.
[39] Maxime Rodinson, 'The Western Image and Western Studies of Islam', *The Legacy of Islam*, ed. Joseph Schacht and C.E. Bosworth, 2nd edn. (Oxford: Clarendon Press, 1974), p. 11.
[40] W.B. Patterson, *King James VI and I and the Reunion of Christendom* (Cambridge: Cambridge University Press, 1997).
[41] McAlindon points out that, according to Knolles, the island fell, not primarily because of Turkish military superiority, but in part because of inadequate leadership on Cyprus (*Shakespeare's Tragic Cosmos*, p. 127).

traditions that it is impossible to say if they are essentially one thing or another. A more useful question to ask is what the play has to say about the contemporary debate on civilized values. Whether heroic masculinity and the ideals it represents have any place in a civilized society is an essential ingredient in that debate. However, because Othello is more than just a type of Senecan *furor*, any attempt to explain the play's symbolic patterns must also consider the passions that lead its hero to such 'preposterous conclusions'.

METAMORPHOSIS

One of the most puzzling aspects of Othello's transformation in Act III is the sheer speed with which doubt takes possession of his mind. It would be wrong to apply realistic criteria to a poetic drama that is patently the product of self-conscious artistic design. But the dramatic effect of such exceptional economy and compression is to emphasize the horror of Othello's quasi-Ovidian metamorphosis. Before Desdemona petitions him on Cassio's behalf there has been not the slightest suggestion that Othello suspected that his wife was capable of indiscretion. Yet within a few lines of Iago's hint that her conversation with Cassio may not be what it seems, he refers to her as 'Excellent wretch' and speaks of primal chaos returning with the death of his own love (III.iii.91–3). The belief that if love should leave the earth, chaos would return, is a commonplace of medieval and Renaissance thought.[42] So too is the knowledge that evil is supremely skilful at disguising itself as virtue. The first thirty lines of Act I Scene iii present the latter theme in a mode that is mainly realistic, but also, given the popular association of the Turks with Antichrist, inevitably partly symbolic. Sifting and weighing conflicting evidence of the movements of the Turkish fleet, the Venetian senators conclude that the 'general enemy' is putting up a pageant to deceive them (20). For a brief moment Othello also seems to be thinking symbolically as he voices the suspicion that Iago may be the devil in

---

[42] See for example John Gower's *Confessio Amantis*, Prologue, 168–79, *The Complete Works*, 4 vols, ed. G.C. Macaulay (Oxford: Clarendon Press, 1899–1902), vol. II (1901), p. 9. The *locus classicus* for the idea that love is the basis of social order is Boethius' *Consolation of Philosophy*. Boethius writes: 'If thys dyvine or godly love shuld slacke the brydell . . . whatsoever thynge now lovyth together, and agreith, would be at contynual varyance and dyscorde' (*Boethius' Consolation of Philosophy*, trans. George Colville (1556), ed. Ernest Belfort Bax (London: David Nutt, 1897), p. 52).

disguise (v.ii.292–3). But by then it is too late. In Act III Scene iii he does not pause to weigh Iago's evidence.

Once the seeds of doubt have been sown, the transformation is complete within a matter of 300 lines. In the play's final scene Othello says that he did 'naught . . . in hate, but all in honour' (v.ii.301). But to claim that hatred was not one of his motives is simply not true. It would be difficult to imagine a more vivid and terrible image of pure hatred than Othello's solemn vow of vengeance against his wife in Act III Scene iii. At the beginning of this speech he seems to be thinking primarily of the man he believes has cuckolded him: 'O that the slave had forty thousand lives! / One is too poor, too weak for my revenge'(447–8). But as he develops his theme it is obvious that his desire for vengeance encompasses Desdemona too:

> Look here, Iago.
> All my fond love thus do I blow to heaven – 'tis gone.
> Arise, black vengeance, from the hollow hell.
> Yield up, O love, thy crown and hearted throne
> To tyrannous hate! Swell, bosom, with thy freight,
> For 'tis of aspics' tongues. (449–54)

In what looks like a cunning parody of Amphitryon's attempt to persuade his son to calm his 'furious rage' and put away 'thoughts that ought not to be spoake' (973–5),[43] Iago urges patience. But Othello is implacable. The speech that follows is pure Senecan *furor* in which all that is sacred is inverted as Othello offers up to whatever evil god is now haunting his imagination a travesty of his marriage vow:

> Never, Iago. Like to the Pontic Sea,
> Whose icy current and compulsive course
> Ne'er knows retiring ebb, but keeps due on
> To the Propontic and the Hellespont,
> Even so my bloody thoughts with violent pace
> Shall ne'er look back, ne'er ebb to humble love,
> Till that a capable and wide revenge
> Swallow them up.
> (*He kneels*)
>   Now, by yon marble heaven,
> In the due reverence of a sacred vow
> I here engage my words. (456–65)

---

[43] Seneca, *Hercules furens*, trans. Heywood, vol. I, p. 34.

A mere 200 lines earlier Othello had imagined that Desdemona might be reverting to feral ways like a half-trained hawk (264). The speed with which he himself degenerates from self-possessed military commander to murderer reveals the full irony of his suspicions.

By Act v the Senecan passion has abated, and in its place is a determination to see through to its conclusion the grim task he has set himself. It is a task that has been dictated by Othello's sense of masculine honour[44] and the view of women which that honour code entails.

Valerie Wayne points out that at the beginning of Act II we hear two radically opposed views of women: first Cassio's courtly tribute to Desdemona's miraculous beauty (II.i.62–6), and second, Iago's jesting slander of women (II.i.112–15).[45] They are opposite sides of the same ideological coin. Only a culture that entertains such wildly exaggerated views of what it thinks women should be is going to distort with such malicious hyperbole the reality of what they actually are. However, it is not Iago but Othello who offers the most damaging criticism of women. All Iago says is that women are irritating in their contrariness: 'Bells in your parlours; wildcats in your kitchens, / Saints in your injuries; devils being offended' – in other words, conventional misogynist tittle-tattle. The case that Othello puts against women is far more grave. It is the old argument, deriving from a long line of anti-feminist tracts going back to St Paul (Eph. 5:22–4), that libidinous women represent a dangerous threat to social order. Once one accepts the analogical premise of the medieval cosmos, it follows logically that patriarchy is as much a part of the natural order of things as monarchy. As Sir John

---

[44] Norman Council argues that *Othello* dramatizes the Moor's abandonment of a virtuous notion of honour for a corrupt inversion of that ideal (*When Honour's at the Stake: Ideas of Honour in Shakespeare's Plays* (London: Allen & Unwin, 1973), pp. 113–35). The present chapter owes much to Council's essay. See also Charles Barber, *The Theme of Honour's Tongue: A Study of Social Attitudes in the English Drama from Shakespeare to Dryden* (Göteborg: University of Göteborg Press, 1985), p. 82.

[45] 'Historical Differences: Misogyny and *Othello*', *The Matter of Difference: Materialist Feminist Criticism of Shakespeare*, ed. Wayne (New York and London: Harvester Wheatsheaf, 1991), p. 160. See also Carol Thomas Neely, 'Women and Men in *Othello*', *SStud*, 10 (1977), 133–58, repr. in Carolyn Ruth Swift Lenz, Gayle Greene, and Carol Thomas Neely, *The Woman's Part: Feminist Criticism of Shakespeare* (Urbana, Chicago, and London: University of Illinois Press, 1980), pp. 211–39; Coppélia Kahn, *Man's Estate: Masculine Identity in Shakespeare* (Berkeley, Los Angeles, and London: University of California Press, 1981), pp. 140–6; Marilyn French, *Shakespeare's Division of Experience* (London: Jonathan Cape, 1982), pp. 204–19; Newman, '"And wash the Ethiop white": Femininity and the Monstrous in *Othello*', *Shakespeare Reproduced: The Text in History and Ideology*, (see note 18 above), pp. 143–62.

Hayward put it in 1603: 'As one God ruleth the world, one master the family . . . so it seemeth no less natural that one state should be governed by one commander'.⁴⁶ Endorsing this analogical argument was the claim that men embodied the principle of rational intelligence, while women represented the capricious emotions which, since the Fall, have threatened to usurp the rightful jurisdiction of reason, a commonplace that Langland summed up with typical bluntness in *Piers Plowman* when he wrote: 'The wif is oure wikked flessh þat wol noȝt be chastised / For kynde clyveþ on hym evere to contrarie þe soule' (Passus XVII, 334–5).⁴⁷ So powerful is the logic that underwrites the misogynist position that in 'Orpheus and Erudices' Henryson was able to turn an act of male violence into a solemn allegory of the soul's fall from grace. The fact that Erudices' attacker, Aristius, is a goatherd; that goats symbolize lechery; and that therefore the man who looks after the goats represents reason controlling the lascivious affections, does not make Henryson's *moralitas* any less inherently absurd: Aristius is still a rapist.

It is the same misogynist view of women's moral frailty, or something very like it, that allows Othello to persuade himself that Desdemona's death is necessary in order to prevent her from corrupting more men. The reason why women, like emotions, must be controlled, ruthlessly if necessary, is that failure to do so could have such disastrous consequences. What was the cause of the greatest civic and military catastrophe of the ancient world? The question hardly needed to be asked: as everyone knew, it was a woman. 'Where Hellen is, there will be Warre; / For, Death and Lust, Companions are', wrote George Wither in the inscription to an emblem illustrating the dangers of harlotry.⁴⁸ In *Lepanto* James had referred to the Troy story, comparing the victorious Christian navy to the Grecian fleet.⁴⁹ But at Cyprus the Christians were defeated. Like Troy, the island is a community under siege; Cyprus is the last outpost of Christian civilization, a world beleaguered by the forces of barbarity. In circumstances such as these, 'in a town of war / Yet

---

⁴⁶ *An Answer to the First Part of a Certaine Conference Concerning the Succession* (London, 1603), Sig. Bi^v.
⁴⁷ *Piers Plowman: The B Version*, ed. George Kane and E. Talbot Donaldson (London: Athlone Press, 1975), p. 605.
⁴⁸ *A Collection of Emblemes, Ancient and Moderne* (1635), facsimile edn. (Columbia, S.C.: University of South Carolina Press, 1975), p. 27.
⁴⁹ *The Poems of James VI of Scotland*, ed. Craigie, p. 216.

wild, the people's hearts brimful of fear' (II.iii.206–7), you cannot have another Helen corrupting your troops.

In the tenth book of the *Metamorphoses*, a few pages after the tale of Orpheus and Eurydice, there is another story about lascivious women, one that Shakespeare knew well.[50] Pygmalion's story is also set in Cyprus. It is Pygmalion's revulsion from the behaviour of the Propoetides, a race of women whose shameful behaviour causes horns to grow on their husbands' foreheads, that makes him decide, like Orpheus, to shun women. Convinced that all women are irredeemably tainted by corruption, he carves his own flawless woman out of ivory. Inevitably, he falls in love with his creation, kissing the cold statue and caressing its lifeless limbs. Enchanted by the result of his own artistry, Pygmalion prays to the goddess of the island, petitioning Venus to bring his idealized bride to life. His prayers are answered, and the statue begins to breathe.

Othello too grows horns on his forehead, at least he imagines he does (III.iii.288). But in what looks like another parody of Ovid, he reverses Pygmalion's prayer, believing that he can transform a living woman into alabaster perfection:

> Let me not name it to you, you chaste stars.
> It is the cause. Yet I'll not shed her blood,
> Nor scar that whiter skin of hers than snow,
> And smooth as monumental alabaster.
> Yet she must die, else she'll betray more men. (v.ii.2–6)

Realization of the truth about his ghastly mistake produces another outburst of Senecan *furor*:

> cursèd, cursèd slave!
> Whip me, ye devils,
> From the possession of this heavenly sight.
> Blow me about in winds, roast me in sulphur,
> Wash me in steep-down gulfs of liquid fire! (283–7)

But in all this extravagant spectacle of Herculean suffering, Othello displays little sign of the mortification that Cassio shows when he acknowledges his crass stupidity. 'One unperfectness shows me another,' Cassio confesses, 'to make me frankly despise myself'

---

[50] Shakespeare alludes to the Pygmalion myth in *Measure for Measure* (III.i.313), and adapts it imaginatively in *The Winter's Tale* where he links it, as in Ovid, with the Orpheus story (it is Orpheus who tells the story in the *Metamorphoses*). As she awakens the statue Paulina tells Leontes: 'Do not shun her / Until you see her die again, for then / You kill her double' (*WT*, v.iii.105–7).

(II.iii.290–1). When Othello had broken up the quarrel between Cassio and Montano in Act II Scene iii, comparing them to barbarous Turks and appealing to their Christian shame, he had asked how they could think of creating civil disturbance under such dangerous conditions. Now Othello has become involved in his own 'private and domestic quarrel' in the very 'court and guard of safety' (II.iii.208–9). But if Cassio's awareness of his stupidity reflects unfavourably on Othello, the comparison between the two men also reminds us of the powers of leadership that Cassio lacks. I will return to the latter point in the final section of this chapter.

Both Cassio and Othello are soldiers of high reputation and both are concerned at the loss of their good name. 'Reputation, reputation, reputation', cries Cassio when he realizes that he has just destroyed his career, 'O I ha' lost my reputation! I ha' lost the immortal part of myself, and what remains is bestial! My reputation, Iago, my reputation' (II.iii.256–9). Though Othello claims to be concerned only to limit the damage that Desdemona may do to other men, it is reputation too that is his overriding concern. What will be the consequences of losing his wife? Othello's farewell to innocence is an extraordinary piece of rhetoric, remarkable as much for what it does not say – no mention is made of the loss of a marriage companion – as for its eloquent celebration of the 'Pride, pomp, and circumstance of glorious war' (III.iii.359).

Defenders of Othello's essential nobility of character usually refer to his final speech as evidence of his true greatness of spirit as he faces with unflinching courage the truth of what he has done. In his introduction to the Arden edition of the play M.R. Ridley writes: 'In the brief interval between his belated conviction of the truth and his death he recaptures all our earlier admiration and more than our earlier sympathy'.[51] Eldred Jones says that 'Othello's final speech has a note of deep humility'.[52] Richard Ide argues that in Othello's valediction we see the hero 'reaffirming the transcendent value of the love that he has once again enthroned in his heart'.[53] It is true that in his speech Othello expresses infinite regret for what has happened, and he does it in the most marvellously stirring language. But nowhere does he express that sense of shame which Cassio sums

---

[51] M.R. Ridley, ed., *Othello*, Arden edn. (London: Methuen, 1958), p. lvi.
[52] Eldred Jones, *Othello's Countrymen*, p. 106.
[53] Richard S. Ide, *Possessed with Greatness: The Heroic Tragedies of Chapman and Shakespeare* (London: Scolar Press, 1980), p. 74.

up in those three brief, unadorned phrases of self condemnation: 'To be now a sensible man, by and by a fool, and presently a beast' (II.iii.298–9). Nowhere does he seem to show any sense of the wider social and political ramifications of his actions. Nor does he show much understanding of the kind of love that Sonnet 116 calls 'the marriage of true minds' – the kind of love that 'alters [not] when it alteration finds'.

Othello's final speech is, in effect, a funeral oration. It is usual on such occasions for the speaker to praise the deceased.[54] In an extended prolepsis, Othello speaks of his service to the state; he mentions his bad luck; he characterizes himself as a man of high integrity and powerful emotions; and, almost incidentally, he mentions his wife. But he refers to her, neither as a lover, nor as a friend, nor even as a human being, but as an object. She is like a pearl thrown away by someone who did not appreciate its true value. When Iachimo compares Imogen to a diamond in *Cymbeline*, Posthumus rejects the comparison. 'You are mistaken', he tells Iachimo, 'The one may be sold or given, or if there were wealth enough for the purchase or merit for the gift. The other is not a thing for sale, and only the gift of the gods' (I.iv.80–3). In modern Islamic societies the jewel image is still used to express a husband's rights. 'The Muslim woman is a precious jewel whom only her rightful owner can possess', said a Saudi court advisor recently in opposition to a proposed easing of the ban on *ikhtilat*, or 'mixing' of the sexes in public places.[55] Like Othello, Posthumus swears vengeance on the wife he thinks has betrayed him, threatening to tear her limb from limb (II.iv.147). But when he realizes his error, his reaction is very different from Othello's. Though he longs for death, and resolves to die fighting for Imogen and her country's cause, he does so with no heroic gestures and no thought of fame:

> so I'll die
> For thee, O Innogen, even for whom my life
> Is every breath a death; and, thus unknown,
> Pitied nor hated, to the face of peril
> Myself I'll dedicate.   (v.i.25–9)

---

[54] In *The Arte of Rhetorique* (1560) Thomas Wilson follows Quintilian in giving advice on how to compose a funeral oration in praise of a noble person: in the main part of his oration the speaker should deal with his subject's gifts of mind and body, and advert to his accomplishments (ed. G.H. Mair (Oxford: Clarendon Press, 1909), pp. 12–13).

[55] Reported by David Hirst, *The Guardian*, 3 August 1999.

Othello's final speech, by contrast, is largely about himself, his character, and his achievements.

ALL IN HONOUR

As Othello kisses the sleeping Desdemona he fears that his resolve may not be strong enough to see him through the task before him:

> O balmy breath, that dost almost persuade
> Justice to break her sword! One more, one more.
> Be thus when thou art dead, and I will kill thee
> And love thee after. One more, and that's the last.
> *(He kisses her)*
> So sweet was ne'er so fatal. I must weep,
> But they are cruel tears. This sorrow's heavenly,
> It strikes where it doth love.   (v.ii.16–22)

So tender are his words that audiences are apt to forget the thinking that has led to this pass. Othello speaks of justice. But what kind of justice is it that demands death by strangulation as payment for adultery? Certainly not Venice's. Norman Rabkin puts a familiar point of view when he says that, 'given Iago's alarming skill in marshalling pseudo-evidence, Othello seems to have but little choice'.[56] The extraordinary assumption behind this remark seems to be that, had Iago's accusations been true, Othello's actions would have been justified, his error being merely that he acted precipitately on false evidence. Such an argument would have carried little weight in an Elizabethan court of law.

It is usually assumed that Othello's fatal flaw is his jealousy, with those who are impressed by the hero's moral rehabilitation arguing that his rage is a measure of the strength of his former idealistic faith in Desdemona. 'The paradox of the tragedy is that the faith which makes Othello great makes him helpless as well', writes Rabkin (73). 'Othello's immense capacity for total . . . commitment to an ideal . . . causes him to react violently to the belief that he was wrong in so doing', writes Norman Sanders.[57] That Othello should be jealous is entirely understandable, the more so since, as a member of a vilified ethnic group, he is vulnerable to the humiliation that would result from public knowledge of the fact that his Venetian wife is

---

[56] Norman Rabkin, *Shakespeare and the Common Understanding* (1967; repr. Chicago and London: University of Chicago Press, 1984), p. 72.
[57] Norman Sanders, ed., *Othello* (Cambridge: Cambridge University Press, 1984), p. 29.

apparently having an affair with a compatriot. But though susceptibility to sexual jealousy may be universal, the way people act on their feelings varies between cultures. The question at issue in *Othello* is not jealousy, but vengeance and the honour code that sanctions it.

Katharine Maus has argued that the typical revenge tragedy deals with the private redress of wrong in a society where corrupt or inefficient legal institutions are incapable of delivering justice; 'indeed', she writes, 'the defectiveness of the status quo is virtually a precondition of the genre'.[58] Though this is true of most Elizabethan and Jacobean revenge plays, in *Othello* there is no suggestion that the Senate is corrupt, or that Venice's trusted general would not have been given a fair hearing if he had taken his case to court. Quite the reverse. Having threatened Othello with 'the bloody book of law' (1.iii.67) in response to Brabantio's charges, the duke listens with exemplary impartiality to both sides of the case, deciding finally in Othello's favour. Shakespeare is here drawing on Venice's well-established reputation for political and legal wisdom. In *The Classical Republicans* Zera S. Fink writes: 'when the Duke promises Brabantio that the abductor of his daughter will be punished even though the culprit should turn out to be the Duke's own son, Shakespeare was writing in the spirit of that inexorable administration of justice which was a prominent feature in the contemporary reputation of the [Venetian] republic'.[59] In another essay Maus considers the peculiar emphasis in *Othello* on quasi-legal questions of evidence, noting that Othello's demand for 'ocular proof' of Desdemona's adultery seems to echo contemporary legal practice.[60] She explains that although ecclesiastical courts – the usual venue for dealing with sexual misdemeanours in Elizabethan England – were able to convict on the basis of circumstantial evidence they much preferred eye-witness evidence. Persuaded by Iago to accept supposition in place of hard evidence, Othello thus 'lives out the epistemological dilemma of the English juryman to whom everything is supposed to be manifest, but who is nonetheless forced to depend upon clues and surmises, who must treat as clearly visible that which is inevitably beyond sight' (120); the plot, she says, 'replicates the difficulties with

---

[58] Katharine Eisaman Maus, ed., *Four Revenge Tragedies* (Oxford: Clarendon Press, 1995), p. ix.
[59] *The Classical Republicans: An Essay in the Recovery of a Pattern of Thought in Seventeenth-Century England* (1945), 2nd edn. (Evanston, Ill.: Northwestern University Press, 1962), pp. 42–3.
[60] Katharine Eisaman Maus, in *Inwardness and Theater in the English Renaissance* (Chicago: University of Chicago Press, 1995), pp. 104–27.

which the English criminal courtroom often had to deal' (118). Shrewd as it is, Maus' analysis seems somehow to miss the ironic point of the analogy. The dramatic significance of Othello's judicial language is surely that he speaks as if he were already in a court of law when in fact what he is actually doing is arming himself with the kind of evidence that in normal circumstances would merely enable someone to bring an adultery case to court. But Othello has no intention of doing this. By arrogating to himself the roles of plaintiff, witness, jury, judge, and executioner all in one, he is in effect denying her the kind of hearing that he himself received at the beginning of the play. In *Othello* the question of vengeance arises, not because of a conflict between an individual and a corrupt legal system, but because the code of values by which the avenger lives makes it imperative: 'naught I did in hate, but all in honour', he explains in justification of his actions (v.ii.301). It is his sense of honour that demands that an adulteress be killed.

One of the defining features of civilized states that distinguishes them from many primitive societies and a few modern fundamentalist religious ones, is the existence of laws that deny individuals the right to prosecute crime or injury in a private capacity. 'The instant slaying of wife or adulterer on discovery was part of the early law of every land', wrote Fredson Bowers in *Elizabethan Revenge Tragedy*.[61] Though this is almost certainly an exaggeration, it is true that in an heroic society such as that described in Saxo Grammaticus' *History of the Danes* (see Chapter 2, pp. 74–5) vengeance for an insult to oneself or a member of one's family is a sacred duty; dereliction of that responsibility is sure to result in divine punishment. A strong sense of family and tribal honour combined with a belief in the legitimacy of retaliation is also a feature of early Islamic societies, stoning to death being the traditional penalty for adultery.[62] By contrast, the essence of Christian morality is charity: 'defye the adulter[y]', wrote Erasmus in his *Handbook of a Christian Knight*, 'not the man'.[63] Though the Koran placed strict limits on retaliatory action, honour killings are still a feature of some modern Islamic societies. In April 1999 it was reported in *The Observer* that a

---

[61] Fredson Thayer Bowers, *Elizabethan Revenge Tragedy 1587–1642* (Gloucester, Mass.: Peter Smith, 1959), p. 49.
[62] N.J. Coulson, *A History of Islamic Law* (Edinburgh: Edinburgh University Press, 1964), p. 150.
[63] Desiderius Erasmus, *Enchiridion Militis Christiani: An English Version*, ed. Anne M. O'Donnell, SND (Oxford: Early English Text Society, 1981), p. 152.

teenage rape victim in a remote Pakistani mountain village had been publicly executed by the *jirga*, or council of elders, for bringing shame on the community. The article claimed that such honour killings are not uncommon in remote mountain regions of Pakistan.[64] In exceptional cases, such as that of the Saudi princess Misha'il bint Fahd bin Mohammad whose execution in 1977 was the subject of the controversial television documentary *Death of a Princess*, the law may still officially be evoked to execute adulterers in modern Islamic societies. But though Misha'il's trial was conducted in accordance with Saudi law, the court would not have insisted on the death penalty if her grandfather had not demanded it. According to Prince Muhammad ibn Abdul Aziz it was the ancient Bedouin tribal principle of family honour that was invoked.[65] It was the same sense of family honour for which Moors were renowned in Elizabethan England. In his *History and Description of Africa* Leo Africanus reported that in Morocco 'the men beare a most savage minde, being so extremely possessed with jelousie, that whomsoever they finde but talking with their wives, they presently goe about to murther them'.[66]

But honour in the pre-civilized sense of personal prestige or reputation was not just about adultery. As a code of values that emphasized masculine physical prowess, self-assertion, and the willingness to use violence in the defence of personal, family, or national integrity, it was a highly political issue in Elizabethan and Jacobean England. When Samuel Daniel praised Essex for reviving 'ancient honor neere worne out of date' he was referring to that neo-chivalric code of values that the Elizabethan armorist Gerard Legh defined as 'glory gotten by courage of manhood' (see Chapter 1, p. 34). The fiasco of the 1601 rebellion ensured that the ideals that drove the earl to take the drastic step of challenging the crown's authority received maximum publicity. To those who had offered their support to a man who was prepared to draw his sword against his queen, Tybalt's fleering at Romeo – 'Now, by the stock and honour of my kin, / To strike him dead I hold it not a sin' (I.v.57–8) – would probably not have sounded outrageous.

---

[64] Jason Burke, 'Teenage Rape Victim Shot', *The Observer*, 18 April 1999.
[65] Jan Goodwin, *Price of Honor: Muslim Women Lift the Veil of Silence on the Islamic World* (Boston, New York, Toronto, and London: Little, Brown & Co, 1994), p. 219.
[66] *The History and Description of Africa*, trans. John Pory, ed. Robert Brown, 3 vols. (London: Hakluyt Society, 1896), vol. II, p. 233.

Whether a man of exceptional talents and accomplishments who murders an innocent wife is truly noble or a barbarian at heart is a question that would be difficult enough to answer in real life; in drama it is impossible. Othello is not a real person, but a fictional creation who forms part of a complex dramatic pattern that is at once psychologically plausible and symbolic. When he stages his own suicide, prefacing it with a reference to the story of how he had once dealt with 'a malignant and a turbaned Turk' who posed a threat to the state (v.ii.362), he is both making a Senecan gesture of self-assertion that is entirely in keeping with his heroic character, and at the same time returning us to the play's fundamental symbolic opposition between barbarism and civilization.

James VI had characterized the battle of Lepanto as an apocalyptic conflict between 'the baptiz'd race, / And circumsised Turband Turkes'. In *Othello* that symbolic contrast between order and barbarity is elaborated in a complex pattern of antinomies. Describing the 'symbolic geography' of the play, Alvin Kernan lists all the qualities with which the Turks are associated in the play: barbarism, cunning, treachery, ruthlessness, violence. At the other extreme is Venice and all that it stands for: civility, order, law, and reason. Between them is Cyprus, a beleaguered military outpost defending civilization against the barbarian. As we move from Venice to Cyprus, says Kernan, we move from '*The City* to barbarism, from Christendom to the domain of the Turks, from order to riot, from justice to wild revenge and murder, from truth to falsehood',[67] though it should be added that Venice is not just any city. In keeping with the myth of a republic of such legendary stability that it seemed, in the words of Contarini's English translator, to be 'as it were entertaining a league of intelligence with heavenly powers',[68] Shakespeare represents the Venetian senate, in ironic contrast to Othello himself, as the very embodiment of cautious deliberation. As is usually the case in Shakespeare, apparently clear-cut binary oppositions turn out to be anything but simple, and it is a super-subtle Venetian who exemplifies 'Turkish' cruelty in

---

[67] *Othello*, ed. Kernan (New York: New American Library, 1963), p. xxix.
[68] Lewes Lewkenor, Introduction to Gaspar Contarini, *The Commonwealth and Government of Venice* (1543), trans. Lewkenor (London, 1599), Sig. Aiii. The stability of the Venetian republic was attributed to the fact that it was the supreme example in the modern world of the classical ideal of the mixed state. On the mixed state see Zera S. Fink, *The Classical Republicans*.

its most gratuitous form. 'Nay, it is true, or else I am a Turk' (II.i.117), says Iago when Desdemona accuses him of slandering women. The fact that his vilification of her is entirely false logically confirms the identification he wants to deny. For Othello too the Turks are the symbolic antithesis of civilized order. 'Are we turned Turks,' he cries as he breaks up the street fight between Cassio and Montano, 'and to ourselves do that / Which heaven hath forbid the Ottomites? / For Christian shame, put by this barbarous brawl' (II.iii.163–5). In the sixteenth century Turks were a byword for barbaric behaviour. When Erasmus put the case for Christian charity he argued that we should condemn the sin, not the sinner: 'lette a christen man ... dispyse the commytter of sacrylege, not the man; let hym kyll the turke, not the man'.[69] In *Othello* the second part of Erasmus' maxim is turned into symbolic action while the first is forgotten. As Othello appeals in defence of his actions to the honour code, finally stabbing himself as he had once stabbed a treacherous Turk, it is as if the similarity between his own name and that of the 'woorthy and warlike *Othoman*',[70] founder of the Turkish empire, was indeed an inauspicious omen. Symbolically, hero and barbarian have become one.

Many critics have argued that, having metamorphosed from loving husband into homicidal barbarian, Othello undergoes another remarkable transformation in the play's final scene. 'The essence of Othello's finale in the theatre is that he wrings from his tragic perception a renewed dignity', writes Marvin Rosenberg.[71] 'It is ... the absolute value of ... love and trust ... that are triumphantly vindicated in the last scene in spite of the hero's fatal blindness', says Dieter Mehl.[72] The fact that so many critics have been moved to pay homage to Othello's courage and dignity means that this response cannot simply be written off as the politically unenlightened reaction of a pre-feminist era. Indeed, if, with Leavis, we deny Othello his extraordinary mystique we are left, not with a tragedy, but an unpleasantly sordid tale of battery and murder. Harold Bloom is in one sense right when he says that we need to

---

[69] *Enchiridion Militis Christiani*, p. 152.
[70] For Knolles' account of Othoman see *The Generall Historie of the Turkes*, pp. 131–77. On the possible link between the 'Othoman' Turks and the name of Shakespeare's hero see F.N. Lees, 'Othello's Name', *NQ*, n.s. 8 (1961), 139–41.
[71] *The Masks of Othello* (Berkeley, Los Angeles, and London: University of California Press, 1961), p. 191.
[72] *Shakespeare's Tragedies: An Introduction* (Cambridge: Cambridge University Press, 1986), p. 77.

restore to Othello some sense of the 'dignity and glory' that much modern criticism has deprived him of.[73] To be capable of persuading intelligent critics that this wife-battering soldier is a paragon of love and trust, there must be some powerful force at work in the play's final scene. And there is. It is the persuasive power of the heroic ideal. In acknowledging Othello's exotic grandeur Helen Gardner says that there is even something heroic in Desdemona's murder: it is 'heroic in its absoluteness, disinterestedness, and finality'.[74] She too is right, though perhaps not quite in the sense she intended. But the fact that Othello's grandeur is an essential aspect of his dramatic character does not mean that we have to accept this kind of 'nobility' at face value.

In Chapter 2, I compared Shakespeare's dialectical treatment of the heroic ideal with Conrad's anatomy of heroism. Conrad was suspicious of heroes because it seemed to him that the charismatic idealism that is capable of inspiring followers and admirers can so often have destructive consequences. He describes it as a kind of madness. The sense of conviction, characteristic of the heroic idealist, in the absolute rightness of a sacred cause is like a 'form of dementia the gods send upon those they wish to destroy', says Martin Decoud in *Nostromo*.[75] It is Othello's sense of the sanctity of his cause, as he swears, with all the 'reverence of a sacred vow', to avenge the slight to his honour, that is so chilling. What is at issue in this play is not the hero's professional competence, or his dignity of bearing, or even his 'free and open nature', for these things are indisputable. Rather, it is a code of values that demands death as the unavoidable payment for adultery. And that is something which he takes with him to the grave. At the core of the heroic ideal is a masculine sense of honour. The heroic principles that dictated vengeance for an act of adultery now demand suicide; it is the same heroic sense of masculine honour that has guided all Othello's actions. Just as he had denied Desdemona the benefit of a court of law, so the honour code demands, not scrupulous weighing of evidence and careful measuring of his own motives and actions

---

[73] *Shakespeare: The Invention of the Human* (London: Fourth Estate, 1999), p. 433. Cf Eugene Waith: 'When Othello's nobility and idealism are underplayed, as they occasionally are, an important dimension of the play is lost' (*Ideas of Greatness: Heroic Drama in England* (London: Routledge & Kegan Paul, 1971), p. 105).

[74] Gardner, 'The Noble Moor', p. 174.

[75] *Nostromo: A Tale of the Seaboard* (Harmondsworth: Penguin, 1983), p. 188.

against a civilized code of conduct in a publicly convened court of law, but a heroic death that will leave his reputation intact.[76]

And as far as the characters who are left alive at the end of the play are concerned it *is* intact. Emilia is the one person who openly voices her disgust at Othello's behaviour: 'O gull, O dolt, / As ignorant as dirt!' (v.ii.170–1). Is her exasperated outburst merely a hasty and understandably partisan response? Does Shakespeare intend us to respond sympathetically to Othello's heroic death? Kenneth Muir believes he does: 'when Othello or Antony makes his final apologia, these characters are not meant to be indulging in self-pity or vanity: they are used by the dramatist to guide the feelings of the audience'.[77] However, it is possible to read this final scene in another way. The fact that not one of the men on stage questions the honour code to which Othello appeals in justification of his actions may be meant not as an endorsement of heroic masculinity, but as an ironic comment both on the power of charismatic heroism to inveigle its admirers, and on the potential for political destabilization which that ideal had recently demonstrated in such a public way.

OTHELLO'S OCCUPATION

The hero we see in the first act of *Othello* may look like a noble savage, but as he degenerates from dignified general and loving husband to embittered avenger it is clear that the passions that drive him are more savage than noble. The point of Shakespeare's deflation of the sentimental ideal of primitive nobility is not to calumniate Moors, Turks, or any other racio-religious group, but rather to suggest the inherently barbaric nature of pre-civilized heroic values. To use a black man of Islamic origins to symbolize those values is dramaturgical shorthand. D.H. Lawrence used a similar device when he put Sir Clifford Chatterley in a wheelchair. Chatterley's physical immobility is not being used to make a

---

[76] John Holloway notes that Othello's final speech belongs to a clearly recognizable convention of heroic valediction (*The Story of the Night: Studies in Shakespeare's Major Tragedies* (London: Routledge & Kegan Paul, 1961), pp. 55–6); see also Peter Mercer, *'Othello* and the Form of Heroic Tragedy', *CQ*, 11 (1969), 45–61; Reuben A. Brower, *Hero and Saint: Shakespeare and the Graeco-Roman Heroic Tradition* (Oxford: Clarendon Press, 1971), pp. 29–30; James C. Bulman, *The Heroic Idiom of Shakespearean Tragedy* (Newark, N.J.: University of Delaware Press, 1985), pp. 123–4. The fact that Shakespeare is using a well worn convention does not of course necessarily mean that he is endorsing its values.

[77] Introduction to *Richard II* (New York: New American Library, 1963), p. xxxi.

statement about the disabled in modern society. It symbolizes rather the emotional paralysis of the man and what Lawrence believed was the parasitic character of the class he belongs to. The novel would probably have been a better one if Lawrence had dealt with the problem of women's sexual needs without recourse to such unsubtle symbolism. Shakespeare uses a comparably convenient symbol in *Othello*. In the twenty-first century it would be inexcusable to use an African to represent the darker side of human nature. But what rightly shocks a modern actor like Hugh Quarshie (see note 18 above) did not have the same meaning for an early-modern audience with no qualms whatsoever about crude racial stereotyping. Coleridge seems to have felt no embarrassment about voicing rooted objection to the idea of Shakespeare's hero being an African;[78] neither did Lamb, though he put the matter more delicately.[79] Even in the twentieth century A.C. Bradley was willing to admit that he found it 'monstrous' that we should be expected to believe that Desdemona could love a black man.[80] There is no evidence to suggest that four centuries ago playgoers were any more sensitive to racial issues than Bradley was. Queen Elizabeth felt sufficiently strongly about 'Negars and Blackamoors' to give orders for the city to be ethnically cleansed. Judging from his remarks about the primitive in his *Daemonologie* (1597) it would appear that James shared her distaste for people that she clearly regarded as savages. In 'the wild partes of the worlde', he wrote in his treatise on *Daemonologie*, 'the Devill findes greatest ignorance and barbaritie, there assayles he grosseliest'.[81] We also know that James disliked the heroic military values that very nearly resulted in the deposition of his predecessor in 1601 and that were to be the cause of such an embarrassingly public rift with his own son a few years later (see Chapter 5). The link between savagery and the heroic in *Othello* suggests that Shakespeare was also sceptical of those values. Into the mouth of his avenging hero he put what must be the most vivid evocation of heroic military values to be found anywhere in the period. Othello's

---

[78] *Coleridge's Shakespearean Criticism*, 2 vols., ed. T.M. Raysor (London: Dent, 1960), vol. 1, p. 42.
[79] Lamb wrote: 'I appeal to every one that has seen Othello played . . . whether he did not find something extremely revolting in the courtship and wedded caresses of Othello and Desdemona; whether the actual sight of the thing did not overweigh all the beautiful compromise we make in reading' (*Lamb as Critic*, ed. Roy Park (London and Henley: Routledge & Kegan Paul, 1980), p. 97).
[80] *Shakespearean Tragedy*, p. 165.
[81] James VI and I, *Daemonologie* (1597) (Edinburgh: Edinburgh University Press, 1966), p. 69.

response to the news that Desdemona has apparently been unfaithful to him sounds less like a lament for a loving wife than the kind of sentiments that Essex must have felt when he knew that he had destroyed his own career in a moment of irrevocable folly:

> Farewell the tranquil mind, farewell content,
> Farewell the plumèd troops and the big wars
> That makes ambition virtue! O, farewell,
> Farewell the neighing steed and the shrill trump,
> The spirit-stirring drum, th' ear-piercing fife,
> The royal banner, and all quality,
> Pride, pomp, and circumstance of glorious war!
> And O, you mortal engines whose rude throats
> Th' immortal Jove's dread clamours counterfeit,
> Farewell! Othello's occupation's gone. (III.iii.353–62)

Othello is at once an evocation of the persuasive power of heroic masculinity and a repudiation of a world of pre-civilized values that, in James' view at least, had no place in a post-humanist Europe. Opposed to war, as he was in principle, James would probably not have responded sympathetically to the idea of an 'erring barbarian' extolling the big wars that makes ambition virtue.

But though his own ambition was to see a Europe united by humanistic values, James shared Erasmus' belief that exceptions had to be made when it came to defending Christendom against the Turk (see Introduction, p. 13). Indeed the subject of his own *Lepanto* was the providential victory of Christian forces over barbarian hordes. *Othello* thus leaves us with a conundrum similar to that at the end of *Hamlet*. *Henry V* asks us to consider the paradox of an idealistic and highly capable Christian leader uniting his country in an expansionist European war that was to have disastrous consequences for England. But *Hamlet*, like *Othello*, is about a Christian community defending itself against pagan forces. In such circumstances a country needs strong leadership. With his military experience and knowledge of Cyprus, his 'unbookish' eloquence, and his commanding presence, Othello seems perfectly fitted for that role. Presumably Hamlet thinks that, despite his 'unimprovèd mettle', Fortinbras would be too. Yet in both plays the very qualities that ensure effective leadership in time of war are bound up with other traits that at times seem indistinguishable from the barbarism against which the civilized world is defending itself. In the next chapter I will deal with Shakespeare's treatment of the question of how far, and in what circumstances, it is legitimate to use violence in the pursuit of peaceful ends. In *Macbeth* that problem typically takes the form of a question that is implicit in *Hamlet* and *Othello*, but which the play's characters now address explicitly, namely, what it means to say of someone that he lived or died 'like a man' (*Mac.*, v.xi.9).

CHAPTER 4

'Arms and the Man': *Macbeth*

> For I shall sing of Battels, Blood, and Rage,
> Which Princes, and their People did engage.
> Dryden's translation of Virgil's *Aeneid*, VII.60–1

> Blood hath been shed ere now, i' th' olden time,
> Ere human statute purged the gentle weal.
> *Macbeth*, III.iv.74–5

For a play designed to compliment a self-proclaimed anti-militarist, *Macbeth* has something decidedly odd about it. While apparently celebrating such eirenic 'king-becoming graces' as 'justice, verity, temp'rance, stableness, / Bounty, perseverence, mercy, lowliness, / Devotion, patience, courage, fortitude' (IV.iii.93–5), the play shows men defending those virtues, not with reluctant resort to force, or even 'industrious soldiership' (V.iv.16), but with vengeance, rage, and passionate violence. Symptomatic of this confusion of values is the appeal – repeated throughout the play – to manhood. For Lady Macbeth true manhood is synonymous with heroic violence; for Macduff manly valour must be tempered by the more 'civilized' virtues of feeling and compassion. But it is not just Macbeth and his wife who associate manliness with violence. Though the play's characters seem to be divided into those associated with 'Good things of day' and those who act as 'night's black agents' (III.ii.53–4), the former also think of true manhood in terms of violent action. This studied ambivalence on the question of manhood points to a larger ethical and political problem in *Macbeth*. Whether or not it is legitimate to use violence in the pursuit of peaceful ends is a question that preoccupied Elizabethan political writers (see Chapter 2, pp.70–1). It may be one reason why Virgil's *Aeneid* – another fictionalized national history offering an ambivalent view of manhood and warfare – seems to have spoken so directly to the early seventeenth century. The *Aeneid* was one of King James' favourite poems. Judging by the use he made of it in a number of plays, it was also a favourite of Shakespeare's. Together with Ovid's *Metamorphoses*[1] and Seneca's *Hercules furens*,[2] it forms a significant part of *Macbeth*'s intertextual provenance.

BLESSED ARE THE PEACEMAKERS

In *The Trew Law of Free Monarchies* King James argued that, because wicked kings are God's way of punishing a sinful people, rebellion can never be justified, even against a tyrannical ruler.[3] Applied to *Macbeth*, this principle means that, once Duncan has been assassinated and Macbeth crowned, those who oppose the new dispensation become rebels themselves against an anointed ruler. As if in confirmation of the anomaly, both sides justify their actions in terms of a heroic conception of manhood.

The heroic world of *Macbeth* is quickly established in Scene ii with the account of Macdonwald's death. The Captain who reports the event does not simply announce that the leader of the rebel forces has been killed by Macbeth. Echoing Virgil's description of Turnus' slaughter of Pandarus[4] – one of the bloodiest passages in the *Aeneid* –

---

[1] Zara Bruzzi, 'Instruments of Darkness: *Macbeth*, Ovid, and Jacobean Political Mythologies', *Shakespeare and History*, Shakespeare Yearbook 6, ed. Holger Klein and Rowland Wymer (Lewiston, Queenstown, and Lampeter: Edwin Mellen Press, 1996) pp. 215–44.

[2] Robert S. Miola, *Shakespeare and Classical Tragedy: The Influence of Seneca* (Oxford: Clarendon Press, 1992), pp. 92–121.

[3] James VI and I, *Political Writings*, ed. Johann P. Sommerville (Cambridge: Cambridge University Press, 1994), p. 79.

[4]
       sublatum alte consurgit in ensem
       et mediam ferro gemina inter tempora frontem
       dividit impubesque volnere malas.
       Fit sonus, ingenti concussa est pondere tellus;
       conlapsos artus atque arma cruenta cerebro
       sternit humi moriens atque illi partibus aequis
       huc caput atque illuc umero ex utroque pependit.

(*Aeneid*, IX.749–55, ed. H. Rushton Fairclough (London: Heinemann, 1922), pp. 162–4). Dryden translates these lines as follows:
       Then rising, on his utmost stretch he stood:
       And aim'd from high: the full descending blow
       Cleaves the broad Front, and beardless Cheeks in two:
       Down sinks the Giant with a thund'ring sound,
       His pond'rous Limbs oppress the trembling ground;
       Blood, Brains, and Foam, gush from the gaping Wound.
       Scalp, Face, and Shoulders, the keen Steel divides;
       And the shar'd Visage hangs on equal sides.

(*The Works of John Dryden*, 20 vols., ed. Edward Niles Hooker, Alan Roper, and H.T.

he describes, with the obscene detail of epic convention, how these two heroic warriors grappled with each other until the triumphant Macbeth had sliced open Macdonwald's head and torso like a butcher in an abattoir:

> brave Macbeth – well he deserves that name! -
> Disdaining fortune, with his brandished steel
> Which smoked with bloody execution,
> Like valour's minion
> Carved out his passage till he faced the slave,
> Which ne'er shook hands nor bade farewell to him
> Till he unseamed him from the nave to th' chops. (I.ii.16–22)

Just as Virgil recreates all the unconscionable horror of Homeric warfare by imitating the *Iliad*,[5] so Shakespeare evokes Virgil's epic style as a way of establishing Macbeth as a warrior of heroic *virtus*. It is that manly courage which Lady Macbeth questions when she challenges her husband on his reluctance to murder Duncan, asking him if he is afraid to turn words into action. Protesting that he 'dare do all that may become a man' (I.vii.46), Macbeth argues that there are bounds even to manly action: 'Who dares do more is none' (47). But she resists his suggestion of limit, implying that true manhood knows no bounds:

> When you durst do it, then you were a man;
> And to be more than what you were, you would
> Be so much more the man. (49–51)

During the banquet Lady Macbeth again questions her husband's courage, asking 'Are you a man?' (III.iv.57), and suggesting that there is something shameful in such womanish fear of ghosts:

> O, these flaws and starts,
> Impostors to true fear, would well become
> A woman's story at a winter's fire
> Authorized by her grandam. (62–5)

To Lady Macbeth there is something pitiful in the spectacle of a warrior thus 'unmanned in folly' (72). Again, Macbeth protests his masculine courage: 'What man dare, I dare' (98). But it is not until

---

Swedenborg, Jr. (Berkeley, Los Angeles, and London: University of California Press, 1956–89), vols. v–vi (ed. William Frost, 1987), vol. vi, p. 673.)
[5] On Virgil's debt to Homer see W.K. Gransden, *Virgil's 'Iliad': An Essay on Epic Narrative* (Cambridge: Cambridge University Press, 1984).

the ghost has disappeared that he feels his courage return: 'Why, so, being gone, / I am a man again' (106–7).

In *Hamlet* Christian-Stoic values are contrasted with those of a heroic society. One might have expected to see a similar antinomy in *Macbeth*, with the usurper's opponents subscribing to principles that are the antithesis of his own. But this is not the case. As he seeks to oust his father's murderer, Malcolm shares Macbeth's sense of the need to combat treason with 'manly readiness' (II.iii.32). The man destined to kill Scotland's warrior–tyrant is Macduff. What provides Macduff with the personal motive for tyrannicide is the murder of his wife and children. But without Malcolm's incitement to vengeance it is doubtful whether this gentle and unwarlike noble would have had the resolution to kill his country's enemy. When he learns of the slaughter of his family Macduff is at first too stunned to speak, so Malcolm urges him to give voice to his feelings:

> What, man, ne'er pull your hat upon your brows.
> Give sorrow words. The grief, that does not speak
> Whispers the o'er fraught heart, and bids it break.
>
> (IV.iii.209–11)

But Macduff can only whisper feebly, 'My children too? . . . My wife kill'd too?' (212; 214). When it is clear that there is no hope, Macduff is once more silent. So again Malcolm tries to stir him into action, urging him to turn grief to vengeance:

> Be comforted.
> Let's make us medicines of our great revenge
> To cure this deadly grief.   (214–16)

Roused by Malcolm's words, Macduff curses the tyrant who has destroyed his family. But even as he does so his thoughts turn tearfully to his 'pretty chickens, and their dam' (219), all slaughtered by Macbeth's hired murderers. When Malcolm tells him to confront his grief 'like a man', Macduff replies that he must also 'feel it as a man'; with these words he sinks into maudlin self-condemnation, blaming himself for the deaths of his wife and children:

> Sinful Macduff,
> They were all struck for thee. Naught that I am,
> Not for their own demerits but for mine
> Fell slaughter on their souls. Heaven rest them now.   (226–9)

Earlier in the scene Malcolm, mistrustful by now of all Scottish noblemen, had tested Macduff's integrity with an elaborate pretence of villainy, denying in effect all that he holds most dear. So great is the wickedness he feigns that he claims that in the pursuit of self interest he would not hesitate to turn universal peace into uproar and confound all unity on earth (100–1). Macduff is a natural appeaser, admitting that tyranny thrives on subjects' desire for self-preservation: 'Great tyranny . . . goodness dare not check thee!' (34–5). But not even he can submit to such villainy. When Macduff admits that he cannot follow so egregious a tyrant, Malcolm reveals the truth, confessing himself the dutiful servant of his country (115ff). But now, as he urges Macduff once more to avenge the murder of his family, the pacific virtues he had tacitly endorsed through his charade of denial are apparently forgotten: 'let grief / Convert to anger; blunt not the heart, enrage it', he tells Macduff (230–1). Shamed by Malcolm's words, Macduff at last resolves to seek out the murderer of his family and engage him in personal combat:

> Cut short all intermission. Front to front
> Bring thou this fiend of Scotland and myself.
> Within my sword's length set him.   (234–6)

These are the kind of heroic words that Malcolm had wanted to hear: 'This tune goes manly', he tells Macduff (237). Inflamed by Malcolm's violent words, Macduff resolves to seek out Macbeth on the battlefield, like Aeneas searching for Turnus.

In his final battle Macbeth fights with the same 'valiant fury' (v.ii.14) that had won him honour in his defeat of the rebel Macdonwald. But with 'revenges burn[ing]' in him (3), the enraged Macduff is his equal. Having defeated the usurper in personal combat, he presents Malcolm with the tyrant's severed head, crying 'the time is free' (v.ix.21). Malcolm answers him with a valedictory speech in which he speaks of the 'love', 'grace' and 'measure' that will be the keynotes of the new dispensation (27, 38–9). The contrast between the severed head, symbol of heroic violence, and Malcolm's pacific words echoes a similar contrast in the play's second scene. Duncan's response to the Captain's story of how Macbeth had 'unseamed' Macdonwald's body 'from the nave to th' chops' and fixed his head on the castle battlements is to praise him, not as the epitome of heroic valour, but as a 'worthy *gentle*man!' (24). The conventional honorific, invisible in normal use, is thrown into startling prominence by its incongruity. Where *Hamlet* shows us a hero torn between mutually incompatible value systems, *Macbeth* presents us with the paradox of men acting with heroic savagery in defence of eirenic principles.

`MACBETH´, KING JAMES, AND THE BRITISH MYTH

That Shakespeare's treatment of ethical and political problems is radically ambivalent is a commonplace of modern criticism. Rejecting E.M.W. Tillyard's view of Shakespeare as the patriotic upholder of supposedly orthodox political opinion, a long line of critics from Helen Gardner and A.P. Rossiter in the 1950s to Graham Bradshaw in 1987 and 1993 emphasized the dialectical structure of the plays (see Introduction, note 103). According to Norman Rabkin it is Shakespeare's ambivalence that puts the plays 'out of the reach of the narrow moralist, the special pleader for a particular ideology, the intellectual historian looking for a Shakespearean version of a Renaissance orthodoxy'.[6] Despite the repeated rejection, over four decades, of the notion of a politically orthodox Shakespeare acting as a spokesman for government opinion, Alan Sinfield insists that traditional Shakespearean criticism assumes that *Macbeth* is an endorsement of James I's character and policies.[7] Challenging this unidentified 'Jamesian reading' of the play, Sinfield proposes that *Macbeth* should be seen, not as an endorsement of James' character and policies, but as an implicit critique of state violence at a time of transition from feudalism to absolutism.[8] Because there are certain 'structural difficulties' inherent in the absolutist state (which Sinfield defines as 'the monarch versus the rest'),[9] tyrants must inevitably resort to force in order to suppress dissidents. James may have compared a king with a loving father caring for his children,[10] but, Sinfield argues, the benign image is misleading. In reality, there is little to choose between James and a tyrant like Macbeth. Just as Macbeth employs ruthless measures to maintain himself in power, so James could only survive by executing those who dared resist his rule: 'Macbeth is a murderer and oppressive ruler, but he is one version of [James] the absolutist ruler,

---

[6] Norman Rabkin, *Shakespeare and the Common Understanding* (1967; repr. Chicago and London: University of Chicago Press, 1984), p. 12.
[7] Alan Sinfield, 'Macbeth: History, Ideology, and Intellectuals' in *Faultlines: Cultural Materialism and the Politics of Dissident Reading* (Oxford: Clarendon Press, 1992), p. 99.
[8] 'Macbeth: History, Ideology, and Intellectuals', p. 95.
[9] Ibid., p. 98.
[10] *The Trew Law of Free Monarchies, Political Writings*, ed. Sommerville, p. 65.

not the polar opposite'.[11] 'Oppositional' readings which claim that *Macbeth* exposes the corruption of James' political and social world have now become, in effect, a new orthodoxy. For Terry Eagleton the play exposes 'a reverence for hierarchical order for what it is, as the pious self-deception of a society based on routine oppression and incessant warfare';[12] for Kiernan Ryan it is 'a fierce arraignment of one of the mainsprings of modern Western society . . . the ideology and practice of individualism'.[13]

Sinfield's picture of a Macbeth-like tyrant meting out savage reprisals to dissidents who tried to resist state oppression is an extreme form of the traditional view of James as intransigent autocrat. It is a view that originated in the work of James' own contemporaries. Three books in particular were responsible for the traditional negative view of James: Sir Anthony Weldon's *Court and Character of King James* (1650), Arthur Wilson's *The Life and Reign of King James* (1653), and Francis Osborne's *Traditional Memoirs of the Reigns of Queen Elizabetha and King James the First* (1658). Weldon was a disaffected courtier; Wilson and Osborne were aristocratic opponents of James. Not published until after Charles' execution, their books were welcomed by republicans seeking to justify the overthrow of the monarchy. It was their negative picture of James that formed the basis of Macaulay's familiar character assassination. Macaulay's caricature of the 'stammering, slobbering [pedant] shedding unmanly tears, trembling at a drawn sword, and talking in the style alternately of a buffoon and a pedagogue'[14] survived unchallenged until comparatively recently.[15] However, over the past twenty years revisionist historians have produced a very different picture of England's first Stuart king.

James may have sounded like an autocrat in *The Trew Law of Free Monarchies*, but revisionists argue that, for all his faults, he was an astute and humane politician who, unlike Elizabeth, combined a grasp of abstract theory with an ability to work with radicals who were opposed to his ideal of Christian unity.[16] Indeed it is ironic, in view of Sinfield's objections to James' allegedly savage treatment of

---

[11] Sinfield, 'Macbeth: History, Ideaology and Intellectuals', p. 102.
[12] Terry Eagleton, *William Shakespeare* (Oxford: Basil Blackwell, 1986), p. 2.
[13] Kiernan Ryan, *Shakespeare*, 2nd edn. (New York and London: Prentice Hall, 1995), p. 93.
[14] *The History of England from the Accession of James the Second*, 8 vols. (London: Longman, Brown, Green, 1858–62), vol. 1 (1858), p. 76.
[15] Roger Lockyer, *James VI and I* (London and New York: Longman, 1998), pp. 1–6.
[16] Kenneth Fincham and Peter Lake, 'The Ecclesiastical Policy of James I', *JBS*, 24 (1985),

religious dissidents, that one of the causes of friction between him and parliament was his policy of accommodating extreme religious elements in the state. Far from persecuting Catholics, he consulted with them, employed them as ambassadors, and even knighted them. It was only those who supported the pope's call to Catholics to depose their king whom he was determined to exclude. Even after the Gunpowder Plot he continued to resist parliamentary demands for a harsher policy towards Catholics. Jenny Wormald notes that, at a time when Catholics had for half a century been oppressed, dispossessed, and disfranchised, James was unusually humane.[17] According to an interpretation promoted by James and his advisors, the Gunpowder Plot was the work of Antichrist aimed at destroying the Reformation in England and averting a predestined union of kingdoms that had been foretold by ancient prophecy.[18] To twenty-first-century minds this might sound like ideological mystification. But James had good reasons for believing that his escape was providential.

That James survived to manhood at all is something of a miracle. Indeed few public figures can have had such a terrible childhood. With his father murdered before he was a year old, probably with the connivance of his mother, James was effectively an orphan from the age of two. During a regency in which Scotland was at times close to anarchy, he was the subject of repeated kidnappings and plots against his life. These were not popular uprisings, but sectarian feuds between violent nobles determined to wrest control from James' regents. Little wonder that, despite the watering down of James' original plan for a perfect union of the two kingdoms,[19] the mood of the English parliament was opposed to formal ties with what what was perceived as a barbaric nation,[20] and that full union did not take place until 1707. Nor is it surprising that James was so

169–207. See also Marc L. Schwarz, 'James I and the Historians: Toward a Reconsideration', *JBS*, 13 (1974), 114–34.

[17] Jenny Wormald, 'Gunpowder, Treason, and Scots', *JBS*, 24 (1985), 141–68.
[18] Garry Wills, *Witches and Jesuits: Shakespeare's 'Macbeth'* (New York and London: Oxford University Press, 1995), pp. 15–16. See also Lilian Winstanley, *'Macbeth', 'King Lear' and Contemporary History* (Cambridge: Cambridge University Press, 1922), p. 31.
[19] See Brian P. Levack, *The Formation of the British State: England, Scotland, and the Union 1603–1707* (Oxford: Clarendon Press, 1987), p. 8.
[20] On the constitutional debate over the question of union see Levack, *The Formation of the British State*, pp. 31–4; Jenny Wormald, 'One King, Two Kingdoms' in *Uniting the Kingdom: The Making of British History*, ed. Alexander Grant and Keith J. Stringer (London and New York: Routledge, 1995), pp. 123–32.

deeply shocked when, in circumstances eerily similar to those in which his own father had died, yet another Catholic plot against his life was discovered in 1605. Since he narrowly escaped so many plots both in childhood and maturity, it is understandable that he should have feared a repetition of his father's fate. In an age when typology was still a key to the understanding of history, it is perhaps inevitable that the parallels between his father's death and his own apparently providential escape from a similar fate should have convinced him that the powers of darkness were in league against him, and more importantly, that heaven was protecting him.

When Elizabethan writers revived the myth of Britain's Trojan origins and traced the queen's ancestry back to the legendary Brutus, great-grandson of Aeneas, they conflated the Troy story with the prophecies of Virgil's fourth *Eclogue*: Astraea had returned to the earth, and Troynovaunt was about to witness a restoration of the legendary golden age of antiquity.[21] Like Elizabeth, James actively cultivated the British Myth.[22] The Astraea story had suited Elizabeth perfectly because, as a woman, she could be represented as a reincarnation of the virgin goddess of justice. James could not represent himself as Astraea, though she was a prominent symbolic figure in his pageants. But there was an important ingredient in the British Myth that did suit his purposes. According to Arthurian legend, the country would be reunited and Arthur's empire would live again when the ancient British line was restored. That myth could be made to serve the cause of his own commitment to unification of the two kingdoms. On 17 April 1603 the Venetian Secretary in London reported: 'It is said that he is disposed to abandon the titles of England and Scotland, and to call himself King of Great Britain, and like that famous and ancient King Arthur to embrace under one name the whole circuit of one thousand seven hundred mile which includes the United Kingdom now possessed by His Majesty in that island'.[23] When James visited Oxford in 1605,

[21] A.E. Parsons, 'The Trojan Legend in England', *MLR*, 24 (1929), 243–64; Edwin Greenlaw, *Studies in Spenser's Historical Allegory* (Baltimore: Johns Hopkins University Press, 1932); Charles Bowie Millican, *Spenser and the Table Round* (Cambridge, Mass.: Harvard University Press, 1932); Sydney Anglo, 'The British Myth in Early Tudor Propaganda', *BJRL*, 44 (1951), 17–48; S.K. Heninger Jr., 'The Tudor Myth of Troy-novaunt', *SAQ*, 61 (1962), 378–87.

[22] See Millican, *Spenser and the Table Round*, pp. 127–41; Graham Parry, *The Golden Age Restor'd: The Culture of the Stuart Court, 1603–42* (Manchester: Manchester University Press, 1981), pp. 1–39.

[23] *Calendar of State Papers* (Venetian), 17 April 1603.

Matthew Gwynne, the University's first Professor of Physic, flattered the king's interest in his own genealogy with some Latin verses which reminded him of the legend that fate had foretold that Banquo's descendants would be the inheritors of an 'endless empire' (*imperium sine fine*).[24] Though Gwynne did not mention Macbeth, his reign was of particular interest to contemporary historians because it represented a turning point in Scottish history when the old anarchic tanistry system of elective succession gave way to a stable hereditary monarchy. By attempting to avert destiny, Macbeth himself was ironically instrumental in ensuring that Merlin's prophecy of a united kingdom would be realized. In *Poly-Olbion* Drayton explained how, by murdering Banquo and causing Fleanch (Shakespeare's Fleance) to flee to Wales, Macbeth was indirectly responsible for bringing about a marriage that would unite the houses of Plantagenet and Tudor. For Fleanch married the daughter of Llewellin, the Prince of Wales. His descendant, Henry VII, married Elizabeth of York, and it was their eldest daughter, Margaret, who married James IV.[25] James could thus claim both to unite the houses of York and Lancaster, and to restore the ancient British line. In his 1603 panegyric on 'The Majesty of King James' Drayton praised England's new king as the fulfilment of Merlin's prophecy of a reunited Britain.

> An ancient Prophet long agoe fore-told,
> (Though fooles their sawes for vanities doe hold)
> A King of Scotland, ages comming on,
> Where it was found, be crown'd upon that stone,
> Two famous Kingdoms seperate thus long,
> Within one Iland, and that speake one tongue,
> Since *Brute* first raign'd, (if men of *Brute* alow)
> Never before united untill now.[26]

By revealing the Gunpowder Plot and thwarting the Antichrist, providence had clearly signalled its protection of a prince predestined to bring peace to a warring world.[27]

---

[24] Quoted by Henry N. Paul, *The Royal Play of 'Macbeth'* (1948; repr. New York: Octagon Books, 1971), p. 163.
[25] *The Works of Michael Drayton*, 5 vols., ed. J. William Hebel (Oxford: Basil Blackwell, 1931–41), vol. IV (1933), p. 167.
[26] 'To the Majesty of King James', 133–40, *The Works*, vol. I (1931), p. 474.
[27] Wills, *Witches and Jesuits: Shakespeare's 'Macbeth'*, p. 16.

AUGUSTUS REDIVIVUS

Addressing parliament in March 1604 James reminded the house of his grand political ambition. 'At my comming here,' he told the Commons, 'I found the State embarqued in a great and tedious warre, and onely by mine arrivall here, and by the Peace in my Person, is now amitie kept, where warre was before.'[28] In contrast to Essex, who in his *Apologie* of 1598 had evoked the warlike spirit of Henry V and compared the unheroic present with 'those former gallant ages' when England did not hesitate to 'atchieve great conquests in Fraunce' (see Introduction, note 60), James represented himself as a prince of peace.[29] In doing so he was consciously rejecting the traditional image of the heroic prince promoted by the Elizabethan war party. Though there was wide support for the 1604 settlement with Spain, the chivalric ideals espoused by Essex were by no means dead.[30] To win over opponents of his pacifist policies James drew, as Elizabeth's poets had done in support of hers, on the resources of myth and historical analogy. But where Spenser had celebrated England's imperial aspirations in the figure of a fully armed warrior–maiden, James turned not to medieval chivalry, but to the classical world for his image of the ideal prince.

The unifying theme of James' coronation entry was peace, symbolized by the goddess Eirene, with Mars at her feet, 'his armour scattered upon him in severall pieces, and sundrie sorts of weapons broken about him'.[31] Amplifying this theme was a series of interlocking motifs from classical, biblical, and British mythology. In his notes for the pageant Dekker rehearsed the myth, told by Drayton in his poem on 'The Majesty of King James', of how the old kingdom of Britain that had been divided by Brutus in ancient times would one day be reunited. That prophecy had now been fulfilled. Through James Britain's empire has been restored: 'All are againe

---

[28] *Political Writings*, ed. Sommerville, pp. 133–4.
[29] Parry, *The Golden Age Restor'd*, p. 4.
[30] Malcolm Smuts, 'Cultural Diversity and Cultural Change at the Court of James I' in *The Mental World of the Jacobean Court*, ed. Linda Levy Peck (Cambridge: Cambridge University Press, 1991), p. 110. See also Norman Council, 'Ben Jonson, Inigo Jones, and the Transformation of Tudor Chivalry', *ELH*, 47 (1980), 259–75.
[31] 'Part of the Kings entertainment, in passing to his Coronation', *Ben Jonson*, 11 vols, ed. C.H. Herford and Percy and Evelyn Simpson (Oxford: Clarendon Press, 1925–52), vol. VII (1941), p. 97.

united and made One'.³² Combining biblical and British myth, Dekker explained how Troynovaunt, the mythical new Troy built by Brutus in the old kingdom of Albion, had now become a 'Sommer Arbour' and 'Bridall Chamber' ready to receive its new bridegroom. In an allusion to John 3:29, James was invited to 'Come . . . as a glorious Bridegroome through your Royall Chamber'.³³

In his 1604 speech to parliament James himself adapted the biblical theme of Christ as husband of the church when he declared that he was wedded to the state: 'What God hath conjoyned . . . let no man separate. I am the Husband, and all the whole Isle is my lawfull Wife'.³⁴ The marriage theme was elaborated in the fifth of the triumphal arches that marked James' progress through the city. Dekker's notes describe the clusters of exotic fruits, flowers, and vegetables that decorated the fifth arch and the figures that peopled it. Chief among these were Eirene and Euporia, goddesses of peace and plenty. Eirene had a garland of olive and laurel branches, a dove on her lap, and other 'ensignes and furnitures of Peace'; Euporia wore a crown of poppy and mustard seed, 'the antique badges of Fertilitie and Abundance', and held a cornucopia filled with flowers and fruits.³⁵ Developing the two motifs of James as both biblical bridegroom and restorer of the ancient British dynasty, the fifth coronation arch celebrated the idea of a fruitful marriage of kingdoms that promised to restore a golden age of peace and plenty.

James' coronation pageant was rich in biblical and classical allusion. But in addition to the mythical figures that adorned the mock-Roman triumphal arches there was a powerful historical figure whose presence was implied by the pageantry. That figure was Augustus, or rather Augustus as portrayed by James' favourite poet, Virgil. In his collection of sonnets of 1584 James had immodestly compared himself with the author of the *Aeneid*. Favour me with your blessing, he tells the Muses in the well worn epideictic formula, and my verse will record your praise: 'I shall your names from all oblivion bring. / I lofty *Virgill* shall to life restore'.³⁶ The claim was nothing if not audacious: James was to combine the roles of royal

---

[32] Thomas Dekker, *The Whole Magnifycent Entertainment Given to King James* (London, 1604), Sig. I.
[33] Ibid., Sigs. F3–F3ᵛ.
[34] *Political Writings*, ed. Sommerville, p. 136.
[35] Dekker, *The Whole Magnifycent Entertainment*, Sigs. Gᵛ-G2.
[36] 'The Essayes of a Prentice' (1584), *The Poems of James VI of Scotland*, ed. James Craigie (Edinburgh and London: William Blackwood, 1955), p. 14.

patron and national poet. It was fitting therefore that prophetic motifs from Virgil should be a key element in his coronation pageant.[37]

Writing during the peace that followed the civil wars that had plagued the last years of the Republic, Virgil had represented his patron as a descendant of the gods, destined to pacify a warring world. In the great visionary speech in the sixth book of the *Aeneid* Anchises interprets for his son the significance of the long line of descendants passing before him, explaining, in an allusion to the famous prophetic lines of the fourth *Eclogue*, that the final figure in the procession was

> *Caesar* himself, exalted in his Line;
> *Augustus*, promis'd oft, and long foretold,
> Sent to the realm that *Saturn* rul'd of old;
> Born to restore a better Age of Gold.[38]

Spenser had already firmly re-established the myth of Britain's Trojan origins in the national mind. What better way for James to confirm his own credentials as a peacemaker than to suggest typological parallels with Augustus, most illustrious descendant of the Trojan remnant, one branch of which had colonized Albion? Because legend had it that James' 'Grandsire Brute',[39] the legendary founder of the ancient kingdom of Britain, was himself descended from Aeneas, it meant that James could, in a poetic fiction, claim lineal descent from Troy. Developing this Virgilian allusion, Dekker quoted the famous lines from the fourth *Eclogue* – 'Iam redit et virgo, redeunt Saturnia regna' – in which Virgil imagines Astraea returning to the earth under a new enlightened dispensation.[40] Dekker claimed that the 'fruitfull glories' of the newly united Britain 'shine so far and even, / They touch not onely earth, but they kisse heaven, / From whence Astraea is descended hither'.[41] In his own notes for the coronation pageant, Jonson also quoted the talismanic phrase, 'redeunt Saturnia regna', adding, 'out of *Virgil*, to shew that now those golden times were returned againe'.[42]

Taking their cue from these public hints, court poets dutifully

[37] See Parry, *The Golden Age Restor'd*, p. 4.
[38] *Aeneid*, VI.1078–81, *The Works of John Dryden*, ed. Hooker, Roper and Swedenborg, vol. V, p. 564.
[39] Dekker, *The Whole Magnifycent Entertainment*, Sig. F^v.
[40] Ibid., Sig. H4^v.
[41] Ibid., Sig. I.
[42] 'Part of the Kings entertainment', p. 100.

confirmed the parallel between Augustus and their own prince of peace. 'Renowned Prince,' wrote Drayton in his panegyric to James,

> when all these tumults cease,
> Even in the calme, and Musick of thy peace,
> If in thy grace thou deigne to favour us,
> And to the Muses be propitious,
> Caesar himselfe, Roomes glorious wits among,
> Was not so highly, nor divinely sung.[43]

Some years later, in *Prince Henry's Barriers* (1610), Jonson again evoked Virgilian parallels in his celebration of James' historic destiny:

> Here are kingdoms mixed
> And nations joined, a strength of empire fixed
> Coterminate with heaven; the golden vein
> Of Saturn's age is here broke out again.
> Henry but joined the roses ensigned
> Particular families, but this hath joined
> The rose and thistle, and in them combined
> A union that shall never be declined.[44]

The public message was clear: just as the god-like Augustus was the subject of ancient prophecy, destined by providence to bring Rome's internal wars to an end and restore the golden age, so James fulfilled the ancient British prophecy of a king who would reconcile international conflicts, reunite the kingdom, and usher in an age of universal peace. The grand historical plan that had begun with Troy was about to be completed: 'redeunt Saturnia regna'.

VIRGIL'S AMBIVALENCE

It is easy to see why the *Aeneid* should have appealed so strongly to James. Here was a poem about his favourite themes: prophecy, empire, the predestined peacemaker, the return of a golden age. But though Rome's imperial destiny may be Virgil's grand theme, the *Aeneid* is a deeply ambivalent poem. At its centre is a conundrum. The *pax romana* – ultimate justification for the wars that took place so many centuries ago in Latium – was bought at a terrible cost. For Roman imperialists the justification of war was peace.[45] In the *De*

---

[43] 'To the Majesty of King James', lines 159–60, p. 475.
[44] Ben Jonson, *The Complete Masques*, ed. Stephen Orgel (New Haven, Conn. and London: Yale University Press, 1969), lines 331–8, p. 155.
[45] R.O.A.M. Lyne, 'Vergil and the Politics of War', in *Oxford Readings in Vergil's 'Aeneid'*, ed. S.J.

Officiis Cicero argued that wars were to be undertaken for one reason alone, namely, 'that without injury we may live in peas'.⁴⁶ Like Cicero, Virgil justified war in terms of its results: from the conquest of Latium there would follow in the distant future a time when

> dire Debate, and impious War shall cease,
> And the stern Age be softned into Peace:
> Then banish'd Faith shall once again return,
> And Vestal Fires in hallow'd Temples burn. (1.396)

Virgil portrays Aeneas, not as a latter-day Homeric hero glorying in his martial skills, but as a reluctant warrior, disinclined to engage in battle, and piously accepting his role as the instrument of destiny. In complete contrast is Turnus, the very type of unreflecting *furor* full of 'Revenge, and jealous Rage, and secret Spight' (XII.110).

In an interesting discussion of the *Aeneid* Gary Schmidgall reminds us of the connotations of Virgil's antinomies: *pietas* – the virtue conventionally associated with Aeneas – implies the dutiful subjugation of personal feelings to a higher cause, while *furor* signifies those forces that threaten civilized order. 'In the *Aeneid*', writes Schmidgall, 'the "furious" are invariably at odds with the "pious" . . . Virgil's is a world of political absolutes in which good and evil are easily discerned. On the side of civic decency and harmony is Aeneas. On the other side are Juno and her factors Dido, Turnus, and Alecto.'⁴⁷ It is true that the *Aeneid* is built on a symbolic contrast between chaos, represented by the fall of Troy, and order, signified by the founding of a new civilization. But Virgil's binary oppositions do not work in the neat way that Schmidgall describes. One of the great ironies of the *Aeneid* is that, as his final encounter with Turnus draws near, Aeneas seems increasingly to take on the characteristics of his aggressive adversary. When, in violation of the league established with Latinus, fighting breaks out once more between Trojans and Rutulians, Aeneas appeals to his compatriots to 'cease / From impious arms, nor violate the Peace' (XII.473–4). This is the 'pious Aeneas' of medieval and Renaissance iconography, the epitome of wise and responsible leadership. But even while Aeneas is addressing his troops, he is hit by an arrow. The fragile truce is broken, and Turnus, like some terrible god of war, wreaks havoc on the battlefield. As Aeneas, his wound now healed by Venus, seeks out his rival, there is apparently little to choose between the two men: 'With like impetuous Rage the Prince appears . . . nor less Destruction bears' (XII.671–2). But more atrocities are to be committed before the two men finally meet in battle. Incensed by what he sees as the treachery of the Rutulians, Aeneas resolves to raze their 'perjur'd City' (XII.837). While the battle continues to rage, the unprotected city is an easy target. 'Gaping, gazing Citizens' (XII.844) are killed in cold blood, and their houses set on fire. The destruction complete, Aeneas then appeals to the gods in an act of bizarre self-justification:

> Advancing to the Front, the Heroe stands,
> And stretching out to Heav'n his Pious Hands;
> Attests the Gods, asserts his Innocence,
> Upbraids with breach of Faith th' Ausonian Prince:
> Declares the Royal Honour doubly stain'd,
> And twice the Rites of holy Peace profan'd.   (XII.849–54).

As in *Henry V*, the contrast between the reality of war and the pious sentiments that are used to justify it are too sharply and too shockingly juxtaposed to be ignored. Virgil does not comment on the irony, but sustains it unresolved to the very end of the poem.

The outcome of the contest with Turnus is decided by fate: Jupiter and Juno agree that, if Aeneas is allowed to win, the Latins will be permitted to keep their name, their customs, and their language. For a time it looks as if our final view of Aeneas will be that of the humane military leader reasserting civilized values as the conflict is at last concluded. As he stands over his defeated enemy, he hesitates, torn between vengeance and mercy:

> In deep Suspence the Trojan seem'd to stand;
> And just prepar'd to strike repress'd his Hand.
> He rowl'd his Eyes, and ev'ry Moment felt
> His manly Soul with more Compassion melt.   (XII.1360–3)

But in the very act of sparing his rival in love and war, he happens, by another trick of fate, to catch sight of the belt that Turnus had earlier torn from Aeneas' dead friend Pallas on the battlefield. In a moment of blind rage Aeneas plunges his sword deep into Turnus' heart. The poem that had set out to celebrate Rome's imperial destiny and to honour the man who epitomized the superiority of eirenic values thus ends with a vision, not of universal peace, but of primal savagery.

When Virgil died the *Aeneid* was unfinished, and the final scene is probably not how he planned to end the poem. Nevertheless, the image of 'pious Aeneas' plunging his sword into the heart of a disarmed and helpless enemy is a fitting emblem for the whole poem. The *Aeneid* is not simply a celebration of 'the long Glories of Majestick Rome'; it is also about 'Arms, and the Man'. Cicero argued that true valour will never allow itself to be contaminated by frenzy, 'for there is no bravery that is devoid of reason'.[48] In an ideal world no doubt this is true. But for all the idealistic sentiments of the *Aeneid*'s most celebrated passages about Rome's imperial destiny, the military world that Virgil portrays is far from ideal. As he represents it, 'Arms' is inevitably a savage business, and the 'Man' who becomes involved in it, however unwillingly, is unavoidably contaminated by its brutality. Where imperial apologists like Cicero justified war in terms of its results, Virgil shows that one cannot employ violence in defence of peace without somehow compromising the values one is defending.

'MACBETH' AS ROYAL COMPLIMENT

How far James was aware of these anomalous elements in the *Aeneid* we cannot tell. We do know, however, that he was both a genuine peacemaker whose dearest ambition was to see a united Europe, and also a realist who knew that a militaristic aristocracy must be controlled. Contrary to the impression that Sinfield gives of a tyrant determined at whatever cost to hang on to power in the face of popular unrest, James actually enjoyed considerable popularity in the early part of his reign. After the deep disaffection that characterized the final years of Elizabeth's reign with the inbred factionalism of the court and the aggressively militant nationalism fostered by the war party,[49] James' manifest desire to promote 'pietie, peace and learning'[50] was widely welcomed. At a time, moreover, when the

---

[48] *Tusculan Disputations*, trans. J.E. King (London and New York: Heinemann (London) and Putnam (New York), 1927), IV.xxii, p. 383.
[49] See Joel Hurstfield, 'The Succession Struggle in late Elizabethan England' in Elizabethan Government and Society, ed. S.T. Bindoff, J. Hurstfield, and C.H. Williams (London: Athlone Press, 1961), pp. 369–96.
[50] *Basilicon Doron, Political Writings*, ed. Sommerville, p. 27.

English had recently had cause for extreme anxiety over the problem of uncertain succession, his direct descent from Banquo, unrivalled in length by any English dynasty, represented a real hope of political stability.[51] In *Basilicon Doron* James characterized the wise ruler as one who tempers justice with mercy, and who respects parliament as 'the honourablest and highest judgment in the land'.[52] At the same time he emphasized the importance of limiting the power of anarchic elements in the state. Having been a victim himself of the 'rough wooing' of Scotland during the Reformation, it is not surprising that he had little time for 'the fierie spirited men in the ministerie [who] got such a guiding of the people at that time of confusion'.[53] But James was equally contemptuous of the nobility who justified violence as a legitimate way of defending personal and family honour. He wrote:

The naturall sickenesse that I have perceived this estate subject to in my time, hath beene, a fectlesse arrogant conceit of their greatnes and power; drinking in with their very nourish-milke, that their honor stood in committing three points of iniquitie: to thrall by oppression, the meaner sort that dwelleth neere them . . . to maintain their servants and dependers in any wrong . . . and . . . to bang it out bravely, hee and all his kinne, against him and all his [kin].[54]

Applied to questions of foreign policy, it was this same honour code that led Essex to propose the opening up of a potentially disastrous land war with Spain. In *Basilicon Doron* James comes across as a pragmatic realist, naturally favouring peace, but recognizing the need to curb the violence of aggressive aristocrats eager for war. It is these problems that Shakespeare turns into dialectical drama.

In presenting James with an 'imperial theme' (1.iii.128) featuring a history of his own ancestors, Shakespeare, like Virgil, makes use of prophecy and fate. Despite the epic style of the second scene and the allusion to Virgil in Act 1 Scene iii,[55] the *Aeneid* is not a source for *Macbeth* in the way that it is clearly for *Titus Andronicus*, and less

---

[51] 'In what part of the world,' asked George Marcelline, 'is to be found, so long a succession of Kinges in the right line, without interruption or breach?' (*The Triumphs of James the First* (London, 1610), p. 59).
[52] *Basilicon Doron*, p. 21.
[53] Ibid., p. 26.
[54] Ibid., p. 28.
[55] 'Strange images of death' (1.iii.97) echoes Virgil's 'plurima mortis imago', *Aeneid*, 11.369 (*Virgil*, revised edn., 2 vols., trans. H. Rushton Fairclough (London: Heinemann, 1935–6), vol. 1 (1935), p. 318).

clearly for *The Tempest*.⁵⁶ However, it is apparent from the Virgilian allusions in his coronation pageant that James was interested in the poem's epideictic possibilities. Shakespeare puts those possibilities to use in his own dramatic compliment to a new monarch. As Virgil recreated the world of heroic epic from the perspective of a latter-day urban civilization, so *Macbeth* looks back from the modern world to the founding moment of the present dynasty in a barbarous, heroic age. Macbeth's talk of blood having been shed in 'th' olden time, / Ere human statute purged the gentle weal' (III.iv.74–5) seems incongruous coming, as it does, from a warrior-member of a heroic society. But it evokes very vividly the sense that James must have had, as he watched the play, of an heroic culture viewed from the relatively civilized present. And as the *Aeneid* compliments Augustus by showing him a prophetic vision of himself, 'promis'd oft, and long foretold', so Shakespeare alludes to the Virgilian idea of a time of 'universal peace' (IV.iii.99). Like Virgil, he offers his patron oblique compliment in the form of a parade of kings stretching out to the crack of doom and culminating in a vision of his own coronation (IV.i.128–40).

For Macbeth the Virgilian parallels are of course ironic. Where Anchises presents his son with a vision of his own descendants, the witches taunt Macbeth with the 'horrible sight' (IV.i.138) of another man's royal progeny. By causing Banquo's son to escape into exile where, like Aeneas, he would marry a foreign princess, Macbeth is the unwitting agent of that historical destiny. While Banquo will be 'the root and father / Of many kings' (III.i.5–6), the 'unlineal' Macbeth's own crown will be 'fruitless' and his sceptre 'barren' (62–4). In James' coronation pageant Euporia's cornucopia symbolized the idea of a fecund marriage between England and her new bridegroom. In another metaphor James was compared to a sun 'whose new beames make our Spring'.⁵⁷ The coronation theme of spring-time renewal is echoed in the fourth act of *The Winter's Tale*, where Perdita plays the part of Flora, seeming to re-enact the Proserpina myth (IV.iv). It is also echoed in Juno's song of 'barns and

---

⁵⁶ See Heather James, 'Cultural Disintegration in *Titus Andronicus*: Mutilating Titus, Vergil and Rome', *TD*, 13 (1991), 123–40. For discussion of Shakespeare's use of the *Aeneid* in *The Tempest*, see Chapter 6, n.39. See also Robert S. Miola, *Shakespeare's Rome* (Cambridge: Cambridge University Press, 1983), *passim*; John W. Velz, '"Cracking Strong Curbs Asunder": Roman Destiny and the Roman Hero in *Coriolanus*', *ELR*, 13 (1983), 58–69.

⁵⁷ Dekker, *The Whole Magnifycent Entertainment*, Sig. G4ᵛ.

garners never empty' in *The Tempest* (IV.i.111). In *Macbeth* too there are repeated images of springtime, procreation, and harvest. House martins build their 'procreant cradles' under the eaves of Macbeth's castle where 'heaven's breath / Smells wooingly' (I.vi.4–10); images of planting, growth, and harvest (I.iv.28–33) are used to suggest that the bond between king and subject – another favourite theme of James'[58] – is as natural as the cycle of the seasons; a crowned baby with a tree in its hand symbolizes the future birth of a new kingdom (s.d. following IV.i.102).[59] Duncan and Banquo's images of planting and growth are picked up by Malcolm in the final scene of the play: 'What's more to do, / Which would be planted newly with the time . . . We will perform in measure, time, and place' (V.xi.30–9).

These natural processes are corrupted or perverted by Macbeth and his wife. The house martins, traditional symbol of innocence deceived,[60] have made their nests in a place of death; 'innocent flowers' have serpents under them (I.v.64–5); honoured guests are 'provided for' with daggers (66). In this world of inverted values, where even a suckling infant can have its brains dashed out as a sacrifice to ambition (I.vii.54–7), Macbeth is associated with crows, bats, beetles, and other things of 'yawning' night (III.ii.41–5). In contrast to the spring-making James entering into his flower-decked bridal bower, the 'unlineal' Macbeth has 'fallen into the sere, the yellow leaf' (V.iii.25). The effect of these images of fecundity and of nature perverted is both to compliment James by echoing one of the central themes of the coronation pageant, and to suggest the sacrilegious nature of regicide. Killing a king, the imagery implies, is a violation of one of nature's most sacred laws. To break that law is to invite catastrophe, as the play's unnatural portents imply (II.iii.53–60; II.iv.5–18). However, the fact that *Macbeth* appears to confirm James' own understanding of natural law does not mean that the play is a simple endorsement of his policies.

Recent historical criticism of *Macbeth* has focused on the early-

---

[58] The subtitle of *The Trew Law of Free Monarchies* is *The Reciprock and mutuall duetie betwixt a free King and his naturall Subjects*.

[59] D.J. Gordon interprets the figure of the crowned child in the North panel of Rubens' allegorical tribute to James in the Whitehall Banqueting House as the birth of a new united kingdom ('Rubens and the Whitehall Ceiling', *The Renaissance Imagination*, ed. Stephen Orgel (Berkeley, Los Angeles, and London: University of California Press, 1975) p. 40). It seems probable that Shakespeare intended a similar symbolism by the Third Apparition.

[60] Caroline Spurgeon, *Shakespeare's Imagery and What it Tells Us* (1935; repr. Cambridge: Cambridge University Press, 1990), pp. 187–8.

modern political debate on obedience and tyrannicide. David Norbrook and Alan Sinfield both read the play in the context of Buchanan's resistance theory.[61] The debate on resistance is certainly relevant to Shakespeare's only Scottish play. But unlike *Richard II* and *Henry IV*, where the problem is dramatized in such a way as to admit of no easy solution, *Macbeth* presents the question of resistance in more polarized form. For a playwright wanting to offer a defence of the right to resist tyranny, the Macbeth story that Shakespeare read in Holinshed would be suitable material, but not ideal: a strong and successful ruler deposes an ineffectual one and is himself deposed when, many years after the usurpation, he becomes tyrannical. Shakespeare modifies his principal source in two important ways. First, he telescopes the usurper's reign. He omits altogether Holinshed's account of the way Macbeth restores justice and law to the country,[62] and turns him instead into a stage villain – albeit a subtle and psychologically realistic one – linked with witches and all the gothic paraphernalia associated with them (in Holinshed they are described merely as 'three women ... resembling creatures of elder world').[63] Second, he transforms Duncan from a weak and ineffectual ruler who showed 'overmuch slacknesse in punishing offenders',[64] into a saintly martyr. The effect of this rewriting of the story is twofold: it intensifies the horror of regicide, but it also shows that a usurping tyrant must be removed. The first part of the play's political message is clearly in line with James' own ideas on kingship and obedience; the second is a contradiction of them. In this respect *Macbeth* is like *Cymbeline* and *The Tempest*, both of which pay compliment to James while at the same time offering oblique, but pointed criticism.[65] The problematic aspect of *Macbeth* is not, as in the English historical plays, its treatment of constitutional questions, but what it has to say about heroic manhood.

---

[61] David Norbrook, '*Macbeth* and the Politics of Historiography' in *Politics of Discourse: The Literature and History of Seventeenth-Century England*, ed. Kevin Sharpe and Steven N. Zwicker (Berkeley, Los Angeles, and London: University of California Press, 1987), pp. 78–116; Sinfield, 'Macbeth: History, Ideology, and Intellectuals'.

[62] *Holinshed's Chronicles*, revised edn. (1587) ed. John Vowell, 6 vols. (London, 1807–8), vol. v (1808), p. 266.

[63] Ibid., p. 268.

[64] Ibid., p. 265.

[65] See Peggy Muñoz Simonds, *Myth, Emblem, and Music in Shakespeare's 'Cymbeline': An Iconographic Reconstruction* (Newark, N.J.: University of Delaware Press, 1992); Robin Headlam Wells, *Elizabethan Mythologies: Studies in Poetry, Drama and Music* (Cambridge: Cambridge University Press, 1994), ch. 3.

SHAKESPEAREAN DIALECTIC

In Act III Scene vi we learn that Macduff has fled to England to enlist King Edward's support in the war against Macbeth (29–33). But Lady Macduff does not know this and cannot understand why her husband has apparently abandoned her and their children without telling her. Rosse tells her to be patient. But she is in no mood for patience: 'He had none. / His flight was madness' (IV.ii.3–4). Rosse tells her that it is impossible to say whether it was wisdom or fear that made him flee. She is incredulous: 'Wisdom,' she cries, 'to leave his wife, to leave his babes, / His mansion, and his titles in a place / From whence himself does fly?' (4–8). She then appeals to nature: 'He loves us not, / He wants the natural touch' (8–9). In Act I Scene vi Banquo had used the tranquil image of house martins building their 'pendent beds and procreant cradles' under the eaves of Macbeth's castle to evoke a sense of natural harmony. But now Lady Macduff uses the image of nesting birds to suggest that fighting too is natural:

> the poor wren,
> The most diminutive of birds, will fight,
> Her young ones in her nest, against the owl.
> All is the fear and nothing is the love;
> As little is the wisdom, where the flight
> So runs against all reason.   (9–14)

After some banter between Lady Macduff and her son about the prevalence of evil-doers in the world – grotesque in its seeming flippancy – a messenger brings news that her life is also at risk. 'Whither should I fly?' she asks herself,

> I have done no harm. But I remember now
> I am in this earthly world, where to do harm
> Is often laudable, to do good, sometime
> Accounted dangerous folly.   (74–8)

Lady Macduff has apparently been betrayed by a pusillanimous husband and now she and her children are about to be murdered by Macbeth's hired assassins. Her ironic words express a sense of the futility of a world in which all values have been, as Nietzsche would say, transvalued. But there is a larger sense in which what she says is potentially true, not just of Macbeth's tyrannical rule, but of any society. When, after testing Macduff's allegiance, Malcolm assures him of his own integrity, he tells him that the Earl of Northumberland, with 'ten thousand warlike men', is already on his way to give England's support to the rebel cause: 'Now we'll together', says Malcolm, 'and the chance of goodness / Be like our warranted quarrel' (IV.iii.135–8). For Lady Macduff the wren's right to fight the owl is indubitable; it is part of nature's law. But for Malcolm there are no certainties, only risks to be weighed in the balance: out of a bloody battle between thousands of 'warlike men' there is a chance that good will come; out of a 'warranted quarrel' with a tyrant – a warrant denied by James – a better order may emerge. Not surprisingly, Macduff's response is puzzlement: 'Such welcome and unwelcome things at once, / 'Tis hard to reconcile' (139–40).

These things are hard to reconcile because in the world of the play there are no certainties. There may be absolutes – 'justice, verity, temp'rance, stableness, / Bounty, perseverence, mercy, lowliness, / Devotion, patience, courage, fortitude' on one side, and Macbeth's violence on the other – but these binary opposites are not as mutually exclusive as the play's apocalyptic imagery would seem to suggest. *Macbeth* may appear to offer a stark contrast between 'Good things of day' and 'night's black agents', but at a deeper level these antinomies each embody rival virtues and vices that are incommensurable. The result is a world in which 'to do harm / Is often laudable, to do good, sometime / Accounted dangerous folly'. This ambivalence concerning fundamental values can be seen most clearly in the way the play's characters conceive of manhood.

Although Shakespeare's Duncan, unlike the 'feeble and slouthfull' king described by Holinshed,[66] is a saintly figure renowned for his piety, the play reminds us that this is a heroic age when Scotland was still at the mercy of warring nobles and Norse invaders. Its champion is a warrior of Homeric courage who disdains fortune (I.ii.17). When they are under pressure, it is not Malcolm's 'king-becoming graces', but heroic manhood that is of paramount concern to the actors in this drama of usurpation and rebellion; for heroes and villains alike, manhood is a way of defining virtue and integrity. And to be a man means to be 'bloody, bold and resolute' (IV.i.95). Among the soldiers killed in the play's final battle is young Siward, the Earl of Northumberland's son. Informing Siward's father, Rosse consoles the general with the thought that his son died a hero's death:

[66] *Holinshed's Chronicles*, p. 269.

> Your son, my Lord, has paid a soldier's debt.
> He only lived till he was a man,
> The which no sooner had his prowess confirmed,
> In the unshrinking station where he fought,
> But like a man he died. (v.xi.5–9)

But Old Siward is not satisfied and, like a Roman father, asks Rosse how his son died: 'Had he his hurts before?' Rosse confirms that they were indeed 'on the front' (12–13). Content that his son's death was that of a true hero, Old Siward's mind is now at rest:

> Why then, God's soldier be he.
> Had I as many sons as I have hairs
> I would not wish them to a fairer death. (13–15)

In the heroic world of *Macbeth* manhood is a kind of touchstone by which an individual's true worth can be measured. What defines and characterizes this quality is above all prowess in battle; to die a hero's death is confirmation of manhood. Yet each time the term is used it generates more anomalies. On hearing of Macbeth's heroic exploits on a Golgotha-like battlefield, the saint-like Duncan praises him for his gentlemanly honour; yet Golgotha, the place of the skull, is renowned solely for the death of a famous pacifist. When Macbeth tests the resolve of his hired murderers, asking them if they are so patient, and so steeped in the Gospels, that they are afraid of violence, they boast, 'We are men' (III.i.92); yet Malcolm too urges Macduff not to shrink from 'manly' violence. Lady Macbeth and Lady Macduff both appeal to an heroic conception of manhood; yet one is urging the ultimate act of treachery, the other regretting her husband's failure to defend wife and children as nature commands.

Within *Macbeth* there are two mutually opposed conceptions of manhood. One is based on heroic epic, the other on the Gospels. But the play is not simply claiming the superiority of one set of values over another. The closer one looks, the less easy it is to separate them. It is not just that Duncan's piety would be helpless without Macbeth's ferocity, and Macbeth's *virtus* mere barbarism without Duncan's *civilitas*. Civilized values must be defended; but the use of barbaric means to do so seems inevitably to result in contamination of the very ideals that are being upheld. It might appear at first sight as if Rubens was making a similar point in his allegorical portrait of King James in the Whitehall Banqueting House. In front of the enthroned James are two mythological tableaux. On the right is a heroic figure triumphing over a defeated enemy; on the left are two embracing women representing Peace and Plenty. James is shown turning from war to peace. As D.J. Gordon explained, James rejects the military victor because, although the enemy is clearly evil, the triumphant hero is also a barbaric figure carrying the flaming torch of discord: 'The dangerous victories of war, then, are rejected in favour of the victories of wisdom or prudence and peaceful suasion'.[67] *Macbeth* too considers the problem of the contaminating nature of military values, though unlike Rubens' allegory, it does not reject the military option. Instead it shows us the paradox of men defending civilized principles with heroic action. In this respect it is like the *Aeneid*. The contrast that Virgil makes between the heroic values of Homeric epic and the civilized values of the Roman world eventually breaks down, so that in his conduct on the battlefield Aeneas is virtually indistinguishable from Turnus. Shakespeare's heroes and villains are also sometimes hard to tell apart; at least, like Aeneas and Turnus, they fight according to the same rules. Theirs is a world in which 'Fair is foul, and foul is fair'.

Virgil's *Aeneid* provided a model for countless Renaissance poets who wanted to compliment a royal patron. But it was the poem's agonistic vision, rather than its form, that seems to have spoken to Shakespeare's imagination. It is a vision perhaps best characterized by John Gray's term 'cultural pluralism'. In contrast to the Cultural Materialist, who posits a world of 'true and false discourses'[68] where writers must be judged according to whether they are for or against authority, the cultural pluralist believes that political and ethical problems are rarely reducible to a simple formula. In his book on Isaiah Berlin, Gray explains that pluralism is not to be confused with ethical relativism. The relativist holds that, however internally consistent particular value systems may be, they are always the product of a specific society and cannot be the object of rational adjudication.[69] However, Berlin insists that human value systems are, by their very nature, inherently conflictual. It is obvious that there is an unbridgeable gulf between the opposing views of humanity that one finds in Homeric epic and the Sermon on the Mount. But Berlin argues, not that it would be futile to attempt to

[67] 'Rubens and the Whitehall Ceiling', p. 42.
[68] Jonathan Dollimore, *Radical Tragedy: Religion, Ideology and Power in the Drama of Shakespeare and his Contemporaries* (1984; repr. Brighton: Harvester Press, 1986), p. 229.
[69] John Gray, *Isaiah Berlin* (London: Harper Collins, 1995), p. 44.

adjudicate between them, but that *within* each of these value systems there will always be irresolvable conflict. 'The cornerstone of [Berlin's] thought', writes Gray, 'is his rejection of monism in ethics – his insistence that fundamental human values are many, that they are often in conflict and rarely, if ever, necessarily harmonious, and that some, at least of these conflicts are among incommensurables – conflicts among values for which there is no single, common standard or arbitration.'[70] Sinfield writes of a radical alternative to our present system of state-authorized violence,[71] though what form this alternative society would take, or how it would solve the kind of problems that beset the United Nations Security Council in the final decade of the twentieth century he does not say. Unlike the Cultural Materialist, the cultural pluralist knows that there can be no certainties in ethical and political questions, no overarching truth, no universal panacea.

It might be argued that a sense of human values as inherently conflictual is one of the characteristics of most great literature. Certainly it seems to be one of the most distinctive features of Virgil's art. It also seems to be the fundamental ordering principle of Shakespeare's plays. James' *Trew Law of Free Monarchies*, published in 1598 when James was only thirty-two, is a book that deals in certainties: kings are God's deputies on earth; monarchy is the most perfect form of government; rebellion is never justified; a king is like a father to his people; unjust rulers are God's way of punishing the wicked and must not be resisted; lineal succession is a sacred principle originating in primal antiquity. *Macbeth* problematizes all these principles. The idea that James, like Elizabeth, could trace his ancestry to the ancient world was an important ingredient in Stuart political mythology. The fact that not even those who promulgated the myth believed in its literal truth[72] does not mean that it lacked serious typological value. James seems genuinely to have believed that the Stuart dynasty, with its promise of a united Europe enjoying a new age of peace and plenty, was the realization of a divine plan. But if that providentialist interpretation of history was true, it would

---

[70] Ibid., p. 6.
[71] 'Macbeth: History, Ideology, and Intellectuals', p. 108.
[72] Although Spenser makes extensive use of the British Myth in *The Faerie Queene*, he speaks with scorn of those who treat the myth as literal truth, 'it being impossible to proove, that there was ever any such Brutus of England' (*A View of the Present State of Ireland*, *The Prose Works*, Variorum edn., ed. Rudolf Gottfried (Baltimore: Johns Hopkins University Press, 1949), p. 82.

mean that heaven's plan must have included, not just Macbeth's tyranny and Fleance's escape to Wales, but also the overthrow of a usurper by men who had good cause to feel 'revenges burn in them'. Macbeth himself says that 'Blood hath been shed ere now, i' th' olden time, / Ere human statute purged the gentle weal'. However, the play suggests that in this case it was not civic legislation, but an act of heroic violence which, in the hatch and brood of time, was to result in the creation of a gentler weal. *Macbeth* is neither a defence nor an 'arraignment' of James' rule; like Virgil's *Aeneid*, the play is an anatomy of heroic values that offers no solution to the conundrum it dramatizes.

CHAPTER 5

'Flower of warriors': Coriolanus

Unhappy the land that is in need of heroes.
> Brecht, *The Life of Galileo*, p. 108

The city needs a hero, just as the hero needs a city.
> Paul A. Cantor, *Shakespeare's Rome*, p. 123

What the world needs is an end to the ethic of heroism in its leadership for good and all.
> John Keegan, *The Mask of Command*, p. 350

It is when the tribunes accuse him of being a traitor to the people that Martius' self-control finally breaks. Despite all his mother's careful coaching in the art of 'policy', he is no more capable of restraining his fury than a child in a tantrum. Hurling insults at the ungrateful plebeians, he resolves to avenge his injured pride by destroying the city that has shown so little gratitude to its most magnificent warrior. Like all Shakespeare's martial heroes, Caius Martius Coriolanus is a liability to the state he serves. The honour code that is so valuable to Rome in time of war comes very close to ensuring the destruction of the city.[1]

But at the beginning of Act IV we see a new Martius. Gone is the raging scorn for the feckless plebeians, and in its place is a restrained and dignified stoicism. Bidding his mother summon her 'ancient courage', he tells Menenius to remind the weeping valediction party that "Tis fond to wail inevitable strokes / As 'tis to laugh at 'em'

---

[1] Paul N. Siegel writes: 'it is precisely Coriolanus' sense of honor which causes him to seek revenge against the country that has wronged him' ('Shakespeare and the Neo-Chivalric Cult of Honor', *CR*, 8 (1964), 61). On the honour code in early-modern England see Mervyn James, *Society, Politics and Culture: Studies in Early Modern England* (1978; repr. Cambridge: Cambridge University Press, 1986), pp. 308–415; On honour and fame in *Coriolanus* see D.G. Gordon, 'Name and Fame: Shakespeare's *Coriolanus*', *Papers Mainly Shakespearean*, ed. G.I. Duthie (Edinburgh and London: University of Aberdeen, 1964), pp. 40–57.

(IV.i.27–8). As he makes his last farewell, his words have an elegiac tenderness that is rare in *Coriolanus*:

> Fare ye well.
> Thou hast years upon thee, and thou art too full
> Of the wars' surfeits to go rove with one
> That's yet unbruised. Bring me but out at gate.
> Come, my sweet wife, my dearest mother, and
> My friends of noble touch. When I am forth,
> Bid me farewell, and smile. I pray you come.
> While I remain above the ground you shall
> Hear from me still, and never of me aught
> But what is like me formerly. (IV.i.45–54)

Paradoxically, this new eloquent Martius is far more dangerous than the old volatile, aggressive upholder of patrician military values. The danger lies in his ability to win our sympathy in spite of so much negative evidence. For all his political ineptitude, this is something that Martius himself is at least partially aware of. Echoing Octavius' reflections on the fickleness of political reputation ('the ebbed man, ne'er loved till ne'er worth love, / Comes deared by being lacked', *Ant.*, I.iv.43–4), Martius predicts the revival of his own reputation: 'I shall be loved when I am lacked', he tells his mother (IV.i.16). True to his prophecy, the play ends, not with sober reflection on the perils of unreliable leadership, but with sentimental tribute to the memory of a man who, for all his vaunted Roman constancy,[2] and his contempt for the capriciousness of the mob, has brought two cities to the brink of destruction through his own double treachery. 'Let him be regarded / As the most noble corpse that ever herald / Did follow to his urn' (V.vi.143–5) says an unnamed Volscian Lord in the expected conventional tribute. But the final speech of the play is no mere epideictic formula. 'My rage is gone, / And I am struck with sorrow', says Aufidius with obvious feeling,

> Though in this city he
> Hath widowed and unchilded many a one,
> Which to this hour bewail the injury,
> Yet he shall have a noble memory. (147–8; 151–4)

---

[2] On Martius' constancy see Geoffrey Miles, *Shakespeare and the Constant Romans* (Oxford: Clarendon Press, 1996), pp. 149–68. As Miles rightly says, 'Coriolanus is proud that everyone knows what to expect of him, and that he is seen to be always the same' (p. 152). See also Charles and Michelle Martindale, *Shakespeare and the Uses of Antiquity: An Introductory Essay* (London and New York: Routledge, 1990), pp. 179–81.

The least sympathetic of Shakespeare's heroes, Martius is nevertheless capable of inspiring awe and admiration in friends and enemies alike. It is the power of the charismatic leader to inspire devotion that is his most dangerous quality. And it is this phenomenon that the theatre is uniquely capable of reproducing. As Emrys Jones argues in *Scenic Form in Shakespeare*, a theatre audience is like a 'charmed crowd': just as a crowd can turn law-abiding citizens into credulous barbarians, so intelligent, civilized people become susceptible in the theatre to feelings which in other circumstances they would probably disown.[3] Martius' greatest conquest is not Corioli, but the hearts of theatre audiences and critics alike. Responding to his final explosion of rage at Aufidius' taunts (v.vi.103–17), one recent critic of the play writes: 'it is impossible to hear this in the theatre without a sense of exhilaration, and without sensing too that this is a noble anger and a noble pride . . . here is a solitary hero defying his inevitable fate'.[4] And he is right. The fall of a man whose heart is 'too great for what contains it' (104) cannot but be a moving spectacle. But as Oscar Wilde put it, the advantage of the emotions is that they lead us astray. Like all Shakespeare's tragic heroes, Martius is a warning of the seductive charm of the charismatic hero. To offer that warning by evoking the *sentimental* reactions of one's audience is risky dramaturgy. But if it is bound to backfire with at least some playgoers, it has the advantage of making it possible to glance at matters of state without too much risk of attracting the attentions of the censor.

THE POLITICS OF VIRTUE

Coriolanus is Shakespeare's most political play. It is also, despite its austere Roman authenticity,[5] his most topical. The Midlands corn riots of 1607, and the arguments in parliament three years earlier

---

[3] *Scenic Form in Shakespeare* (Oxford: Clarendon Press, 1971), pp. 6, 132.
[4] T. McAlindon, '*Coriolanus*: An Essentialist Tragedy', *RES*, 44 (1993), 517. Cf A.C. Bradley: 'the pride and self-will of Coriolanus . . . are scarcely so in quality; there is nothing base in them, and the huge creature whom they destroy is a noble, even a lovable, being' (*Shakespearean Tragedy*, 2nd edn. (1905; repr. London: Macmillan, 1963), p. 64), and Hermann Heuer: 'With all his want of polish, his revulsion from the mob and his naive display of unbounded vitality, the solitary protagonist is meant to claim our sympathies as a tragic figure' ('From Plutarch to Shakespeare: A Study of *Coriolanus*', *ShS*, 10 (1957), 57).
[5] For a valuable discussion of Shakespeare's unique combination of anachronism and calculated *Romanitas* see Charles and Michelle Martindale, *Shakespeare and the Uses of Antiquity*, pp. 121–64.

over the right of the House of Commons to initiate legislation, form a well-documented part of the play's political context.[6] But there was another political problem that was being hotly debated in the years immediately preceding the writing of *Coriolanus*, one that had international, rather than purely domestic, implications, and that may help to answer Geoffrey Bullough's question: 'What led Shakespeare to write this play on a comparatively minor and early figure in Roman history?'[7] This is that most vexed of Jacobean foreign-policy issues – the question of war and peace.

Martius' defining characteristic is his heroic *virtus*. In his tribute to Rome's most terrible warrior, Cominius declares,

> It is held
> That valour is the chiefest virtue, and
> Most dignifies the haver. If it be,
> The man I speak of cannot in the world
> Be singly counterpoised. (II.ii.83–7)

As Cominius defines it, 'virtue' means above all manly prowess in battle. Whatever contemporary audiences might have thought of an ethical system that placed paramount value on *virtus* – and the way Cominius phrases his speech suggests that it was a matter of debate – they would have known, at least if they had read their Plutarch, that such a code of values was intrinsic to the greatest military society of the ancient world.[8] Without explicitly revealing his own Greek distaste for Roman military values at their harshest, Plutarch explains in his 'Life of Caius Martius Coriolanus' that in the early days of the Republic 'valliantnes was honoured in Rome above all other virtues: which they called *Virtus* by the name of vertue [it]selfe, as including in that generall name, all other speciall vertues

---

[6] See E.C. Pettett, '*Coriolanus* and the Midlands Insurrection of 1607', *ShS*, 3 (1950), 34–42; W.Gordon Zeeveld, '*Coriolanus* and Jacobean Politics', *MLR*, 57 (1962), 321–4; Annabel Patterson, *Shakespeare and the Popular Voice* (Cambridge, Mass. and Oxford: Blackwell, 1989), pp. 127–46; Richard Wilson, *Will Power: Essays on Shakespearean Authority* (New York and London: Harvester Wheatsheaf, 1993), pp. 88–117.

[7] *Narrative and Dramatic Sources of Shakespeare*, 8 vols. (1957–75), vol. v (Roman Plays) (London: Routledge & Kegan Paul, 1964), 454. Cf Bruce King: 'Does *Coriolanus* represent . . . a feudal order remembered with nostalgia?'; 'why should this come up in Shakespeare's work at this time?' (*Coriolanus* (Basingstoke and London: Macmillan, 1989), pp. 65–6).

[8] See Reuben A. Brower, *Hero and Saint: Shakespeare and the Graeco-Roman Heroic Tradition* (Oxford: Clarendon Press, 1971), pp. 358, 372–5. See also Eugene M. Waith, *The Herculean Hero in Marlowe, Chapman, Shakespeare and Dryden* (London: Chatto & Windus, 1962); Siegel, 'Shakespeare and the Neo-Chivalric Cult of Honor'; Paul A. Cantor, *Shakespeare's Rome: Republic and Empire* (Ithaca and London: Cornell University Press, 1976).

besides. So that *Virtus* in the Latin, was asmuche as valliantnes'.[9] Eugene Waith has argued that the pride and the arrogance that modern audiences find objectionable in Martius are inseparable aspects of that Roman *virtus*. In portraying a valour that is almost godlike in its terrible single-mindedness, Shakespeare was not asking us to make moral or political judgments, says Waith; in the face of such Herculean *superbia* 'both approval and disapproval give way to awe'.[10]

Waith is concerned to restore to Shakespeare's hero something of the grandeur that modern criticism, with its sceptical distaste for martial heroism, has tended to belittle; his achievements, says Waith, 'border on the supernatural'.[11] The evidence is compelling. Named after the Roman god of war and patron deity of Rome,[12] and compared by Cominius to Hercules, the mythological founder of war (IV.vi.103-4), Martius is repeatedly likened to some implacable force of nature (I.v.27-32; II.ii.99; II.ii.108-22; IV.vi.94-6; V.iv.18-21). Believing that he has been killed inside the gates of Corioli, Titus Lartius pays tribute, not to Martius' bravery (which must entail some measure of fear), but to his seemingly godlike powers of destruction:

> Thou wast a soldier
> Even to Cato's wish, not fierce and terrible
> Only in strokes, but with thy grim looks and
> The thunder-like percussion of thy sounds
> Thou mad'st thine enemies shake as if the world
> Were feverous and did tremble.   (I.v.27-32)

Of Martius' apparently superhuman qualities there is no question: even in a society that holds that 'valour is the chiefest virtue', he is regarded as exceptional. 'Thou hast affected the fine strains of honour, / To imitate the graces of the gods', his mother tells him (V.iii.150-1). But in claiming that Martius is in some mysterious way beyond good and evil, Waith does not consider the fact that the heroic ideal was a highly politicized topic at the time Shakespeare was writing *Coriolanus*. Indeed so contentious had the issue become by 1608 that dramatic treatment of such a sensitive subject would

---

[9] 'The Life of Caius Martius Coriolanus', *Plutarch's Lives of the Noble Grecians and Romans*, 6 vols., trans. Sir Thomas North (London: David Nutt, 1895–6), vol. II (1895), p. 144.
[10] *The Herculean Hero*, p. 127.
[11] Ibid., p. 125.
[12] On the significance of Martius' name see T. McAlindon, '*Coriolanus*: An Essentialist Tragedy', pp. 507–8. See also Peggy Muñoz Simonds, '*Coriolanus* and the Myth of Juno and Mars', *Mosaic*, 18 (1985), 33–50.

have required careful avoidance of anything that might have struck a censor as tactless topical allusion. It was a matter that went to the heart of government foreign policy and involved dispute within the Royal Family on the wider question of fundamental social and political values.

'LIKE MARS IN ARMOR CLAD'

In November 1612 England was in deep mourning for an eighteen-year-old national hero. Shortly after Prince Henry's death, the Venetian ambassador in London sent a dispatch in which he described the man who had touched the nation's heart. His portrait is not particularly flattering and sounds oddly familiar: according to the ambassador, the prince's 'whole talk was of arms and war'; he was 'grave, severe, reserved, brief in speech'; he was keenly interested in extending his country's territories; and he was 'athirst for glory if ever any prince was'.[13]

Henry had been interested in the martial arts from his earliest years. With his passion for history,[14] he would doubtless have found inspiration in Plutarch's description of the young Caius Martius Coriolanus, who like himself, 'beganne from his Childehood to geve him self to handle weapons, and daylie dyd exercise him selfe therein'.[15] In his *Life and Death of our late most incomparable heroic Prince* John Hawkins describes Henry's obsession with all things military:

He did also practise Tilting, Charging on Horseback with Pistols, after the Manner of the Wars, with all other the like Inventions. Now also delighting to confer, both with his own, and other strangers, and great Captains, of all Manner of Wars, Battle, Furniture, Arms by Sea and land, Disciplines, Orders, Marches, Alarms, Watches, Strategems, Ambuscades, Approaches, Scalings, Fortifications, Incamping; and having now and then Battles of Head-men appointed both on Horse and Foot, in a long Table; whereby he

---

[13] *Calendar of State Papers* (Venetian), quoted by J.W. Williamson, *The Myth of the Conqueror: Prince Henry Stuart: A Study of 17th-Century Personation* (New York: AMS Press, 1978), p. 162. The following paragraphs are based on Williamson, and Roy Strong, *Henry, Prince of Wales* (London: Thames & Hudson, 1986). See also Frances A. Yates, *Shakespeare's Last Plays: A New Approach* (London: Routledge & Kegan Paul, 1975), pp. 19ff; Norman Council, 'Ben Jonson, Inigo Jones, and the Transformation of Tudor Chivalry', *ELH*, 47 (1980), 259–75; David M. Bergeron, *Royal Family, Royal Lovers: King James of England and Scotland* (Columbia and London: University of Missouri Press, 1991), pp. 92–109.
[14] Strong, *Henry, Prince of Wales*, p. 145.
[15] 'The Life of Caius Martius Coriolanus', pp. 144–5.

might in a manner, View the right ordering of a Battle . . . Neither did he omit, as he loved the *Theorick* of these Things, to practise . . . all manner of Things belonging to the Wars.[16]

The Prince's public career began officially with his investiture as Prince of Wales in June 1610. To mark his entry into the life of the nation Henry commissioned Ben Jonson and Inigo Jones to produce a series of mythological entertainments, the first of which was performed on Twelfth Night, 1610. *Prince Henry's Barriers* was designed as a public statement of the role that the new Prince of Wales intended to play in national and international affairs. Henry was going to be a holy warrior. Introduced by the spirit of King Arthur as a fulfilment of Merlin's prophecy that a prince would one day restore the glories of ancient Britain, Henry is discovered 'like Mars . . . in armor clad'.[17] After a roll call of English monarchs from 'warlike Edward' to 'great Eliza . . . fear of all the nations nigh' (179, 200–2), the sleeping figure of Chivalry is roused by Merlin to invite combatants to the lists. 'Break, you rusty doors / That have so long been shut,' cries Chivalry,

> and from the shores
> Of all the world come knighthood like a flood
> Upon these lists to make the field here good,
> And your own honours that are now called forth
> Against the wish of men to prove your worth! (385–90)

There then followed the Barriers proper with all the pageantry of medieval warfare: pavilions, plumed helmets, heraldic devices, swords, pikes, and lances. In the *Annales* John Stow described how 'the Prince performed his first feates of armes, that is to say, at Barriers against all commers . . . with wonderous skill, and courage, to the great joy and admiration of all the beholders'.[18] After the tournaments were over, Merlin delivered a final encomium to James in which he prophesied that the young prince would in time relieve the king of his cares in government and 'shake a sword / And lance against the foes of God and you' (416–17). Although in deference to James' pacifist principles (and, it may be presumed, his own inclinations), Jonson qualified the warlike tone of the *Barriers* by claiming that 'Defensive arms th'offensive should forego' (99), Henry's

---

[16] Quoted by Strong, *Henry, Prince of Wales*, p. 68.
[17] Ben Jonson, 'Prince Henry's Barriers', lines 137–8, *The Complete Masques*, ed. Stephen Orgel (New Haven, Conn. and London: Yale University Press, 1969), p. 147.
[18] John Stow, *Annales* (London, 1631), Sig. Ffff4^v quoted by Williamson, p. 65.

message was transparent: as an enthusiastic believer in chivalric values, the Prince of Wales would realize the ambitions of the old Elizabethan war party by actively pursuing an anti-Habsburg crusade in Europe. After his death the Venetian ambassador spoke of how the Prince had aspired to lead a confederation of Protestant princes,[19] while George Wither imagined the role he might have played as head of an anti-Catholic army:

> Me thought ere-while I saw Prince *Henries* Armes
> Advanc't above the Capitoll of *Rome*,
> And his keene blade, in spight of steele or charmes,
> Give many mighty enemies their doome.[20]

All this took place after the first performance of *Coriolanus* (probably in late 1608 or early 1609).[21] But there was nothing new in the iconography of the *Barriers*. From infancy Henry had been portrayed by militant Protestants as a future warrior–hero.[22] Invoking, not James' own patron deity, Eirene, but Mars, the Roman god of war,[23] and Hercules his champion, Protestant iconographers surrounded their young prince with images of chivalry and arms, representing him, even at the improbable age of nine, as a conquering hero. In the portrait of 1603 by Robert Peake the Elder (Metropolitan Museum of Art, New York), Henry is shown in belligerent posture with drawn sword, and an impresa on his tunic depicting St George slaying the dragon.[24] In the miniature by Isaac Oliver in the Fitzwilliam Museum, Cambridge, he is shown in the guise of a Roman general.[25] The military theme continued throughout Henry's teenage years. A year before the investiture, when Henry was still only fifteen, George Marcelline described him

---

[19] *Calendar of State Papers* (Venetian), 23 November 1612.
[20] George Wither, 'Prince Henries obsequies', *Juvenilia* (Manchester: Spenser Society, 1871), p. 394.
[21] See R.B. Parker, ed., Introduction to *The Tragedy of 'Coriolanus'* (Oxford: Clarendon Press, 1994), pp. 2–7. See also John Ripley, *Coriolanus on Stage in England and America, 1609–1994* (Cranbury, N.J. and London: Associated University Presses, 1998), pp. 34–5.
[22] Williamson, *The Myth of the Conqueror*, pp. 8–10.
[23] On Mars' association with war in Roman mythology see Georges Dumézil, *Archaic Roman Religion*, 2 vols.; trans. Philip Krapp (Chicago and London: University of Chicago Press, 1970), vol. I, pp. 205–13.
[24] Roy Strong, *The English Icon: Elizabethan and Jacobean Portraiture* (London: Routledge & Kegan Paul, 1969), p. 234. In the Hampton Court version of this portrait (1605) Prince Henry is shown with Robert Devereux, 3rd Earl of Essex, instead of the 3rd Lord Harington of Exton (p. 246).
[25] Ibid., p. 55.

as 'a COMMET of dreadfull terrour to [England's] enemies'.²⁶ 'This young Prince,' wrote Marcelline,

> is a warrior alreadie, both in gesture and countenance, so that in looking on him, he seemeth unto us, that in him we do yet see Ajax before Troy, crowding among the armed Troops . . . Honour [is] all his nouriture, and Greatnesse his pastime (as it was saide of Alexander) and Triumph the ordinary end of al his Actions.²⁷

In the same year the Venetian cleric Paolo Sarpi wrote: 'from all sides one hears about the great *virtù* of the Prince'.²⁸ As J.W. Williamson remarks, 'rarely had such a young boy managed to surround himself so with the odor of masculinity'.²⁹

The blatant advertisement of Prince Henry's military ambitions by his Protestant supporters was bound to cause friction between him and his father. Indeed their differences were public knowledge. Noting that James was not 'overpleased to see his son so beloved and of such promise that his subjects place all their hopes in him', the Venetian ambassador wrote: 'It would almost seem, to speak quite frankly, that the King was growing jealous'.³⁰ Though his dearest wish was to see Europe at peace, James was not an uncompromising pacifist. Following early sixteenth-century humanists like Erasmus and Vives,³¹ he recognized that defensive wars were sometimes necessary.³² But he was implacably opposed to wars of expansion. Henry, by contrast, was an enthusiastic supporter of the militant-Protestant campaign for a renewal of the war against Spain and even drew up strategic plans for a naval blockade of the Spanish fleet in the West Indies.³³ Matters came to a head in 1608 when a group of Henry's military advisors, by whom the Prince was, according to the

---

26 *The Triumphs of King James the First* (London, 1610), Sig. A2, quoted by Williamson, p. 77. *The Triumphs* was first published in French in 1609.
27 Ibid, p. 66, quoted by Williamson, p. 34.
28 Quoted by Strong, *Henry, Prince of Wales*, p. 76.
29 *The Myth of the Conqueror*, p. 32.
30 *Calendar of State Papers* (Venetian), quoted by Williamson, p. 41.
31 See Robert P. Adams, *The Better Part of Valor: More, Erasmus, Colet, and Vives on Humanism, War, and Peace 1496–1535* (Seattle: University of Washington Press, 1962); Philip C. Dust, *Three Renaissance Pacifists: Essays on the Theories of Erasmus, More, and Vives* (New York: Peter Lang, 1987).
32 Advising Henry on preparations for war James wrote 'Let first the justnesse of your cause be your greatest strength; and then omitte not to use all lawfull meanes for backing of the same' (*Basilicon Doron*, *Political Writings*, ed. Johann P. Somerville (Cambridge: Cambridge University Press, 1994), p. 32).
33 Strong, *Henry, Prince of Wales*, p. 72.

Venetian ambassador, 'obeyed and lauded',[34] put together a pamphlet titled 'Arguments for Warre'. The 'Arguments' is a lightweight document that does little more than rehearse well worn apologies for war: namely, that arms are the original foundation of civilization; that states which lack an external enemy will all too easily rush 'from arms to pleasures, from employment to idleness'; and that 'when people have no enemies abroad, they find some at home'.[35] The most contentious part of the 'Arguments' is its concluding call for an expansionist policy towards Europe. Claiming that the rewards that accrued from England's wars with France and Spain far exceeded the costs involved, the pamphlet concludes by summarizing the advantages of an aggressively expansionist policy:

> Our *Honour*, as the Stile of our Kings, by confluence of so many Titles increased; and by accession of so many territories as we held in *France*, our dominions and liberties so far inlarged. The facilities to effect this being now more than ever by the addition of strength, and substraction [*sic*] of diversions, in this happy union of the *Britain Empire*'.[36]

Alarmed by such a provocative challenge to his own humanist belief in a united Europe in which he himself would act the part of mediator and peacemaker, James commissioned his trusted advisor, the parliamentarian Sir Robert Cotton,[37] to write a reply warning of the dangers of the new cult of chivalric honour associated with the young prince. Unlike the 'Arguments for Warre', Cotton's ninety-page 'Answer' is a scholarly document citing classical authority and historical example in a measured refutation of the claims of the militarists. It is particularly pointed in its allusion to recent history. Among the claims of Henry's militant-Protestant supporters was that he was the spiritual heir of the second Earl of Essex,[38] who had himself been compared to Caius Martius Coriolanus.[39] Alluding to

---

[34] *Calendar of State Papers* (Venetian), 23 November 1612.
[35] 'Propositions of Warre and Peace delivered to his Highness Prince Henry by some of his Military servants: Arguments for Warre', printed in Sir Robert Cotton, *An Answer made by Command of Prince Henry, to Certain Propositions of Warre and Peace, Delivered to his Highness by some of his Military Servants* (London, 1655), pp. 1–2.
[36] Ibid., pp. 3–4.
[37] Before the accession Cotton had supported James' claim to the English throne and as an antiquary enthusiastically endorsed the idea of an ancient kingdom of Great Britain (see Kevin Sharpe, *Sir Robert Cotton 1586–1631: History and Politics in Early Modern England* (Oxford: Oxford University Press, 1979), p. 227).
[38] Strong, *Henry, Prince of Wales*, p. 14.
[39] In 1601 Bishop William Barlow referred to Martius as a 'discontented Romane, who might make a fit parallel for the late Earle [of Essex]' (quoted by Clifford Chalmers Huffman, *'Coriolanus' in Context* (Lewisburg: Bucknell University Press, 1971), p. 25).

the earl's rebellion, Cotton warned of the dangers posed by over-ambitious nobles who identified themselves with the honour code:

> Our own times can afford some, whose spirit improved by *Military imployment*, and made wanton with popular applause, might have given instance of these dangers . . . And every age breeds some exorbitant spirits, who turn the edge of their own sufficiency upon whatsoever they can devour in their ambitious apprehensions, seeking rather a great then a good Fame; and holding it the chiefest Honour to be thought the Wonder of their times.[40]

The pamphlet concludes with a restatement of James' belief in the importance of his own role as international mediator:

> Since then by *Situation* and Power we are the fittest, either to combine or keep severall the most potent and warlike Nations of the *West*, it is the best for *Safety*, and the most for *Honour*, to remain . . . Arbiters of Europe, and so by Neutralitie sway still the Ballance of our mightiest Neighbours.[41]

But Cotton's admonitions did nothing to dampen the prince's interest in war, or his enthusiastic support for expansionist ventures. The following year saw a new expedition to Virginia. Commemorating the event, Michael Drayton wrote a poem for his young patron praising colonial conquest as an expression of the heroic spirit and suggesting, like the authors of the 'Arguments for Warre', that there is something shameful in peace:

> You brave Heroique Minds,
> Worthy your countries name;
> That Honour still pursue,
> Goe, and subdue,
> Whilst loy'tring Hinds
> Lurke here at home, with shame.[42]

The appeal of the Virginia expedition to a neo-medievalist like Henry is obvious: as Drayton imagines it, the voyage sounds like a combination of Homeric peregrination mediated through Spenser, and the achieving of a chivalric quest. Commenting on the prince's enthusiastic interest in colonial expansion, the Venetian Ambassador wrote: 'To the ears of the Prince, who is keen for glory, come suggestions of conquests far greater than any made by the kings of

---

[40] *An Answer . . . to Certain Propositions of Warre and Peace*, p. 22.
[41] Ibid., p. 95.
[42] 'To the Virginian Shore', *The Works of Michael Drayton*, 5 vols., ed. J. William Hebel (Oxford: Basil Blackwell, 1931–41), vol. II (1932), p. 363, quoted by Strong, *Henry, Prince of Wales*, p. 61.

Spain'.⁴³ Ironically, Henry never had the opportunity to win the military glory he craved. As Erasmus wryly put it, 'dulce bellum inexpertis'⁴⁴ – war is a beautiful thing to those who have not experienced it.

In the tense political situation that existed between Whitehall and St James' Palace in 1608–9, praise of 'Heroique Minds' could mean only one thing: it was a coded indication that you subscribed to the ideals of militant Protestantism and that you were a supporter of its charismatic and bellicose young patron. So when a character in a contemporary play declares 'It is held / That valour is the chiefest virtue', contemporary audiences could hardly fail to make connections, however oblique, with the conflicts that were currently being played out in such a public way in London, particularly when the precocious youthfulness of the heroic mind in question is given such pointed emphasis.

There is no particular reason why Cominius should dwell on Martius' youth. Plutarch simply mentions briefly how Martius first went to war as 'a stripling'.⁴⁵ But in commending Martius to the tribunes, Cominius spends a dozen lines rehearsing, not, as one would expect, the leadership qualities of the mature general, but the exploits of a sixteen-year-old. After telling us his precise age (roughly a year older than Henry when *Coriolanus* was first performed), he goes on repeatedly to emphasize his boyish appearance and his 'pupil age':

> At sixteen years,
> When Tarquin made a head for Rome, he fought
> Beyond the mark of others. Our then dictator,
> Whom with all praise I point at, saw him fight
> When with his Amazonian chin he drove
> The bristled lips before him. He bestrid
> An o'erpressed Roman, and, i' th' consul's view,
> Slew three opposers. Tarquin's self he met,
> And struck him on his knee. In that day's feats,
> When he might act the woman in the scene,
> He proved best man i' th' field, and for his meed
> Was brow-bound with the oak. His pupil age

---

⁴³ *Calendar of State Papers* (Venetian), quoted by Strong, p. 63.
⁴⁴ 'Dulce bellum inexpertis' is the title of Erasmus' most celebrated pacifist essay (*The 'Adages' of Erasmus*, ed. and trans. Margaret Mann Phillips (Cambridge: Cambridge University Press, 1964), pp. 308–53).
⁴⁵ 'The Life of Caius Martius Coriolanus', p. 145.

>   Man-entered thus, he waxèd like a sea,
>   And in the brunt of seventeen battles since
>   He lurched all swords of the garland.   (II.ii.87–101)

None of this has any special bearing on Martius' suitability for political office and is not the subject of thematic development in the play (Aufidius' taunt of 'Boy' that so enrages Martius in the play's final scene does not depend for its effect on what Cominius has told us about the hero's adolescence). In the absence of any structural or thematic reason for dwelling on his hero's youth, we have to assume that Shakespeare meant to remind his audience that, half a dozen or so years after Essex's death, and the apparent demise of the neo-chivalric values he stood for, support was growing once more for the old heroic ideal, this time embodied in a charismatic young warrior–hero-in-the-making. In his account of Martius' entry into Rome following the sack of Corioli, Brutus reports how 'All tongues speak of him, and the bleared sights/Are spectacled to see him' (II.i.202–3). So stirring is this triumphal display that it seems to the Roman populace 'As if that whatsoever god who leads him / Were slily crept into his human powers/And gave him graceful posture' (216–18). It has been suggested that, in his description of Martius' triumphal return, Shakespeare was echoing contemporary accounts of James' delayed coronation entry of 1604.[46] But as David George admits, any comparison between a middle-aged pacifist and Shakespeare's charismatic, battle-hardened warrior–hero is inherently implausible. What seems far more probable is that, like Wither, Shakespeare was using his own imagination (as he did in the final chorus of *Henry V* when he pictured Essex returning like a conquering Caesar, with plebeians swarming at his heels) and evoking an image, not of an unathletic pacifist, but of an altogether more youthful and warlike royal hero.

Volumnia too puts special emphasis on Martius' precociousness, recalling for Virgilia the time 'when youth / with comeliness plucked all gaze his way' (I.iii.7–8). Again, Plutarch says little about Martius' childhood, and merely reports that as an adult he 'dyd not only content him selfe to rejoyce and honour [his mother], but at her desire tooke a wife also'.[47] The long conversation with Virgilia in Act I Scene iii in which Volumnia tells of her concern for her son's

---

[46] David George, 'Coriolanus' Triumphal Entry into Rome', *NQ*, 241 (1996), 63–5.
[47] Ibid., p. 147.

honour; of how she sent him when still 'tender-bodied' to a 'cruel war'; and how if she had had a dozen sons she 'had rather had eleven die nobly for their country/than one voluptuously surfeit out of action' (5–25) – all this is invention on Shakespeare's part and is reminiscent more of contemporary panegyrics to Prince Henry than of Plutarch. (Like Shakespeare's Martius, Henry had from an early age been encouraged in his military obsessions by an unusual mother. According to James' eighteenth-century biographer Thomas Birch, Queen Anne 'used all her efforts to corrupt the mind of the Prince by flattering his passions, diverting him from his [academic] studies and exercises, representing to him, out of contempt for his father, that learning was inconsistent with the character of a great General and Conqueror'.)[48]

The plays that Shakespeare wrote after 1603 contain many indirect allusions to James I: *Measure for Measure*, *Macbeth*, *Cymbeline* and *The Tempest* all touch on issues that were of keen interest to the king, or else portray authority figures whose problems resemble those that James himself was grappling with.[49] These plays are not *pièces à clef*. But they do deal with topics of contemporary political concern. If *Coriolanus* makes oblique allusion to the vogue for heroic values that was rapidly gaining support at St James' Palace, this does not mean that the play's warrior-hero represents the austere and arrogant Henry any more than he stands for the prince's peace-loving father, as Jonathan Goldberg has rather implausibly suggested.[50] What it does mean is that, along with the flood of militaristic books and pamphlets dedicated to Prince Henry, the play forms part of a public debate on the contentious question of war and peace. For his last anatomy of military values[51] Shakespeare chose,

---

[48] Thomas Birch, *The Life of Henry, Prince of Wales* (London, 1760), p. 46, quoted by Williamson, p. 40.
[49] Alvin Kernan, *Shakespeare, the King's Playwright: Theater in the Stuart Court 1603–1613* (New Haven, Conn. and London: Yale University Press, 1995), pp. xix–xx.
[50] Goldberg describes Martius as an 'absolutist', claiming that 'it is on such absolutist models as the king . . . that Coriolanus is imagined' (*James I and the Politics of Literature: Jonson, Shakespeare, Donne, and Their Contemporaries* (Baltimore and London: Johns Hopkins University Press, 1983), p. 193.
[51] In a revisionist article on 'Shakespeare's Pacifism' Steven Marx writes: 'I believe that, as political satire, [*Coriolanus*] makes most sense when it is regarded . . . as an attack on the bellicose policies that create the war that provides the framework of the play's action' (*RenQ*, 45 (1992), 80). Like Adelman, Kahn, and Sprengnether, Marx looks for an explanation of those 'policies' in the hero's psychology rather than in contemporary events (see Janet Adelman, '"Anger's My Meat": Feeding, Dependency and Aggression in *Coriolanus*', *Representing Shakespeare: New Psychoanalytic Essays*, ed. Murray Schwartz and

appropriately enough, a story from the state noted above all other politically advanced societies in the ancient world for its ferocious expansionism. As Livy put it, 'such is the renowmed martiall prowess of the Romans, that all nations of the world may as well abide them to report Mars above the rest, to the stockefather both of themselves and their first founder'.[52]

REPUBLICAN ROME

After completing his cycle of English history plays dealing with dynastic conflict in fifteenth-century England, Shakespeare turned to Roman history for a new perspective on the problems of a society emerging from civil war to a new order.[53] *Julius Caesar* and *Antony and Cleopatra* dramatize events from the most momentous period in Roman history – the transition from republic to empire. In *Coriolanus* Shakespeare goes back 500 years to the semi-legendary early years of the Republic. His knowledge of this period of Roman history was based largely on Florus, Livy, and Sallust – staple authors of the Elizabethan grammar-school curriculum[54] – and of course Plutarch. Machiavelli's *Discourses*, several translations of which were circulating in manuscript in Elizabethan England,[55] provided a heterodox modern view of republican Rome. Though these writers differ from one another in their view of the early Republic, they all emphasize one fact of overriding significance: this was a time of rapid expansion when the Roman people acquired a reputation throughout Italy for their ferocity in battle. In his abridgement of Livy's *Roman History* Florus contrasts the Augustan period, when Octavian 'settled peace thorow all the world', with the early years of the Republic. The latter was, in the words of his seventeenth-century translator, 'a time most

---

Coppélia Kahn (Baltimore: Johns Hopkins University Press, 1980), pp. 129–50; Coppélia Kahn, *Man's Estate: Masculine Identity in Shakespeare* (Berkeley, Los Angeles, and London: University of California Press, 1981), pp. 151–72; Kahn, *Roman Shakespeare: Warriors, Wounds, and Women* (London and New York: Routledge, 1997), pp. 144–59); Madelon Sprengnether, 'Annihilating Intimacy in *Coriolanus*', *Women in the Middle Ages and the Renaissance: Literary and Historical Perspectives*, ed. Mary Beth Rose (Syracuse, N.Y.: Syracuse University Press, 1986), pp. 89–111).

[52] *The Romane Historie*, trans. Philemon Holland (London, 1600), p. 2.
[53] See J. Leeds Barroll, 'Shakespeare and Roman History', *MLR*, 53 (1958), 327–43.
[54] T.W. Baldwin, *William Shakespere's Small Latine and Less Greeke*, 2 vols. (Urbana: University of Illinois Press, 1944), vol. II, p. 564.
[55] See Felix Raab, *The English Face of Machiavelli: A Changing Interpretation 1500–1700* (London: Routledge & Kegan Paul, 1964), p. 53.

famous for manhood, and deeds of Chevalrie' when, having freed themselves from the tyranny of the Tarquins, Romans took up arms against alien peoples, 'till running like a plague through every nation . . . they brought all Italie at last to be under their subjection'.[56] This is the relentless Roman military machine that Shakespeare evokes in Menenius' speech to the citizens in the opening scene of *Coriolanus*:

> Roman state, whose course will on
> The way it takes, cracking ten thousand curbs
> Of more strong link asunder than can ever
> Appear in your impediment.   (1.i.67–70)

Sallust also describes the period following the overthrow of the Tarquins as one of aggressive expansion when *virtus* and *gloria* came to be the defining values of Roman society. 'It is incredible to report', wrote Sallust,

> in howe short a time, the Citty, having obtained . . . Liberty in Government . . . so infinite a desire of glory, had possessed the minds of al sorts . . . Valor was resolute, & at times victorious. Their emulation was glorious: Every mans strife was, who should first attack the enemy. . . These exploits they accounted Riches, Reputation, and true Nobility . . . [they were] desirous of glory above measure.[57]

Machiavelli, rebutting Plutarch's claim that the Romans owed their extraordinary successes as much to good fortune as to military valour, insisted that it was *virtù* alone that enabled the early Republic to expand so rapidly: 'if never any Republique made the same progress, that Rome made; it is because never hath any Republique beene so order'd to make its advantage, as Rome was: the valour [*virtù*] of their armyes gain'd them their Empire'.[58]

During the early years of the Republic Rome was more or less continuously at war. Plutarch, less enthusiastic than Florus and Sallust about the military ethos of republican Rome, attributed the grain crisis he described in the 'Life of Coriolanus' to this state of perpetual warfare, reporting that one of the grievances of the plebeians was the fact that they were never free from war service: 'Moreover, they sayed, to dwell at Rome was nothing els but to be slaine, or hurte with continuall warres'.[59] This plebeian complaint

---

[56] *The Roman Histories*, trans. E.M. Bolton (London, 1619), Sig. B3, pp. 36–7.
[57] *The Conspiracie of Catiline*, trans. Thomas Heywood (London, 1608), pp. 7–8.
[58] *Machiavels discourses upon the first Decade of T. Livius*, trans. E. Dacres (London, 1636), p. 252.
[59] 'The Life of Caius Martius Coriolanus', pp. 156 and 148–9 respectively.

about unremitting war is echoed in the reponse of Shakespeare's First Citizen to Menenius' unconvincing professions of social concern: 'If the wars eat us not up, they will; and there's all the love they bear us' (1.i.83–4). As Sallust explained, Rome's national culture of violence fed on a system of social values that placed paramount importance on *gloria*. Since eligibility for public office depended on reputation, and since the kind of reputation that mattered most was the glory of victory in battle, the military ethos was self-perpetuating.[60] Describing the vicious circle of military honour leading to desire for further glory, Plutarch wrote:

Valliant mindes . . . esteeme, not to receave reward for service done, but rather take it for a remembraunce and encoragement, to make them doe better in time to come: and be ashamed also to cast their honour at their heeles, not seeking to increase it still by like deserte of worthie valliant dedes.

He went on to describe how, as a product of this system of *laus* and *gloria*, Martius 'strained still to passe him selfe in manlines'.[61]

It is this expansionist military society with its exaggerated regard for 'manlines' that Shakespeare evokes in *Coriolanus*. For those who had spent many hours translating Florus, Livy, and Sallust at school, Cominius' words about valour being counted the chiefest virtue would have had an immediate resonance. If one was a supporter of the Prince of Wales and one believed in an heroic ideal of what Florus' translator called 'manhood and Chevalrie', they would be like a rallying cry to military action; if one was of the king's party, they would be more likely to sound like a threat to international stability.

One of the most frequently rehearsed arguments of the war party was that peace, as Aufidius' servingman puts it, 'makes men hate one another' (IV.v.234–5): hence the belief that an astute prince should busy giddy minds with foreign quarrels. 'When Wars are ended abroad,' wrote Sir Walter Ralegh, 'Sedition begins at home, and when Men are freed from fighting for Necessity, they quarrel through Ambition'.[62] This familiar claim is echoed by Paul Jorgensen, who argues that *Coriolanus* shows 'the domestic hazards of peace'.[63] That Shakespeare himself may have felt some sympathy

---

[60] See William V. Harris, *War and Imperialism in Republican Rome, 327–70 BC* (Oxford: Clarendon Press, 1979), pp. 11–12.
[61] 'The Life of Caius Martius Coriolanus', p. 146.
[62] 'A Discourse of War', *The Works of Sir Walter Ralegh*, 2 vols. (London, 1751), vol. II, p. 65.
[63] *Shakespeare's Military World* (Berkeley and Los Angeles: University of California Press, 1956), p. 184.

with this view is suggested by the fact that it is one of his most saintly characters – Imogen – who says that 'Plenty and peace breeds cowards' (*Cym.*, III.vi.21). But it would be wrong to attribute to heroic values that quasi-religious sense of common purpose which is so often generated by war. Many writers and diarists in the First World War habitually used the language of medieval chivalry in describing their experiences and feelings.[64] However, it was not a culture of violence that gave rise to the extraordinary acts of civilian as well as military courage and altruism that are part of the social history of the time, and that held even pacifists and suffragettes in its euphoric grip, but something more deeply rooted in our human metaculture. Discussion of the question of what atavistic causes may be responsible for the universal tendency to sacralize war is beyond the scope of this book (Barbara Ehrenreich deals brilliantly with it in *Blood Rites*).[65] What is clear, however, is that one effect of choosing a story from the early republican period (to answer Bullough's question) is to show that a heroic culture does not promote social cohesion: *Coriolanus*' opening scenes of civil discord take place, not in a 'weak piping time of peace' (*R3*, 1.i.24), but during Rome's 'present wars' against the Volsci (1.i.258). Considered in the context of the contemporary quarrel between militarists and pacifists, the Martius story is significant because it concerns a time, not just of 'continuall warres', but also, as Appian tells us, when civil order *within* the city broke down altogether.[66] One of the most striking messages that *Coriolanus* has to offer is that, far from uniting people against a common enemy, heroic military values in their most exaggerated form are inherently divisive, setting citizen against citizen, and obliging warrior–aristocrats to assert their superiority over lower orders in the relentless competition for *laus* and *gloria*.

FLOWER OF WARRIORS

At the battle of Corioli, Martius is in his true element. Cursing the 'common file' for their cowardice, and performing deeds of extraordinary daring, he impresses even his fellow warrior-nobles with his

---

[64] See Paul Fussell, *The Great War and Modern Memory* (London, Oxford, and New York: Oxford University Press, 1975), p. 114.
[65] *Blood Rites: Origins and History of the Passions of War* (London: Virago Press, 1997).
[66] *An Aunciect Historie*, trans. 'W.B.' (London, 1578), Sig. A3.

manly valour. During a lull in the battle he greets his old friend Cominius:

> O, let me clip ye
> In arms as sound as when I wooed, in heart
> As merry as when our nuptial day was done,
> And tapers burnt to bedward! (I.vii.29–32)

These lines, together with those in which Aufidius greets Martius at Antium (IV.v.102–36), have caught the attention of critics looking for evidence of homoeroticism in Shakespeare.[67] Bruce Smith finds it odd that Shakespeare should apparently be talking about a male friendship in erotic terms. He says it is surprising for two reasons: first, because 'Renaissance writers ordinarily contrasted, not likened, the friendly ties between man and man with the sexual ties between man and woman'; and second, because 'in legal discourse, sodomy was a capital offence'.[68] In fact it is not at all surprising to find a relationship between warriors described in quasi-erotic language; indeed it was commonplace in chivalric literature. But this does not necessarily mean that Martius and Cominius are sodomites. In his recent *History of Gay Literature* Gregory Woods suggests that it is 'fear and loathing' that leads critics to resist gay readings of such scenes.[69] One would hope that this is not true. The important consideration is surely what language and action tell us about a play's central concerns, rather than what we can deduce from those things about its characters' offstage lives. With a play like *Edward II* homosexuality is a crucial element in the unfolding of the political drama; with *Coriolanus* it is not at all clear that this is so. Since Martius and Cominius are characters in a play, not real people with a life beyond the stage, it makes more

---

[67] There is a widespread assumption in recent gay and feminist studies that homosexuality, along with human nature, did not exist in early-modern England and was 'invented', according to different scholars, either in the seventeenth, the eighteenth, or the nineteenth century (see Alan Bray, *Homosexuality in Renaissance England* (London: Gay Men's Press, 1982); Valerie Traub, *Desire and Anxiety: Circulations of Sexuality in Shakespearean Drama* (London and New York: Routledge, 1992)). This counter-intuitive claim has been effectively demolished by Joseph Cady who shows that the Renaissance had a very clear sense of homosexuality as a distinct category ('"Masculine Love," Renaissance Writing, and the "New Invention" of Homosexuality' in *Homosexuality in Renaissance England: Literary Representations in Historical Context*, ed. Claude J. Summers (New York, London, and Norwood (Australia): Haworth Press, 1992), pp. 9–40).

[68] *Homosexual Desire in Shakespeare's England: A Cultural Poetics* (Chicago: University of Chicago Press, 1991), p. 35. On the 'quasi-homosexual relationship' between Martius and Aufidius see also Ralph Berry, 'Sexual Imagery in *Coriolanus*', *SEL*, 13 (1973), 301–16.

[69] *A History of Gay Literature: The Male Tradition* (New Haven, Conn. and London: Yale University Press, 1998), p. 99.

sense to enquire what their metaphors have to do with war, military values and social conflict, than to ask how these men spend their hypothetical private moments. The key to the significance of Martius' imagery lies in Cominius' reply: 'Flower of warriors!' (I.vii.33). These three words may not tell us very much about Martius' and Cominius' private lives, but they tell us a great deal about the kind of leader Martius is and the values he subscribes to.

Although it is not at all uncommon to find knights in medieval romance embracing and kissing with all the apparent fervour of lovers, such extravagant displays of affection are not normally a sign of sexual interest.[70] They echo early Christian social customs. In his Epistles St Paul regularly signs off with the injunction to affirm brotherhood ties by 'salut[ing] one another with a holy kiss' (Rom. 16:16; cf I Cor. 16:20; II Cor. 13:12; I Thess. 5:26). Though the last of the three kisses with which Gawain and Bertilak seal their exchanges of winnings[71] might be thought to echo Judas rather than St Paul, the kiss is a normal way of showing brotherly loyalty in chivalric romance. The recognition scene in the tenth book of the *Morte D'Arthur* is a good example. In Book II Merlin prophesies to King Mark that at the tomb of his son Launceor a great duel will take place. It will be 'the grettist bateyle betwyxte two knyghtes that was or ever shall be, and the trewyst lovers; and yette none of hem shall slee other' (II.viii).[72] Eight books later the mysterious battle takes place. Two knights arrive at Launceor's tomb and immediately start fighting. The battle lasts for four hours, during which time neither says a word. When they can fight no longer they pause on the bloodsoaked grass and ask each other's name. It turns out that one is Launcelot, the other Trystram. When Trystram realizes whom he has been fighting he says 'Alas! what have I done! For ye ar the man

---

[70] See Reginald Hyatte, *The Arts of Friendship: The Idealization of Friendship in Medieval and Early Renaissance Literature* (Leiden, New York, and Cologne: E.J. Brill, 1994), ch. 3. Hyatte points out that not even the relationship between Galehout and Launcelot in the thirteenth-century *Prose Launcelot* – widely assumed to be homosexual – is consummated on a physical level (p. 103).

[71] In a recent discussion of *Sir Gawain*, Carolyn Dinshaw argues that the kisses that Gawain and Bertilak exchange should be read 'as components of a specific inflection of a broad heterocultural strategy of unintelligibility', by which I *think* she means that the poem is hinting that the relationship between Gawain and Bertilak could, in other circumstances, have been homosexual, but in fact is not ('A Kiss is Just a Kiss: Heterosexuality and its Consolations in *Sir Gawain and the Green Knight*', *Dia*, 24 (1994), 205–6).

[72] *The Works of Sir Thomas Malory*, 3 vols.; ed. Eugène Vinaver; revised by P.J.C. Field (Oxford: Clarendon Press, 1990), vol. I, p. 72

in the worlde that I love beste'. They then take off their helmets and, embracing each other, 'ayther kyste other an hondred tymes' (xv).[73] These men are not homosexuals, or even bisexuals. Both are extravagantly, even compulsively, heterosexual, and Malory does not shrink from relating how they sometimes spend whole nights of passion with their lovers. But there is never any question of them sleeping with other men. Their relationship is the idealized heroic love of brothers-in-arms. What they are in love with is the idea of their own flamboyant chivalry mirrored in another.[74] There are similar scenes in *The Faerie Queene*. In Book IV Triamond and his brothers spend some thirty stanzas fighting Cambell for the hand of Canacee. But no sooner have Triamond and Cambell felt the power of Cambina's magic wand of friendship than hostility gives way to love:

> each other kissed glad,
> And lovely haulst from feare of treason free,
> And plighted hands for ever friends to be. (IV.iii.49–51)[75]

But again, for all the kissing, their love is no more a homosexual love than that of Launcelot and Trystram: the conflict had been over a woman in the first place, and when it has been resolved Triamond marries Canacee and Cambell marries Cambina.

Like Palamon and Arcite, Launcelot and Trystram, Triamond and Cambell, and many other pairs of knights in romance literature, Martius and Cominius are sworn brothers-in-arms. When Martius asks Cominius to let him fight against Aufidius he appeals to their brotherly pact:

> I do beseech you
> By all the battles wherein we have fought,
> By th' blood we have shed together, by th' vows we have made
> To endure friends, that you directly set me
> Against Aufidius and his Antiates. (I.vii.55–9)

[73] Ibid., vol. II, p. 570.
[74] Cf Burton Hatlen: 'both Coriolanus and Aufidius seem to be fixated at Lacan's mirror stage, entranced by a "perfect" image of the self' ('The "Noble Thing" and the "Boy of Tears"': Coriolanus and the Embarrassments of Identity', *ELR*, 27 (1997), 408–9). While it is true that Shakespeare's warriors are fascinated by each other in much the same way that medieval knights and present-day boxers are both attracted and repelled by rivals, it is not easy to see how a purely speculative theory of child development unsupported by empirical evidence helps us to understand this familiar phenomenon. The fact of the matter is that, as Shakespeare's Aeneas points out, warriors love the thing they mean to kill (*Tro.*, IV.i.23–4).
[75] Edmund Spenser, *The Poetical Works*, ed. J.C. Smith and E. de Selincourt (London, New York, and Toronto: Oxford University Press, 1912), p. 230.

As Cominius' greeting, 'Flower of warriors' suggests, their friendship has more to do with medieval chivalric traditions than with either homoerotic desire or with the kind of *amicitia* that plays such an important part in *Julius Caesar*.

In the final years of the Republic friendship was an essential part of the political process. As Plutarch's 'Life of Cicero' so vividly shows, the upheavals of this momentous period were a story of friendships made and broken, of 'betrayals, renewals and re-betrayals'.[76] *Julius Caesar* captures brilliantly the suspicions and the jealousies that are inevitable in a world where friendship, for all its personal rewards, serves a primarily political purpose. It is repeatedly evoked by both conspirators and avengers as evidence of loyalty to a cause. When Cassius tells Brutus,

> I do observe you now of late.
> I have not from your eyes that gentleness
> And show of love as I was wont to have.
> You bear too stubborn and too strange a hand
> Over your friend that loves you.   (*JC*, I.ii.34–8)

both know that he is testing the strength of his friend's political allegiance, and Brutus is quick to apologize for neglecting his 'good friends' and for forgetting those 'shows of love to other men' (45, 49) that are such an important part of republican political life. It is one of the ironies of the conspiracy that the man who wrote so nobly on the subject of friendship was himself executed on account of his own friendship with the leader of an assassination plot. Cicero's *De Amicitia*, that favourite handbook of Tudor humanists,[77] is more than just a popular essay intended for the general reader echoing commonplaces from Plato, Aristotle, Xenophon, and Theophrastus. With its urbane discourse between politicians and statesmen, it enacts an ideal conception of civilization that is far removed from the Machiavellian scheming that was the reality of late republican politics.

Though it is generally agreed that Martius is the most Roman of all Shakespeare's heroes,[78] his friendship with Cominius is as remote

---

[76] Horst Hutter, *Politics as Friendship: The Origins of Classical Notions of Politics in the Theory and Practice of Friendship* (Waterloo, Ontario: Wilfrid Laurier University Press, 1978), p. 136.
[77] Thomas Lupset writes: 'Howe you shall know them that be worthy to be your frendis & by what menes, & what wey frendes be both gotten & also kept, ye shall best lerne in Ciceros littell boke *De Amicitia*', quoted by Laurens J. Mills, *One Soul in Bodies Twain: Friendship in Tudor Literature and Stuart Drama* (Bloomington, Ind.: Principia Press, 1937), p. 96. Mills lists some of the many Tudor translations of *De Amicitia*, pp. 79–80.
[78] Brower, *Hero and Saint*, p. 372.

from the *De Amicitia*, with its idealized conversation between cultured statesmen, as it is from the machinations of a Cassius or an Antony. While those around him, both in Rome and Antium, are busily involved in political scheming, Martius lives in his own heroic world, a world where friendship means, not a strategic alliance between politicians, but a pact of 'manhood and Chevalrie' between heroic brothers-in-arms, and where, despite avowals of heroic patriotism (I.vii.71–3), personal honour is more important than national security. Brutus, the tribune, knows that a more wily career strategist would be content to play second fiddle to his general (I.i.263–70). But Martius lives for the dream of *gloria* won through heroic combat. Confessing his lust for honour, he admits that battle with a worthy opponent is his greatest ambition:

> Were half to half the world by th' ears and he
> Upon my party, I'd revolt to make
> Only my wars with him. He is a lion
> That I am proud to hunt.   (I.i.233–6)

Knowing his man, Aufidius shrewdly appeals to this obsessive passion for chivalric conflict when he welcomes Martius to Antium.

To interpret Aufidius' talk of twining his arms about Martius' body and contesting 'As hotly and as nobly with thy love / As ever in ambitious strength I did / Contend against thy valour' (IV.v.112–14) as evidence of homosexual desire is to divert attention from the important signals that the Volscian general is sending to his enemy. Aufidius wants his old adversary to know that he recognizes in him a kindred spirit who will be a Trystram to his own Launcelot. It is an invitation that Martius cannot resist. In doing so he fails to recognize one of the oldest tricks in the trade. The distinction between true and false friendship is a favourite topic in classical, medieval, and Renaissance writing. A lyric from Timothy Kendall's *Flowers of Epigrams* (1577) is typical of verses on friendship that were produced in their dozens in the sixteenth century:

> Not he so muche annoyes and hurtes
>   that saies I am thy foe:
> As he that beares a hatefull harte,
>   and is a frende to showe.
> Warnde of my foe, I shunne my foe:
>   but how should I take heede
> Of hym that faines himself my frende,
>   when as he hates in deede?

> Moste sure a wretched foe is he,
> > whiche frendship firme doeth faine:
> And sekes by all the shifts he can,
> > his frende to put to paine.[79]

Martius' failure to notice the deceit in Aufidius' declaration of chivalric friendship is the more ironical when he himself has just been reflecting on the vicissitudes of friendship in lines that frankly acknowledge his own act of betrayal:

> O world, thy slippery turns! Friends now fast sworn,
> Whose double bosoms seem to wear one heart,
> Whose hours, whose bed, whose meal and exercise
> Are still together, who twin as 'twere in love
> Unseparable, shall within this hour,
> On a dissension of a doit, break out
> To bitterest enmity . . .
> > So with me.
> My birthplace hate I, and my love's upon
> This enemy town.   (IV.iv.12–24)

But it is not just gullibility that Martius is guilty of. As a class, the patricians in *Coriolanus* show little sympathy for the plight of the plebeians; even Menenius, commonly regarded as a jovial conciliator, is openly sarcastic to them. But as the embodiment of 'manhood and Chevalrie' in its most exaggerated form, it is Martius who is the chief architect of discord in Rome. A measure of his divisiveness as a leader is the gulf between his own conception of heroic manhood and the view of society expressed in the play's ruling image of community – the body/state analogy.

THE BODY POLITIC

When Martius curses the common soldiers for their cowardice at the battle of Corioli the fate he wishes on them is boils and plagues (I.v.2). As a natural ramification of the body/state analogy, disease is an important thematic image in *Coriolanus* and is used by patricians and tribunes alike in their attempts to diagnose Rome's sickness: while Martius regards the tribunes as an infection threatening the health of the body politic, they see him as a gangrenous limb that needs to be cut away (III.i.152–60, 296–309).

---

[79] Quoted by Mills, *One Soul in Bodies Twain*, p. 126.

From its earliest use in Greek antiquity,[80] the anthropomorphic analogy served to illustrate the importance of co-operation of all members of the state for the good of the whole. In the *De Officiis* Cicero wrote:

> if everie parte of the bodie should have this imagination: to think, it might be strong, if it had conveyed to itself the strength of the next limmes: of force it should folowe, that the holle bodie should be weakened, and perish: evenso if everieone of us catche to himself the commodities of other, and pulleth from eche man what he can, for his owne profites sake: the felowship, and common companie of men must needes be overthrowne.[81]

It is this classic ideal of social co-operation in which all members contribute to the good of the whole that Menenius appeals to in his fable of the belly.

Considered from a Marxist point of view, the anthropomorphic analogy is a classic piece of ideological indoctrination: by persuading the lower orders of society to believe that a 'kingly crownèd head' is as much part of the natural order of things as the 'muniments and petty helps/In this our fabric' (1.i.113, 116–17), their willing collusion in maintaining a status quo that favours the aristocracy is assured. For if human society is, in Sir Thomas Elyot's words, 'a body lyvying, compacte or made of sondry estates and degrees of men',[82] then it is as necessary for the state to have a head as a 'great toe' (153); take away either, and the body can no longer function effectively. It is a measure of the hegemonic power of the anthropomorphic analogy and its ability to persuade people that social hierarchies are natural and God-given, it might be argued, that plebeians are still thinking in anachronistic terms of a 'kingly crownèd head' in a republican state (actually more of an aristocratic oligarchy than a true republic) that has banished its ruling dynasty.

While this type of analysis has its own sociological value, it is of limited interest to the historicist. The anthropomorphic analogy has such a long history in antiquity, the Middle Ages, and the Renaissance,[83] and is used in such a wide variety of constitutional

---

[80] David George Hale, 'The Body Politic: A Political Metaphor in Renaissance English Literature' (Duke University, PhD thesis, 1965), p. 14.

[81] *Marcus Tullius Ciceroes thre bokes of duties*, trans. Nicholas Grimald, ed. Gerald O'Gorman (Washington: The Folger Shakespeare Library, 1990) pp. 153–4.

[82] Sir Thomas Elyot, *The Boke Named the Governour*, ed. Foster Watson (London: Dent, 1907), p. 1.

[83] See Hale, *The Body Politic*. See also Leonard Barkan, *Nature's Work of Art: The Human Body as Image of the World* (New Haven, Conn. and London: Yale University Press, 1975); Reuben

contexts, that no analysis which speaks in general terms about strategies of power that are effectively transcultural and transhistorical can tell us much about early seventeenth-century England and the particular political problems it was grappling with. A contemporary playgoer listening to Menenius' fable of the belly would be likely to be struck less by the inherent implausibility of this familiar story,[84] than by the patronizing tone of the Belly. It is not so much that the organic metaphor is too simple a model for dealing with complex political realities, as David Hale argues,[85] as that the meaning of the traditional model has been travestied. The one constant factor in the countless variations on the anthropomorphic analogy is the value to the community of all its members and the importance of co-operation in the corporate enterprise; as Thomas Starkey puts it, 'the strength of the politic body standeth in every part being able to do his office and duty'.[86] In Menenius' version of the classic fable this fundamental principle has been violated.[87] It is not just that the Belly is frankly contemptuous of the 'other instruments', and replies to their complaints with a 'taunting' smile; as Menenius interprets the story, the plebeians are idle recipients of a one-way flow of benefits from patricians to the common people:

> The senators of Rome are this good belly,
> And you the mutinous members. For examine
> Their counsels and their cares, digest things rightly
> Touching the weal o' th' common, you shall find
> No public benefit which you receive
> But it proceeds or comes from them to you,
> And no way from yourselves. (1.i.146–52)

Shakespeare's Menenius is a very different character from the 'mediator for civil attonement', beloved of senators and commoners

---

Brower, Introduction to *The Tragedy of Coriolanus* (New York and Toronto: New American Library, 1966), pp. xlii–xlvi.

[84] Among writers who rehearse the fable of the belly are Aesop, Livy, Plutarch, St Paul, Erasmus, Elyot, Forset, Sidney, and Camden (see Hale, *The Body Politic*, pp. 25–8, 134; Andrew Gurr, '*Coriolanus* and the Body Politic', *ShS*, 28 (1975), 66); Parker, Introduction to *The Tragedy of 'Coriolanus'*, ed. Parker, p. 19.

[85] David G. Hale, '*Coriolanus*: The Death of a Political Metaphor', *SQ*, 22 (1971), 197–202.

[86] Thomas Starkey, *A Dialogue Between Reginald Pole and Thomas Lupset*, ed. K.M. Burton (London: Chatto & Windus, 1948), p. 57.

[87] Cf Gurr, '*Coriolanus* and the Body Politic': 'Menenius is not offering a rationale of the state as a single organism so much as conducting a cynical delaying action' (p. 67).

alike, that Livy describes.[88] In retelling the fable of the belly Menenius transforms the traditional meaning of the anthropomorphic analogy, characterizing the plebeians, not as supporting limbs, but as social parasites sponging off the body politic.

There has been much debate on the question of whether Shakespeare's political sympathies are republican, or monarchist, or whether he favoured a mixed constitution. Contrary to the view, widely expressed in recent criticism, that Shakespeare wrote his later plays under an absolutist regime that was willing to tolerate little freedom of speech,[89] there was lively discussion of constitutional questions in Jacobean England.[90] Francis Bacon is said to have told James personally that Venice, renowned for the longevity of its republican constitution, was the 'wisest state of Europe'.[91] The fact that Shakespeare uses the anthropomorphic analogy in plays about republics (*JC*, II.i.66–9), empires (*Tit.*, v.iii.69–71), hereditary monarchies (*Jn.*, IV.ii.112), usurper monarchies (*2H4*, III.i.37–42), elective monarchies (*Ham.*, I.iii.21–4), and ducal states (*MM*, I.ii.147) suggests that he is concerned more with the underlying causes of social disorder, be it in ancient Rome, medieval England, or Renaissance Europe, than with the merits of any one particular system of government.[92] As the Roman plays show, irresponsible leadership and corrupt government can just as easily be found in a republican democracy as in an hereditary monarchy or a patrician oligarchy. In *Coriolanus* there is no one single cause of the breakdown of order.[93]

---

[88] *The Romane Historie*, p. 66.
[89] See Alan Sinfield, '*Macbeth*: History, Ideology, and Intellectuals', *Faultlines: Cultural Materialism and the Politics of Dissident Reading* (Oxford: Clarendon Press, 1992), pp. 95–108.
[90] See above, Chapter 2, p. 71. Margaret Attwood Judson, *The Crisis of the Constitution: An Essay in Constitutional and Political Thought in England, 1603–1645* (New Brunswick, N.J.: Rutgers University Press, 1949); Huffman, '*Coriolanus' in Context*, p. 135; Barry Coward, *The Stuart Age: A History of England 1603–1714* (London and New York: Longman, 1980), p. 102; Derek Hirst, *Authority and Conflict: England 1603–1658* (London: Edward Arnold, 1986), pp. 40–1; Glenn Burgess, *The Politics of the Ancient Constitution: An Introduction to English Political Thought, 1603–1642* (Basingstoke and London: Macmillan, 1992), pp. 110–12; Patrick Collinson, 'The Monarchical Republic of Queen Elizabeth I', *Elizabethan Essays* (London and Rio Grande: Hambledon Press, 1994), pp. 31–57; Markku Peltonen, *Classical Humanism and Republicanism in English Political Thought 1570–1640* (Cambridge: Cambridge University Press, 1995), pp. 3–4.
[91] Peltonen, *Classical Humanism and Republicanism*, p. 179.
[92] Cf Glenn Burgess, 'Revisionist History and Shakespeare's Political Context', *Shakespeare and History*, Shakespeare Yearbook 6, ed. Holger Klein and Rowland Wymer (Lewiston, Queenstown and Lampeter: Edwin Mellen Press, 1996), pp. 5–36.
[93] Brian Vickers rightly notes that Shakespeare does not offer explicit judgment on the political conflict: 'He votes . . . against both sides' (*Returning to Shakespeare* (London and New York: Routledge, 1989), p. 135).

Of the fickleness of the plebeians there can be no question. It is one of the menial Senate Officers who acknowledges the capriciousness of plebeian opinion: 'there be many that they have loved they know not wherefore, so that if they love they know not why, they hate upon no better a ground' (II.ii.9–11), while the Third Citizen succinctly sums up the futility of relying on plebeian judgment in affairs of state when he admits of the banishment of Martius: 'That we did, we did for the best, and though we willingly consented to his banishment, yet it was against our will' (IV.vi.152–4). However, if the plebeians characterize themselves as hopelessly indecisive, they are at least tolerant and open-minded and can hardly be blamed for the conflict between the orders. That responsibility is shared jointly by the politically astute, but cynical tribunes and the self-serving patricians. But though relations between the orders are tense, it needs Martius' intervention to bring this volatile state of affairs to combustion point. Peggy Muñoz Simonds pointed out that, as a type of Mars, his very existence in the city is inflammatory:[94] since Mars, in Roman mythology, is a god whose purlieus lie beyond the civilized world, his presence *within* the city can be almost guaranteed to cause 'strange insurrections,/the people against the senators, patricians, and nobles' (IV.iii.13–14).

However cynical individuals may be in their interpretation of it, all three orders in Rome do at least agree that the body is a valid analogy for debating political issues. It is Martius alone who rejects the traditional co-operative model, not just refusing to take seriously the plebeians' grievances, but actively 'seek[ing] their hate with greater devotion than they can render it him' (II.ii.18–19). If he had his own way he would eliminate, not just the plebeians' voice in political affairs (III.i.159), but the common people themselves:

> Would the nobility lay aside their ruth
> And let me use my sword, I'd make a quarry
> With thousands of these quartered slaves as high
> As I could pitch my lance.   (I.i.195–8)

Nor is this very surprising. As Erich Auerbach noted, in the world of chivalry the proving of knightly valour is everything, and the

---

[94] '*Coriolanus* and the Myth of Juno and Mars', p. 44.

historically real aspects of daily life are typically ignored.[95] It is such a world to which Martius would like to belong, an idealized world of heroic combat in which the mundane realities of class and politics are refined out of existence.[96]

In one of his more thoughtful speeches Martius warns of the folly of having more than one authority in the state (III.i.112–15), a theme rehearsed by Plutarch and Machiavelli,[97] and dramatized in plays like *Gorboduc* and *King Lear*. In doing so Martius merely shows how incapable he is of providing that responsible leadership himself. 'You speak o' th' people as if you were a god / To punish, not a man of their infirmity'(III.i.85–6), Brutus tells him. But it is Volumnia who articulates most vividly the true meaning of Martius' rejection of the notion of community as expressed in the play's ruling image of the state as living body. Pleading with him to spare Rome, she describes him as a monster 'tearing / His country's bowels out' (v.iii.103–4). But for all his iron-hearted determination, Martius is unable to achieve the break with nature that he strives for. Jonathan Dollimore argues that *Coriolanus* exposes the essentialist belief in a universal human nature for the myth that it is: in reality we are merely the product of social forces, with no underlying core of shared humanity.[98] It would be difficult to imagine a reading that is more completely at odds with the meaning of the play's central thematic image. In the act of denying nature, instinct, and essence, Martius affirms those very things; in the act of suggesting that a man might be his own author (v.iii.36) he demonstrates its impossibility. Confronted by the combined pleas of 'mother, wife and child' (101), the supreme solipsist is unable, finally, to deny the 'bond and privilege of nature' (25). Radical anti-essentialism not only makes nonsense of the early-modern belief in the value of history; it also negates the

---

[95] *Mimesis: The Representation of Reality in Western Literature*, trans. Willard Trask (Garden City, N.Y.: Doubleday Anchor, 1953), p. 119.

[96] For a recent counter-argument to the one I have set out in the last two paragraphs see Thomas Clayton, '"So our virtues lie in the'interpretation of the time"': Shakespeare's Tragic *Coriolanus* and Coriolanus, and Some Questions of Value', *Ben Jonson Journal*, 1 (1994), 147–81. Quoting Ibsen's *Enemy of the People* ('the strongest man in the world is he who stands most alone'), Clayton writes: 'Ibsen obviously saw and valued such a spirit in *Coriolanus*, and there is every reason in the play to think that Shakespeare and probably his "target" audience did, too' (p. 151).

[97] Plutarch, 'The Life of Caius Martius Coriolanus', p. 162; *Machiavels discourses upon the first Decade of T. Livius*, pp. 47–53.

[98] *Radical Tragedy: Religion, Ideology and Power in the Drama of Shakespeare and his Contemporaries* (1984; repr. Brighton: Harvester, 1986), pp. 218–30.

play's most fundamental political principle, namely, that irrespective of the particular constitutional form of the body politic, men and women are by nature social beings who depend on one another for their political as well as their personal well-being.[99] To the modern anti-humanist the anthropomorphic analogy is either pre-scientific make-believe, or a particularly successful form of ideological interpellation, or both. But for Shakespeare's contemporaries it expressed a truth subscribed to by monarchists and republicans alike. Reuben Brower puts it well when he writes, 'metaphors of the body politic keep reminding us that the great natural order is realized in a whole of which the single man is only a part'.[100]

Analysis of *Coriolanus* as political drama has tended to deal with the play either in terms of class warfare[101] or in the context of early-modern debate on constitutional theory.[102] Allusions in the play to the parliamentary wrangles over the winning of the initiative in the early years of James' reign, and to the Midlands riots of 1607, give a uniquely topical flavour to Shakespeare's picture of a society divided against itself. But it is the immediate and controversial issue of martial versus eirenic values, rather than the more academic question of the merits and demerits of republican government, that is the play's central concern. Like Chapman's Byron,[103] the play's hero is a passionate militarist who despises the kind of pageants of peace to which the London populace had been so lavishly treated in 1604: 'plant love among 's', he tells Menenius with undisguised sarcasm, 'Throng our large temples with the shows of peace, / And not our streets with war!' (III.iii.36–8). Martius' whole world revolves around extraordinary feats of masculine prowess, while his marriage appears to be almost non-existent. Anything less like Terry Eagleton's

---

[99] For a recent challenge to anti-essentialist readings of the play see McAlindon, '*Coriolanus*: An Essentialist Tragedy'.
[100] Bower, Introduction to *The Tragedy of Coriolanus*, p. xlvi.
[101] See above note 6.
[102] See Huffman, *'Coriolanus' in Context*; Patricia K. Meszaros, ' "There is a world elsewhere": Tragedy and History in *Coriolanus*', *SEL*, 16 (1976), 273–85. For one of the best recent discussions of the play's engagement with classical and early-modern constitutional debate see Anne Barton, 'Livy, Machiavelli, and Shakespeare's *Coriolanus*', *ShS*, 38 (1985), 115–29. On Shakespeare's use of Machiavelli see also Victoria Kahn, *Machiavellian Rhetoric: From the Counter-Reformation to Milton* (Princeton: Princeton University Press, 1994), pp. 119–24.
[103] Comparing himself to the Earl of Essex, Byron complains of the way 'sensuall peace confounds / Valure' (*The Conspiracie and Tragedie of Charles Duke of Byron*, I.ii.15–16, *The Plays of George Chapman: The Tragedies*, ed. John B. Gabel (Woodbridge, Suffolk and Wolfeboro, N.H.: D.S. Brewer, 1987), p. 339).

'bourgeois individualist'[104] would be difficult to imagine. A warrior to the core of his being, he has no more notion of representing the political interests of lower orders than King Arthur's knights do: his main concern is to prove his masculine honour, and to do this he must show that his fellow citizens are lacking in this quality, leaving, as Sicinius remarks, 'nothing undone that may fully discover him their opposite' (II.ii.20–1). 'Worshipful mutineers,' he sneers at the hungry plebeians, 'Your valour puts well forth' (I.i.250–1). As if in confirmation of his fundamentally asocial cast of mind, Martius' professions of humility after the battle of Corioli are immediately followed by the revealing incident of the Volscian host he claims to want to reward (I.x.81ff). When two common soldiers meet on the plain of Antium after what is presumably a period of months or even years, they have no trouble remembering each other's names, despite their altered appearance (IV.iii.1–7). But in a departure from Plutarch, Shakespeare has Martius find he cannot recall the name of the man whose hospitality he has so recently received. Like his *virtus*, his display of magnanimity serves only one cause – his own reputation. His world is in truth a fantasy world of chivalric deeds in which plebeians play no part. And when he goes into exile, the creature he compares himself to is a lonely dragon (IV.i.31) – a monster that exists only in the worlds of mythology and romance.

While recognizing the importance of courage in defence of one's country, classical humanists cautioned against the dangers of self-seeking ambition.[105] Their warnings were regularly repeated by sixteenth- and seventeenth-century political writers. In *A philosophicall discourse* (1576) Thomas Rogers argued that 'an unmeasurable desire for glory' is 'the most daungerous thing in a common weale'.[106] It was the politically destabilizing effect of neo-chivalric values that concerned Sir Robert Cotton when he warned of the dangers of the cult of masculinity that the Prince of Wales was so eager to promulgate. 'The last mischief is the disposition that military education leaveth in the minds of many,' he wrote in his reply to Henry's Protestant advisors,

for it is not born with them that they so much distaste peace, but proceeds from that custom that hath made in them another nature. It is rarely found

---

[104] Terry Eagleton, *William Shakespeare* (Oxford: Basil Blackwell, 1986), p. 73.
[105] See for example *Ciceroes thre bokes of duties*, pp. 83–4.
[106] *A philosophicall discourse, entituled, the anatomie of the minde* (London, 1576), fols. 10^v-11^v.

that ever Civil troubles of this State were dangerously undertaken, but where the plot and pursuit was made by a spirit so infused.[107]

Shakespeare's Martius is the supreme example of the mischief that Cotton feared in 1608. Whatever naturally aggressive inclinations he may have been born with – and Brutus knows that irascibility is in 'his nature' (II.iii.258) – these qualities have been exacerbated by a mother determined that he should be a model of Roman *virtus* (I.iii.1–25). As Menenius says, 'he has been bred i' th' wars / Since a could draw a sword, and is ill-schooled' (III.i.322–3). The same schooling is now being repeated with Martius' son. Sounding remarkably like Queen Anne in Birch's account of the way Prince Henry was encouraged to believe 'that learning was inconsistent with the character of a great General and Conqueror', Volumnia reports that 'He had rather see the swords and hear a drum / than look upon his schoolmaster' (I.iii.57–8).

WAR AND CHIVALRY

In his discussion of the Roman character Cicero allows himself a moment of national congratulation as he considers his country's extraordinary military successes. 'Specially,' he wrote in the *De Officiis*, 'the people of Rome did exceede in greatnesse of corage. And their desire of martial glorie is declared: in that wee see, their images of honour be set up, for the most parte, in warrlike aray.'[108] But Cicero is aware that there is an intractable problem here. While successful nations need strong leaders, the qualities that make for effective military leadership all too often threaten the very stability that it is the leader's job to safeguard. In a military society masculine values are glorified, often by comparing them unfavourably with their female counterparts. 'That seemes to shine brightest: which is wrought with a greate and lofty corage, despising worldly vanities', said Cicero; and when you want to insult a man you tell him he has a 'womens herte'.[109] But as Cicero himself pointed out, the man who displays 'greatnesse of corage' is likely also to have a keen interest in the rewards of power:

as everie man is of the hyest corage, and disirous of glorie: so is he soonest egged to unjust doinges.

---

[107] *An Answer . . . to Certain Propositions of Warre and Peace*, pp. 20–1.
[108] *Ciceroes thre bokes of duties*, p. 74.   [109] Ibid., p. 74.

Which is indeede a verie slipper place: bicause scase ther is anie man founde, who when he hathe susteined travailes, and aventured daungers, dooth not desire glorie, as reward of his dooinges.[110]

This is a conundrum that interested Shakespeare deeply. Apart from *Coriolanus*, the plays that address the problem most directly are *Hamlet* and *Macbeth*. The former shows a potential national leader torn between military and civic–humanist ideals; the latter considers the problem of the use of violence in the pursuit of peaceful ends. Neither play offers a solution to the problems it poses: a sweet prince gives his dying voice to the Viking irredentist who has been trying to seize Danish territory, and a pacifist monarch who passionately denied the right of resistance is complimented by a story that shows how his ancestors fought tyranny with heroic violence. *Coriolanus* is less equivocal than either of these plays. Written at a time when 'manhood and Chevalrie' were once again acquiring a powerful popular appeal, it is Shakespeare's last and most emphatic denunciation of heroic values.

[110] Ibid., p. 76.

CHAPTER 6

'Rarer action': The Tempest

> Heav'n calls me to the War: Th'expected Sign
> Is giv'n of promis'd Aid, and Arms Divine
>   . . .
>   He said, and, rising from his homely Throne,
> The Solemn Rites of *Hercules* begun:
> And on his Altars wak'd the sleeping Fires.
> <div align="right">Dryden's translation of Virgil's <i>Aeneid</i>, VIII.706–20</div>

> Orpheus with his lute made trees,
> And the mountain tops that freeze,
> Bow themselves when he did sing.
> To his music plants and flowers
> Ever sprung, as sun and showers
> There had made a lasting spring.
> <div align="right"><i>Henry VIII</i>, III.i.3–8</div>

In the brief interval of calm following Martius' exile in the fourth act of *Coriolanus*, Brutus and Sicinius congratulate themselves on their astute handling of a difficult situation. Martius is safely out of the way and the 'world goes well' (IV.vi.5). Then comes news that Martius has joined forces with Aufidius and is about to attack Rome. At first the tribunes cannot believe their ears. 'This is most likely!' says Sicinius, 'The very trick on 't' (70, 73). But Cominius berates them for their stupidity, assuring them that Martius will be merciless in his vengeance. 'He'll shake your Rome about your ears', Cominius tells them. 'As Hercules did shake down mellow fruit', adds Menenius (103–4). Though there are only two allusions to Hercules in *Coriolanus*, Eugene Waith is justified in describing Martius as the supreme Herculean hero. For Hercules is not only the archetypal warrior; he is also famed for his terrible vengeance. Shakespeare's most egregious example of the warrior–hero is truly Herculean, not just in his manly courage, but also in his vindictive rage.

177

In his final play Shakespeare portrays an entirely different kind of leader. If, as Waith suggests, the heroes of the martial tragedies are variations on a Herculean theme, the central mythological figure that dominates the late tragi-comedies is Hercules' symbolic antithesis. That figure is Orpheus, the divinely gifted poet–musician who was able to move even 'moody Pluto' (*Luc.*, line 553) by his eloquence.[1] Though both Hercules and Orpheus are represented as peacemakers in Roman literature, they represent antithetical views of manhood and civilization. 'As the works of wisdom surpass in dignity and power the works of strength,' wrote Bacon in *The Wisdom of the Ancients* (1609), 'so the labours of Orpheus surpass the labours of Hercules.'[2] War is one of the most rigidly gendered of all human activities,[3] and Hercules, the mythological founder of war, is the very type of heroic manhood. Not surprisingly, the values of the warrior-society are masculine values. Orpheus, by contrast, is a type of the creative artist and embodies a very different ideal of manhood.

HERCULES AND ORPHEUS: THE QUEST FOR PEACE

In Ovid's *Metamorphoses* – the most accessible version of the Hercules story for Jacobean readers – the greatest warrior of the ancient world does not come across as a particularly complicated character. Courageous but gullible – he is an easy prey to Nessus' trickery – he shows, as Ovid's sixteenth-century translator Arthur Golding puts it, that 'valiantnesse of hart / Consisteth not in woords, but deedes: and that all slyght [i.e., subterfuge] and Art / Give place to prowesse'.[4] Though the suffering he endures as he tries to escape the

---

[1] Northrop Frye, *A Natural Perspective: The Development of Shakespearean Comedy and Romance* (New York: Columbia University Press, 1965), p. 147. See also David Armitage, 'The Dismemberment of Orpheus: Mythic Elements in Shakespeare's Romances', *ShS*, 39 (1986), 123–33; Robin Headlam Wells, *Elizabethan Mythologies: Studies in Poetry, Drama and Music* (Cambridge: Cambridge University Press, 1994), pp. 63–80; Peggy Muñoz Simonds, *Myth, Emblem, and Music in Shakespeare's 'Cymbeline': An Iconographic Reconstruction* (Newark, N.J.: University of Delaware Press, 1992); Simonds, '"Sweet Power of Music": The Political Magic of "the Miraculous Harp" in Shakespeare's *The Tempest*', *CD*, 29 (1995), 61–90. Jonathan Bate discusses allusions to Orpheus in *Venus and Adonis*, *The Rape of Lucrece* and briefly in *The Winter's Tale* and *Henry VIII* in *Shakespeare and Ovid* (Oxford: Clarendon Press, 1993).
[2] *The Philosophical Works*, ed. John M. Robertson (London: George Routledge, 1905), p. 835.
[3] Barbara Ehrenreich, *Blood Rites: Origins and History of the Passions of War* (London: Virago Press, 1997), p. 125. See also Margaret Loftus Ranald, 'War and its Surrogates: Male Combat Sports and Women's Roles', *TRI*, 23 (1998), 59–68.
[4] 'The Epistle', 199–200, *Shakespeare's Ovid*, trans. Arthur Golding, ed. W.H.D. Rouse (London: Centaur Press, 1961), p. 5.

terrible pain of Nessus' poisoned shirt is truly heroic, it is, by its very excess, almost beyond human comprehension. Even his transmogrification is spectacular rather than moving. W.B. Stanford describes Hercules as a prototype of the muscle-man.[5] But as those fabled muscles are consumed on the sacrificial pyre he has built for himself, revealing the unrecognizable, god-like frame beneath (IX. 262–70), Hercules is reminiscent, not so much of a contestant for the title of Mr Olympia, as of James Cameron's Terminator emerging from the holocaust of a burning fuel tanker, with all living tissue seared away, and nothing remaining but a gleaming titanium endoskeleton. Purified by fire, Ovid's hero is now ready for deification.

More interesting for the dramatist is the way Hercules is portrayed by Virgil and Seneca. In the *Aeneid* Hercules himself appears only in the interpolated story of the slaying of Cacus in Book VIII, itself an adumbration of Aeneas' final battle with Turnus. But he is there in spirit throughout the poem. At each stage of the story Aeneas is compared with Hercules.[6] His trials are described as *labores*, which, like those of Hercules, have been imposed on him by envious Juno. And like Hercules, too, he makes a descent into the underworld. By linking Aeneas with a hero who was deified for his extraordinary *virtus*, Virgil is hinting at Augustus' own deification.[7] Augustus wanted the world to see him as a peacemaker, 'Born to restore a better Age of Gold',[8] and deliberately encouraged the association with Hercules, legendary pacifier of Arcadia.[9] But as Tacitus tells us, the new stability for which Augustus' reign is celebrated was won by ruthless elimination of all opposition.[10] While praising his patron as author of the *pax romana*, Virgil had to find some way of justifying the judicial violence that seems to have been an essential item in Augustus' repertoire of 'imperial Arts' (VI.1177). It is a problem that

---

[5] Foreword to G. Karl Galinsky, *The Herakles Theme: The Adaptations of the Hero in Literature from Homer to the Twentieth Century* (Oxford: Basil Blackwell, 1972), pp. ix–x.
[6] Galinsky, *The Herakles Theme*, pp. 132ff.
[7] Ibid., p. 138.
[8] *Aeneid*,VI.1081, trans. Dryden, *The Works of John Dryden*, 20 vols. ed. Edward Niles Hooker, Alan Roper, and H.T. Swedenborg, Jr. (Berkeley, Los Angeles, and London: University of California Press, 1956–89), vol. v (ed. William Frost, 1987), p. 564.
[9] Galinsky, *The Herakles Theme*, p. 141.
[10] Tacitus writes: 'he drew to himselfe the affairs of the Senate; the duties of magistrates and lawes, without contradiction of any: the stoutest by war or proscriptions alreadie spent, and the rest of the nobilitie . . . did rather choose the present estate with securitie, than strive to recover their old danger' (*The Annales of Cornelius Tacitus*, trans. Richard Grenewey (London, 1598), Sig. A1).

he seems to have pondered deeply. The classic palliative solution is to demonize the enemy. In Book VIII Evander tells Aeneas the story of how Hercules defeated Cacus, a hideous creature who is half man, half beast, and who feeds on human flesh. When Hercules exposes Cacus' lair to the light of day, even the gods are sickened by the horrors within. The implied message is clear: no violence can be too great when one is dealing with a monster of such depravity. To commemorate the defeat, the Rutulians establish an annual festival in Hercules' honour. The whole episode closely parallels Aeneas' struggle against Turnus in Book XII.[11]

In an expedient that is all too familiar in the history of colonialism, we seem to be led to the conclusion that, because there is, by implication, something demonic in Turnus too, Aeneas' brutal killing of an indigenous tribal leader is justified. Yet in reality we know that Turnus is not an inhuman monster. He may be full of 'Revenge, and jealous Rage, and secret Spight' (XII.110), but he has good reason: not only has his country been taken over, but his future bride has been appropriated by the invader. The more effective the thematic and verbal parallels between Cacus and Turnus, the less justified do they seem. Erasmus is probably right when he says that no empire was built without shedding blood.[12] However, because Virgil paints Aeneas' adversary in the blackest colours, this does not mean that he is complacent in his apparent vindication of the violence that seems to be an inescapable part of the colonial enterprise.[13] Heaven may have decreed that Rome's imperial destiny was 'To rule Mankind; and make the World obey' (VI.1174), but that does not make the violence any more acceptable. Aeneas was known to the Middle Ages and the Renaissance by the conventional epithet *pius*. But by repeatedly reminding us of his spiritual affinity with Hercules, Virgil ensures that we are aware that Aeneas is not just the dutiful son who obeys heaven's will and protects his family gods, but also an empire builder 'Whose Martial Fame from Pole to Pole extends' (VII, 143). His heroic *virtus* is just as essential an aspect of his character as his legendary piety. And, as we saw in Chapter 4, it is that Herculean *virtus* that makes the parallel with Turnus such an uncomfortable one.

[11] Galinsky, *The Herakles Theme*, p. 144.
[12] *The 'Adages' of Erasmus*, ed. and trans. Margaret Mann Phillips (Cambridge: Cambridge University Press, 1964), p. 320.
[13] See Edward W. Said, *Culture and Imperialism* (London: Chatto & Windus, 1993), p. xii.

If the ethical and social conundrum confronting the peacemaker who must use force to subdue barbarism is never far from the surface of the *Aeneid*, it is at the very centre of Seneca's *Hercules furens*. Though by no means his best play, *Hercules* has that grim logic that is typical of Seneca. Ostensibly a tragic tale of human error and divine persecution, the play is in truth a deeply pessimistic meditation on the futility of attempting to achieve peace through violent means.

Like Aeneas, Seneca's Hercules is a peacemaker; his greatest ambition is to subdue tyranny and restore harmony to a discordant world: 'Let restful peace kepe nations quietly,' says Seneca's hero on his triumphant return from Hades, 'nor fierce and fell lykewyse / Let tyrantes raygne' (929, 936–7).[14] But even as he makes his appeal for universal peace, Hercules looks for more tasks to perform and new worlds to conquer, boasting that he will tame nature herself, not by *charming* rocks and trees, as Orpheus had done, but by 'smighting' them down (967–8).[15] As he does so, Juno's spell begins its terrible work, and Hercules starts to have fantasies about leading the Titans in a war of liberation against Olympus.

Though Hercules believes that the earth itself has been conquered (955), his triumph is a hollow one. Surveying the wreckage of his family, Amphitryon warns his son of the poisonous consequences of revenge, telling him that true manhood lies in self-control (see Chapter 3, p. 91). Symbolic of the contrast between artist and warrior is the ironic discrepancy between the Chorus' Virgilian evocation of peace at the end of the first act (139–58), and Lycus' vision, in the following act, of a state of endless warfare, with fields lying untilled and the inhabitants of the earth buried by the ashes of their own houses (365–7). For all the hero's honest desire for peace, it is that fate, Seneca implies, which is Hercules' real legacy to humanity. His madness is symbolic of the madness of war itself. At the end of Act II the Chorus rehearses Hercules' exploits and asks Fortune to be kind to the hero in his descent into the underworld. But it concludes its prayer with the story of another descent into Hades by a very different hero. Orpheus had won over the gods of the underworld not with violence but with the power of his song (569–91). The Thracian hero is the antithesis of the Herculean ideal of manhood.

---

[14] *Hercules furens*, trans. Jasper Heywood, *The Tenne Tragedies of Seneca* (1581), 2 vols. (Manchester: The Spenser Society, 1887), vol. I, p. 33.
[15] Ibid., p. 34.

When Renaissance humanists rehearse the myth of the origins of civilization, it is usually the Orpheus story that they tell.[16] Hercules can lay equal claim to the title of founder of civilization, and is sometimes cited in Renaissance discussions of the origins of civilization.[17] But with its commitment to a political and cultural ideal based on a revival of the arts of antiquity, Erasmian humanism naturally looked to the artist rather than the warrior for its model of national leadership. George Puttenham followed Horace (*Ars poetica*, lines 391–401) in allegorizing the Orpheus story. 'It is fayned', he wrote in *The Arte of English Poesie*,

> that . . . Orpheus assembled the wilde beasts to come in heards to harken to his musicke, and by that meanes made them tame, implying thereby, how by his discreete and wholsome lessons uttered in harmonie and with melodious instruments, he brought the rude and savage people to a more civill and orderly life, nothing, as it seemeth, more prevailing or fit to redresse and edifie the cruell and sturdie courage of man then it.[18]

It is this civilizing power of the arts that Shakespeare's Lorenzo alludes to when he tells Jessica that the poet

> Did feign that Orpheus drew trees, stones, and floods,
> Since naught so stockish, hard, and full of rage
> But music for the time doth change his nature.   (*MV*, v.i.80–2)

Since Orpheus' music was responsible, symbolically, for taming the savage heart of fallen man, it is inevitable that images of music and musical harmony should find their way into political debate in Renaissance Europe. In a classic expression of the harmonist view of society the encyclopaedist Pierre de La Primaudaye explained how the well-ordered state is informed by the same principles that govern a musical consort:

> A citie or civill company is nothing else but a multitude of men unlike in estates or conditions, which communicate togither in one place their artes, occupations, workes and exercises, that they may live the better, & are obedient to the same lawes and magistrats . . . Of such a dissimilitude an

---

[16] See Kirsty Cochrane, 'Orpheus Applied: Some Instances of his Importance in the Humanist View of Language', *RES*, 19 (1968), 1–13. See also John Warden ed., *Orpheus: The Metamorphosis of a Myth* (Toronto: University of Toronto Press, 1982); Charles Segal, *Orpheus: The Myth of the Poet* (Baltimore and London: Johns Hopkins University Press, 1989); Neil Rhodes, *The Power of Eloquence and English Renaissance Literature* (New York and London: Harvester Wheatsheaf, 1992), pp. 3–8; Headlam Wells, *Elizabethan Mythologies*, pp. 2–8, 63–80.

[17] See Introduction, p. 26.

[18] *The Arte of English Poesie*, ed. Gladys Doidge Willcock and Alice Walker (Cambridge: Cambridge University Press, 1936), p. 6.

harmonicall agreement ariseth by due proportion of one towards another in their diverse orders & estates, even as the harmonie in musicke consisteth of unequal voyces or sounds agreeing equally togither.[19]

According to the law of correspondence, the same principles that are responsible for social harmony also govern our individual lives. 'Looke upon the frame, & workmanship of the whole worlde,' wrote John Case, 'whether there be not above, an harmony between the spheares, beneath a simbolisme between the elements. Looke upon a man, whome the Philosophers termed a little world, whether the parts accord not one to the other by consent and unity.'[20]

When writers like La Primaudaye talk of 'harmonicall agreement' and 'due proportion' they are not claiming that harmonious equilibrium is the world's natural condition.[21] They are appealing rather to those universal principles which alone could prevent nature's fragile equilibrium from breaking down into the sort of violent confusion that we see in a play like *King Lear*. For a contemporary audience Othello's fateful words, 'Perdition catch my soul / But I do love thee, and when I love thee not, / Chaos is come again' (III.iii.91–3) would have had a resonance that is lost on most modern playgoers.

The fragility of this neo-Pythagorean model of socio-personal harmony is one of the age's most insistent concerns and is reflected everywhere in the literature of the period. If, as Middleton's Isabella says, 'Providence . . . can make a harmony / In things that are most strange to human reason',[22] it is all too easy for men like Iago to 'set down the pegs that make this music' (*Oth.*, II.i.201). Hence the need, expressed by republicans and monarchists alike, for responsible government. 'Where the King doth guide the state and the lawe the King,' wrote Hooker in the *Laws of Ecclesiastical Polity*, 'that common-

---

[19] *The French Academie* (London, 1586), p. 743.
[20] *The Praise of Musique* (Oxford, 1586), p. 2
[21] Stephen L. Collins rehearses a familiar view when he argues that 'traditionally order was founded upon the belief that rest was natural' (*From Divine Cosmos to Sovereign State: An Intellectual History of Consciousness and the Idea of Order in Renaissance England* (New York and Oxford: Oxford University Press, 1989), p. 28). However, as Tom McAlindon has shown, hierarchical order was only one aspect of the pre-modern cosmology that the Renaissance inherited from the Greeks. At least as important was the notion of polarity. The Heraclitean principle of *discordia concors* provided the Renaissance with an essentially dynamic conception of the universe that accommodated strife as well as order (*English Renaissance Tragedy* (Basingstoke and London: Macmillan, 1986), pp. 5–6; McAlindon *Shakespeare's Tragic Cosmos* (Cambridge: Cambridge University Press, 1991), chapter 1).
[22] Thomas Middleton, *Women Beware Women*, I.ii.179–82, Revels Plays, ed. J.R. Mulryne (London: Methuen, 1975), p. 25.

wealth is like an harpe or melodious instrument, the stringes whereof are tuned and handled by one hand, following as lawes the rules and canons of Musicall science.'[23]

There was no doubt an element of personal vanity in James' representation of himself as the musician–king of classical and Christian tradition.[24] But given his sponsorship of the arts, and the unquestioned sincerity of his commitment to 'the Musick of peace',[25] the suggestion that he was a kind of latter-day Orpheus was not entirely fanciful. The clearest statement of the political ideal embodied in the figure of the musician–king is John Gower's evocation of Arion in the Prologue to *Confessio Amantis*. 'Wolde god', wrote Gower, during the period of civil chaos that culminated in Richard II's deposition in 1399,

> that now were on
> An other such as Arion
> Which hadde an harpe of such temprure,
> And therto of so good mesure
> He song, that he the bestes wilde
> Made of his note tame and milde
>
> if ther were such on now,
> Which cowthe harpe as he tho dede,
> He myhte availe in many a stede
> To make pes wher now is hate.[26]

Bacon also evoked the musician–king as a guardian of 'society and peace'. In presenting James with *The Advancement of Learning* in 1605, he warned that 'if [Orpheus'] instruments be silent, or that sedition and tumult make them not audible, all things dissolve into anarchy and confusion'.[27] Four years later George Marcelline appealed, less subtly, to the same traditional image of the musician–king when he praised James as Orpheus *redivivus*:

Behold how like another Orpheus . . . he draweth to the true knowledge of God, very salvage Beasts, Forrests, Trees, and Stones, by the sweet Harmony of his harp, the most fierce and wilde, the most stupid and

---

[23] *The Works of Richard Hooker*, 4 vols., ed. W. Speed Hill (Cambridge, Mass.: Harvard University Press, 1977–93), vol. IV (1981), p. 342.
[24] On the musician-king see Headlam Wells, *Elizabethan Mythologies*, pp. 2–8.
[25] The phrase is Michael Drayton's (see Chapter 4, p. 130).
[26] *Confessio Amantis*, lines 1053–58, 1072–5, *The Complete Works of John Gower*, 4 vols, ed. G.C. Macaulay (Oxford: Clarendon Press, 1899–1902), vol. II (1901), p. 34.
[27] *The Advancement of Learning*, ed. William A. Armstrong (London: Athlone Press, 1975), p. 89.

insenced, the most brutish and voluptuous, are changed and civilized by the delectable sound of his Musicke. The which may transport and ravish our eares, at his mellodious touchinges and concordes, and not tickle them with any delicate noyse, tending unto voluptuous and sensuall pleasure: but rather such, as by well tempered proportions are able to reduce all extravagant rudenesse, and circuites of our soules, though they had wandered from the right way, to the true path of dutie, and settle all thoughts in such a harmony, as is most pleasing unto them.[28]

Marcelline's sycophantic rhetoric is that of the court masque. But behind the hyperbole is a clear political signal: in contrast to Prince Henry, whose ambition was to lead a holy war in Europe, James has chosen to base his rule on an Orphic rather than a Herculean model of kingship, with all that those labels imply. Following his series of pessimistic analyses of the Herculean warrior–hero, Shakespeare now turns, at the end of his writing career, to the question of how to evoke an Orphic political leader. The solution was not a simple one. In the theatre conflict is inherently more interesting than harmony. Moreover, the patron of the King's Men was far from the ideal monarch represented by panegyrists like Marcelline. Although his anti-militarist policies initially won wide support from a country tired of twenty years of war with Spain, politicians became increasingly irritated with James' self indulgence, his pontifical style, and his casual attitude to parliamentary business. While it seems likely that the King's Men would have felt obliged to make at least some gesture of compliment towards their patron, it would be an insult both to their intelligence and to James' to insist that Renaissance writers would inevitably have been either 'for' or 'against' the government. That is not the way politics worked in early-modern England (or indeed in twenty-first-century England), and it is certainly not the way great literature works. It is a measure of Shakespeare's skill as a dramatist that he is able obliquely to compliment his patron as an Orphic ruler, while at the same time reminding him that a prince 'may not, as unvalued persons do, / Carve for himself' (*Ham.*, 1.iii.19–20). In doing so he worked within a long theatrical tradition in which praise and blame were combined as a way of moulding the opinion of rulers who would probably not have been anxious to receive advice from a mere playwright.[29]

[28] *The Triumphs of King James the First* (London, 1610), p. 35 (first published in French in 1609).
[29] See Greg Walker, *Plays of Persuasion: Drama and Politics at the Court of Henry VIII* (Cambridge: Cambridge University Press, 1991).

'THE TEMPEST' AND COLONIALISM

It is widely assumed in modern Shakespeare criticism that *The Tempest* is about colonialism. In a seminal article of 1966 Philip Brockbank argued that what the play seems to offer as perennial truths has its origin in the colonizing enterprises of Shakespeare's England.[30] Ten years later Stephen Greenblatt published the first version of an article called 'Learning to Curse'.[31] Since then it has become an axiomatic principle in New-Historicist criticism that *The Tempest* reflects contemporary colonial activity in Virginia and Ireland, with Prospero's appropriation of what critics assume to be 'Caliban's island'[32] standing for European exploitation of indigenous peoples.[33] The fact that Caliban is himself the son of a North-African immigrant who was banished from Algeria for unspecified atrocities (1.ii.265) is usually passed over, as is the fact that Sycorax

---

[30] '*The Tempest*: Conventions of Art and Empire', in *Later Shakespeare*, ed. John Russell Brown and Bernard Harris (London: Edward Arnold, 1966), p. 183–201.

[31] Stephen Greenblatt, 'Learning to Curse: Aspects of Linguistic Colonialism in the Sixteenth Century', in *First Images of America: The Impact of the New World on the Old*, ed. Fred Chiappelli (Berkeley, Los Angeles, and London: University of California Press, 1976), pp. 561–80.

[32] Thomas Cartelli, 'Prospero in Africa: *The Tempest* as Colonialist Text and Pretext', in *Shakespeare Reproduced: The Text in History and Ideology*, ed. Jean Howard and Marion F. O'Connor (New York and London: Methuen, 1987), p. 108.

[33] Francis Barker and Peter Hulme, '"Nymphs and reapers heavily vanish": the Discursive Con-texts of *The Tempest*', in *Alternative Shakespeares*, ed. John Drakakis (London: Methuen, 1985), pp. 191–205; Paul Brown, '"This thing of darkness I acknowledge mine": *The Tempest* and the Discourse of Colonialism', in *Political Shakespeare: New Essays in Cultural Materialism*, ed. Jonathan Dollimore and Alan Sinfield (Manchester: Manchester University Press, 1985), pp. 48–71; Malcolm Evans, *Signifying Nothing: Truth's True Contents in Shakespeare's Texts* (Brighton: Harvester Press, 1986), pp. 74–9; Joan Pong Linton, *The Romance of the New World: Gender and the Literary Formations of English Colonialism* (Cambridge: Cambridge University Press, 1998), pp. 155–70; Barbara Fuchs, 'Conquering Islands: Contextualizing *The Tempest*', *SQ*, 48 (1997), 45–62. For useful critiques of colonialist readings of *The Tempest* see Meredith Anne Skura, 'The Case of Colonialism in *The Tempest*', *SQ*, 40 (1989), 42–69; Alden T. Vaughan and Virginia Mason Vaughan, *Shakespeare's Caliban: A Cultural History* (Cambridge: Cambridge University Press, 1991), pp. 140–71.

In *Virgil and 'The Tempest': The Politics of Imitation* (Columbus: Ohio State University Press, 1990) Donna B. Hamilton supports a colonialist reading of *The Tempest* by reference to the Irish question, claiming that Irish affairs were the subject of contemporary concern. She shows that in dealing with the history of the English presence in Ulster, the authors of *The Chronicle of Ireland* (included in *Holinshed's Chronicles* of 1587) had been liberal in their citation of Virgil. In this way, writes Hamilton, the *Aeneid* 'functioned as an archive by means of which those involved in plantations could take stock of their project'. She claims that this contemporary interest in colonial matters is reflected in Shakespeare's play (pp. 64–5). Until the Earl of Tyrone's submission in March 1603, the Irish problem had certainly been in the forefront of the nation's political consciousness. But it is difficult to discern evidence of that concern in *The Tempest* eight years later when the war was ended, Tyrone was in self-imposed exile, and plantation was progressing relatively smoothly.

seems to have had no qualms about torturing and enslaving the indigenous inhabitants of the island when they refused to 'act her earthy and abhorred commands' (274).

It is true that James I liked to claim that kings had their origin in those 'who planted and spread themselves in *Colonies* through the world'.[34] Despite his theoretical interest in the subject, he was in practice cautious when it came to supporting colonial ventures in the New World.[35] Recent historical scholarship has suggested that contemporary interest in colonial ventures has been exaggerated by New Historicists who have adapted the myth of a national literature born from the stimulus of imperial enterprise, and used it to underpin post-colonial readings of Shakespeare and other writers of the period. But as David Armitage argues, applying a nineteenth-century model of the relationship between culture and imperialism to early-modern literature 'demands an indifference to context and inevitably courts anachronism'; in reality 'the impress of Empire on English literature in the early-modern period was minimal'.[36] For the major writers of the period colonial activity was not an important theme. Though Shakespeare used William Strachy's account of a shipwreck off Bermuda in 1609 for details of the storm,[37] he seems

---

[34] 'A Speach to Parliament', March 1609, *Political Writings*, ed. Johann P. Sommerville (Cambridge: Cambridge University Press, 1994), p. 182.

[35] Louis B. Wright points out that, although colonial affairs were under the aegis of the king and the Privy Council after 1609, the activity that did take place was 'carried out by joint stock companies with only nominal support from the government'. He writes: 'The reign of James I ended without the development of a well-thought-out colonial policy' ('Colonial Developments in the Reign of James I', *The Reign of James VI and I*, ed. Alan G.R. Smith (London and Basingstoke: Macmillan, 1973), p. 139).

[36] David Armitage, 'Literature and Empire,' in *The Origins of Empire: British Overseas Enterprise to the Close of the Seventeenth Century*, ed. Nicholas Canny, *The Oxford History of the British Empire*, 5 vols., general ed. Wm. Roger Louis (Oxford and New York: Oxford University Press, 1998–99), vol. 1 (1998), pp. 99–123. Canny points out that, although by the end of the seventeenth century the English were the dominant presence in the North Atlantic, the transformation in England's position as a trading and colonizing nation came about more by accident than design: 'people in the seventeenth century had little awareness that they were on the threshold of some great Imperial age' (p. xi). See also Jerry Brotton, '"This Tunis, sir, was Carthage": Contesting Colonialism in *The Tempest*', *Post-colonial Shakespeares*, ed. Ania Loomba and Martin Orkin (London and New York: Routledge, 1998), pp. 23–42. Brotton argues that 'colonial readings [of *The Tempest*] have offered a historically anachronistic and geographically restrictive view of the play, which have [sic] overemphasized the scale and significance of English involvement in the colonization of the Americas in the early decades of the seventeenth century' (p. 24). See also Tristan Marshall, '*The Tempest* and the British Imperium in 1611', *HJ*, 41 (1998), 375–400.

[37] Since the early nineteenth century scholars have been aware that, although Shakespeare set *The Tempest* in the Mediterranean, the play echoes the so-called Bermuda pamphlets (see Frank Kermode, ed., *The Tempest*, Arden edn. (London: Methuen, 1954), p. xxvi).

to have been more interested in *A true reportory of the wracke* as a cautionary tale of mutiny, treason, and effective government than as a call to empire.[38] Far more significant than the Bermuda pamphlets is what Shakespeare does with themes from classical poetry and drama.

One of the most persuasive arguments in support of a colonialist reading of *The Tempest* is the one that compares *The Tempest* with the *Aeneid*.[39] Along with the Bible, the *Aeneid* is one of the great colonizing texts of all time. Virgil's grand theme is Rome's imperial mission. 'To them [the Trojans], no Bounds of Empire I assign; / Nor term of Years to their immortal Line', Jupiter tells Venus; 'The subject World shall *Rome*'s Dominion own' (1.378–9; 84). If the realization of that mission involves a cruel war, the means are apparently justified by the new civilization that heaven has decreed will ultimately arise from the 'sad Relicks of the *Trojan* race' (III.115):

> Then dire Debate, and impious War shall cease,
> And the stern Age be softned into Peace:
> Then banish'd Faith shall once again return,
> And Vestal Fires in hallow'd Temples burn.   (1.396–9)

Whatever doubts Aeneas himself may have about this mission and the violence it involves, he is persuaded to put them aside by the vision that his father's ghost shows him of 'the long Procession of his Progeny' culminating in the 'Youth of Form Divine' who is destined to restore the golden age (VI.1024, 1077–81). Prospero is also an

---

[38] Strachy writes: 'In these dangers and divellish disquiets (whilest the almighty God wrought for us, and sent us miraculously delivered from the calamities of the Sea, all blessings upon the shoure to content and binde us to gratefulnesse) thus inraged amongst our selves, to the destruction each of other, into what mischiefe and misery had wee bin given up, had we not had a Governour with his authority, to have suppressed the same?' (*A true reportory of the wracke and redemption of Sir Thomas Gates*, in *Purchas His Pilgrimes*, 20 vols. (Glasgow: Glasgow University Press, 1905–7), vol. XIX (1906), p. 32.

[39] For Shakespeare's use of the *Aeneid* in *The Tempest* see J.M. Nosworthy, 'The Narrative Sources for *The Tempest*', *RES*, 24 (1948), 281–94; Jan Kott, 'The *Aeneid* and *The Tempest*', *Arion*, n.s. 3, 4 (1976), 424–51; Kott, '*The Tempest*, or Repetition', *Shakespeare Today, Mosaic*, 10 (1977), ed. Ralph Berry, 9–36; Gary Schmidgall, *Shakespeare and the Courtly Aesthetic* (Berkeley, Los Angeles, and London: University of California Press, 1981), pp. 74–5, 165–73; John Pitcher, 'A Theatre of the Future: The *Aeneid* and *The Tempest*', *EC*, 34 (1984), 193–215; Barbara Bono, *Literary Transvaluations: from Vergilian Epic to Shakespearean Tragedy* (Berkeley, Los Angeles, and London: University of California Press, 1984), pp. 220–4; Robert S. Miola, 'Vergil in Shakespeare: from Allusion to Imitation', *Vergil at 2000*, ed. John D. Bernard (New York: AMS Press, 1986), pp. 254–56; Robert Wiltenburg, 'The *Aeneid* in *The Tempest*', *ShS*, 39 (1986), 159–68; Donna B. Hamilton, *Virgil and 'The Tempest'*; Heather James, *Shakespeare's Troy: Drama, Politics, and the Translation of Empire* (Cambridge: Cambridge University Press, 1997), pp. 189–221.

unwilling exile. He too suffers a 'sea-sorrow' (I.ii.171). But unlike
Aeneas, he is not directed by the gods to seek new lands or found a
new civilization; he is hurried away in the dead of night, put on a
rotting boat, and cast adrift, not with a band of doughty warriors,
but only an infant daughter for company. It is true that 'providence
divine' (I.ii.160) brings him safely ashore, but it does not command
him to found a new colony or to smite his enemies. If it has any
plans for 'sweet Revenge' (*Aeneid*, 1.388), it does not mention them to
Prospero.

It is well known that there is an explicit allusion to Aeneas and
Dido at II.i.71–9. In addition, there are a number of evocative
echoes of the *Aeneid* in *The Tempest*, in particular the supernatural
storm that begins the action in both poem and play, the opening of
the city gates at night to admit the enemy (I.ii.129–30), and the
providentially directed sea voyage. But these are not thematic
parallels. The differences between the two works are far more
important than the similarities, and point to a fundamental difference of subject matter and outlook. There are no quarrelling deities
in *The Tempest*; no divine championship of a favoured people; no
chthonic revelations of future racial supremacy; no ethnic migration;
no military conquest; no conflict between love and a national
mission. The only reference in the play to the idea of a master race is
Caliban's less-than-noble vision of an island peopled with the
products of his own repeated rape of Miranda (I.ii.352–3), a fate that
would have been all too likely had Prospero died on the island.
Conversely, in the *Aeneid* there is nothing about books and learning,
or the transforming power of music; nothing about charity and
forgiveness; no reconciliation of dynastic dispute through the romantic love of a younger generation. It cannot be denied that, in the
course of its rich and complex afterlife, *The Tempest* has spoken in a
powerful way to successive generations about the injustices of
colonial rule.[40] But while the play has inevitably changed its
meaning over four centuries, particularly for African and West
Indian readers and audiences, colonial exploitation was not part of

---

[40] Notable among re-readings and reworkings of *The Tempest* by West Indian writers are
George Lamming's *The Pleasures of Exile* (London: Michael Joseph, 1960), Aimé Césaire's
Une Tempête (Paris: Seuil, 1969), and Derek Walcott's *Pantomime* in '*Remembrance*' and
'*Pantomime*': *Two Plays* (New York: Farrer, Straus & Giroux, 1980). See Bill Ashcroft, Gareth
Griffiths, and Helen Tiffin, *The Empire Writes Back: Theory and Practice in Post-Colonial
Literatures* (London and New York: Routledge, 1989), pp. 189–91; Jonathan Bate, *The Genius
of Shakespeare* (London and Basingstoke: Picador, 1997), pp. 248–50.

Shakespeare's original play. Whatever it may have come to mean for later ages, *The Tempest* of 1611 is not about the founding of a new civilization through subjugation of indigenous peoples; it is about the patching up of an old one by peaceful means. The Virgilian parallels are important for two reasons: first, because they show how little *The Tempest* has to do with colonialism; and second, because it was the Virgilian idea of universal peace that seems to have interested both James and Shakespeare.

ORPHEUS REDIVIVUS

In a discussion of West Indian revisionist readings of *The Tempest*, Jonathan Bate remarks that 'Prospero's failure to appreciate Caliban's ear for music vitiates any purely "Prosperian" reading of the play'.[41] To the colonialist mentality musical connoisseurship is the last thing one would expect to find in an illiterate semi-savage islander. But as we have seen, Prospero is not a colonizer; his mind is on quite different matters. In the long speech in which he echoes Ovid's *Metamorphoses* he explains that he has used 'heavenly music . . . / To work mine end upon their senses' (v.i.52–3). Since his whole 'project' (v.i.1) has involved changing people's behaviour through the magical power of music, it would be strange if he imagined that Caliban might be indifferent to its qualities. The fact that Caliban lacks musical education is neither here nor there. It was a well-known commonplace in Renaissance musical lore that even animals are susceptible to music. As Lorenzo tells Jessica,

>   do but note a wild and wanton herd
>   Or race of youthful and unhandled colts,
>   Fetching mad bounds, bellowing and neighing loud,
>   Which is the hot condition of their blood,
>   If they but hear perchance a trumpet sound,
>   Or any air of music touch their ears
>   You shall perceive them make a mutual stand,
>   Their savage eyes turned to a modest gaze
>   By the sweet power of music.   (*MV*, v.i.71–9)

Ariel uses the same bovine image when he tells Prospero how he lured Stephano and Trinculo into a stagnant pool with his tabor:

---

[41] *The Genius of Shakespeare*, p. 247.

like unbacked colts they pricked their ears,
Advanced their eyelids, lifted up their noses
As they smelt music. So I charmed their ears
That calf-like they my lowing followed.   (IV.i.176–9)

Caliban is as susceptible to music as Lorenzo's unhandled colts are; and Prospero is obviously in the habit of using it to keep him quiet when he is taking his own afternoon nap (III.iii.138–48). The trouble is that, although Caliban likes music, it does not seem to civilize him. According to Prospero, his nature is one on which 'Nurture can never stick' (IV.i.188–9). Like Perdita's debate with Polixenes on the selective propagation of plants (*WT*, IV.iv.79–99), Prospero's words about nature and nurture are a signal that Shakespeare is engaging, as he did in *Othello*, in one of the age's great debating *topoi*.

So familiar in medieval folklore, and Renaissance pageantry and iconography, is the figure of the libidinous savage who, despite his knowledge of nature's secrets, is essentially ineducable,[42] that it would be pointless to try to identify a particular source for Caliban. The important question is what Shakespeare does with this familiar figure. The answer seems fairly clear: he is responding to primitivist rewriting of the stereotyped savage. By showing us a savage who is anything but noble, Shakespeare appears to be taking sides in the art / nature debate and debunking the myth of sentimental primitivism (see p. 200, 'The Primitivist Myth'). With hindsight we can see that the way he characterizes Caliban is not very different from the way nineteenth-century colonizers characterized indigenous African, Australasian, and New World peoples.[43] Modern psycho-anthropology has shown that IQ levels vary marginally, if at all, between

---

[42] See Vaughan and Vaughan, *Shakespeare's Caliban*, pp. 62–71. On the mythical figure of the Wild Man see also Richard Bernheimer, *Wild Men in the Middle Ages* (Cambridge, Mass.: Harvard University Press, 1952); Robert H. Goldsmith, 'The Wild Man on the English Stage', *MLR*, 53 (1958), 481–91; Hayden White, 'The Forms of Wildness: Archaeology of an Idea', *The Wild Man Within: An Image in Western Thought from the Renaissance to Romanticism*, ed. Edward Dudley and Maximillian E. Novak (Pittsburgh: University of Pittsburgh Press, 1972), pp. 3–38; Timothy Husband, *The Wild Man: Medieval Myth and Symbolism* (New York: Metropolitan Museum of Art, 1980).

[43] The following nineteenth-century example is remarkable only for its relatively moderate view of primitive peoples. Though familiar with aboriginal customs since childhood, and despite his own detailed accounts of the aborigines' highly sophisticated hunting skills, George Thomas Lloyd writes in *Thirty-Three Years in Tasmania and Victoria* (London: Houlston and Wright, 1862): 'Of that unhappy race it may truly be remarked that their moral and intellectual energies were of the most inferior order' (p. 43). As recently as 1982 a correspondent in the Australian *Bulletin* described Tasmanian aborigines as treacherous, murderous, war-like, filthy, gluttonous, and vermin-infested. The white settlers, whom the writer denies were responsible for the extermination of aborigines, were, by contrast,

those few modern tribes still living in Stone-Age isolation and 'civilized' peoples.[44] But with no comparative anthropology, and little opportunity for even the most casual first-hand observation of New-World societies, it is not surprising that early-modern explorers and writers encountering or imagining primitive peoples for the first time should have a different view of race and class from our own. Their view of the primitive is far more likely to have been formed by classical and medieval authority than by observation.

It is true that Prospero has an unpleasantly autocratic side to him. But unlike the colonizers of Australia, Tasmania, and both North and South America, he has no interest in exterminating natives. To suggest, because he claims that Caliban is ineducable, that Prospero is playing out a parable of 'transatlantic imperialism',[45] is about as reasonable as accusing George Eliot or Elizabeth Gaskell of the suppression of women simply because, like every other middle-class woman in nineteenth-century England, they employed chamber maids and cooks. If anyone in *The Tempest* is guilty of terrorizing and torturing natives, it is Sycorax, not Prospero. She is Shakespeare's invention and he disapproves of her.

With most of the plays we have a source text and can see how Shakespeare modified it in adapting the story for the stage. Despite the claims that have been made for the *Aeneid*, we still have no source for *The Tempest* story. However, we do have a contemporary analogue in the form of an enchanted island filled with magical music where people undergo surprising transformations. Though it is no more a narrative source than the *Aeneid*, Spenser's *Faerie Queene* is probably a more useful guide to the play's central theme than parliamentary exchanges on the Irish question.[46]

Like *The Tempest*, the final canto of Book II opens with a terrifying ordeal at sea in which sailors fear for their lives:

---

peace-loving and of high moral character (cited by Jared Diamond, *The Rise and Fall of the Third Chimpanzee* (1988; repr. London: Vintage, 1992), pp. 254–5).
[44] Matt Ridley, *Genome: The Autobiography of a Species in 23 Chapters* (London: Fourth Estate, 1999), p. 86.
[45] Leslie Fiedler, *The Stranger in Shakespeare* (London: Croom Helm, 1973), p. 209.
[46] In *The Analogy of 'The Faerie Queene'* (Princeton, N.J.: Princeton University Press, 1976), James Nohrnberg compares Prospero with Circe, but does not pursue the parallel. He writes: 'Should the vision of man's potential for . . . self-transformation prove to be a temporary impression, then Miranda might be found awakening not on Prospero's isle, but on Circe's' (p. 790).

>   An hideous roaring farre away they heard,
>   That all their senses filled with affright,
>   And streight they saw the raging surges reard
>   Up to the skyes, that them of drowning made affeard.[47]

Shakespeare's eye may have been caught by these lines when he described the 'wild waters in this roar . . . mounting to th' welkin's cheek' (II.i.2–4). Spenser's description of the sea 'belch[ing] forth his superfluity' (3) may also have suggested Ariel's image of the 'never-surfeited sea' 'belching' up Alonso, Sebastian, and Antonio on the island (III.iii.55–6). But these verbal sea-echoes – if they are echoes – are of no particular importance in themselves. What makes the analogue significant is the transformation motif. As Guyon and his companions explore Acrasia's island they are ravished, like Caliban, by the magical sound of invisible music. Its origin is later revealed: Spenser's Acrasia is an enchantress who uses music to entice her victims into her sexual trap. She is in effect a kind of evil counterpart of Orpheus. According to the ancients, the point of the Orpheus story was to show, as Lorenzo explains to Jessica, that music could change people's nature, 'for the time'. Where Orpheus uses music and song to civilize the savage heart, Acrasia uses those same arts to corrupt men. When she has satisfied her lust, she transforms her victims into wild beasts. What Spenser has 'clowdily enwrapped in Allegorical devise'[48] is a commonplace of Renaissance thought, namely, that man is capable of developing either the rational or the bestial side of his fallen nature.[49]

Until Guyon arrives, Acrasia finds little difficulty in accomplishing her scheme. Since she has the willing co-operation of sailors who are only too eager to accept her sexual invitation, this is not surprising. Prospero has a much more difficult task. It involves persuading clever men to forget past enmities and agree to the establishment of a new political union. But as a magus, his methods are the same as those of Spenser's temptresses. Quoting Alonso's lines about the song of the ocean (III.iii.96–9), David Armitage has suggested that 'This imaginative connection between music ("sing", "organ-pipe",

---

[47] *The Faerie Queene*, II.xii.2, *The Poetical Works*, ed. J.C. Smith and E. de Selincourt (London, New York, and Toronto: Oxford University Press, 1912), p. 131.

[48] Letter to Ralegh, *Poetical Works*, p. 407.

[49] The most famous expression of this principle is in Giovanni Pico della Mirandola's 'Oration on the Dignity of Man', trans. Elizabeth Livermore Forbes, *The Renaissance Philosophy of Man*, ed. Ernst Cassirer, Paul Oskar Kristeller, and John Herman Randall (Chicago: University of Chicago Press, 1948), p. 225.

"bass") and the depths of the ocean is characteristically Shakespearean'.[50] Though it *is* characteristically Shakespearean, the metaphor is not original. When Spenser's mermaids invite Guyon and his companions ashore, their alluring song seems to be echoed by the music of the sea. Like a mixed consort of instruments and voices, the rolling billows provide the bass, the waves breaking on the shore the mean, and the west wind the treble. The result is a 'straunge kind of harmony' that sailors find irresistible:

> With that the rolling sea resounding soft,
> In his big bass them fitly answered,
> And on the rocke the waves breaking aloft,
> A solemne Meane unto them measured,
> The whiles sweet *Zephirus* lowd whistered
> His treble, a straunge kinde of harmony. (II.xii.33)

Prospero too uses his magical powers to move and persuade. As his 'high charms' begin to work on Alonso, his old enemy imagines that nature is singing to him, not of temptation, but of reformation:

> Methought the billows spoke and told me of it,
> The winds did sing it to me, and the thunder,
> That deep and dreadful organ-pipe, pronounced
> The name of Prosper. It did bass my trespass. (III.iii.96–9)

As well as that of bringing his enemies to repentance, Prospero's 'project' involves conquering his own desire for vengeance on the men who usurped his dukedom. In the long speech beginning 'Ye elves of hills, brooks, standing lakes and groves' (v.i.33–57) Prospero admits how he has used 'rough magic' violently to subdue nature. 'I have . . .' he says,

> rifted Jove's stout oak
> With his own bolt; the strong-based promontory
> Have I made shake, and by the spurs plucked up
> The pine and cedar. (41, 45–8)

Prospero's speech is a close imitation of Golding's translation of Medea's supplication of nature to help her rejuvenate her father-in-law Aeson (*Metamorphoses*, VII.192–219).[51] The fact that Shakespeare is apparently linking Prospero with a character who is not just a

---

[50] 'The Dismemberment of Orpheus', p. 129.
[51] Golding's translation reads: 'ye Elves of Hilles, of Brookes, of Woods alone, / Of standing Lakes, and of the Night approche ye everychone' (*Shakespeare's Ovid*, ed. Rouse, p. 142). On Shakespeare's use of both Golding's translation and Ovid's original text in this passage, see Bate, *Shakespeare and Ovid*, p. 8.

sorceress, but an unscrupulous murderess, might appear at first to support colonialist readings of the play that see Prospero as a brutal opportunist intent on depriving Caliban of his birthright. But Prospero is not simply invoking magical powers. As Jonathan Bate points out, 'Medea's powers are summoned up not so that they can be exercised, but so that they can be rejected'.[52] It should be added that Prospero is specifically rejecting the 'rough magic' that calls forth mutinous winds and tears up trees by their roots in favour of an altogether more 'airy charm' (54) that relies on 'heavenly music' (52) for its effects. Seneca makes precisely this comparison between violent and peaceful power over nature in *Hercules furens*. Hercules too destroys trees in his conquest of nature;[53] in his fury he is the epitome of mindless vengeance, and when he pauses for breath, Amphitryon urges him to calm his 'furious rage' (975).[54] As I have shown, Seneca's Chorus later contrasts Hercules with Orpheus, the hero who, instead of *destroying* rocks and trees, charms them with his magical music. It is this Orphic magic to which Prospero now turns. Urged by Ariel to listen to the promptings of his gentler feelings, he resolves to abjure the 'rough magic' of destructive vengeance and employ a gentler art: 'Though with their high wrongs I am struck to th' quick,' he tells Ariel,

> Yet with my nobler reason 'gainst my fury
> Do I take part. The rarer action is
> In virtue than in vengeance.   (v.i.25–8)

Prospero is in effect re-defining masculine *virtus*. For the Herculean hero, virtue means military valour. When Cominius tells Rome's patricians that 'It is held / That valour is the chiefest virtue' (*Coriolanus*, II.ii.84–5), he makes it clear exactly what kind of courage he is talking about: Martius is a warrior who runs 'reeking o'er the lives of men as if / 'Twere a perpetual spoil' (119–20) and whose every motion is timed with the dying cries of the slain (110). Like Martius, Prospero has been exiled from his own country, and would dearly like to be avenged on those who have struck him to the quick with their high wrongs. But at Ariel's prompting, he now resolves to suppress that Herculean fury and espouse a rarer kind of virtue. Mythologically, Hercules has ceded authority to Orpheus.

In the emblem by Vaenius that I discussed in my Introduction

---

[52] *Shakespeare and Ovid*, p. 252.   [53] See above, p. 181.
[54] *Hercules furens*, trans. Heywood, p. 34.

(pp. 29–30), Hercules has been taught by Love that 'the Musick of peace' (to use Drayton's phrase once more) is superior to the might of war. His club abandoned, the feminized hero now devotes himself to the task of learning the arts of civilization. It is a commonplace of medieval and Renaissance harmonist thought that music and love are complementary metaphysical principles. In the *Symposium* Plato explained how 'Music, by implanting mutual love and sympathy, causes agreement between [the] elements . . . and music in its turn may be called a knowledge of the principles of love in the realm of harmony and rhythm'.[55] Plato's principle is echoed by countless medieval and Renaissance writers. Stephen Gosson, for example, wrote: 'The politike lawes in wel governed common wealthes, that treade downe the proude and upholde the meeke; the love of the king and his subjectes, the father and his chylde . . . are excellent maisters to shewe you that this is right musicke, this perfect harmony'.[56] In portraying an Orphic ruler – albeit a seriously flawed one – who seeks to bring about peace through dynastic marriage, Shakespeare turns an abstract metaphysical principle into a political metaphor that would have spoken very directly to the royal audience who saw *The Tempest* when it was performed as part of the betrothal entertainments for Princess Elizabeth and the Elector of the Palatinate in 1613.

DYNASTIC MARRIAGE

The atmosphere in which negotiations for Elizabeth's match with Prince Frederick took place had not been easy. For some years the whole question of royal marriage had been a source of friction between James and his increasingly assertive elder son. Just as the militant-Protestant campaign for a crusade against Spain led to a pamphlet war between Whitehall and St James' Palace in 1608 (see Chapter 5), now the impending marriage question resulted once more in semi-public dispute. On one side, Henry's advisors were anxious to see the northern anti-Catholic alliance strengthened by Protestant marriages for both prince and princess. On the other, James, despite his earlier caveats in *Basilicon Doron* about mixed marriages,[57] inclined increasingly towards a Catholic match for

---

[55] *The Symposium*, trans. W. Hamilton (Harmondsworth: Penguin, 1961), p. 55.
[56] *The Schoole of Abuse* (London: The Shakespeare Society, 1841), p. 16.
[57] *Political Writings*, ed. Sommerville, pp. 40–1.

Henry as a way of uniting Europe's warring nations in peaceful union. The war party was appalled by James' plans. English militant Protestants believed that a Spanish alliance would play straight into the enemy's hands. 'It is the Spaniard that is to be feared,' wrote Sir Walter Ralegh in a pamphlet commissioned by the Prince, 'the Spaniard, who layeth his pretences and practices with a long hand . . . it were a horrible dishonour to be overreached by any of those dry and subtle-headed Spaniards'.[58] However, if Henry were to marry a German princess, this would give him a foothold in Calvinist Europe from which to pursue his great ambition of leading a holy war against Spain. This was the political environment in which negotiations for Princess Elizabeth's marriage were conducted. 'Those last months before the arrival of the Palatine Elector were characterized by an escalation of Protestant agitation against Catholic Europe,' writes J.W. Williamson, 'and at the centre of that aggressive talk sat the image of Prince Henry as the conqueror knight, like a shrine to which the national sacrifice to Mars must be addressed.'[59]

As a national symbol of 'Courage and Heroique sprite',[60] Henry stood for a self-consciously masculine military culture. Austere and reserved, he was noticeably unresponsive to women. To his admirers he was a very type of Roman *virtus*, while his crusading zeal seemed like a living reproach to his father's epicurean self-indulgence. Williamson has shown how, building on this royal image of masculine asceticism, Protestant pamphleteers developed an anti-feminist rhetoric that sought to portray all potential Catholic brides as deceivers intent on corrupting their Prince's high-minded purity. 'A woman's tongue caused Peter to deny his Master, and Dalila persuaded Sampson to betray his strength and life to her', wrote Sir John Holles, 'This is the surest engine and instrument the devil hath, and the pope and his ministers for the planting his kingdom employ not other'.[61] Summing up his warning of the way even the most austere of men may be brought down by a temptress, Sir John Holles

---

[58] 'A Discourse Touching a Marriage Proposed between Prince Henry and a Daughter of Savoy', quoted in J.W. Williamson, *The Myth of the Conqueror: Prince Henry Stuart: A Study of 17th-Century Personation* (New York: AMS Press, 1978), p. 135.
[59] *The Myth of the Conqueror*, p. 141.
[60] Henry Peacham the Younger, 'The period of mourning', quoted by Elkin Calhoun Wilson, *Prince Henry and English Literature* (Ithaca, N.Y.: Cornell University Press, 1946), p. 140.
[61] 'Speech of Sir John Holles, concerning Prince Harry's Marriage', quoted by Williamson, *The Myth of the Conqueror*, p. 136.

cited the example of John the Baptist, the anchorite with the camel's-hair shirt (Matt., 3:4), who was beheaded as a result of the wiles of a seductive woman: 'Christ sent before him John the masculine but the pope delights more in Jone the feminine'.[62]

Cautious, as he was, of involving the government in high-risk plantation ventures, James would have been unlikely to have seen *The Tempest* as pro-colonialist polemic, especially since the play ends with all its European characters abandoning the island and returning to their courts. But as a tale of reconciliation and reunion involving a marriage alliance between former enemies, it could hardly have been more topical. Here was a story that touched on his own most dearly held policies.[63] Indeed he must have wished that his own son had been more like the gentle and tractable Ferdinand who falls in so readily with Prospero's plans. In contrast to the coldly aloof Prince Henry, Ferdinand has an eye for female beauty: 'Full many a lady / I have eyed with best regard,' he tells Miranda,

> and many a time
> Th' harmony of their tongues hath into bondage
> Brought my too diligent ear. For several virtues
> Have I liked several women; never any
> With so full soul but some defect in her
> Did quarrel with the noblest grace she owed
> And put it to the foil.   (III.i.39–46)

Though Prince Henry was keenly interested in negotiating a marriage contract that would help him realize his political ambitions in

---

[62] Ibid., quoted by Williamson, p. 136.
[63] I take a different view of *The Tempest* from Frances Yates, who sees the play as part of 'an archaising revival, a deliberate return to the past by an old Elizabethan living in the Jacobean age' (*Shakespeare's Last Plays: A New Approach* (London: Routledge & Kegan Paul, 1975), pp. 79–80). It was Henry, not James, who wanted to bring about a return to England's heroic past, an ambition with which Shakespeare would seem to have had little sympathy. David M. Bergeron discusses *The Tempest* as a 're-presentation of the politics of the Stuart royal family' in *Shakespeare's Romances and the Royal Family* (Lawrence, Kans.: University Press of Kansas, 1985), (p. 178), but does not consider the political issues that divided James and Henry. However, in an important essay published after this chapter was written, David Bevington argues for a topical reading along the lines I have suggested: the play's wedding masque 'is a means of preserving a balance of power and a reconciliation of warring principalities' ('*The Tempest* and the Jacobean Court Masque', *The Politics of the Stuart Court Masque*, ed. David Bevington and David Holbrook (Cambridge: Cambridge University Press, 1998), p. 221. In *Shakespeare's Monarchies: Ruler and Subject in the Romances* (Ithaca and London: Cornell University Press, 1997) Constance Jordan, notes that 'The future of both [Prospero's] dukedom and [Alonso's] kingdom is at last secured by the marriage of the two heirs Miranda and Ferdinand; the romance of *The Tempest* concludes with a political union' (p. 148).

Europe, and even made secret plans for a Protestant match, he seems to have shown little romantic interest in the various princesses that were presented to him as potential brides.[64] Writing to his father, he said, 'my part . . . which is to be in love with any of them, is not yet to hand'.[65] By contrast, Ferdinand conveniently falls in love 'At the first sight' (I.ii.443) with the very woman who will serve Prospero's grand scheme of uniting Milan and Naples:

> Hear my soul speak.
> The very instant that I saw you did
> My heart fly to your service; there resides
> To make me slave to it.   (III.i.63–6)

Though Ferdinand uses the old Petrarchan cliché about the enslaved heart, we have moved on from Romeo's imagined world of disdainful mistresses and unrequited passion. Miranda is no cruel tyrant, but a gentle-hearted fourteen-year-old who weeps to see her aristocratic lover being forced by her 'crabbed' father to perform menial tasks. Though he says that it is the 'sweet thoughts' of her tears that persuade him to continue playing the 'patient log-man' (67), it is difficult to imagine Ferdinand asserting his right to the woman he loves in the way that Othello does. When we see him in private conversation with Miranda, he comes across, not as a warrior-hero, but as a man of sensibility. On hearing of Prospero's marriage plans, he admits that the height of his own ambition is 'quiet days, fair issue, and long life' (IV.i.24). And when Prospero's masque is concluded, he and his bride declare in symbolic unison, 'We wish your peace' (IV.i.163). Anything less like the recalcitrant and fiercely masculine Henry it would be difficult to imagine.

As if to suggest the providential nature of the match that Prospero hopes will bring about peace in Italy, Shakespeare invests the meeting between the young lovers with portentous emblematic overtones. Tom McAlindon has shown how a commonplace of Greek and medieval romance – the hero's mis-identification of the heroine as a goddess – is transformed into a solemn act of mutual homage whose language forms part of a rich pattern of liturgical imagery in the play.[66] Prayer is one of *The Tempest*'s central motifs. Beginning with the mariners' cries: 'To prayers, to prayers!' (I.i.49), the play

---

[64] Williamson, *Myth of the Conqueror*, pp. 132–3.
[65] Quoted by Williamson, p. 139.
[66] 'The Language of Prayer in *King Lear* and *The Tempest*', forthcoming, *SEL*.

ends with Prospero supplicating the prayers of his audience (Epil. 16). When Ferdinand and Miranda first meet, he asks her to accept his humble prayer (I.ii.425–8). Heaven's blessing is repeatedly invoked in the play. The fact that some of the references to prayer in *The Tempest* are to specifically Catholic forms of liturgy[67] may be an oblique but tactful allusion to a potentially far-reaching foreign-policy decision, namely, James' plans to bring about peace in Europe by arranging a Catholic match for his son. Unlike Alonso, who chose not to 'bless Europe' with his daughter (II.i.130), James hoped that through diplomatic marriage Prince Henry would realize the peace plans that he himself had spent so many years devising. It is one of the cruellest ironies of James' reign, not just that Henry did not survive to marry,[68] but that it was James' own son-in-law who, as King of Bohemia and leader of the anti-Habsburg coalition, was a key figure in precipitating the catastrophe of the Thirty Years War.[69]

THE PRIMITIVIST MYTH

As a 'delicate and tender prince' – epithets more appropriate to Ferdinand than to Fortinbras (*Ham.* IV.iv.39) – Miranda's wooer

[67] Prospero's words to Alonso – 'I rather think / You have not sought her help, of whose soft grace / For the like loss I have her sovereign aid' (V.i.143–5) – echo the Catholic practice of intercession of the Virgin Mary, while Gonzalo's final speech – 'O rejoice / Beyond a common joy! And set it down / With gold on lasting pillars' (V.i.209–11) recalls the Compline (see Peter Milward, *Shakespeare's Religious Background* (Bloomington and London: Indiana University Press, 1973), pp. 26, 29). When Ariel alludes to St Paul's voyage to Rome (Acts 27:34) in reporting how the survivors of the shipwreck were miraculously spared with 'Not a hair perished' (I.i.218), it is the Catholic Rheims Testament from which he is quoting (Milward, p. 86). On Shakespeare's possible Catholic upbringing see Milward, pp. 15–23. See also J.S. Smart, *Shakespeare: Truth and Tradition* (London: Arnold, 1928), pp. 69–71; John Henry De Groot, *The Shakespeares and the Old Faith* (1946; repr., Freeport, N.Y.: Books for Libraries Press, 1968); E.A.J. Honigmann, *Shakespeare: The 'Lost Years'* (Manchester: Manchester University Press, 1985); Richard Wilson, 'Shakespeare and the Jesuits', *TLS*, 19 December 1997, p. 11.
[68] Following angry correspondence over his negative response to the various matches proposed by his father, Henry devised a secret plan: he would accompany Elizabeth and Frederick back to Germany after their wedding and there find a suitable Protestant bride for himself. Henry's journey never took place. Three weeks after Frederick arrived in England (on 18 October 1612), Henry died of a mysterious fever (Williamson, *The Myth of the Conqueror*, pp. 138–42).
[69] The outbreak of war in 1618 exacerbated existing tensions between James and the more militant-Protestant elements in Parliament: 'The King was now more than ever convinced of the need for a negotiated settlement, of which the Spanish marriage [for Prince Charles] would form an integral part. But public opinion in England, as reflected in Parliament, was in favour of armed intervention to advance the protestant cause' (Roger Lockyer, *James VI and I* (London and New York: Longman, 1998), p.131).

sounds like a forerunner, not so much of the foppish heroes of Caroline romance, as of the feminized eighteenth-century man of sensibility, recognizable by 'the glowing Cheek, the mild dejected Air, / The soften'd Feature, and the beating Heart',[70] all qualities conventionally associated with women rather than warriors. The man of sensibility is perhaps the best example we have of the literary androgyne whose masculinity is softened by compassion, and who has no inhibitions about expressing his emotions. Developing Coleridge's throwaway remark about great minds being androgynous,[71] Virginia Woolf argued that truly creative writers seem to combine masculine and feminine characteristics; for her Shakespeare is the epitome of the 'manly-womanly mind'.[72] Whatever Shakespeare's views were on the ancient myth of the androgyne – and he was certainly familiar with it[73] – it is clear, judging from the evidence of the plays at least, that he was particularly interested in the idea of strong, independent-minded women like Beatrice, Portia, and Rosalind, and distrustful of the more exaggerated pretensions of his heroic characters. But though he is sceptical of the heroic ideal, and offers the sensitive Ferdinand as a contrast to the harsh masculinity of the warrior–hero, there is no question of his subscribing to the sentimental primitivism that informs much of the literature of sensibility.[74]

Among the books and pamphlets that Shakespeare had been reading at the time he wrote *The Tempest* was Montaigne's essay 'Of the Caniballes' (see Chapter 3). When Gonzalo imagines the ideal commonwealth he would like to establish on the island (II.i.153–70), he echoes not just Montaigne's words about 'a nation . . . with no kinde of trafficke, no knowledge of Letters . . . no name of magistrate',[75] but also his provocative claim that South-American Indian

---

[70] James Thomson, *The Seasons* ('Autumn', 1007–8), ed. James Sambrook (Oxford: Clarendon Press, 1981), p. 186.

[71] *The Collected Works of Samuel Taylor Coleridge*, 16 vols., Bollingen Series 75, general ed. Kathleen Coburn, (London and Princeton: Routledge and Princeton University Press, 1969–), *Table Talk*, 2 vols., ed. Carl Woodring (1990), vol. II, pp. 190–1.

[72] *A Room of One's Own* (London: Hogarth Press, 1931), p. 148.

[73] As Robert Kimbrough rightly argues, Shakespeare would undoubtedly have been familiar with the classical myth of man's androgynous origins (*Shakespeare and the Art of Humankindness: The Essay Toward Androgyny* (Highlands, N.J. and London: Humanities Press, 1990), pp. 5–6).

[74] See Lois Whitney, *Primitivism and the Idea of Progress in English Literature of the Eighteenth Century* (Baltimore: Johns Hopkins University Press, 1934), ch. 1.

[75] 'Of the Caniballes', *The Essayes of Montaigne*, trans. John Florio, 3 vols. (1910; repr. London: Dent, 1928), vol. I, p. 220.

society was superior even to the life that poets claimed people led in the mythical golden age. Montaigne's description of primitive Brazilian society is a mixture of imagination, second-hand report, and his reading of the classics. He is seeing the Indian through Ovid's eyes and comparing what his servant has told him about primitive Brazilian society with poetic accounts of the golden age. But as I have explained elsewhere, though Montaigne alludes to Ovid, he omits any mention of Ovid's account of the fall from innocence that followed the passing of the golden age, or of the divine vengeance that ensued.[76]

Familiar to sixteenth-century readers from writers like Tacitus, primitivist ideas had been the subject of debate in England long before Montaigne's essays were published.[77] At the heart of More's *Utopia* is a dispute between Hythloday the idealist and 'More' the pragmatist. The former endorses Utopian belief in humanity's natural virtue; the latter believes that men have an innate flaw in their nature that will inevitably defeat the best intentions of idealistic social planners. Anticipating a central principle in Marxist thought, Hythloday argues that, because 'nature dothe allure and provoke men one to healpe another to lyve merily',[78] all that is necessary to realize the just society is to abolish money and private property, the cause of all social evil.[79] But 'More' is a realist. He knows that human beings are not naturally given to virtue: 'it is not possible for all things to be well onles all men were good', he tells Hythloday, 'Whych I thinke wil not be yet thies good many yeares'.[80] Though More (the author) does not resolve the argument, he gives a broad hint as to where his own sympathies lie in Hythloday's final impassioned speech against pride, the only thing, according to Hythloday, that prevents the rest of the world from adopting Utopian principles of social organization. Having admitted that pride is 'so depely roted in mens brestes, that she can not be plucked out', Hythloday then contradicts himself by declaring that in Utopia

---

[76] *Elizabethan Mythologies*, pp. 74–5.
[77] On More's debt to Tacitus see W.H. Fyfe, 'Tacitus' *Germania* and More's *Utopia*', *PTRSC*, 30 (1936), 57–9. Arthur O. Lovejoy and George Boas use the term 'chronological primitivism' for what I have called 'sentimental primitivism' (*Primitivism and Related Ideas in Antiquity* (Baltimore: Johns Hopkins University Press, 1935), pp. 23–102).
[78] Thomas More, *Utopia*, trans. Raphe Robinson (1551), with an introduction by John O'Hagan (London and Toronto: Dent, 1910), p. 73.
[79] Ibid., p. 44.
[80] Ibid., p. 42.

alone (in other words, nowhere) it has been 'plucked up by the rootes'.[81] Readers are left to draw their own conclusions.

More's sceptical treatment of primitivist ideas is echoed some fourteen years later in Thomas Starkey's *Dialogue Between Pole and Lupset*.[82] Like *Utopia*, Starkey's *Dialogue* contains some damning criticism of contemporary social and political abuses. Before setting out his radical proposals for a constitutional oligarchy, Starkey establishes his premises. This involves disposing of the sentimental belief in natural virtue. The primitivist argument is put into the mouth of Pole. Pointing to the corruption in England's towns and cities, Pole argues that, since men lived more virtuously in the primitive world, it is clear that human beings are by nature unfitted for civic life:

> yf thys be cyvyle lyfe & ordur to lyve in cytes & townys wyth somuch vyce & mysordur me seme man schold not be borne therto, but rather to lyfe in the wyld forest, ther more folowyng the study of vertue, as hyt ys sayd men dyd in the golden age where in man lyvyd accordyng to hys natural dygnyte.[83]

But Lupset replies that, if corruption is rife in the modern world, that is due not to the contaminating effect of civilization, but to a flaw in human nature itself: 'the faut ys nother in the cytes nor townys nother in the lawys ordeynyd therto, but hyt is in the malyce of man, wych abusyth & turnyth that thyng wych myght be to hys welth & felycyte to hys owne dystructyon & mysery'.[84]

More and Starkey's views on human nature in the raw are based not on first- or even second-hand experience of primitive peoples, but largely on classical and Christian authority. Though Tacitus had described the Germani as a virile race whose virtuous simplicity compared favourably with the decadence of imperial Rome,[85] it was Ovid's disillusioned view of a world contaminated by the effects of human wickedness that was the dominant classical influence on

---

[81] Ibid., p. 114.
[82] The most likely date for the *Dialogue* is 1529–32 (see T.F. Mayer, ed., *A Dialogue Between Pole and Lupset* (London: The Royal Historical Society, 1989), p. x.
[83] *A Dialogue*, pp. 6–7.
[84] Ibid., p. 7.
[85] Tacitus wrote: 'They live in most straite chastitie, uncorrupted with the allurements of shewes and spectacles, or provocations in banketting . . . No man laugheth at vices . . . They grow to have these great lims and bodies which we marvell at . . . Every mother nurseth her owne children with her owne breasts' (*The Description of Germanie*, *The Annales of Cornelius Tacitus*, trans. Grenewey, p. 263).

medieval thinking about the nature of man. The golden age is passed, justice has fled from the earth, and we now live in the dregs of time, said Gower in a conflation of Christian and Ovidian ideas: 'thus stant all the worldes werk / After the disposicioun / Of man and his condicioun', he wrote at the end of his great *planctus* on mutability.[86] But as first-hand reports of primitive peoples became more widely available in sixteenth-century Europe, the possibility began to suggest itself that the legendary golden age might be more than just a myth. So impressed is Montaigne by what he says he has heard of South-American Indians, that he claims that their society exceeds 'all the pictures wherewith licentious Poesie had proudly embellished the golden age'.[87] Whether or not there is any truth in Montaigne's claim that his description of the lives of primitive Brazilians was based on a traveller's report, there were sufficient authentic records in Hakluyt's heterogeneous collection of *Voyages* (1582–1600) to allow comparisons to be made between primitive and civilized societies. However, although it is Montaigne's words that Shakespeare gives to Gonzalo when Prospero's benevolent old courtier imagines the ideal commonwealth that he would establish on the island, his own position would appear to be closer to that of 'More' and Lupset. While Caliban's primary symbolic function in the play is to give the lie to the sentimental myth of the noble savage, the sardonic interruptions of Antonio and Sebastian make it clear that, with such men around, the survival prospects of a benign anarchy could never be promising. As 'More' points out in *Utopia*, abolishing private property does not automatically result in the perfect society: first you have to perfect human nature, which, he says, 'I thinke will not be yet thies good many yeares'.

THE FINAL END OF POESY

Acknowledging the barbaric elements in our nature that have survived from the dark backward and abysm of time,[88] Renaissance

---

[86] *Confessio Amantis*, 942–4, *Complete Works*, ed. Macaulay, vol. II, pp. 30–1.
[87] 'Of the Caniballes', trans. Florio, vol. I, p. 220.
[88] So powerful has been the impact of materialism's anti-humanist rhetoric that many liberal intellectuals now find it embarrassing to talk of universals: to admit to a belief in something called human nature is to confess to the crassest kind of intellectual naiveté. Neo-Darwinism has removed that embarrassment. Darwinism has been described as 'amongst the most comprehensively successful achievements of the human intellect' (Helena Cronin, *The Ant and the Peacock: Sexual Selection from Darwin to Today* (Cambridge: Cambridge University Press,

humanists argue that we are capable of choosing to develop either the rational or the non-rational side of our nature. Even Hercules, type of the warrior–hero, can be taught by the Orphic arts of music and song to restrain his violent nature, or so Vaenius claimed (Introduction p. 29). Eloquence, it was believed, is the very basis of civilization. Thomas Wilson wrote: 'Neither can I see that men could have beene brought by any other meanes, to live together in fellowship of life, to maintaine Cities, to deale truely, and willingly obeye one an other, if men at the first had not by art and eloquence, [been] perswaded [of] that which they full oft found out by reason'.[89] That is why literature is so highly valued in the Renaissance. The final end of poesy, said Sidney in a famous passage from his *Apology*, 'is to lead and draw us to as high a perfection as our degenerate souls . . . can be capable of'.[90]

Despite attempts to discover a republican subtext in *The Tempest*,[91] there is little evidence that will enable us reliably to pin down Shakespeare's views on the constitution. As with *Coriolanus*, that argument is probably a red herring; insofar as they deal with politics, both plays are more concerned with foreign-policy issues than with constitutional problems. But if Shakespeare was not a covert republican, he was conscious of the dangerous power of the demagogue. He was also conscious of the power of the theatre and its ability to work on people's imaginations. And he built into his plays a self-reflexive concern with how far, and under what conditions, the theatre is capable of working its magic on us. *The Tempest*, more than any of the plays, is concerned with the power of theatrical illusion. It reminds its audiences that what drama offers us is at best a make-believe world. When Ferdinand, enchanted by Prospero's wedding masque, says 'Let me live here ever! / So rare a wondered father and a wise / Makes this place paradise' (IV.i.122–4), Prospero

---

1991), p. 431). The evolutionary psychology that Darwin himself hinted at (Cronin, p. 74), but which has taken off in such a remarkable way only over the last twenty years, offers a thought model powerful enough and sufficiently well-established to give us the confidence to challenge the new orthodoxies that are seldom questioned in student primers on modern theory, and to re-endorse the humanism without which literature cannot exist, and criticism is reduced simply to recording the history of reception. But that is another story for another book.

[89] *The Arte of Rhetorique*, ed. G.H. Mair (Oxford: Clarendon Press, 1909), Preface, Sig. Avii.
[90] *An Apology for Poetry*, ed. Geoffrey Shepherd (London: Nelson, 1965), p. 104.
[91] See David Norbrook, '"What cares these roarers for the name of king?": Language and Utopia in *The Tempest*', *The Politics of Tragi-Comedy: Shakespeare and After*, ed. Gordan McMullan and Jonathan Hope (London and New York: Routledge, 1992), pp. 21–54.

reminds him that his spectacle has merely been a conjuror's illusion. Utopias exist only in the imagination. At the end of the play Prospero, speaking now for Shakespeare, supplicates *our* prayers, asking us to adjudicate his performance. If we are persuaded by his vision of a harmonious society based on Orphic rather than Herculean values, the rest is up to us. But we cannot begin to act on that vision if, like Ferdinand, we confuse it with reality. That would be to mistake romance for kitsch. *The Tempest* is Shakespeare's most self-conscious essay on changing, not human nature, but human behaviour.

This book has been about Shakespeare's heroes: their folly and their greatness, their cruelty and their tenderness, their destructiveness and their charm. Irrespective of whether there is any ancestral reason for our fascination with charismatic leaders, history has provided ample proof of their universal appeal. Writing at a time when it looked as if a powerful war lobby, led first by the Earl of Essex and then a few years later by Prince Henry, might succeed in pushing England into another war with Europe, Shakespeare offers us a series of portraits of the charismatic warrior–hero. Charismatic heroes are dangerous because they are capable of causing us to suspend rational judgment and revert to the values of heroic society, where the honour code is a substitute for the rule of law. 'He was great of heart', says Cassio of the man who, in the name of honour, has just murdered his wife; 'He has my dying voice', says Hamlet of the Viking marauder who has no inhibitions about finding quarrel in a straw when honour is at the stake. Both speak for the masculine principle of honour in a society under threat from barbaric forces. Even pacifists like Erasmus acknowledge that states may have to defend themselves against aggressors. But in using force to defend civilization we do not have to let martial values rule our lives. As the much maligned James I showed in his coronation pageant, we are capable of choosing our own gods.

Afterword: historicism and 'presentism'

It will be plain to most historians and literary scholars that my approach to Shakespeare is, broadly speaking, historicist. My aim has been to describe some of the conflicting views that Shakespeare's contemporaries held on the subject of heroic masculinity, to show what part those views played in the political debates of late Elizabethan and early Jacobean England, and to use that information to help interpret Shakespeare's plays as they engage with topics of public controversy. In general I have tried to keep my own views out of the picture, though doubtless they will have surfaced from time to time. (Like John Keegan, I think the 'ethic of heroism' has no place in the modern world. Though I cannot prove it, I suspect that Shakespeare probably felt the same.)

But since historicism is a confusing term, I had better explain what I mean by it. It is confusing for two reasons: first, because in the earlier part of the twentieth century it was used by different writers to mean diametrically opposite views of history; and second, because in the final two decades of the century there was a surprising ignorance among literary critics concerning debates that took place half a century earlier. One result of this unfamiliarity with English's own history as an academic discipline is a lack of consensus about the current meaning of historicism.

For historians writing in a tradition of empiricism going back to the German historian Leopold von Ranke (1795–1886) in the nineteenth century, historicism meant a commitment to objective methods of enquiry, combined with the belief that historians should not allow their own assumptions, attitudes, and beliefs to enter into their judgment of the past: every epoch, each cultural moment, is unique and must be interpreted in terms of its own values. However, in *The Poverty of Historicism* (published in 1957, but originating in the 1930s) the philosopher Karl Popper used the term historicism in a sense that was the opposite of its usual meaning. As Popper used the term, historicism referred to any deterministic, theoretical, and predictive historical science, such as Marxism or Christianity, that was dedicated to uncovering general laws of historical development (what would now be called 'grand narratives'). But Popper's usage did not win general acceptance, and since the 1950s the Rankean meaning of historicism has become the received sense among professional historians.[1]

From the early years of the twentieth century there was lively debate on the limits of Rankean empiricism. In the 1930s a group of so-called 'New Historians' led by Charles Beard and Carl Becker argued that, while historians should strive for accurate knowledge of the past, in practice it was impossible to prevent their own opinions and prejudices from contaminating their narratives.[2] While historians will continue to rely on scientific methods of enquiry in recovering the past, they are bound to acknowledge that any written history inevitably reflects the thought of the author in his time and cultural setting. 'The supreme issue before the historian now', wrote Beard,

> is the determination of his attitude to the disclosures of contemporary thought. He may deliberately evade them for reasons pertaining to personal, economic, and intellectual comfort . . . Or he may proceed to examine his own frame of reference, clarify it, enlarge it by acquiring knowledge of greater areas of thought and events, and give it consistency of structure.[3]

Beard's caveats were repeated by literary theorists. In 1942 René Wellek and Austin Warren explained that, with historicist principles well established in literature departments, scholars like Hardin Craig, E.E. Stoll, and Rosemond Tuve were arguing that we must 'enter into the mind and attitude of past periods and accept their standards, deliberately excluding the intrusions of our own conceptions'.[4] However, Wellek and Warren also made it clear that the first

---

[1] Georg G. Iggers, *Historiography in the Twentieth Century: From Scientific Objectivity to the Postmodern Challenge* (Hanover, N.H.: Wesleyan University Press, 1997). See also Paul Hamilton, *Historicism* (London and New York: Routledge, 1996).
[2] Peter Novick, *That Noble Dream: The 'Objectivity Question' and the American Historical Profession* (Cambridge: Cambridge University Press, 1988), ch. 9.
[3] Charles A. Beard, 'Written History as an Act of Faith', *AHR*, 39 (1934), 221, 228.
[4] *Theory of Literature* (New York: Harcourt, Brace & Co, 1942), p. 32.

three decades of the century were a period of active debate: nineteenth-century empiricism had been questioned by Ernst Troeltsch and others from the earliest years of the twentieth century. Following New Historians like Beard and Becker, Wellek and Warren asserted that, although the past must be judged in terms of its own values and principles, it is impossible in practice to exclude the critic's own attitudes and assumptions:

> It is simply not possible to stop being men of the twentieth century while we engage in a judgment of the past: we cannot forget the associations of our own language, the newly acquired attitudes, the impact and import of the last centuries . . . There will always be a decisive difference between an act of imaginative reconstruction and actual participation in a past point of view . . . If we should really be able to reconstruct the meaning which *Hamlet* held for its contemporary audience, we would merely impoverish it. We should suppress the legitimate meanings which later generations found in *Hamlet*. We would bar the possibility of a new interpretation.[5]

Wellek and Warren's concern to distance themselves from the literary empiricists who were still working in the Rankean tradition was shared by a number of English critics. For them it was E.M.W. Tillyard who represented the dangers of uncritical assumptions about our ability to reconstruct the past. Tillyard's influential *Shakespeare's History Plays* was published in 1944. With his claim that Elizabethan political thought was 'so simple that there is not much to do beyond stating the obvious and trying to make it emphatic', and his belief that Shakespeare's history plays were doctrinally 'entirely orthodox',[6] Tillyard was exceptional even in the 1940s: no modern historical scholar had previously offered quite such a schematic view of Shakespeare. Four years earlier, in *The State in Shakespeare's Greek and Roman Plays*, James Phillips had made it clear that the later sixteenth century was a period of vigorous intellectual and political debate in England.[7] That intellectual complexity had now been reduced to a set of axiomatic principles concerning hierarchy, order, and obedience to which every educated Elizabethan was supposed to have subscribed. Not surprisingly, Tillyard's contemporaries objected to the new simplified version of Elizabethan intellectual life. Reviewing *Shakespeare's History Plays* in 1945, Geoffrey Tillotson wrote: 'I do not think Dr Tillyard's

---

[5] Ibid., p. 34.
[6] E.M.W. Tillyard, *Shakespeare's History Plays* (London: Chatto & Windus, 1944), pp. 64, 261.
[7] See Chapter 2, p. 71.

Elizabethans are human enough. He has become interested in certain notions of theirs, and he tends to think of them as repositories of those notions'.[8] In 1950 Hiram Haydn argued that if there was a ruling principle in Elizabethan writing it was not hierarchical order but paradox: 'inconsistency runs through all their work'.[9] In the following year a lecturer in Tillyard's own college challenged the notion of an intellectually orthodox Shakespeare acting as spokesman for the Elizabethan establishment. 'To me', wrote A.P. Rossiter in a lecture entitled 'Ambivalence: The Dialectic of the Histories', the pattern of these plays 'is obscure, ironic, and – as far as Shakespeare shows us the scheme of things – seemingly endless'.[10] Two years later Helen Gardner also lectured on the issues raised by Tillyard's brand of empiricist scholarship, warning that 'the "Elizabethan World Picture" tidily presented to us as a system of thought cannot tell us how much of that picture had truth and meaning for any Elizabethan'.[11]

Gardner's 1953 lecture was titled 'The Historical Approach'. In it she challenged the empiricist claim to objective knowledge of the past: since 'the historical imagination . . . is itself historically conditioned',[12] any attempt to define the past will inevitably reflect the historian's own prejudices and preconceptions. 'In the last hundred years the conception of "the Elizabethans" has been as unstable as the conception of *Hamlet*', she wrote,

> To Froude and Kingsley they were God-fearing, Protestant, and patriotic. In the nineties they were Italianate and much less manly and God-fearing. In the twenties they were subtle, sensual, and sceptical. Recently they have become pious again, but in a different way, obsessed with the idea of hierarchy, the Great Chain of Being and Natural Law.[13]

She went on to argue that although notions of period are too unstable and too conjectural to provide us with an objective field of reference, this does not mean that we should abandon the quest for

---

[8] Review of Tillyard's *Shakespeare's History Plays*, *English*, 5 (1944–5), 160.
[9] *The Counter-Renaissance* (New York: Grove Press, 1950), p. 7.
[10] *Angel with Horns: Fifteen Lectures on Shakespeare*, ed. Graham Storey (1961); repr. with an introduction by Peter Holland (London and New York: Longman, 1989), p. 43. 'Ambivalence' was delivered at the Shakespeare Summer School, Stratford-upon-Avon in 1951 and first published in *Talking of Shakespeare*, ed. John Garrett (London: Hodder & Stoughton, 1954).
[11] Helen Gardner, *The Business of Criticism* (Oxford: Clarendon Press, 1959), p. 34.
[12] *The Business of Criticism*, p. 32.
[13] Ibid., p. 33.

historical understanding. The important thing is to avoid letting our sense of history 'harden into a fixed background'. 'We are rightly sceptical when we read statements about modern man and the modern mind and dismiss both as figments of journalism', she wrote. 'We ought to be at least as sceptical about statements about "the Elizabethan mind".'[14] If, Gardner argued in another lecture, we simply impose our own critical paradigms on the past we are in danger of 'emptying it of its own historical reality';[15] historical scholars have a responsibility to safeguard their own age against the chronological 'provincialism'[16] that inevitably results from recruiting past writers as spokesmen and women for their own beliefs and theories.

By the 1950s literary critics on both sides of the Atlantic were familiar with the debate on relativism that had begun with the New Historians two decades earlier. While there were certainly exceptions, there was widespread scepticism regarding a literary–historical empiricism, exemplified in its most exaggerated form by Tillyard, that seemed old-fashioned even by Troeltsch's standards.[17] After the Second World War a long line of critics including Rossiter, Rabkin, Elton, McElroy, Jones, and Grudin[18] replaced Tillyard's unified 'Elizabethan World Picture' with a more complex view of the relationship between the writer and his world. 'The kind of vision I have tried to point at', wrote Rabkin in *Shakespeare and the Common Understanding* (1967), 'is what puts Shakespeare's plays out of the reach of the narrow moralist, the special pleader for a particular ideology, the intellectual historian looking for a Shakespearean version of a Renaissance orthodoxy.'[19] The post-war view of what it meant to be a literary historicist is summed up in Peter Milward's introduction to his *Shakespeare's Religious Background* (1973). The following is an abstract of his argument: critics sometimes deal with great works of literature without reference to the historical circumstances in which they were written; to some extent this

---

[14] Ibid., p. 34.
[15] 'The Historical Sense', in *The Business of Criticism*, p. 135.
[16] Ibid., p. 156.
[17] For discussion of Tillyard's influence see Robin Headlam Wells, 'The Fortunes of Tillyard: Twentieth-Century Critical Debate on Shakespeare's History Plays', *ES*, 46 (1985), 391–403.
[18] See Introduction, note 103.
[19] Norman Rabkin, *Shakespeare and the Common Understanding* (1967; repr. Chicago and London: University of Chicago Press, 1984), p. 12.

approach is justifiable; after all, the value of great works seems undiminished by time and may even gain something from the varied interpretations of successive ages; but while masterpieces may be 'monuments more lasting than bronze', they are also 'abstracts and brief chronicles of the time'; present critical fashions need to be complemented by historical knowledge and an understanding of the possible meanings the text may have had for its contemporary readers; though we can never achieve complete objectivity – the choices and selections we make are bound to be affected by modern assumptions and preferences – nevertheless, as historicists we must strive for as much objectivity as we are humanly capable of if we are to rise above the mere voicing of personal prejudice.[20]

In contrast to the historicist approach, with its qualified ideal of impartiality and its belief in the importance of interpreting the past in its own terms, is what might be called a 'presentist' approach to history.[21] A recent example of the latter is Mark Breitenberg's *Anxious Masculinity in Early Modern England*. In his Introduction Breitenberg explains that 'masculine subjectivity' – that is to say the sense that men have of themselves as conscious, thinking individuals with a unique personal identity and the ability to make rational choices – is to some extent an illusion. In reality their selfhood is the product of social forces. They are, as Louis Althusser put it, 'interpellated' by ideology.[22] Breitenberg explains that, where you have a patriarchal society based on unequal distribution of power and authority, men's 'subjectivity' will be equivocal: on the one hand, tradition, authority, and example all proclaim men's natural superiority to women; on the other, the obvious injustice of this state of affairs is bound to make men feel anxious. But since practically all

---

[20] *Shakespeare's Religious Background* (Bloomington and London: Indiana University Press, 1973), pp. 7–8.
[21] J.G. Merquior uses the term 'presentism' in his discussion of Foucault's interpretation of Nietzsche's historiography (*Foucault*, 2nd edn. (London: Fontana, 1991), p. 26). In *Shakespeare's Universal Wolf: Studies in Early Modern Reification* (Oxford: Clarendon Press, 1996), Hugh Grady writes: 'At present the trend toward historicizing Shakespeare appears to have become so dominant in the field and therefore so highly valued that more "presentist" approaches – that is those oriented towards the text's meaning in the present, as opposed to "historicist" approaches oriented to meanings in the past – are in danger of eclipse' (pp. 4–5). For a critical discussion of some of the logical problems in presentist historiography see Graham Good, 'The Hegemony of Theory', *UTQ*, 65 (1996), 534–5.
[22] Mark Breitenberg, *Anxious Masculinity in Early Modern England* (Cambridge: Cambridge University Press, 1996), p. 3.

known forms of human society throughout history, and certainly all non-human social primate societies,[23] involve unequal distributions of power, it is safe to say that anxiety will be 'a necessary and inevitable condition' of masculinity in general. If Breitenberg's premises are correct, it would mean that, wherever you chose to look – in the ancient or the modern world, in pre-civilized or civilized societies, in feudal or capitalist economies, in the Developing World or in metropolitan centres – you would find men anxious about their masculinity. Though Breitenberg describes himself as a historicist,[24] his approach might better be described as presentist: what he is finally concerned with is not the otherness of the past, but what Dr Johnson called 'general and transcendental truths which will always be the same'.[25] Breitenberg's particular field of enquiry is early-modern literature. Though he emphasizes that he wishes to engage in 'dialogue' with the past, listening to what its texts have to say and interpreting them in the light of modern psychological theory, he already knows what those texts are going to tell him. Forearmed with the knowledge that writers in this period are going to be feeling anxious about their masculinity, his methodology is in one sense relatively straightforward: 'select a text or textual moment that displays an excessive response to a specifically masculine anxiety', he explains, 'search for the cultural tensions or contradictions that inform the response, then consider the function of the articulation within a specifically textual (or literary) context as well as in the general context of early modern patriarchy'.[26] The result, which Breitenberg knows in advance, will be to reveal 'the fissures and contradictions of partriarchal systems'.[27] Analysis of a play like *Othello*, for example, can thus be expected 'to demonstrate once again that masculine anxiety . . . is endemic to early modern

---

[23] See, for example, Frans de Waal, *Chimpanzee Politics: Power and Sex among Apes* (London: Jonathan Cape, 1982). See also Irenhäus Eibl-Eibesfeldt, 'The Myth of the Aggression-Free Hunter and Gatherer Society' in *Primate Aggression, Territoriality, and Xenophobia: A Comparative Perspective*, ed., Ralph L. Holloway (New York and London: Academic Press, 1974), pp. 435–57; John Paul Scott, 'Agonistic Behavior of Primates: A Comparative Perspective' in *Primate Aggression*, ed. Holloway, pp. 417–34.
[24] *Anxious Masculinity*, p. 6.
[25] *Rasselas*, ed. Gwin J. Kolb, *The Yale Edition of the Works of Samuel Johnson*, 16 vols., general eds. Allen T. Hazen and John H. Middendorf (New Haven, Conn. and London, 1958–1990), vol. XVI (1990), p. 44.
[26] *Anxious Masculinity*, p. 17.
[27] Ibid., p. 2.

patriarchy'.[28] Endemic, indeed, to all human societies at every point in history.

How does Breitenberg know that anxiety is an inescapable part of the male condition? This is partly a matter of common sense, and thus so obvious as not to require justification: 'Masculine subjectivity constructed and sustained by a patriarchal culture – infused with patriarchal assumptions about power, privilege, sexual desire, the body – inevitably engenders varying degrees of anxiety in its male members'.[29] But at a deeper level we are now, thanks to Freud, in a better position than early-modern writers were to diagnose the ills of patriarchal society and interpret the aetiology of its characteristic neuroses. 'Freud's understanding of anxiety', writes Breitenberg, 'leads us to a useful way of thinking about the pervasive masculine anxiety... that is so common in early modern texts.'[30] The story of Freud's evolving theory of anxiety neurosis is a complex and highly controversial one.[31] But leaving aside the question of the validity of Freud's theories and the integrity of his methodology, it is clear that psychoanalysis is here being used to confirm an *a priori* conviction that anxiety is 'a necessary and inevitable condition' of masculinity.

Since the 1930s most historicists have acknowledged that it is impossible in practice to prevent personal factors entering into our interpretation of the past. At the same time they have affirmed the Rankean principle of basing interpretation on the way other cultures conceptualized their world, however misguided those models may seem to us, rather than treating past writers as our own intellectual precursors. There may perhaps be room for both historicist and presentist readings of history.[32] But if, instead of listening to the

---

[28] Ibid., p. 31.   [29] Ibid., p. 1.   [30] Ibid., p. 5.
[31] See Malcolm Macmillan, *Freud Evaluated: The Completed Arc* (Amsterdam: North-Holland, 1991), pp. 122–43; Richard Webster, *Why Freud Was Wrong: Sin, Science and Psychoanalysis* (London: Harper Collins, 1996), Part I, 'The Creation of a Pseudo-Science'. Webster writes: 'From a scientific point of view all Freud's theories about the sexual aetiology of neurasthenia were, it need scarcely be said, completely spurious' (p.189).
[32] In its more radical form, presentism does not restrict itself simply to *interpretation* of the past. In a tradition running from Nietzsche, through Foucault and Hayden White, to postmodern historiographers like Keith Jenkins, it is claimed not just that it is impossible to avoid imposing our own values on the past, but that in doing so we actually *construct* the past. Historical narratives, White claims, are in reality no more than 'verbal fictions, the contents of which have more in common with their counterparts in literature than they have with those in the sciences' (*Tropics of Discourse: Essays in Cultural Criticism* (Baltimore: Johns Hopkins University Press, 1985), p. 82). For discussion of the logical fallacies in this position see Peter Lamarque and Stein Haugom Olsen, *Truth, Fiction, and Literature: A Philosophical Perspective* (Oxford: Clarendon Press, 1994), pp. 279–81. See also Robin Headlam Wells,

voices from the past, we insist on being ventriloquists, always putting our own theories and values and beliefs into the mouths of earlier writers, there is a risk of relegating ourselves to that intellectual provincialism that Helen Gardner warned against half a century ago. At the very least, academic historians and critics owe it to their readers to be clear about the differences between the two approaches, and to show how their work relates to the scholarship of the past. Failure to do so can result in some rather embarrassing confusions.

Given the familiarity among earlier twentieth-century literary critics with the terms of the debate on historicism, and the very clear sense they had of the limitations of Rankean empiricism, it is puzzling to find it so widely asserted over the past two decades that traditional literary–historical scholars were scarcely aware of the problems involved in recovering the past. Indeed it is even claimed that traditional literary criticism was not interested in socio-historical considerations *tout court*. In the Introduction to *Renaissance Self-Fashioning* Stephen Greenblatt set up an opposition between his own form of politicized historicism (based on Geertz's version of the constructionism that dominated social studies for much of the twentieth century), and a caricature of traditional criticism. Greenblatt claims that the latter involves either 'a conception of art as addressed to a timeless, cultureless, universal human essence' or else a conception of it as 'a self-regarding, autonomous, closed system'. In both forms of traditional criticism 'art is opposed to social life'.[33]

It might be supposed that unfounded generalizations of this kind would have little impact in the academy. In practice the opposite has happened. Greenblatt is probably the most influential critic currently working in the field of early-modern literature. His characterization of traditional criticism as sealed off in its own world of timeless verities and indifferent to social reality has been echoed by materialist critics on both sides of the Atlantic. 'The New Historicists combat empty formalism by pulling historical considerations to the center stage of literary analysis', writes H. Aram Veeser.[34] 'The

---

Glenn Burgess, and Rowland Wymer, eds., Introduction to *Neo-Historicism: Studies in English Renaissance Literature, History and Politics* (Woodbridge, Suffolk: D. S. Brewer Ltd, 2000).
[33] *Renaissance Self-Fashioning From More to Shakespeare* (Chicago and London: University of California Press, 1980), p. 4.
[34] H. Aram Veeser, ed., *The New Historicism* (New York and London: Routledge, 1989), p. xi.

traditional literary critic . . . imaginarily occupies a transcendent, virtual point outside of history', claims Scott Wilson.[35] Inevitably these misrepresentations find their way into student primers. In a recent textbook entitled *Beginning Theory* students are taught that, before the advent of 'Theory', criticism eschewed contextual considerations of any kind, and focused instead on literature's 'timeless significance'.[36]

Even those materialists who do acknowledge the existence of a historicist tradition in twentieth-century criticism seem to be unaware that since the Second World War criticism had moved on from naive empiricism, or that what was being produced in literature departments in the 1920s and 1930s was not as simplistic as modern caricatures of this work suggest.[37] Graham Holderness claims that, 'Where the old historicism relied on a basically empiricist form of historical research, confident in its capacity to excavate and define the events of the past, New Historicism drew on post-structuralist theory, and accepted "history" only as a contemporary activity of narrating or representing the past'.[38] Jeffrey Cox and Larry Reynolds similarly argue that New Historicism 'rejects the idea of "History" as a directly accessible, unitary past, and substitutes for it the conception of "histories", an ongoing series of human constructions'.[39] Hugh Grady asserts that traditional historians of Renaissance culture posit a 'single-minded authoritarian culture' in which cultural documents have 'stable, affirmative, and unitary meanings'. But now, he argues, thanks to the 'clarity of focus provided by the new critical paradigms of our own day' we have left behind such notions as 'the transcendent author . . . and transparent, single-levelled meaning'.[40] Catherine Belsey also attributes to modern theory the perception that past ages were not intellectually homo-

---

[35] *Cultural Materialism: Theory and Practice* (Oxford, and Cambridge, Mass.: Blackwell, 1995), p. 5.
[36] Peter Barry, *Beginning Theory: An Introduction to Literary and Cultural Theory* (Manchester: Manchester University Press, 1995), p. 17.
[37] Lilian Winstanley might be said to typify pre-Second World War literary historicism. In the Introduction to *'Hamlet' and the Scottish Succession* (Cambridge: Cambridge University Press, 1921) she wrote: 'We [cannot] judge Shakespeare completely by the effect produced on our own minds . . . the psychology of the sixteenth century is bound to differ from that of the nineteenth century, and it is important to show in what its differences consist' (pp. 2, 31).
[38] *Shakespeare Recycled: The Making of Historical Drama* (Hemel Hempstead: Harvester Press, 1992), p. 32.
[39] Jeffrey N. Cox and Larry J. Reynolds, eds., *New Historical Literary Study: Essays on Reproducing Texts, Representing History* (Princeton, N.J.: Princeton University Press, 1993), p. 1.
[40] *Shakespeare's Universal Wolf*, pp. 7–8.

geneous: 'nostalgia still tempts us to imagine a previous culture as a consensual realm, in which the important meanings and values could be taken for granted', she writes; however, 'current theory permits us to see meaning as heterogeneous'.[41] But perhaps most remarkable of all is John Drakakis' claim in 1996 that the ideological bias of Tillyard's Elizabethan World Picture had been revealed '*over the past decade*'.[42]

Taken together, these remarks represent a striking phenomenon: the history of twentieth-century historicism has in effect been rewritten so that credit for the revision of Rankean empiricism is now accorded, not to the historians and critics of the 1930s and 1940s, but to 'the new critical paradigms of our own day'. In a widely cited article on New Historicism Jean Howard writes: 'it seems to me that the historically-minded critic must increasingly be willing to acknowledge the non-objectivity of his or her own stance . . . [and to] acknowledge as well that any move into history is an . . . attempt to reach from the present moment into the past'.[43] Ivo Kamps writes with a similar sense of missionary urgency in *Materialist Shakespeare*: 'The critic's task, as it is currently defined, is . . . a difficult and paradoxical one: to study a distant past that is shrouded in/by the present'.[44] Hugh Grady agrees, arguing that, 'at the present juncture' in Renaissance studies, we must 'define an adequate dialectic' between past and present.[45] The same arguments are rehearsed by Ania Loomba and Martin Orkin in *Post-Colonial Shakespeares*: 'we read the past to understand our own lives, and equally, our own commitments direct us to the "truth" about the past'.[46] Catherine Belsey similarly argues that there can be no 'single, correct interpretation' of the past; 'reading takes place from

---

[41] *Shakespeare and the Loss of Eden* (Basingstoke and London: Macmillan, 1999), p. 15.
[42] John Drakakis, 'Afterword', *Alternative Shakespeares 2*, ed. Terence Hawkes (London and New York: Routledge, 1996), p. 240 [my italics]. In *Misrepresentations: Shakespeare and the Materialists* (Ithaca and London: Cornell University Press, 1993), p. 5, Graham Bradshaw took Grady to task for excluding one of the central strands in modern criticism from his historical study of Shakespeare in the twentieth-century (Hugh Grady, *The Modernist Shakespeare: Critical Texts in a Material World* (Oxford: Clarendon Press, 1991)). Grady had claimed that it was only over the previous twenty years that Tillyard had been dethroned. Drakakis then halved that twenty years, thus effectively bringing the Great Deposition forward to the mid 1980s.
[43] Jean Howard, 'The New Historicism in Renaissance Studies', *ELR*, 16 (1986), 43.
[44] Ivo Kamps, ed., *Materialist Shakespeare: A History* (London and New York: Verso, 1995), p. 3.
[45] *Shakespeare's Universal Wolf*, p. 7.
[46] Ania Loomba and Martin Orkin, eds., *Post-Colonial Shakespeares* (London and New York: Routledge, 1998), p. 6.

a position in the present'.⁴⁷ The puzzling thing about all these statements is not their content – they contain nothing that would surprise traditional literary historicists like Gardner or Wellek – but their evangelical tone. In calling for a recognition of the fact that the empiricist's belief in scientific objectivity is an unattainable ideal, that our view of the past is unavoidably coloured by the present, and that in writing history we are in effect commenting on our own world, Belsey, Howard, Kamps, Grady, Loomba, and Orkin seem to be unaware of the fact that all these things have been said many times before, or indeed that they have been said by the very traditionalists against whom these critics are in reaction.

Marc Bloch, co-founder of the *Annales d'histoire économique et sociale*, once wrote: 'Misunderstanding of the present is the inevitable consequence of ignorance of the past'.⁴⁸ If there is a lesson to be learnt from these confusions about the nature of literary historicism in the twentieth century, it probably lies in the historicist principle of rational reconstruction. Despite the inadmissibility of empiricist claims to complete scientific objectivity, accurate knowledge of the past is arguably still the best means of providing a perspective on the present. As Johnson put it, 'To judge rightly of the present we must oppose it to the past'.⁴⁹ Charles Beard went further. Fifteen years before Orwell wrote *Nineteen Eighty-Four*, he argued that the empirical method 'is the chief safeguard against the tyranny of authority, bureaucracy, and brute power'.⁵⁰

---

⁴⁷ *Shakespeare and the Loss of Eden*, p.12.
⁴⁸ *The Historian's Craft*, trans. Peter Putnam (Manchester: Manchester University Press, 1954), p. 43.
⁴⁹ *Rasselas*, p. 112.
⁵⁰ 'Written History as an Act of Faith', p. 227.

Select bibliography

PRIMARY SOURCES

Africanus, Leo. *The History and Description of Africa*, trans. John Pory, ed. Robert Brown, 3 vols. (London: Hakluyt Society, 1896).

Anon. *Propositions of Warre and Peace delivered to his Highness Prince Henry by some of his Military servants: Arguments for Warre* (London, 1655).

The Mirrour of Maiestie: or, The Badges of Honour (1618), facsimile edn., ed. Henry Green and James Croston (London, 1870).

The Return from Parnassus, or the Scourge of Simony, ed. Edward Arber (London: English Scholar's Library, 1879).

Gesta Henrici Quinti: The Deeds of Henry the Fifth, ed. and trans. Frank Taylor and John S. Roskell (Oxford: Clarendon Press, 1975).

Appian. *An Auncient Historie*, trans. 'W.B.' (London, 1578).

Aristotle. *Poetics*, trans. W. Hamilton Fyfe (London: Heinemann, 1927).

Ascham, Roger. *The Scholemaster*, ed. W.A. Wright (Cambridge: Cambridge University Press, 1904).

Ashley, Robert. *Of Honour*, ed. with an introduction by Virgil B. Heltzel (San Marino, Calif.: The Huntington Library, 1947).

Augustine, St *Confessions*, trans. William Watts (1631), 2 vols. (London: Heinemann, 1992–5).

Augustine of Hippo, St *Of the Citie of God*, trans. J. Healey (London, 1610).

Bacon, Francis. *The Works of Francis Bacon*, ed. James Spedding, Robert Leslie Ellis, and Douglas Denon Heath, 7 vols. (London: Longman, 1879–87).

The Philosophical Works, ed. John M. Robertson (London: George Routledge, 1905).

The Essayes or Counsels Civill or Morall (London: Dent, 1906).

The Advancement of Learning, ed. William A. Armstrong (London: Athlone Press, 1975).

Bartholomaeus Anglicus. *On the Properties of Things: John Trevisa's Translation of Bartholomaeus Anglicus 'De Proprietatibis Rerum'*, ed. M.C. Seymour, 3 vols. (Oxford: Clarendon Press, 1975–1988).

Birch, Thomas. *The Life of Henry, Prince of Wales* (London, 1760).
Bodin, Jean. *Six Books of the Commonwealth*, trans. M.J. Tooley (Oxford: Blackwell, 1955).
Browne, Sir Thomas. *The Religio Medici* (London: Dent, 1962).
Bryskett, Lodowick, *A Discourse of Civil Life* (London, 1606).
Buchanan, George. *The Art and Science of Government among the Scots: being George Buchanan's 'De jure regni apud Scotos'*, trans. with a commentary by Duncan H. MacNeill (Glasgow: William McLellan, 1964).
Bullough, Geoffrey, ed. *Narrative and Dramatic Sources of Shakespeare*, 8 vols. (London: Routledge & Kegan Paul, 1957–75).
Calendar of State Papers (Venetian), ed. Horatio F. Brown (London: HM Stationery Office, 1897–1905).
Case, John. *The Praise of Musique* (Oxford, 1586).
Castiglione, Baldassare. *The Book of the Courtier*, trans. Sir Thomas Hoby, ed. W.H.D. Rouse (London: Dent, 1928).
Césaire, Aimé. *Une Tempête* (Paris: Seuil, 1969).
Chapman, George, *The Poems of George Chapman*, ed. Phyllis Brooks Bartlett (New York: Russell & Russell, 1962).
  The Plays of George Chapman: The Comedies, ed. Allan Holaday and Michael Kiernan (Urbana, Chicago, and London: University of Illinois Press, 1970).
  The Plays of George Chapman: The Tragedies, ed. Allan Holaday (Woodbridge, Suffolk and Wolfeboro, N.H.: D.S. Brewer, 1987).
Chaucer, Geoffrey. *The Works of Geoffrey Chaucer*, 2nd edn., ed. F.N. Robinson (London: Oxford University Press, 1957).
Cicero. *De Officiis*, trans. Walter Miller (London and New York: Heinemann and Macmillan, 1913).
  Tusculan Disputations, trans. J.E. King (London and New York: Heinemann and Putnam, 1927).
  De Amicitia, trans. William Armistead Falconer (London and New York: William Heinemann, 1927).
  Marcus Tullius Ciceroes thre bokes of duties, trans. Nicholas Grimald, ed. Gerald O' Gorman (Washington: The Folger Shakespeare Library, 1990).
Coleridge, Samuel Taylor. *Coleridge's Shakespearean Criticism*, ed. T.M. Raysor, 2 vols. (London: Dent, 1960).
Contarini, Gaspar. *The Commonwealth and Government of Venice*, trans. Lewes Lewkenor (London, 1599).
Copley, Anthony. *A Fig for Fortune* (1596), facsimile edn. (London: The Spenser Society, 1883).
Cotton, Sir Robert. *An Answer made by Command of Prince Henry, to Certain Propositions of Warre and Peace, Delivered to his Highness by some of his Military Servants* (London, 1655).
Daniel, Samuel. *The Complete Works in Verse and Prose of Samuel Daniel*, ed. Alexander B. Grosart, 5 vols. (London, 1885–96).

The Civile Wars, ed. Lawrence Michel (New Haven, Conn.: Yale University Press, 1958).
Davies, John of Hereford. *Microcosmos* (London, 1603).
Davies, Sir John. *The Poems of Sir John Davies*, ed. Robert Krueger (Oxford: Clarendon Press, 1975).
Day, Angel. *Upon the life and death of the most worthy, and thrise renowmed knight, Sir Phillip Sidney* (London, 1586).
Dekker, Thomas. *The Whole Magnifycent Entertainment Given to King James* (London, 1604).
Dent, Arthur. *The ruine of Rome* (London, 1603).
Devereux, Robert, 2nd Earl of Essex. *An Apologie of the Earl of Essex* (London, 1603).
Drayton, Michael. *The Works of Michael Drayton*, ed. J. William Hebel, 5 vols. (Oxford: Basil Blackwell, 1931–41).
Elyot, Sir Thomas. *The Boke Named the Governour*, ed. Foster Watson (London: Dent, 1907).
Erasmus, Desiderius. *The Education of a Christian Prince*, trans. with an introduction by Lester K. Born (New York: Columbia University Press, 1936).
  The 'Adages' of Erasmus, ed. with a translation by Margaret Mann Phillips (Cambridge: Cambridge University Press, 1964).
  Enchiridion Militis Christiani: An English Version, ed. Anne M. O'Donnell, SND (Oxford: Early English Text Society, 1981).
Fletcher, Giles. *Christ's Victory and Triumph* (London: Griffith, Farran, Okeden, and Welsh, n.d.).
Florus, Lucius Annaeus. *Epitome of Roman History*, trans. Edward Seymour Forster (London: Heinemann, 1929).
  The Roman Histories, trans. E.M. Bolton (London, 1619).
Gifford, George. *Sermons upon the Whole Booke of the Revelation* (London, 1596).
Gorges, Sir Arthur. *The Poems of Sir Arthur Gorges* (Oxford: Clarendon Press, 1953).
Gosson, Stephen. *The Schoole of Abuse* (London: The Shakespeare Society, 1841).
Gower, John. *The Complete Works of John Gower*, ed. G.C. Macaulay, 4 vols. (Oxford: Clarendon Press, 1899–1902).
Grafton, Richard. *Grafton's Chronicle* (1569), 2 vols. (London, 1809).
Greene, Robert. *Friar Bacon and Friar Bungay*, ed. J.A. Lavin (London: Ernest Benn, 1969).
Hall, Edward. *Hall's Chronicle* (1548; repr. London, 1809).
Harvey, Gabriel. *Gabriel Harvey's Marginalia*, ed. G.C. Moore Smith (Stratford-upon-Avon: Shakespeare Head, 1913).
Hayward, Sir John. *The First and Second Part of John Hayward's 'The Life and Raigne of King Henrie IIII'*, ed. with introduction by John J. Manning, Camden Fourth Series, vol. XLII (London: Royal Historical Society, 1991).

An Answer to the First Part of a Certaine Conference Concerning the Succession (London, 1603).

Henryson, Robert. *The Poems of Robert Henryson*, ed. Denton Fox (Oxford: Clarendon Press, 1981).

Hoccleve, Thomas. *Hoccleve's Works*, ed. Frederick J. Furnival, 3 vols. (London: Early English Text Society, 1892–7).

Holinshed, Raphael. *Holinshed's Chronicles*, revised edn. (1587), ed. John Vowell, 6 vols. (London, 1807–8).

Hooker, Richard. *The Works of Richard Hooker*, ed. W. Speed Hill, 4 vols. (Cambridge, Mass.: Harvard University Press, 1977–93).

James VI. *The Poems of James VI of Scotland*, ed. James Craigie (Edinburgh and London: William Blackwood, 1955).

James VI and I. *Daemonologie* (1597) (Edinburgh: Edinburgh University Press, 1966).

Political Writings, ed. Johann P. Sommerville (Cambridge: Cambridge University Press, 1994).

Johnson, Samuel. *The Yale Edition of the Works of Samuel Johnson*, general eds. Allen T. Hazen and John H. Middendorf, 16 vols. (New Haven, Conn. and London: Yale University Press, 1958–1990).

Johnson's Shakespeare, ed. Graham Frederick Parker (Oxford: Clarendon Press, 1989).

Jonson, Ben. *Ben Jonson*, ed. C.H. Herford and Percy and Evelyn Simpson, 11 vols. (Oxford: Clarendon Press, 1925–52).

Ben Jonson: The Complete Masques, ed. Stephen Orgel (New Haven, Conn. and London: Yale University Press, 1969).

Poems, ed. Ian Donaldson (London, Oxford, and New York: Oxford University Press, 1975).

Knolles, Richard. *The Generall Historie of the Turkes* (London, 1603).

Langland, William. *Piers Plowman: The B Version*, ed. George Kane and E. Talbot Donaldson (London: Athlone Press, 1975).

Languet, Hubert. *The Correspondence of Sir Philip Sidney and Hubert Languet*, ed. S.A. Pears (London, 1845).

La Primaudaye, Pierre de. *The French Academie* (London, 1586).

Legh, Gerard. *The Accedens of Armory* (1562; repr. London, 1597).

Livy. *The Romane Historie*, trans. Philemon Holland (London, 1600).

Livy, trans. B.O. Foster, 13 vols. (London and New York: Heinemann, 1919–59).

Lull, Ramón. *The Book of the Ordre of Chyvalry*, trans. William Caxton (London: Early English Text Society, 1926).

Lydgate, John. *Lydgate's Troy Book*, ed. Henry Bergen, 4 vols. (London: Early English Text Society, 1906–35).

Lydgate's Siege of Thebes, ed. Axel Erdmann and Eilert Ekwall, 2 vols. (London: Early English Text Society, 1911–30).

Lyly, John. *The Complete Works of John Lyly*, ed. R. Warwick Bond, 3 vols. (Oxford: Clarendon Press, 1902).

Machiavelli, Niccolò. *Machiavels discourses upon the first Decade of T. Livius*, trans. E. Dacres (London, 1636).
The Discourses of Niccolò Machiavelli, ed. and trans. Leslie J. Walker, 2 vols. (London: Routledge & Kegan Paul, 1950).
The Life of Castruccio Castracani of Lucca, in *Machiavelli: The Chief Works*, trans. Allan Gilbert, 2 vols. (Durham, N.C.: Duke University Press, 1965).
The Prince, ed. Quentin Skinner and Russell Price (Cambridge: Cambridge University Press, 1988).
Malory, Sir Thomas. *The Works of Sir Thomas Malory*, ed. Eugène Vinaver; revised by P.J.C. Field, 3 vols. (Oxford: Clarendon Press, 1990).
Marcelline, George. *The Triumphs of King James the First* (London, 1610).
Markham, Gervase. *Honour in his Perfection* (London, 1624).
Marlowe, Christopher. *The Complete Works of Christopher Marlowe*, ed. Fredson Bowers, 2 vols. (Cambridge: Cambridge University Press, 1981).
Middleton, Thomas. *Women Beware Women*, Revels Plays, ed. J.R. Mulryne (London: Methuen, 1975).
Milles, Thomas. *The Treasurie of Auncient and Moderne Times* (London, 1613).
Milton, John. *The Poetical Works of John Milton*, ed. Helen Darbishire, 2 vols. (Oxford: Clarendon Press, 1952-55).
Complete Prose Works of John Milton, ed. Douglas Bush and others, 8 vols. (New Haven, Conn. and London: Yale University Press and Oxford University Press, 1953-82).
Montaigne, Michel de. *The Essayes of Montaigne*, trans. John Florio, 3 vols. (1910; repr. London: Dent, 1928).
More, Thomas. *Utopia*, trans. Raphe Robinson (1551), with an introduction by John O' Hagan (London and Toronto: Dent, 1910).
Myers, James P. Jr., ed. *Elizabethan Ireland: A Selection of Writings by Elizabethan Writers on Ireland* (Hamden, Conn.: Arcon Books, 1983).
Nichols, John, ed. *The Progresses and Public Processions of Queen Elizabeth*, 3 vols. (London: Society of Antiquaries, 1823).
ed. *The Progresses, Processions, and Magnificent Festivities of King James the First*, 4 vols. (London: Society of Antiquaries, 1828).
Ovid. *Shakespeare's Ovid*, trans. Arthur Golding, ed. W.H.D. Rouse (London: Centaur Press, 1961).
Peacham, Henry, the Elder. *The Garden of Eloquence* (1593), with an introduction by William G. Crane (Gainesville, Fla.: Scholars' Facsimiles and Reprints, 1954).
Peele, George. *The Life and Works of George Peele*, general ed. Charles Tyler Prouty (New Haven, Conn. and London: Yale University Press, 1952-70).
Plutarch. *Plutarch's Lives of the Noble Grecians and Romans*, trans. Sir Thomas North, 6 vols. (London: David Nutt, 1895-6).
Ponet, John. *A Short Treatise of Politic Power* (1556), facsimile edn. (Menston: Scolar Press, 1970).

Puttenham, George. *The Arte of English Poesie*, ed. Gladys Doidge Willcock and Alice Walker (Cambridge: Cambridge University Press, 1936).
Ralegh, Sir Walter. *The Works of Sir Walter Ralegh*, 2 vols. (London, 1751).
Rich, Barnaby. *Rich's Farewell To Military Profession*, ed. Thomas Mabry Cranfill (Austin: University of Texas Press, 1959).
Rogers, Thomas. *A philosophicall discourse, entituled, the anatomie of the minde* (London, 1576).
Sackville, Thomas and Norton, Thomas. *Gorboduc, or Ferrex and Porrex*, ed. Irby B. Cauthen, Jr. (Lincoln, Nebr.: University of Nebraska Press, 1970).
Sallust, Caius Crispus. *The Conspiracie of Catiline*, trans. Thomas Heywood (London, 1608).
Saxo Grammaticus. *The History of the Danes*, ed. H.E. Davidson, trans. P. Fisher, 2 vols. (Cambridge: D.S. Brewer, 1979).
Seneca, Lucius Annaeus. *Seneca's Tragedies*, trans. Frank Justus Miller, 2 vols. (London: Heinemann, 1927).
  The Tenne Tragedies of Seneca, trans. Jasper Heywood (1581), 2 vols. (Manchester: The Spenser Society, 1887).
Shakespeare, William. *The Complete Works*, ed. Stanley Wells and Gary Taylor (Oxford: Clarendon Press, 1986).
Sidney, Sir Philip. *The Poems of Sir Philip Sidney*, ed. William A. Ringler, Jr. (Oxford: Clarendon Press, 1962).
  An Apology for Poetry, ed. Geoffrey Shepherd (London: Nelson, 1965).
  The Countess of Pembroke's Arcadia, ed. Maurice Evans (Harmondsworth: Penguin, 1977).
Spenser, Edmund. *The Poetical Works*, ed. J.C. Smith and E. de Selincourt (London, New York, and Toronto: Oxford University Press, 1912).
  A View of the Present State of Ireland, The Prose Works, ed. Rudolf Gottfried (Baltimore: Johns Hopkins University Press, 1949).
Starkey, Thomas, *A Dialogue Between Pole and Lupset*, ed. T.F. Mayer (London: The Royal Historical Society, 1989).
Stow, John. *Annales* (London, 1631).
Strachy, William. *A true reportory of the wracke and redemption of Sir Thomas Gates*, in *Purchas His Pilgrimes*, ed. Samuel Purchas, 20 vols. (Glasgow: Glasgow University Press, 1905–7), vol. XIX (1906), pp. 5–72.
Tacitus. *The Annales of Cornelius Tacitus*, trans. Richard Grenewey (London, 1598).
Tasso, Torquato, *Prose Filosofiche* (Florence: Alcide Parenti, 1847).
Veen, Otto van. *Amorum Emblemata* (Antwerp, 1608).
Virgil. *The Works of Virgil in English*, trans. John Dryden, ed. William Frost, vols. 5–6 of *The Works of John Dryden*, general eds. Edward Niles Hooker, Alan Roper, and H.T. Swedenborg, Jr., 20 vols. (Berkeley, Los Angeles, and London: University of California Press, 1956–89).
Webster, John. *The Duchess of Malfi*, Revels Plays, ed. John Russell Brown (London: Methuen, 1964).

Whetstone, George. *An Heptameron of Civill Discourses* (London, 1582).
Whitney, Geffrey. *A Choice of Emblemes* (1586) (New York: Benjamin Blom, 1967).
Wilson, Thomas. *The Arte of Rhetorique*, ed. G.H. Mair (Oxford: Clarendon Press, 1909).
Wither, George. *Juvenilia* (Manchester: Spenser Society, 1871).
  A Collection of Emblemes, Ancient and Moderne (1635), facsimile edn. (Columbia, S.C.: University of South Carolina Press, 1975).
Worcester, William of. *The Boke of Noblesse: Addressed to King Edward IV on his Invasion of France*, with an introduction by John Gough Nicholas (London: J.B. Nichols, 1860).

SELECTED SECONDARY SOURCES

Adams, Robert P. *The Better Part of Valor: More, Erasmus, Colet, and Vives on Humanism, War, and Peace 1496–1535* (Seattle: University of Washington Press, 1962).
Adamson, J.S.A. 'Chivalry and Political Culture in Caroline England', in *Culture and Politics in Early Stuart England*, ed. Kevin Sharpe and Peter Lake (Basingstoke and London: Macmillan, 1994), pp. 161–97.
Allmand, C.T. 'Henry V the Soldier, and the War in France', in *Henry V: The Practice of Kingship*, ed. G.L. Harriss (Oxford: Oxford University Press, 1985), pp. 117–35.
  Henry V (London: Methuen, 1992).
Altman, Joel B. *The Tudor Play of Mind: Rhetorical Inquiry and the Development of Elizabethan Drama* (Berkeley, Los Angeles, and London: University of California Press, 1978).
Anglo, Sydney. 'The British Myth in Early Tudor Propaganda', *BJRL*, 44 (1951), 17–48.
  Spectacle, Pageantry, and Early Tudor Policy (Oxford: Clarendon Press, 1969).
  ed. *Chivalry in the Renaissance* (Woodbridge, Suffolk: Boydell Press, 1990).
Armitage, David. 'The Dismemberment of Orpheus: Mythic Elements in Shakespeare's Romances', *ShS*, 39 (1986), 123–33.
  'Literature and Empire', in *The Origins of Empire: British Overseas Enterprise to the Close of the Seventeenth Century*, ed. Nicholas Canny, *The Oxford History of the British Empire* (1998–99), general ed. Wm. Roger Louis, 5 vols. (Oxford and New York: Oxford University Press, 1998), vol. I, pp. 99–123.
Ashton, Robert, ed. *James I by his Contemporaries* (London: Hutchinson, 1969).
Baker-Smith, Dominic. ' "Inglorious glory": 1513 and the Humanist Attack on Chivalry', in *Chivalry in the Renaissance*, ed. Sydney Anglo (Woodbridge, Suffolk: Boydell Press, 1990), pp. 129–44.

Barber, Charles, *The Theme of Honour's Tongue: A Study of Social Attitudes in the English Drama from Shakespeare to Dryden* (Göteborg: University of Göteborg Press, 1985).

Barkan, Leonard. *Nature's Work of Art: The Human Body as Image of the World* (New Haven, Conn. and London: Yale University Press, 1975).

The Gods Made Flesh: Metamorphosis and the Pursuit of Paganism (New Haven, Conn. and London: Yale University Press, 1986).

Barker, Francis and Hulme, Peter. '"Nymphs and reapers heavily vanish": The Discursive Contexts of *The Tempest*', in *Alternative Shakespeares*, ed. John Drakakis (London: Methuen, 1985), pp. 191–205.

Barroll, J. Leeds. 'Shakespeare and Roman History', *MLR*, 53 (1958), 327–43.

Politics, Plague, and Shakespeare's Theater: The Stuart Years (Ithaca and London: Cornell University Press, 1991).

Barton, Anne. 'The King Disguised: Shakespeare's *Henry V* and the Comical History', in *The Triple Bond: Plays, Mainly Shakespearean, in Performance*, ed. Joseph G. Price (University Park and London: Pennsylvania State University Press, 1975), pp. 92–117.

'Livy, Machiavelli, and Shakespeare's *Coriolanus*', *ShS*, 38 (1985), 115–29.

Bate, Jonathan. *Shakespeare and Ovid* (Oxford: Clarendon Press, 1993).

The Genius of Shakespeare (London and Basingstoke: Picador, 1997).

Bauckham, Richard. *Tudor Apocalypse: Sixteenth-Century Apocalypticism, Millenarianism and the English Reformation* (Abingdon: Sutton Courtenay, 1978).

Baumer, Franklin le van. *The Early Tudor Theory of Kingship* (New Haven, Conn. and London: Yale University Press, 1940).

Belsey, Catherine. *Shakespeare and the Loss of Eden* (Basingstoke and London: Macmillan, 1999).

Bergeron, David M. *Shakespeare's Romances and the Royal Family* (Lawrence, Kans.: University Press of Kansas, 1985).

Royal Family, Royal Lovers: King James of England and Scotland (Columbia and London: University of Missouri Press, 1991).

Bernheimer, Richard. *Wild Men in the Middle Ages* (Cambridge, Mass.: Harvard University Press, 1952).

Bevington, David. *Tudor Drama and Politics: A Critical Approach to Topical Meaning* (Cambridge, Mass.: Harvard University Press, 1968).

'The Tempest and the Jacobean Court Masque', in *The Politics of the Stuart Court Masque*, ed. Bevington and Holbrook (Cambridge: Cambridge University Press, 1998), pp. 218–43.

Bevington, David and Holbrook, David, eds. *The Politics of the Stuart Court Masque* (Cambridge: Cambridge University Press, 1998).

Bloomfield, Morton W. 'The Problem of the Hero in the Later Medieval Period', in *Concepts of the Hero in the Middle Ages and the Renaissance*, ed. Norman T. Burns and Christopher J. Reagan (Albany: State University of New York Press, 1975), pp. 27–48.

Bolgar, R.R. 'Hero or Anti-Hero: The Genesis and Development of the

Miles Christianus', in *Concepts of the Hero in the Middle Ages and the Renaissance*, ed. Norman T. Burns and Christopher J. Reagan (Albany: State University of New York Press, 1975), pp. 120–46.
Bono, Barbara. *Literary Transvaluations: From Vergilian Epic to Shakespearean Tragedy* (Berkeley, Los Angeles, and London: University of California Press, 1984).
Boris, Edna Zwick. *Shakespeare's English Kings: The People and the Law* (Rutherford, N.J.: Fairleigh Dickinson University Press, 1978).
Bowers, Fredson Thayer. *Elizabethan Revenge Tragedy 1587–1642* (Gloucester, Mass.: Peter Smith, 1959).
Box, Ian. 'Politics and Philosophy: Bacon on the Values of War and Peace', *SC*, 7 (1992), 113–27.
 'Bacon's Moral Philosophy', *The Cambridge Companion to Bacon*, ed. Markku Peltonen (Cambridge: Cambridge University Press, 1996), pp. 260–82.
Boynton, Lindsay. *The Elizabethan Militia 1558–1638* (London: Routledge & Kegan Paul, 1967).
Braden, Gordon. *Renaissance Tragedy and the Senecan Tradition: Anger's Privilege* (New Haven, Conn. and London: Yale University Press, 1985).
Bradley, A.C. *Shakespearean Tragedy* (1905; repr. London: Macmillan, 1963).
Bradshaw, Graham. *Shakespeare's Scepticism* (Brighton: Harvester Press, 1987).
 Misrepresentations: Shakespeare and the Materialists (Ithaca and London: Cornell University Press, 1993).
Bray, Alan. *Homosexuality in Renaissance England* (London: Gay Men's Press, 1982).
Brecht, Bertolt, *The Life of Galileo*, trans. Desmond I. Vesey (London: Methuen, 1963).
Bredbeck, Gregory. *Sodomy and Interpretation: From Marlowe to Milton* (Ithaca, N.Y.: Cornell University Press, 1991).
Breitenberg, Mark. *Anxious Masculinity in Early Modern England* (Cambridge: Cambridge University Press, 1996).
Brockbank, Philip. '*The Tempest*: Conventions of Art and Empire', in *Later Shakespeare*, ed. John Russell Brown and Bernard Harris (London: Edward Arnold, 1966), pp. 183–201.
Brotton, Jerry. ' "This Tunis, sir, was Carthage": Contesting Colonialism in *The Tempest*' in *Post-colonial Shakespeares*, ed. Ania Loomba and Martin Orkin (London and New York: Routledge, 1998), pp. 23–42.
Brower, Rueben. *Hero and Saint: Shakespeare and the Graeco-Roman Heroic Tradition* (Oxford: Clarendon Press, 1971).
Brown, Paul, ' "This thing of darkness I acknowledge mine": *The Tempest* and the Discourse of Colonialism', in *Political Shakespeare: New Essays in Cultural Materialism*, ed. Jonathan Dollimore and Alan Sinfield (Manchester: Manchester University Press, 1985), pp. 48–71.

Bruzzi, Zara. 'Instruments of Darkness: *Macbeth*, Ovid, and Jacobean Political Mythologies', in *Shakespeare and History*, Shakespeare Yearbook 6, ed. Holger Klein and Rowland Wymer (Lewiston, Queenstown, and Lampeter: Edwin Mellen Press, 1996), pp. 215–44.

Bulman, James C. *The Heroic Idiom of Shakespearean Tragedy* (Newark, N.J.: University of Delaware Press, 1985).

Burgess, Glenn. 'Revisionist History and Shakespeare's Political Context', *Shakespeare and History*, ed. Klein and Wymer (1996), pp. 5–36.

Burns, Norman T. and Reagan, Christopher J., eds. *Concepts of the Hero in the Middle Ages and the Renaissance* (Albany: State University of New York Press, 1975).

Cantor, Paul. *Hamlet* (Cambridge: Cambridge University Press, 1989).

Shakespeare's Rome: Republic and Empire (Ithaca and London: Cornell University Press, 1976).

Capp, Bernard. 'The Political Dimension of Apocalyptic Thought', in *The Apocalypse in English Renaissance Thought and Literature*, ed. C.A. Patrides and Joseph Wittreich (Manchester: Manchester University Press, 1984), pp. 93–124.

Chew, Samuel S. *The Crescent and the Rose: Islam and England During the Renaissance* (New York: Oxford University Press, 1937).

Christianson, Paul. *Reformers and Babylon: English Apocalyptic Visions from the Reformation to the End of the Civil War* (Toronto: University of Toronto Press, 1978).

'Royal and Parliamentary Voices on the Ancient Constitution c. 1604–1621', in *The Mental World of the Jacobean Court*, ed. Linda Levy Peck (Cambridge: Cambridge University Press, 1991), pp. 71–95.

Clark, Arthur Melville. *Murder Under Trust or the Topical 'Macbeth' and other Jacobean Matters* (Edinburgh: Scottish Academic Press, 1981).

Clarke, Aiden. 'Pacification, Plantation, and the Catholic Question, 1603–23', in *Early Modern Ireland, 1534–1691*, ed. T.W. Moody, F.X. Martin, and F.J. Byrne (Oxford: Clarendon Press, 1976–), pp. 187–232.

Clayton, Thomas. 'So our virtues lie in the "interpretation of the time"': Shakespeare's Tragic *Coriolanus* and Coriolanus, and Some Questions of Value', *BJJ*, 1 (1994), 147–81.

Cochrane, Kirsty. 'Orpheus Applied: Some Instances of his Importance in the Humanist View of Language', *RES*, n.s. 19 (1968), 1–13.

Coles, Paul. *The Ottoman Impact on Europe* (London: Thames & Hudson, 1968).

Colie, Rosalie. *Paradoxica Epidemica* (Princeton: Princeton University Press: 1966).

Shakespeare's Living Art (Princeton, N.J.: Princeton University Press, 1974).

Collinson, Patrick. 'The Monarchical Republic of Queen Elizabeth I', *Elizabethan Essays* (London and Rio Grande: Hambledon Press, 1994), pp. 31–57.

Corbin, Peter and Sedge, Douglas, eds., *The Oldcastle Controversy: Sir John*

Oldcastle, Part I and the Famous Victories of Henry V (Manchester and New York: Manchester University Press, 1991).
Coulson, N.J. *A History of Islamic Law* (Edinburgh: Edinburgh University Press, 1964).
Council, Norman. *When Honour's at the Stake: Ideas of Honour in Shakespeare's Plays* (London: Allen & Unwin, 1973).
'Ben Jonson, Inigo Jones, and the Transformation of Tudor Chivalry', *ELH*, 47 (1980), 259–75.
Curtius, Ernst Robert. *European Literature and the Latin Middle Ages*, trans. Willard R. Trask (London: Routledge & Kegan Paul, 1953).
Cust, Richard and Hughes, Ann, eds. *Conflict in Early Stuart England: Studies in Religion and Politics 1603–1642* (London and New York: Longman, 1989).
Daniel, Norman. *Islam, Europe and Empire* (Edinburgh: Edinburgh University Press, 1966).
The Arabs and Medieval Europe (London: Longman, 1975).
Dash, Irene. *Wooing, Wedding, and Power: Women in Shakespeare's Plays* (New York: Columbia University Press, 1981).
Dodsworth, Martin. *'Hamlet' Closely Observed* (London: Athlone Press, 1985).
Dollimore, Jonathan. *Radical Tragedy: Religion, Ideology and Power in the Drama of Shakespeare and his Contemporaries* (1984; repr. Brighton: Harvester Press, 1986)
Dollimore, Jonathan and Sinfield, Alan. 'History and Ideology: the Instance of *Henry V*', *Alternative Shakespeares*, ed. John Drakakis (London and New York: Methuen, 1985), pp. 206–27.
eds. *Political Shakespeare: New Essays in Cultural Materialism* (Manchester: Manchester University Press, 1985).
Donner, Fred McGraw. *The Early Islamic Conquests* (Princeton: Princeton University Press, 1981).
Dubrow, Heather and Strier, Richard, eds. *The Historical Renaissance: New Essays on Tudor and Stuart Literature and Culture* (Chicago and London: University of Chicago Press, 1988).
Dumézil, Georges. *Archaic Roman Religion*, trans. Philip Krapp, 2 vols. (Chicago and London: University of Chicago Press, 1970).
Dusinberre, Juliet. *Shakespeare and the Nature of Women* (London: Macmillan, 1975).
Dust, Philip C. *Three Renaissance Pacifists: Essays on the Theories of Erasmus, More, and Vives* (New York: Peter Lang, 1987).
Eliot, T.S. 'Shakespeare and the Stoicism of Seneca', in *Selected Essays* (London: Faber & Faber, 1932), pp. 126–40.
Ellis-Fermor, Una. *The Frontiers of Drama*, 2nd edn. (London: Methuen, 1964).
Elton, G.R. *Studies in Tudor and Stuart Politics and Government, Vol IV: Papers and Reviews 1982–1990* (Cambridge: Cambridge University Press, 1992).
Erickson, Peter. *Patriarchal Structures in Shakespeare's Drama* (Berkeley, Los Angeles, and London: University of California Press, 1985).

Fairchild, Hoxie Neale. *The Noble Savage: Essays in Romantic Naturalism* (New York: Columbia University Press, 1928).
Ferguson, Arthur B. *The Indian Summer of English Chivalry: Studies in the Decline and Transformation of Chivalric Idealism* (Durham, N.C.: Duke University Press, 1960).
  The Chivalric Tradition in Renaissance England (Washington, London, and Toronto: The Folger Shakespeare Library, 1986).
Fincham, Kenneth and Lake, Peter. 'The Ecclesiastical Policy of James I', *JBS*, 24 (1985), 169–207.
Fink, Zera S. *The Classical Republicans: An Essay in the Recovery of a Pattern of Thought in Seventeenth-Century England*, 2nd edn. (Evanston, Ill.: Northwestern University Press, 1962).
Firth, Katharine R. *The Apocalyptic Tradition in Reformation Britain 1530–1645* (Oxford: Oxford University Press, 1979).
Fletcher, Anthony. *Gender, Sex and Subordination in England, 1500–1800* (New Haven, Conn.: Yale University Press, 1995).
Fowler, Alastair. 'Hamlet and Honour', in *New Essays on 'Hamlet'*, ed. Mark Thornton Burnett and John Manning (New York: AMS Press, 1994), pp. 3–6.
Foyster, Elizabeth A. *Manhood in Early Modern England: Honour, Sex and Marriage* (London and New York: Longman, 1999).
Frye, Roland Mushat. *The Renaissance 'Hamlet': Issues and Responses in 1600* (Princeton: Princeton University Press, 1984).
Fuchs, Barbara. 'Conquering Islands: Contextualizing *The Tempest*', *SQ*, 48 (1997), 45–62.
Fyfe, W.H. 'Tacitus' *Germania* and More's *Utopia*', *PTRSC*, 30 (1936), 57–9.
Gajowski, Evelyn. 'The Female Perspective in *Othello*' in *'Othello': New Perspectives*, ed. Virginia Mason Vaughan and Kent Cartwright (London and Toronto: Associated University Presses, 1991), pp. 97–114.
  The Art of Loving: Female Subjectivity and Male Discursive Traditions in Shakespeare's Tragedies (Newark, N.J.: University of Delaware Press, 1992).
Galinsky, G. Karl. *The Herakles Theme: The Adaptations of the Hero in Literature from Homer to the Twentieth Century* (Oxford: Basil Blackwell, 1972).
Gardner, Helen. *The Business of Criticism* (Oxford: Clarendon Press, 1959).
  'The Noble Moor', in *Interpretations of Shakespeare: British Academy Shakespeare Lectures*, ed. Kenneth Muir (Oxford: Clarendon Press, 1985), pp. 161–79.
Gilbert, Felix. *Machiavelli and Guicciardini: Politics and History in Sixteenth-Century Florence* (Princeton: Princeton University Press, 1965).
Goldberg, Jonathan. *James I and the Politics of Literature: Jonson, Shakespeare, Donne, and Their Contemporaries* (Baltimore and London: Johns Hopkins University Press, 1983).
  Sodometries: Renaissance Texts/Modern Sexualities (Stanford: Stanford University Press, 1992).

ed. *Queering the Renaissance* (Durham, N.C. and London: Duke University Press, 1994).
Goldsmith, Robert H. 'The Wild Man on the English Stage', *MLR*, 53 (1958), 481–91.
Gordon, D.J. 'Name and Fame: Shakespeare's *Coriolanus*' in *Papers Mainly Shakespearean*, ed. G.I. Duthie (Edinburgh and London: University of Aberdeen, 1964), pp. 40–57.
  'Hymenaei: Ben Jonson's Masque of Union', in *The Renaissance Imagination: Essays and Lectures*, ed. Stephen Orgel (Berkeley, Los Angeles, and London: University of California Press, 1975), pp. 157–84.
  'Rubens and the Whitehall Ceiling', in *The Renaissance Imagination*, ed. Stephen Orgel (Berkeley, Los Angeles, and London: University of California Press, 1975), pp. 24–50.
Grady, Hugh. *The Modernist Shakespeare: Critical Texts in a Material World* (Oxford: Clarendon Press, 1991).
  Shakespeare's Universal Wolf: Studies in Early Modern Reification (Oxford: Clarendon Press, 1996).
Greenblatt, Stephen. 'Learning to Curse: Aspects of Linguistic Colonialism in the Sixteenth Century', in *First Images of America: The Impact of the New World on the Old*, ed. Fred Chiappelli (Berkeley, Los Angeles, and London: University of California Press, 1976), pp. 561–80.
  Renaissance Self-Fashioning From More to Shakespeare (Chicago and London: University of Chicago Press, 1980).
  'Invisible Bullets: Renaissance Authority and its Subversion, *Henry IV* and *Henry V*', *Political Shakespeare: New Essays in Cultural Materialism*, ed. Jonathan Dollimore and Alan Sinfield (Manchester: Manchester University Press, 1985), pp. 18–47.
  Shakespearean Negotiations: The Circulation of Social Energy in Renaissance England (Oxford: Clarendon Press, 1988).
Greene, Thomas M. *The Light in Troy: Imitation and Discovery in Renaissance Poetry* (New Haven, Conn. and London: Yale University Press, 1982).
Greenlaw, Edwin. *Studies in Spenser's Historical Allegory* (Baltimore: Johns Hopkins University Press, 1932).
Grudin, Robert. *Mighty Opposites: Shakespeare and Renaissance Contrariety* (Berkeley, Los Angeles, and London: University of California Press, 1979).
Gurr, Andrew. '*Coriolanus* and the Body Politic', *Shakespeare Survey*, 28 (1975), 63–9.
  '*Henry V* and the Bees' Commonwealth', *ShS*, 30 (1977), 61–72.
  ed. *Introduction to 'King Henry V'* (Cambridge: Cambridge University Press, 1992).
Hale, David G. '*Coriolanus*: The Death of a Political Metaphor', *ShQ*, 22 (1971), 197–202.
Hamilton, Donna B. *Virgil and 'The Tempest': The Politics of Imitation* (Columbus: Ohio State University Press, 1990).

Handover, P.M. *The Second Cecil: The Rise to Power 1563–1604 of Sir Robert Cecil* (London: Eyre & Spottiswoode, 1959).
Hansen, William F. *Saxo Grammaticus and the Life of Hamlet* (Lincoln, Nebr. and London: University of Nebraska Press, 1983).
Harris, William V. *War and Imperialism in Republican Rome, 327–70 BC* (Oxford: Clarendon Press, 1979).
Harrison, G.B. *The Life and Death of Robert Devereux, Earl of Essex* (London, Toronto, Melbourne, and Sydney: Cassell, 1937).
Harriss, G.L. *Henry V: The Practice of Kingship* (Oxford: Oxford University Press, 1985).
Hatlen, Burton, 'The "Noble Thing" and the "Boy of Tears": Coriolanus and the Embarrassments of Identity', *ELR*, 27 (1997), 393–420.
Heninger, S.K., Jr. 'The Tudor Myth of Troy-novaunt', *SAQ*, 61 (1962), 378–87.
Highley, Christopher. *Shakespeare, Spenser, and the Crisis in Ireland* (Cambridge: Cambridge University Press, 1997).
Hirst, Derek. *Authority and Conflict: England 1603–1658* (London: Edward Arnold, 1986).
Holbrook, Peter. 'Jacobean Masques and the Jacobean Peace', in *The Politics of the Stuart Court Masque*, ed. David Bevington and David Holbrook (Cambridge: Cambridge University Press, 1998), pp. 67–87.
Honigmann, E. A. J. 'The Politics of *Hamlet* and the "World of the Play" ', in *Hamlet*, Stratford-upon-Avon Studies 5, ed. John Russell Brown and Bernard Harris (London: Edward Arnold, 1963), pp. 129–47.
Howard, Jean. 'The New Historicism in Renaissance Studies', *ELR*, 16 (1986).
Howard, Jean E. and Rackin, Phyllis. *Engendering a Nation: A Feminist Account of Shakespeare's English Histories* (London and New York: Routledge, 1997).
Howarth, Herbert. *The Tiger's Heart: Eight Essays on Shakespeare* (London: Chatto & Windus, 1970).
Huffman, Clifford Chalmers. *'Coriolanus' in Context* (Lewisburg: Bucknell University Press, 1971).
Huizinga, J. *The Waning of the Middle Ages* (1924; repr. Harmondsworth: Penguin, 1982).
Hulliung, Mark. *Citizen Machiavelli* (Princeton: Princeton University Press, 1983).
Hunter, G.K. 'The Heroism of Hamlet', in *Hamlet*, Stratford-upon-Avon Studies 5, ed. John Russell Brown and Bernard Harris (London: Edward Arnold, 1963), pp. 90–109.
'Othello and Colour Prejudice', *PBA*, 53 (1967), 139–63.
Hurstfield, Joel. 'The Succession Struggle in Late Elizabethan England', in *Elizabethan Government and Society*, ed. S.T. Bindoff, J. Hurstfield, and C.H. Williams (London: Athlone Press, 1961), pp. 369–96.
Freedom, Corruption and Government in Elizabethan England (London: Jonathan Cape, 1975).

Husband, Timothy. *The Wild Man: Medieval Myth and Symbolism* (New York: Metropolitan Museum of Art, 1980).
Hutter, Horst. *Politics as Friendship: The Origins of Classical Notions of Politics in the Theory and Practice of Friendship* (Waterloo, Ontario: Wilfrid Laurier University Press, 1978).
Hyatte, Reginald. *The Arts of Friendship: The Idealization of Friendship in Medieval and Early Renaissance Literature* (Leiden, New York, and Cologne: E.J. Brill, 1994).
Ide, Richard S. *Possessed with Greatness: The Heroic Tragedies of Chapman and Shakespeare* (London: Scolar Press, 1980).
Inalcik, Halil. *The Ottoman Empire: The Classical Age 1300–1600*, trans. Norman Itzkowitz and Colin Imber (New Rochelle, N.Y.: Orpheus Publishing, 1989).
James, D.G. *The Dream of Prospero* (Oxford: Clarendon Press, 1967).
James, Heather. *Shakespeare's Troy: Drama, Politics, and the Translation of Empire* (Cambridge: Cambridge University Press, 1997).
James, Mervyn. *Society, Politics and Culture: Studies in Early Modern England* (1978; repr. Cambridge: Cambridge University Press, 1986).
Jardine, Lisa. *Reading Shakespeare Historically* (London and New York: Routledge, 1996).
Jones, Eldred. *Othello's Countrymen: The African in English Renaissance Drama* (London: Oxford University Press, 1965).
  The Elizabethan Image of Africa (Washington: The Folger Shakespeare Library, 1971).
Jones, Emrys. '*Othello*, "Lepanto" and the Cyprus Wars', *ShS*, 21 (1968), 47–52.
  Scenic Form in Shakespeare (Oxford: Clarendon Press, 1971).
  The Origins of Shakespeare (Oxford: Clarendon Press, 1977).
Jordan, Constance. *Renaissance Feminism: Literary Texts and Political Models* (Ithaca and London: Cornell University Press, 1990).
  Shakespeare's Monarchies: Ruler and Subject in the Romances (Ithaca and London: Cornell University Press, 1997).
Jorgensen, Paul. *Shakespeare's Military World* (Berkeley and Los Angeles: University of California Press, 1956).
Kahn, Coppélia. *Man's Estate: Masculine Identity in Shakespeare* (Berkeley, Los Angeles, and London: University of California Press, 1981).
  Roman Shakespeare: Warriors, Wounds, and Women (London and New York: Routledge, 1997).
Kaiser, Walter. *Praisers of Folly: Erasmus, More, Shakespeare* (London: Gollancz, 1964).
Keegan, John. *The Mask of Command* (London: Jonathan Cape, 1987).
Keen, M.H. *England in the Later Middle Ages: A Political History* (London: Methuen, 1973).
  Chivalry (New Haven, Conn. and London: Yale University Press, 1984).
Kelso, Ruth. *Doctrine for the Lady of the Renaissance* (Urbana: University of Illinois Press, 1956).

Kermode, Frank, ed. *The Tempest* (London: Methuen, 1954).
Kernan, Alvin, ed. *Othello* (New York: New American Library, 1963).
  Shakespeare, the King's Playwright: Theater in the Stuart Court 1603–1613 (New Haven, Conn. and London: Yale University Press, 1995).
Kimbrough, Robert. *Shakespeare and the Art of Humankindness: The Essay Toward Androgyny* (Highlands, N.J. and London: Humanities Press, 1990).
Kott, Jan. 'The *Aeneid* and *The Tempest*', *Arion*, n.s. 3, 4 (1976), 424–51.
  '*The Tempest*, or Repetition', *Shakespeare Today*, ed. Ralph Berry (1977), pp. 9–36.
Kurland, Stuart M. '*Hamlet* and the Scottish Succession?', *SEL*, 34 (1994), 279–300.
Lacey, Robert. *Robert, Earl of Essex: An Elizabethan Icarus* (London: Weidenfeld and Nicolson, 1971).
Laqueur, Thomas. *Making Sex: Body and Gender from the Greeks to Freud* (Cambridge, Mass. and London: Harvard University Press, 1990).
Larner, Christina. 'James VI and I and Witchcraft', in *The Reign of James VI and I*, ed. Alan G.R. Smith (London: Macmillan, 1973), pp. 74–90.
Lawrence, D.H., *Apocalypse* (London: Martin Secker, 1932).
Leavis, F.R. 'Diabolical Intellect and the Noble Hero', in *The Common Pursuit* (London: Chatto & Windus, 1958), pp. 136–59.
Lenz, Carolyn Ruth Swift, Greene, Gayle and Neely, Carol Thomas, eds. *The Woman's Part: Feminist Criticism of Shakespeare* (Urbana, Chicago, and London: University of Illinois Press, 1980).
Levin, Harry. *The Myth of the Golden Age in the Renaissance* (London: Faber & Faber, 1970).
Levy, F.J. *Tudor Historical Thought* (San Marino, Calif.: The Huntington Library, 1967).
Lockyer, Roger. *James VI and I* (London and New York: Longman, 1998).
Loomba, Ania. *Gender, Race, Renaissance Drama* (Manchester: Manchester University Press, 1989).
Loomba, Ania and Orkin, Martin, eds. *Post-Colonial Shakespeares* (London and New York: Routledge, 1998).
Lord, George deForest. *Heroic Mockery: Variations on Epic Themes from Homer to Joyce* (Newark, N.J.: University of Delaware Press, 1977).
Lovejoy, Arthur O. and Boas, George. *Primitivism and Related Ideas in Antiquity* (Baltimore: Johns Hopkins University Press, 1935).
Lyne, R.O.A.M. 'Vergil and the Politics of War', in *Oxford Readings in Vergil's 'Aeneid'*, ed. S.J. Harrison (Oxford and New York: Oxford University Press, 1990), pp. 316–18.
Macaulay, Lord. *The History of England from the Accession of James othe Second*, 8 vols. (London: Longman, Brown, Green, 1852–62).
MacCraffey, Wallace T. *Elizabeth I: War and Politics 1588–1603* (Princeton: Princeton University Press, 1992).

McAlindon, T. 'Language, Style, and Meaning in *Troilus and Cressida*', *PMLA*, 84 (1969), 29–41.
  English Renaissance Tragedy (Basingstoke and London: Macmillan, 1986).
  Shakespeare's Tragic Cosmos (Cambridge: Cambridge University Press, 1991).
McCoy, Richard C. *Sir Philip Sidney: Rebellion in Arcadia* (Hassocks: Harvester, 1979).
  The Rites of Knighthood: The Literature and Politics of Elizabethan Chivalry (Berkeley, Los Angeles, and London: University of California Press, 1989).
  'Old English Honour in an Evil Time: Aristocratic Principle in the 1620s', in *The Stuart Court and Europe: Essays in Politics and Political Culture*, ed. R. Malcolm Smuts (Cambridge: Cambridge University Press, 1996), pp. 133–55.
McElroy, Bernard. *Shakespeare's Mature Tragedies* (Princeton: Princeton University Press, 1973).
McLuskie, Kathleen. 'The Patriarchal Bard: Feminist Criticism and Shakespeare', in *Political Shakespeare: New Essays in Cultural Materialism*, ed. Jonathan Dollimore and Alan Sinfield (Manchester: Manchester University Press, 1985), pp. 88–108.
Mallin, Eric S. 'Emulous Factions and the Collapse of Chivalry: *Troilus and Cressida*', *Rep*, 29 (1990), 145–79.
Marshall, Tristan. '*The Tempest* and the British Imperium in 1611', *HJ*, 41 (1998), 375–400.
  '"That's the Misery of Peace": Representations of Martialism in the Jacobean Public Theatre, 1608–1614', *SC*, 13 (1998), 1–21.
Marx, Steven. 'Shakespeare's Pacifism', *RenQ*, 45 (1992), 49–95.
  'Holy War in *Henry V*', *ShS*, 48 (1995), 85–97.
Mason, Roger A. 'Rex Stoicus: George Buchanan, James VI and the Scottish Polity', in *New Perspectives on the Politics and Culture of Early Modern Scotland*, ed. John Dwyer, Roger A. Mason, and Alexander Murdoch (Edinburgh: John Donald, 1982), pp. 9–33.
Matar, Nabil. *Islam in Britain 1558–1685* (Cambridge: Cambridge University Press, 1998).
Matchinske, Megan. *Writing, Gender and State In Early Modern England: Identity Formation and the Female Subject* (Cambridge: Cambridge University Press, 1998).
Maus, Katharine Eisaman. *Inwardness and Theater in the English Renaissance* (Chicago: University of Chicago Press, 1995).
Mercer, Peter. '*Othello* and the Form of Heroic Tragedy', *CQ*, 11 (1969), 45–61.
Meron, Theodor. *Henry's Wars and Shakespeare's Laws: Perspectives on the Law of War in the Later Middle Ages* (Oxford: Clarendon Press, 1993).
  Bloody Constraint: War and Chivalry in Shakespeare (New York and Oxford: Oxford University Press, 1998).

Meszaros, Patricia K. '"There is a world elsewhere": Tragedy and History in *Coriolanus*', *SEL*, 16 (1976), 273–85.
Miles, Geoffrey. *Shakespeare and the Constant Romans* (Oxford: Clarendon Press, 1996).
Mills, Laurens J. *One Soul in Bodies Twain: Friendship in Tudor Literature and Stuart Drama* (Bloomington, Ind.: Principia Press, 1937).
Milward, Peter. *Shakespeare's Religious Background* (Bloomington and London: Indiana University Press, 1973).
Miola, Robert S. 'Vergil in Shakespeare: From Allusion to Imitation', in *Vergil at 2000*, ed. John D. Bernard (New York: AMS Press, 1986), pp. 254–56.
  'Othello Furens', *SQ*, 41 (1990), 49–64.
  Shakespeare's Rome (Cambridge: Cambridge University Press, 1983).
  Shakespeare and Classical Tragedy: The Influence of Seneca (Oxford: Clarendon Press, 1992).
Neale, J.E. *Elizabeth I and her Parliaments 1584–1601* (London: Jonathan Cape, 1957).
Neely, Carol Thomas. 'Women and Men in *Othello*', *SStud*, 10 (1977), 133–58.
  Broken Nuptials in Shakespeare's Plays (New Haven, Conn. and London: Yale University Press, 1985).
Norbrook, David. '*Macbeth* and the Politics of Historiography', in *Politics of Discourse: The Literature and History of Seventeenth-Century England*, ed. Kevin Sharpe and Steven N. Zwicker (Berkeley, Los Angeles, and London: University of California Press, 1987), pp. 78–116.
  '"What cares these roarers for the name of king?": Language and Utopia in *The Tempest*', in *The Politics of Tragi-Comedy: Shakespeare and After*, ed. Gordan McMullan and Jonathan Hope (London and New York: Routledge, 1992), pp. 21–54.
Novy, Marianne. *Love's Argument: Gender Relations in Shakespeare* (Chapel Hill: University of North Carolina Press, 1984).
Orgel, Stephen, ed. *The Tempest* (Oxford: Clarendon Press, 1987).
Orkin, Martin. 'Othello and the "plain face" of Racism', *SQ*, 38 (1987), 166–88.
Ornstein, Robert. *The Moral Vision of Jacobean Tragedy* (Madison and Milwaukee: University of Wisconsin Press, 1965).
Otis, Brooks, *Virgil: A Study in Civilized Poetry* (Oxford: Clarendon Press, 1964).
Parel, Anthony J. *The Machiavellian Cosmos* (New Haven, Conn. and London: Yale University Press, 1992).
Parker, R.B., ed. *The Tragedy of 'Coriolanus'* (Oxford: Clarendon Press, 1994).
Parry, Graham. *The Golden Age Restor'd: The Culture of the Stuart Court, 1603–42* (Manchester: Manchester University Press, 1981).

Parsons, A.E. 'The Trojan Legend in England', *MLR*, 24 (1929), 243–64.
Patterson, Annabel. *Shakespeare and the Popular Voice* (Cambridge, Mass. and Oxford: Blackwell, 1989).
Patterson, W.B. *King James VI and I and the Reunion of Christendom* (Cambridge: Cambridge University Press, 1997).
Paul, Henry N. *The Royal Play of 'Macbeth'* (1948; repr. New York: Octagon Books, 1971).
Peck, Linda Levy, ed. *The Mental World of the Jacobean Court* (Cambridge: Cambridge University Press, 1991), pp. 1–17.
Peltonen, Markku. 'Politics and Science: Francis Bacon and the True Greatness of States', *HJ*, 35 (1992), 279–305.
  Classical Humanism and Republicanism in English Political Thought 1570–1640 (Cambridge: Cambridge University Press, 1995).
Perry, Curtis. *The Making of Jacobean Culture: James I and the Renegotiation of Elizabethan Literary Practice* (Cambridge: Cambridge University Press, 1997).
Pettett, E.C. '*Coriolanus* and the Midlands Insurrection of 1607', *ShS*, 3 (1950), 34–42.
Phillips, James Emerson, Jr. *The State in Shakespeare's Greek and Roman Plays* (1940; repr. New York: Octagon Books, 1972).
Pitcher, John. 'A Theatre of the Future: The *Aeneid* and *The Tempest*', *EC*, 34 (1984), 193–215.
Proser, Matthew N. *The Heroic Image in Five Shakespearean Tragedies* (Princeton: Princeton University Press, 1965).
Prosser, Eleanor. *'Hamlet' and Revenge*, 2nd edn. (Stanford: Stanford University Press, 1971).
Proudfoot, Richard 'Shakespeare and the New Dramatists of the King's Men 1606–1613', in *Later Shakespeare*, Stratford-upon-Avon Studies 8, ed. John Russell Brown and Bernard Harris (London: Edward Arnold, 1966), pp. 235–61.
Quarshie, Hugh. *Second Thoughts about 'Othello'*, International Shakespeare Association Occasional Paper 7 (Stratford-upon-Avon: International Shakespeare Association, 1999).
Raab, Felix. *The English Face of Machiavelli: A Changing Interpretation 1500–1700* (London: Routledge & Kegan Paul, 1964).
Rabkin, Norman. *Shakespeare and the Problem of Meaning* (Chicago and London: University of Chicago Press, 1981).
  Shakespeare and the Common Understanding (1967; repr. Chicago and London: University of Chicago Press, 1984).
Rossiter, A.P. *Angel with Horns: Fifteen Lectures on Shakespeare*, ed. Graham Storey, 1961; repr. with an introduction by Peter Holland (London and New York: Longman, 1989).
Roy, Emil. 'War and Manliness in Shakespeare's *Troilus and Cressida*', *Comparative Drama*, 7 (1974), 107–20.

Russell, Conrad. *The Crisis of Parliaments: English History 1509–1660* (Oxford: Oxford University Press, 1971).
  Parliaments and English Politics, 1621–1629 (Oxford: Oxford University Press, 1979).
  Unrevolutionary England, 1603–1642 (London and Ronceverte: Hambledon Press, 1990).
Said, Edward W. *Culture and Imperialism* (London: Chatto & Windus, 1993).
Sanders, Norman, ed. *Othello* (Cambridge: Cambridge University Press, 1984).
Savage, James E. '*Troilus and Cressida* and Elizabethan Court Factions', *UMSE*, 5 (1964), 413–66.
Schmidgall, Gary S. *Shakespeare and the Courtly Aesthetic* (Berkeley, Los Angeles, and London: University of California Press, 1981).
Schwarz, Marc L. 'James I and the Historians: Toward a Reconsideration', *JBS*, 13 (1974), 114–34.
Segal, Charles. *Orpheus: The Myth of the Poet* (Baltimore and London: Johns Hopkins University Press, 1989).
Seward, Desmond. *Henry V as Warlord* (London: Sidgwick & Jackson, 1987).
Seznec, Jean. *The Survival of the Pagan Gods: The Mythological Tradition and its Place in Renaissance Humanism and Art*, trans. Barbara F. Sessions (New York: Pantheon Books, 1953).
Shalvi, Alice. *The Relationship of Renaissance Concepts of Honour to Shakespeare's Problem Plays* (Salzburg: University of Salzburg, 1972).
Sharpe, Kevin, ed. *Faction and Parliament: Essays on Early Stuart History* (Oxford: Clarendon Press, 1978).
Sharpe, Kevin and Lake, Peter, eds. *Culture and Politics in Early Stuart England* (Basingstoke and London: Macmillan, 1994).
Shaw, Stanford, *History of the Ottoman Empire and Modern Turkey*, 2 vols. (Cambridge: Cambridge University Press, 1976).
Siegel, Paul N. 'Shakespeare and the Neo-Chivalric Cult of Honor', *CR*, 8 (1964), 39–70.
Simmons, J.L. '*Antony and Cleopatra* and *Coriolanus*: Shakespeare's Heroic Tragedies', *ShS*, 26 (1973), 95–101.
  Shakespeare's Pagan World: The Roman Tragedies (Hassocks: Harvester, 1974).
Simonds, Peggy Muñoz. '*Coriolanus* and the Myth of Juno and Mars', *Mosaic*, 18 (1985), 33–50.
  'The Herculean Lover in the Emblems of Cranach and Vaenius', *Acta Conventius Neo-Latini Torontonensis: Proceedings of the Seventh International Congress of Neo-Latin Studies*, ed. Alexander Dalzell, Charles Fantazzi, and Richard J. Schoeck (Binghamton, N.Y.: Medieval and Renaissance Texts and Studies, 1991), pp. 697–710.
  '"Sweet Power of Music": The Political Magic of "the Miraculous Harp", in Shakespeare's *The Tempest*', *CD*, 29 (1995), 61–90.
  '"My charms crack not": The Alchemical Structure of *The Tempest*', *CD*, 31 (1998), 538–70.

Sinfield, Alan. *Faultlines: Cultural Materialism and the Politics of Dissident Reading* (Oxford: Clarendon Press, 1992).
Skretkowicz, Victor. 'Chivalry in Sidney's *Arcadia*', in *Chivalry in the Renaissance*, ed. Sydney Anglo (Woodbridge, Suffolk: Boydell Press, 1990), pp. 161–74.
Skura, Meredith Anne. 'The Case of Colonialism in *The Tempest*', *SQ*, 40 (1989), 42–69.
Smith, Alan G.R. 'Constitutional Ideas and Parliamentary Developments in England 1603–1625', in *The Reign of James VI and I*, ed. Alan G.R. Smith (London: Macmillan, 1973), pp. 160–76.
Smith, Bruce. *Homosexual Desire in Shakespeare's England: A Cultural Poetics* (Chicago: University of Chicago Press, 1991).
Smuts, Malcolm. 'Cultural Diversity and Cultural Change at the Court of James I', in *The Mental World of the Jacobean Court*, ed. Linda Levy Peck (Cambridge: Cambridge University Press, 1991), pp. 99–112.
  'Court-Centred Politics and the Uses of Roman Historians c.1590–1630', in *Culture and Politics in Early Stuart England*, ed. Kevin Sharpe and Peter Lake (Basingstoke and London: Macmillan, 1994), pp. 21–43.
  Court Culture and the Origins of a Royalist Tradition in Early Stuart England (Philadelphia: University of Pennsylvania Press, 1987).
Sommerville, J.P. 'James I and the Divine Right of Kings: English Politics and Continental Theory', in *The Mental World of the Jacobean Court*, ed. Linda Levy Peck (Cambridge: Cambridge University Press, 1991), pp. 55–70.
Southern, R.W. *Western Views of Islam in the Middle Ages* (Cambridge, Mass.: Harvard University Press, 1962).
Spear, Gary. 'Shakespeare's "Manly" Parts: Masculinity and Effeminancy in *Troilus and Cressida*', *SQ*, 44 (1993), 409–22.
Spencer, Janet M. 'Princes, Pirates, and Pigs: Criminalizing Wars of Conquest in *Henry V*', *SQ*, 47 (1996), 160–77.
Spencer, T.J.B. 'Shakespeare and the Elizabethan Romans', *ShS*, 10 (1957), 27–38.
  'The Decline of Hamlet', in *Hamlet*, Stratford-upon-Avon Studies 5, ed. John Russell Brown and Bernard Harris (London: Edward Arnold, 1963), pp. 185–99.
Starkey, David, ed. *The English Court from the Wars of the Roses to the Civil War* (London: Longman, 1987).
Steadman, John M. 'Heroic Virtue and the Divine Image in *Paradise Lost*', *JWCI*, 22 (1959), 88–105.
  Milton and the Paradoxes of Renaissance Heroism (Baton Rouge and London: Louisiana State University Press, 1987).
Strong, Roy. *Henry, Prince of Wales* (London: Thames & Hudson, 1986).
Talbert, Ernest William. *The Problem of Order: Elizabethan Political Commonplaces and an Example of Shakespeare's Art* (Chapel Hill, N.C.: University of North Carolina Press, 1962).

Taylor, Gary, ed. *Henry V* (Oxford and New York: Oxford University Press, 1982).
Thompson, Ann. ' "The warrant of womanhood": Shakespeare and Feminist Criticism', in *The Shakespeare Myth*, ed. Graham Holderness (Manchester: Manchester University Press, 1988), pp. 74–88.
  'Are There Any Women in *King Lear*', in *The Matter of Difference: Materialist Feminist Criticism of Shakespeare*, ed. Valerie Wayne (New York and London: Harvester Wheatsheaf, 1991), 117–28.
Tillyard, E.M.W. *Shakespeare's History Plays* (London: Chatto & Windus, 1944).
  Shakespeare's Last Plays (London: Chatto & Windus, 1962).
  The Elizabethan World Picture (1943; repr. Harmondsworth: Penguin, 1970).
Tinkler, John F. 'Bacon and History', in *The Cambridge Companion to Bacon*, ed. Markku Peltonen (Cambridge: Cambridge University Press, 1996), pp. 232–59.
Vale, Malcolm. *War and Chivalry: Warfare and Aristocratic Culture in England, France and Burgundy at the End of the Middle Ages* (London: Duckworth, 1981).
Vaughan, Alden T. and Vaughan, Virginia Mason. *Shakespeare's Caliban: A Cultural History* (Cambridge: Cambridge University Press, 1991).
Vaughan, Virginia Mason. *'Othello': A Contextual History* (Cambridge: Cambridge University Press, 1994).
Velz, John W, ' "Cracking Strong Curbs Asunder": Roman Destiny and the Roman Hero in *Coriolanus*', *ELR*, 13 (1983), 58–69.
Voegelin, Eric. 'Machiavelli's Prince: Background and Formation', *RP*, 13 (1951), 142–68.
Waith, Eugene M. 'Manhood and Valor in Two Shakespearean Tragedies', *ELH*, 17 (1950), 262–73.
  The Herculean Hero in Marlowe, Chapman, Shakespeare and Dryden (London: Chatto & Windus, 1962).
  Ideas of Greatness: Heroic Drama in England (London: Routledge & Kegan Paul, 1971).
  'Heywood's Women Worthies', in *Concepts of the Hero in the Middle Ages and the Renaissance*, ed. Norman T. Burns and Christopher J. Reagan (Albany: State University of New York Press, 1975), pp. 222–38.
Walker, Greg. *Plays of Persuasion: Drama and Politics at the Court of Henry VIII* (Cambridge: Cambridge University Press, 1991).
Walter, J.H., ed. *Henry V* (London and Cambridge, Mass.: Methuen and Harvard University Press, 1954).
Warden, John, ed. *Orpheus: The Metamorphosis of a Myth* (Toronto: University of Toronto Press, 1982).
Wardropper, Bruce W. 'The Epic Hero Superseded', in *Concepts of the Hero in the Middle Ages and the Renaissance*, ed. Norman T. Burns and Christopher J. Reagan (Albany: State University of New York Press, 1975), pp. 197–221.
Watson, Curtis Brown. *Shakespeare and the Renaissance Concept of Honor* (Princeton: Princeton University Press, 1960).

Watt, W. Montgomery. *The Influence of Islam on Medieval Europe* (Edinburgh: Edinburgh University Press, 1972).
Wayne, Valerie, ed. *The Matter of Difference: Materialist Feminist Criticism of Shakespeare* (New York and London: Harvester Wheatsheaf, 1991).
  'Historical Differences: Misogyny and *Othello*', in *The Matter of Difference: Materialist Feminist Criticism of Shakespeare*, ed. Valerie Wayne, pp. 153–79.
Wells, Robin Headlam. 'The Fortunes of Tillyard: Twentieth-Century Critical Debate on Shakespeare's History Plays', *ES*, 66 (1985), 391–403.
  Elizabethan Mythologies: Studies in Poetry, Drama and Music (Cambridge: Cambridge University Press, 1994).
Wells, Robin Headlam, Burgess, Glenn and Wymer, Rowland, eds. *Neo-Historicism: Studies in English Renaissance Literature, History and Politics* (Woodbridge, Suffolk: D. S. Brewer Ltd, 2000).
Wells-Cole, Anthony. *Art and Decoration in Elizabethan and Jacobean England: The Influence of Continental Prints, 1558–1625* (New Haven, Conn. and London: Yale University Press, 1997).
Wernham, R.B. *The Making of Elizabethan Foreign Policy, 1558–1603* (Berkeley, Los Angeles, and London: University of California Press, 1980).
Whitaker, Virgil K. *Shakespeare's Use of Learning* (San Marino, Calif.: The Huntington Library, 1953).
White, Hayden. 'The Forms of Wildness: Archaeology of an Idea', in *The Wild Man Within: An Image in Western Thought from the Renaissance to Romanticism*, ed. Edward Dudley and Maximillian E. Novak (Pittsburgh: University of Pittsburgh Press, 1972), pp. 3–38.
Williams, Andrew P. ed. *The Image of Manhood in Early Modern Literature: Viewing the Male* (Westport, Conn. and London: Greenwood Press, 1999).
Williams, Penry. *The Later Tudors: England 1547–1603*, The New Oxford History of England (Oxford: Clarendon Press, 1995).
Williams, R.D. *Aeneas and the Roman Hero* (Basingstoke and London: Macmillan, 1973).
Williamson, J.W. *The Myth of the Conqueror: Prince Henry Stuart: A Study of 17th-Century Personation* (New York: AMS Press 1978).
Wills, Garry. *Witches and Jesuits: Shakespeare's 'Macbeth'* (New York and London: Oxford University Press, 1995).
Wilson, Elkin Calhoun, *Prince Henry and English Literature* (Ithaca, N.Y.: Cornell University Press, 1946).
Wiltenburg, Robert. 'The *Aeneid* in *The Tempest*', *ShS*, 39 (1986), 159–68.
Winstanley, Lilian. *'Hamlet' and the Scottish Succession* (Cambridge: Cambridge University Press, 1921).
  'Macbeth', 'King Lear' and Contemporary History (Cambridge: Cambridge University Press, 1922).
Woodbridge, Linda. *Women and the English Renaissance: Literature and the Nature of Womankind, 1540–1620* (Brighton: Harvester Press, 1984).

Woods, Gregory. *A History of Gay Literature: The Male Tradition* (New Haven, Conn. and London: Yale University Press, 1998).
Worden, Blair. 'Classical Republicanism and the Puritan Revolution', in *History and Imagination: Essays in Honour of H.R. Trevor-Roper*, ed. Hugh Lloyd-Jones, Valerie Pearl, and Blair Worden (London: Duckworth, 1981), pp. 182–200.
  'Ben Jonson Among the Historians', in *Culture and Politics in Early Stuart England*, ed. Kevin Sharpe and Peter Lake (Basingstoke: Macmillan, 1994), pp. 67–89.
  The Sound of Virtue: Philip Sidney's 'Arcadia' and Elizabethan Politics (New Haven, Conn. and London: Yale University Press, 1996).
Wormald, Jenny. 'Gunpowder, Treason, and Scots', *JBS*, 24 (1985), 141–68.
  'One king, two kingdoms', in *Uniting the Kingdom: The Making of British History*, ed. Alexander Grant and Keith J. Stringer (London and New York: Routledge, 1995), pp. 123–32.
  'James VI, James I and the Identity of Britain', in *The British Problem, c.1534–1707: State Formation in the Atlantic Archipelago*, ed. Brendan Bradshaw and John Morrill (Basingstoke and London: Macmillan, 1996), pp. 148–71.
Wright, Louis B. 'Colonial Developments in the Reign of James I', in *The Reign of James VI and I*, ed. Alan G.R. Smith (London and Basingstoke: Macmillan, 1973), pp. 123–39.
Yachnin, Paul. 'The Powerless Theatre', *ELR*, 21 (1991), 49–74.
Yates, Frances. 'Elizabethan Chivalry: The Romance of the Accession Day Tilts', *JWCI*, 20 (1957), 4–25.
  Shakespeare's Last Plays: A New Approach (London: Routledge & Kegan Paul, 1975).
Yeats, W.B. *The Irish Dramatic Movement 1901–1919, Explorations* (London: Macmillan, 1962).
Zeeveld, W. Gordon. '*Coriolanus* and Jacobean Politics', *MLR*, 57 (1962), 321–4.

Index

Aeneas 129, 131–3, 141, 181
Aeneid, see Virgil's *Aeneid*
Africanus, Leo 94, 109
Althusser, Louis 212
androgyne, myth of 201
Anne, Queen 157
anthropomorphic analogy 168–70, 173
  see also body/state analogy
anti-militarism, *see* pacifism
Antichrist 97, 99, 124
  see also Turks
anti-essentialism 172–3
anti-rationalism 53, 55–9
Antony and Cleopatra 158
apocalyptic prophecy 33–4, 48
Appian of Alexandria 161
Aquinas, St Thomas 82n60
Aristotle 2, 165
Armitage, David 178n1, 187, 193–4
Ascham, Roger 14
Ashley, Robert 47–8
Auerbach, Erich 171–2
Augustine of Hippo, S 49
Augustus, Roman emperor 135
Augustus redivivus, James I as 18, 127–30
Averroes 96
Avicenna 96

Bacon, Sir Francis, Viscount St Albans
  and Machiavellianism 19, 21, 22, 26
  on Orpheus and Hercules 1, 26, 28–9, 178, 184
  on state and warfare 19, 21, 22, 170
Barber, Charles 4n8, 101n44
Barkan, Leonard 168n83
Barker, Francis 5, 6n14, 186n14
Barlow, Bishop William 153n39
Bartholomaeus Anglicus 96
Barton, Anne 44n42, 173n102
Bate, Jonathan 178n1, 189n, 190, 194n51
Beard, Charles 208, 209, 218
Beaufort, Henry, Bishop of Winchester 34

Becker, Carl 208, 209
Belsey, Catherine 5, 75, 216–18
Bergeron, David M. 149n13, 198n63
Berlin, Isaiah 141–2
Bevington, David 198n63
Birch, Thomas 157, 175
Blount, Charles (Lord Mountjoy) 27, 63
body/state analogy 167
  see also anthropomorphic analogy
Boethius 88n5, 99n
Bowers, Fredson Thayer 76n, 108
Box, Ian 19n79
Bracciolini, Poggio 20
Bradley, A.C. 66, 80n53, 92n15, 114, 146n4
Bradshaw, Graham 24n103, 32n1, 122, 217n
Breitenberg, Mark 5n, 212–14
British Myth of Trojan origins 52, 122–6, 127, 128–30, 142–3
Brockbank, Philip 186
Brower, Reuben A. 73n, 113n76, 147n8, 165n78, 169n83, 173
Browne, Sir Thomas 98
Bruni, Leonardo 20
Brutus (great-grandson of Aeneas) 125, 127–8, 142n72
Bueil, Jean de 46
Bullough, Geoffrey 147, 161
Bulman, James C. 4n7, 113n76
Burghley, Lord (William Cecil) 10, 17

Cantor, Paul A. 73, 81, 144, 147n8
Capp, Bernard 36n24
Case, John 183
Castiglione, Baldassare 14
Castracani, Castruccio 20
Caxton, William 12
Cecil, Sir Robert 63
Cecil, William, *see* Burghley, Lord 10, 17
Césaire, Aimé 189n
Chapman, George 7, 173
Chaucer, Geoffrey 25, 78
chivalry and chivalric revival 9, 109

243

collapse of 49–51
and *Coriolanus* 154, 156, 159, 160, 171–2, 174, 175–6
and friendship 46–7, 161–7
and *Henry V* and *Troilus and Cressida* 31–60
Christianson, Paul 36n
Cicero, Marcus Tullius 25
  on body/state analogy 168
  on friendship 165
  on warfare 131, 133, 175–6
Cinthio, Giraldi 91
Clarke, Larry R. 58
Cochrane, Kirsty 26n12, 182n16
Coleridge, Samuel Taylor 114, 201
Colet, John 13
Collaert, Hans 97
colonialism 154–5
  and *Tempest* 180, 186–90, 195
Colonne, John Guido delle 51
Conrad, Joseph 77, 80, 83, 84, 112
Contarini, Gaspar 110
Copley, Anthony 8, 10
Coriolanus 27, 144–76
  and body/state analogy 167–75
  and chivalric friendship 161–7
  and Henry, Prince of Wales 149–58
Cotton, Sir Robert 23, 153–4, 174–5
Council, Norman 4n8, 14n55, 101n44, 127n30
Craig, Hardin 208
Cultural Materialism 23, 141–2
Cymbeline 105, 137, 157

Daniel, Samuel 9, 10, 16–17, 18–19, 73, 75, 109
Darwin, Charles/Darwinism 204–5n88
Davies, John, of Hereford 8–9, 18
Day, Angel 9n30
Dekker, Thomas 27n118, 127–8, 129, 135n57
Dent, Arthur 37
Derrida, Jacques 55
Devereux, Robert *see* Essex
Dodsworth, Martin 67
Dollimore, Jonathan 5, 23n100, 141n68, 172
Drakakis, John 217
Drayton, Michael 22, 126, 127, 130, 154, 184n25, 196
Dryden, John 117, 177
Dudley, Edward 191n42
Dumézil, Georges 151n23
Dusinberre, Juliet 4n9
Dust, Philip C. 13n45, 42n37, 152n31

Eagleton, Terry 123, 173–4
Edward IV 11, 52
Edwards, Philip 66, 81n55

Ehrenreich, Barbara 161, 178n
Eliot, T.S. 85, 92n15
Elizabeth I 6, 10, 133
  and Africans 95, 114
  and British myth 125
  and Essex 11, 49, 50–1, 53
  and Spain 36
Elizabeth, Princess (daughter of James I) 28, 196, 197
Ellis-Fermor, Una M. 20n85, 55
Elton, W.R. 24n103, 211
Elyot, Sir Thomas 14, 168, 169n84
empiricism 207–11, 215–16, 218
Erasmus, Desiderius 13, 25, 169n84
  an art 182
  on charity 108, 111
  on chivalry 48
  on Hercules 1, 26, 90n9
  on pacifism and Christian prince 18, 28, 32, 33, 42, 206
  on wars 115, 152, 155, 180
  and women's education 15
  see also humanism
Erickson, Peter 4n9
essentialism 172–3
Essex, 2nd Earl of (Robert Devereux)
  and Elizabeth 11, 49, 53
  and Ireland 31, 49–50
  and James I 63–4, 78
  and Machiavellianism 64
  militarism and heroic ideal 15, 24, 35, 84, 109, 206
  against Spain 11, 17, 36, 37, 78, 134
  coup, failure of 50–1, 59–60, 115
  Sidney-Essex alliance *see under* Sidney
  on Trojan War 78
  on peace 73

Fabyan, Robert 16n65
Ferguson, Arthur B. 12–13
Fink, Zera S. 107, 110n68
Florus, Lucius Annaeus 158, 159, 160
Foucault, Michel 5, 212n21, 214n
Foyster, Elizabeth A. 7
Frederick V, Elector Palatine of Rhine 196, 200
Freud, Sigmund 214
friendship *see* love and friendship
Frye, Northrop 178n1
Frye, Roland Mushat 25n105, 62n4, 67
Fussell, Paul 161n64

Galinsky, G. Karl 26n108, 179nn5, 6 and 9, 180n
Gardner, Helen 24n103, 122, 215, 218

on *Hamlet* 81
on historicism 210–11
on *Othello* 89–90, 112
Geertz, Clifford James 215
Gellner, Ernest 56n67
gender 3–5, 7–8, 15
  see also masculinity
George, David 156
Gifford, George 36–7
Goethe, Johann Wolfgang von 81
Goldberg, Jonathan 6n15, 157
Golding, Arthur 178, 194
Good, Graham 212n
Gordon, D.J. 136n, 141, 144n
Gosson, Stephen 196
Gower, John 99n, 184, 204
Grady, Hugh 55–6, 57, 212n, 216, 217, 218
Grafton, Richard 16n65, 79
Gray, John 57n69, 141–2
Greenblatt, Stephen 32, 37, 38, 186, 215
Grudin, Robert 24n103, 211
Gurr, Andrew 36n23, 41n36, 169n84
Gwynne, Matthew 126

Hakluyt, Richard 204
Hale, David G. 168nn80, 83, 169
Hall, Edward 16n65
Hamilton, Donna B. 186n33
Hamlet 7, 61–85, 176, 210
  and James I 61–5, 78, 85
  and revenge 64–5, 68, 70–2, 74–5, 82
  Viking honour 69, 73–80, 176
Harvey, Gabriel 20–1
Hawes, Stephen 13
Hawkes, Terence 66
Hawkins, John 149–50
Haydn, Hiram 210
Hayward, Sir John 50, 101–2
Henry I, King (Beau Clerke) 14
Henry IV 137
  Part I 7, 38–9, 84
  Part II 50, 170
Henry V 31–49, 52, 115, 132, 156
  holy warrior 37–47
Henry V, king 16, 28, 33–4, 51–2
Henry VII, king 126
Henry VIII 177
Henry VIII, king 13, 16, 28, 63
Henry, Prince (son of James I) 22, 149–58, 174, 185, 206
  father's attitude to and marriage plans for 22–3, 150, 152, 153–4, 196–200 and n68
Henryson, Robert 86, 88, 102

Hercules 25, 28–30
  and *Coriolanus* 148, 151
  Erasmus on 1, 26, 90n
  and Orpheus 23–8
  and *Othello* 89–91
  and *Tempest* and *Aeneid* 177, 178–81, 195
  Virgil on 179–81
  see also Seneca
heroism and heroic manhood 1–2, 22–3, 27
  and *Macbeth* 117–18, 139–41
  see also Hercules;
  masculinity; militarism
Heywood, Jasper 90–1
Highley, Christopher 59n72
historicism 38, 207–12, 215, 216–17
Hoccleve, Thomas 51n57
Holderness, Graham 216
Holinshed, Raphael 16n65, 40, 43, 137, 139
Holles, Sir John 197–8
holy warrior 33–4, 37–47
  see also Henry, Prince; heroism
Homer 119n5
homosexuality 162 and n, 166
Honigmann, E.A.J. 65n18, 200n67
honour 2, 4, 9, 11–12, 15, 206
  and chivalry 51–60
  revival of 31, 32, 34–5, 36, 47–8
  and *Coriolanus* 154, 160
  and *Hamlet* 77
  humanist suspicion of 14, 17
  killings 108–9
  and *Othello* 101, 106–13
  and politics 5–6
  and *Troilus and Cressida* 51–60
  Viking 69, 73–80, 176
Horace (Flaccus, Quintus Horatius) 26
Howard, Jean 4n9, 23n, 217, 218
Huizinga, J. 11n37, 46
humanism 13–15, 17–18, 24–6, 28–9, 38, 73
  and *Tempest* 182, 205
  see also civilization; Erasmus; love and friendship; pacifism
Humphrey, Duke of Gloucester 16n65
Hunter, G.K. 4n7, 6n18, 93n

Ide, Richard S. 4n8, 104
Inalcik, Halil 97
Ireland 31, 35, 49–50
Islam 96–8, 105, 108–9, 113
  see also Turks

James I (VI of Scotland) 6, 19
  accession and coronation 8, 18, 62, 63–4, 127–8, 135, 156, 206
  as *Augustus Redivivus* 18, 127–30

and British Myth of Trojan origins 125–6, 127, 129, 142–3
childhood 62, 124–5
and Christian unity 123–4
and colonialism 187
and daughter's dynastic marriage 196–8
and Essex 63–4, 78
and Gunpowder Plot 124, 126
and *Hamlet* 61–5, 78, 85
Lepanto and Turks 95–6, 98, 102–3, 110, 115
and *Macbeth* 10, 118, 122–30, 133–7, 157
on monarchy and succession 65, 72, 118, 123, 142, 187
as musician-king 27–8, 184–5
pacifism of 18, 63, 123–4, 127, 129, 133–4, 141, 150, 154, 184–5, 190
and *Tempest* 157, 187, 190, 196–8
and Virgil's *Aeneid* 118, 128–30, 134–5
James IV (of Scotland) 126
James, Heather 23n100, 55n62, 135n56, 188n39
James, Mervyn 11n34, 12, 15n61, 50n52, 51n54, 53n60, 144n
Jenkins, Harold 66, 67n23
Johnson, Samuel 213, 218
Jones, Eldred D. 92n18, 94n, 95n20, 104n52
Jones, Emrys 24n103, 146, 211
Jones, Inigo 150
Jonson, Ben 26, 129, 130, 150
Jordan, Constance 6n15, 198n63
Jorgensen, Paul 3, 21n88, 160
Julius Caesar 40, 158, 165, 170
Juvenal (Decimus Junius Juvenalis) 10

Kamps, Ivo 217, 218
Keegan, John 28, 144, 207
Kendall, Timothy 166–7
Kernan, Alvin 6n15, 61, 110, 157n49
King, Bruce 147n7
King John 170
King Lear 172, 183
Knolles, Richard 96, 97–8, 111n70

Lamb, Charles 114 and n79
Langland, William 102
Languet, Hubert 17
Laqueur, Thomas 5n13
Lawrence, D.H. 61, 84, 113–14
Leavis, F.R. 92n15
Legh, Gerard 34, 109
Lewis, C.S. 14
Livio, Tito 16n65
Livy (Titus Livius) 158, 160, 169
Loomba, Ania 93n, 187n, 217, 218
love and friendship 199

chivalric 46–7, 161–7
Cicero on 165
Lovejoy, Arthur O. 202n77
Lull, Ramón 12
Luther, Martin 97
Lydgate, John 16, 31, 48, 51
Lyly, John 8n24, 25n106, 79

McAlindon, Tom 25n104, 37n28, 57n70, 64n15, 92n17, 98n41, 146n4, 148n12, 173n99, 183n21, 199
MacCaffrey, Wallace T. 16n62, 17n70
McCoy, Richard C. 12n40
McElroy, Bernard 24n, 211
Macaulay, Thomas Babington, 1st Baron, 123
Macbeth 116, 117–43, 176
and James I 10, 118, 122–30, 133–7, 157
as royal compliment 133–7
and Virgil's *Aeneid* 117–19, 125, 128–35, 141, 142, 143
see also British Myth
Machiavelli, Niccolò and Machiavellianism 172
and Bacon 19, 21, 22, 26
and Essex 64
and *Hamlet* 69
and *Henry V* 32, 33, 38
and Rome 158, 159, 165
and *virtù* 20, 21–2, 159
Malory, Sir Thomas 13, 14, 164
manliness/manhood 7
see also masculinity/manhood
Marcelline, George 27n117, 134n51, 151–2, 184–5
Markham, Gervase 12, 18, 34
Marlowe, Christopher 20, 25, 76, 78, 84, 162
Marshall, Tristan 6n17, 19n77, 187n36
Martindale, Charles and Michelle 145n2, 146n5
Marx, Steven 13n45, 38, 157n51
Mary, Queen of Scots 62, 63
masculinity/manhood 51–60
major plays discussed *see Coriolanus*; *Hamlet*; *Henry V*; *Macbeth*; *Othello*; *Tempest*; *Troilus and Cressida*
see also chivalry; civilization; courage; heroism; honour; militarism; pacifism; sensibility; *virtus*
Maus, Katharine Eisaman 107–8
Measure for Measure 103n, 157, 170
Merchant of Venice, The 42–3, 54–5, 89, 98, 182, 190

Index

Meron, Theodor 4n8, 43n
Merquior, J.G. 212n
Middleton, Thomas 183
Midsummer Night's Dream, A 87
militant Protestantism 8–9, 15–19, 84
   and *Coriolanus* 151–3, 155
   and *Henry V* 31–2, 36–9
   and *Tempest* 196–7, 200n67
   see also Essex; Sidney
militarism 2, 7–12, 21–4
   and chivalric revival 31, 35–6
   and *Coriolanus* 147–67, 173–6
   and *Hamlet* 69, 73–80
   and *Macbeth* 132–3, 138, 140
   war faction *see* militant Protestantism
millenarianism 33–4, 48
Milton, John 23–4
Milward, Peter 200n, 211–12
Miola, Robert S. 27n116, 75n4, 90, 91, 118n2, 135n56, 188n39
Mirandola, Giovanni Pico della 193n
Montaigne, Michel de 94, 95, 98, 201–2, 204
Montrose, Louis 5
More, Thomas 13, 14, 25, 202–3, 204
Moryson, Fynes 27
Mountjoy, 8th Lord (Charles Blount) 27n115, 63
Muir, Kenneth 113

New Historians 208–9, 211
New Historicism 186, 217
Nietzsche, Friedrich Wilhelm 83, 84, 138, 212n
noble savage 91–9, 113–15
Norbrook, David 137, 205n91
Norton, Thomas 82–3, 172

Octavian, Roman emperor 158
Oliver, Isaac 22, 151
O'Neill, Hugh *see* Tyrone
Orkin, Martin 93n, 217, 218
Ornstein, Robert 80
Orpheus/Orphic arts 1, 29
   and Hercules 23–8
   and *Othello* 87–9, 90, 102–3
   and *Tempest* 178, 181–5, 190–6, 206
Orwell, George 218
Osborne, Francis 123
Othello 86–116, 183, 213–14
   Herculean hero 89–91
   honour 101, 106–13
   noble savage 91–9, 113–15
Ottoman Empire *see* Turks
Ovid (Publius, Ovidius Naso) 48n47
   and *Macbeth* 118

and *Othello* 88, 89n6, 103
and *Tempest* 178, 190, 194n51, 202, 203–4

pacifism and peace 11, 13–14, 15, 20, 42, 73
   versus militarism 23–8
   of Erasmus 18, 28, 32, 33, 42, 206
   of James *see under* James I
Parry, Graham 18n71, 125n22, 127n29, 129n37
Passe, Simon van de 22
Peacham, Henry, the Elder 15n58
Peacham, Henry, the Younger 197n60
Peake, Robert, the Elder 151
Peele, George 12
Peltonen, Markku 19n79, 27n114, 170n91
Perondinus, Petrus 20
Phillips, James Emerson, Jr 71, 209
Plato 165, 196
Plutarch 147–8, 149, 155–60 *passim*, 165, 169n, 172, 174
Ponet, John 71–3
Popper, Karl 207–8
postmodernism 55–6
presentism 212–14, 216, 218
Primaudaye, Pierre de la 41n35, 182–3
primitivism
   noble savage 91–9, 113–15
   and *Othello* 91–9
   and *Tempest* 191 and n42, 200–4
Proser, Matthew N. 4n8, 92
Prosser, Eleanor 66, 67, 70
Protestantism *see* James I; militant Protestantism
Puttenham, George 1, 26n113, 182
Pygmalion 103

Quarshie, Hugh 92n18, 114
Quintilian (Marcus Fabius Quintilianus) 105n54

Raab, Felix 19n80, 158n55
Rabkin, Norman 24n103, 32, 33n7, 106, 122, 211
Ralegh, Sir Walter 23n99, 51, 160, 197
Ranke, Leopold von 207, 209, 214, 217
relativism 54–8, 141, 211
revenge 195
   and *Hamlet* 64–5, 68, 70–2, 74–5, 82
   and *Macbeth* 117, 120–1
   and *Othello* 100, 107–8
Reynolds, Larry J. 216
Richard II 50, 113n77, 137
Richard II, king 184
Ridley, Matt R. 104, 192n44
Riggs, David 4n
Rogers, Thomas 174

Romeo and Juliet 109, 199
Rossiter, A.P. 24n103, 122, 210, 211
Rubens, Peter Paul 136n59, 140–1

Sackville, Thomas 82–3, 172
Said, Edward W. 180n13
Sallust, Caius Crispus 158, 159, 160
Salutati, Coluccio 20
Saxo Grammaticus 70, 74–5, 79, 83, 108
Schmidgall, Gary 131, 188n39
Seneca, Lucius Annaeus: *Hercules furens* 27
  and *Hamlet* 75n41
  and *Macbeth* 118
  and *Othello* 90, 91, 99, 100n43, 101, 103
  and *Tempest* 181, 195
  and *Troilus and Cressida* 59
sensibility, Man of 81–5, 200–1
Shalvi, Alice 4n7
Sidney, Sir Philip 18, 169n84
  and Essex 9, 18, 19, 22
  see also militant Protestantism
  on Hercules 30n124
  and heroic ideal 2, 84
Siegel, Paul N. 17n68, 144n, 147n8
Simonds, Peggy Muñoz 30n124, 137n63, 148n12, 171, 178n1
Sinfield, Alan 18, 122, 123–4, 133, 137, 170n89
Smith, Bruce 162
Spenser, Edmund
  and British Myth 129, 142n72
  on chivalric friendship 164
  on Essex 11, 19
  on Hercules 26
  on Omphale, 30n123
  and *Tempest* 192–4
Starkey, Thomas 169, 203
Steadman, John M. 23n101
Stoicism 25, 73, 120, 144
Stoll, E.E. 208
Stow, John 150
Strachy, William 187, 188n
Strong, Roy 12n40, 22n97, 149n13, 150n16, 151n24, 152n,28 153n38, 154n42, 155n43
subjectivity 212, 214

Tacitus, Publius Cornelius 10, 179, 202, 203
Tallis, Raymond 56n68
Tasso, Torquato 2
Taylor, Gary 32, 44, 47
Tempest, The 27–8, 30, 186–206
  and civilization 181–5, 189–90, 196, 205
  and colonialism 180, 186–90, 195
  dynastic marriage 196–200
  and James I 157, 187, 190, 196–8
  and Orpheus 178, 181–5, 190–6

  primitivism 191 and nn, 200–4
Theophrastus 165
Tiffin, Helen 189n
Tillyard, E.M.W. 23, 55, 70, 122, 209–10, 211, 217
Titus Andronicus 94, 134, 170
Trevet, Nicholas 88n5
Trevisa, John 96
Troeltsch, Ernst 208, 211
Troilus and Cressida 6, 19, 34, 42, 52–60, 84
  and chivalry 58–9
  and *Henry V* linked 52
  manhood and honour 51–60
Troy and Trojan War 77–8, 102
  as origin of British monarchy *see* British Myth
  see also Troilus and Cressida; Virgil's *Aeneid*
Turks and Ottoman Empire 13, 90, 97, 99, 111
  and James I 95–6, 98, 102–3, 110, 115
Tuve, Rosemond 208
Twelfth Night 52
tyrannicide and regicide 64, 70–2, 136–7
  see also Hamlet; *Macbeth*
tyranny 72, 118, 122
Tyrone, 2nd Earl of (Hugh O'Neill) 35, 49, 186n33

Vaenius (Otto van Veen) 29–30, 195–6, 205
valour *see virtus*
Vaughan, Alden T. 186n33, 191n42
Vaughan, Virginia Mason 92n17, 186n33, 191n42
Veen, Otto van *see* Vaenius
Veeser, H. Aram 215
Viking honour 69, 73–80, 176
Virgil's *Aeneid* 75
  ambivalence 130–3
  Hercules in 179–81
  and James I 118, 128–30, 134–5
  and *Macbeth* 117–19, 125, 128–35, 141, 142, 143
  and *Tempest* 188–90
virtus/virtue/*virtù* 2, 6, 9, 14, 19–23, 88n5, 195
  and *Coriolanus* 146–9, 155, 159–60, 174
  and *Macbeth* 119, 140
  see also Hercules; masculinity; militarism
Vives, Juan Luis 15, 152

Waith, Eugene M. 26n108, 147n8
  on *Coriolanus* 148, 177
  on Herculean hero 2–3, 89, 178
  on *Othello* 112n73
Walker, Greg 185n29

Index

Walter, J.H. 32, 41n36, 42
Warden, John 182n16
Warren, Austin 208, 209
Watson, Curtis Brown 3n7, 7n21
Wayne, Valerie 5n13, 101
Weldon, Sir Anthony 123
Wellek, René 208, 209, 218
Wells, Robin Headlam 23n100, 26n112, 27n117, 38n31, 47n44, 137n65, 178n1, 182n16, 184n24, 211n17, 215n32
Wernham, R.B. 11n34, 16n62, 35
West, Rebecca 85
Whetstone, George 8n24
White, Hayden 191n, 214n32
Wilde, Oscar 146
William of Worcester 49n50
   on chivalry 11–12
   and Edward 52
   and Henry VIII 16n65
   on Hercules 26, 28
Williamson, J.W. 22n97, 149n13, 150n18, 151n122, 152, 197, 198n62, 199n64, 200n168
Wilson, Arthur 123
Wilson, John Dover 84–5
Wilson, Scott 216
Wilson, Thomas 105n54, 205
Wiltenburg, Robert 188n39
Wind, Edgar 48n47
Winstanley, Lilian 62n4, 64, 124n18, 216n37
Winter's Tale, The 88, 103n, 135, 191
Wither, George 151, 156
women 7–8
   and education 15
   idealized 53, 101
   killed by men 3n, 86, 88, 89, 91, 109, 112
   as objects 105
   seductive and libidinous 78, 88 and n5, 101–3, 108–9, 193, 197–8
Woodbridge, Linda 8n25
Woods, Gregory 162
Worcester *see* William of Worcester
Worden, Blair 9n28, 10n33, 15n59
Wormald, Jenny 124

Xenophon 165

Yachnin, Paul 6n16
Yates, Frances 12n40, 60n, 149n13, 198n63
Yeats, W.B. 61, 83–4, 84n64